SEVEN THEORIES OF RELIGION

SEVEN THEORIES OF RELIGION

Daniel L. Pals

New York   Oxford
OXFORD UNIVERSITY PRESS
1996

For Phyllis and Katharine

Oxford University Press

Oxford   New York
Athens   Auckland   Bangkok
Calcutta   Cape Town   Dar es Salaam   Delhi
Florence   Hong Kong   Istanbul   Karachi
Kuala Lumpur   Madras   Madrid   Melbourne
Mexico City   Nairobi   Paris   Singapore
Taipei   Tokyo   Toronto

and associated companies in
Berlin   Ibadan

Published by Oxford University Press, Inc.
198 Madison Avenue, New York, New York 10016

Oxford is a registered trademark of Oxford University Press, Inc.

Library of Congress Cataloging-in-Publication Data
Pals, Daniel L.
Seven theories of religion / Daniel L. Pals.
p.   cm. Includes index.
ISBN 0-19-508724-0
ISBN 0-19-508725-9 (pbk.)
1. Religion—Study and teaching—History—19th century.
2. Religion—Study and teaching—History—20th century.   I. Title.
BL41.P36   1996   207—dc20   95-18026

1   3   5   7   9   8   6   2

Printed in the United States of America
on acid-free paper

PREFACE

This book is designed for general readers who have an interest in religion and who wish to know what ideas certain leading thinkers of the modern era have put forward in their attempts to understand it. Specialists in these matters—those who work in the "methodology" of religious studies—will no doubt find in these pages much that is familiar and relatively little that is new, but that is largely by design. The discussions that follow are not really meant for them. Nonetheless, my hope is that even experts may find some profit in what is presented here if they use it to step back from the details they know so well and consider again the classic strategies of interpretation that have defined their subject as it faces them today. If nothing else, such a look backward at the landscape of earlier explanation should place in olearer outline some of the classic interpretive paths (and pathfinders) that have taken them, perhaps even unknowingly, to the present moment and thereby give them a better sense of where they may now expect to go.

That having been said, the first concern of the following chapters is to address other audiences, who come to the subjects of explanation and religion with perhaps less background and focus than professionals but with no less compelling questions of their own. Among such readers might be any of the following: fellow scholars in the field of Religious Studies who are unacquainted with issues of method and theory and may choose this work to fill a gap in their learning; scholars in fields other than religion, who may have a vague acquaintance with the theories considered here, but feel they do not have a fresh memory of the arguments or a firm grasp of their historical impact and current standing; interested general readers who are curious to know the place not only of religion itself in human endeavor but also the role of opinions *about* religion in the general course of contemporary discussion; and finally, but no less importantly, students, both undergraduate and graduate, whose program of study requires them to know at least the main outlines of these "classic" theories for their work in religious studies or other fields, but whose other academic commitments leave them only limited hours for the task. If readers in any of these groups, or others unmentioned, can here gain a first broad grasp of the issues at stake in these important theoretical discussions, this book will have more than served its purpose. I should add that while the text as a whole traces a broadly chronological and intellectual progression, its individual chapters have been constructed so that they can also be read independently as the need arises, though not without some loss of their intellectual context and comparative value.

Most books are the products of many hands, and this one is no exception. I am especially grateful to Cynthia Read, senior editor at Oxford University Press, for the enthusiastic response she gave to this project when it was first suggested and for the timely advice she and her assistant Peter Ohlin supplied as the work proceeded. Heidi Thaens, copy editor, and Ellen B. Fuchs, managing editor, have proven just as efficient and skilled in the later stages of the publishing process. My colleagues in the Department of Religious Studies at the University of Miami—John Fitzgerald, David Kling, and Steve Sapp—not only showed considerable patience with their chair when he was absent from his office, but also offered much in the way of encouragement and criticism. Each has read either all or part of the manuscript and furnished thoughtful suggestions for improvement. Steve Sapp in particular gave the text a meticulous reading for errors of style, diction, punctuation, and typography while also suggesting important revisions on matters of substance. These efforts were matched by those of my wife Phyllis, who also proofread most of the manuscript in various stages of its growth, making thoughtful comments throughout on style, substance, and clarity of presentation.

With regard to substantive issues in the theory of religion, I am immensely indebted to my sister-in-law Eve Brouwer Cronk for her insightful comments on both Durkheim and Freud, to Douglas Allen of the University of Maine, who offered authoritative commentary and patient criticism on the work of Mircea Eliade, and to two other scholars the breadth of whose learning on these topics is rivaled only by the depth of their generosity in sharing it: Professor James Livingston of the College of William and Mary, and Professor Robert Segal of Lancaster University in England. Both read this manuscript in its entirety and offered numerous criticisms that were both thoughtful and persuasive. Whatever its surviving imperfections, this is clearly a better book than it could ever have been without them.

Though decades have now intervened, I do not think it either too late or too sentimental to extend an appreciation to Mr. Bruce Leep and Mr. Vern Boerman, two sterling mentors during high school years whose love of both learning and the English language has been for me a lifelong inspiration. Indirectly their mark is on many of these pages. Among those who helped in more immediate and specific ways, I wish to acknowledge Professor Edward Baker of the University of Miami, who read the chapter on Marx, Mrs. Nancy Helmick, who did the same for my account of Evans-Pritchard, and the students in my spring 1995 senior seminar and independent study courses at the University of Miami—in particular, Fernando Erhardt, Tiffany Field, Lisa Nasser, and Gerl Newburge—who commented on the text from the perspective of young readers new to its subject. Shereen Andrasek and her assistants in the interlibrary loan department of the University of Miami's Richter Library, all of whom seem to specialize in uncomplaining quick action on short notice, also deserve words of appreciation. In some ways, no expression of thanks is sufficient to acknowledge the extraordinary work of Ms. Ada Orlando, our departmental secretary, who tirelessly helped to manage our office of Religious Studies at Miami during a year when I delegated much and she cheerfully accepted all.

Finally, and above all, there is the formidable debt of thanks owed to my wife Phyllis and to my daughter Katharine. During the year and a half of direct labor on this manuscript, they donated in abundant measure what a family should not even be asked to give—the irreplaceable gift of its time together. This book is dedicated to them.

Coral Gables, Fla.   *D.L.P.*
July 1995

CONTENTS

SEVEN THEORIES OF RELIGION

Introduction

On a February day in the winter of 1870, a middle-aged German scholar rose to the stage of London's prestigious Royal Institution to deliver a public lecture. At the time, German professors were famous for their deep learning, and this one was no exception, though as it happened he had also become very English. His name was Friedrich Max Müller. He had first come to Britain as a young man to study the religious writings of ancient India, but soon he settled down, learned the language, married an English wife, and managed to acquire a position at Oxford University. Müller was admired for his knowledge of ancient Hinduism and for his very popular writings on language and mythology. On this occasion, however, he proposed a different subject. He wished to promote something he called the science of religion.

The phrase "science of religion" doubtless struck some in Müller's audience as puzzling in the extreme. After all, he was speaking at the end of a decade marked by a furious debate over Charles Darwin's *Origin of Species* (1859) and its startling theory of evolution by natural selection. Thoughtful Victorians had heard so much of science pitted *against* religion that the phrase "science *of* religion" fell on the ears as a very curious combination, to say the least. How could the age-old certainties of faith ever mix with a program of study devoted to experiment, revision, and change? How could these opposing systems, these two apparently mortal enemies, meet without the one, the other, or both being destroyed? Müller, of course, was certain that the two could be joined. He believed that a scientific study of religion had much to offer on both sides, and his lecture—the first in a series later published as *Introduction to the Science of Religion* (1873)—was designed to prove just that point. He reminded his listeners that the words which the poet Goethe once wrote about human language could also be applied to religion: "He who knows one, knows none."[1] And if that is so,

3

he continued, then perhaps it was time for a new and objective look at this very old subject. Instead of following the theologians, who wanted only to prove their own religion true and all others false, the time had come to take a less partisan approach, seeking out those elements, patterns, and principles that could be found uniformly in the religions of all times and places. Much could be gained by proceeding like any good scientist, gathering the various facts—the customs, rituals, and beliefs—of religions throughout the world and then offering theories to account for them, just as a biologist or chemist might attempt to explain the workings of nature.

Ancient Theories

Although the idea may have seemed new to his audience at the time, part of what Müller proposed in his lecture was in fact very old. Questions as to what religion is and why people practice it probably reach back as far as the human race itself. The earliest theories would have been framed when the first travelers ventured outside their own clans or villages and discovered that their neighbors had other gods with different names. When, on his travels, the ancient historian Herodotus (484–425 B.C.E.) tried to explain that the gods Amon and Horus, whom he encountered in Egypt, were the equivalents of Zeus and Apollo in his native Greece, he was actually offering at least the beginning of a general theory of religion. So did the writer Euhemerus (330–260 B.C.E.) when he claimed that the gods were simply outstanding personages from history who began to be worshipped after their death. In similar fashion, certain Stoic philosophers explained the gods as personifications of the sky, sea, and other natural forces. After viewing the facts of religion, these observers tried, often quite creatively, to explain how it had come to be what it was.[2]

Judaism and Christianity

Thinkers such as these lived in the classical civilizations of ancient Greece and Rome, where many divinities were worshipped and the idea of comparing or connecting one god with another was a natural habit of mind. Judaism and Christianity, however, took a very different view of things. To the great prophets of ancient Israel there was no such thing as a variety of gods and rituals, each with a different and perhaps equal claim on human interest or devotion. For them there was only the one true God, the Lord of the Covenant, who had appeared to Abraham, Isaac, and Jacob and had revealed the divine law to Moses on Mt. Sinai. Since this God alone was real and all others were mere figments of the human imagination, there was very little about religion that needed either comparison or explanation. The people of Israel were to trust in Yahweh because he had chosen only them and had spoken to them directly; all other nations worshipped idols because their eyes had been darkened by ignorance, wickedness, or both. Christianity, which arose out of later Judaism, took over this perspective, found in prophets like Isaiah, almost without change. For the apostles and theologians of the early church, God had put himself on clear display in the human person of Jesus Christ. Those who believed in him had found the truth; those who did not could only be regarded as victims of the great Deceiver, Satan—souls destined to pay the bitter price of eternal suffering in Hell. As Christianity spread throughout the ancient world and later converted the peoples of Europe, this view came to dominate Western civilization throughout most of the medieval era. There were occasional exceptions, of course, but the prevailing attitude was expressed most clearly in the great struggle against Islam during the age of the crusades. Christians, the children of light, were commanded to struggle against the children of darkness. The beauty and truth of God's revelation explained the faith of Christendom; the machinations of Satan explained the beliefs of its enemies.[3]

For the better part of a thousand years in the West, this militant perspective on religions other than Christianity did not significantly change. But around the year 1500, as the epoch of world explorations and the effects of the Protestant Reformation set in, the signs of a rather different outlook began slowly to make an appearance. The voyages of explorers, traders, missionaries, and adventurers to the New World and to the Orient opened the eyes of Christians to people who managed to build impressive civilizations without ever knowing God's revelation in the Bible or in Jesus Christ. Contact with the highly ethical principles of such religions as Hinduism, Buddhism, and Confucianism and the apparent discovery of belief in something like a Supreme Being among certain American "Indian" tribes created a call for a comparative study of these belief systems alongside Judaism and Christianity. Increasingly, in thoughtful circles, the condemnation of such people as disciples of the Devil began to look inappropriate and misguided. China's Confucians, one could reason, might not know Christ, but somehow, without even a Bible to guide them, they had produced a culture that was very civilized, well mannered, and moral—a society that Jesus and the apostles, had they visited, would have been compelled to admire. At the very same moment when these contacts were being made, moreover, the Christian society that Jesus presumably *had* founded was itself plunged into bloody and violent turmoil. Led by the monk Martin Luther in Germany and the lawyer John Calvin in Switzerland and France, the new Protestant movements of northern Europe challenged the power of the church and rejected its interpretations of biblical truth. While the explorers traveled, their homelands were often ablaze with the fires of persecution and war. Communities were split apart by ferocious quarrels over theology, first between Catholics and Protestants and later among the scores and hundreds of different religious groups that began to appear in Europe. Amid this whirl of ecclesiastical conflict and political confusion, which convulsed the societies of the sixteenth and seventeenth centuries, it is not surprising that thoughtful Christians on all sides grew less and less certain that they alone had God's final truth in their grasp. The deadly, destructive wars of religion, which persisted for more than a hundred years in some lands, led people to believe that the truth about religion could not possibly be found in sects that were prepared to torture and execute their opponents, all in the name of the same God. Surely, some said, the truth of religion must lie behind the quarrels of the churches, beyond the tortures of the stake and the rack. Could they not find a new form of religion, a new understanding of its aims and purposes?[4]

The Enlightenment and Natural Religion

It was this great question, set against the bloody background of the previous era, that certain thinkers of the eighteenth century, the age of the Enlightenment, sought to answer by proposing the idea of a single, basic, and original religion shared by the entire human race. Numbered in the circle of these "Deists," as they were then called, were some of the most celebrated names of the day: philosophers like John Toland, Matthew Tindal, and David Hume in Britain; statesmen like Thomas Jefferson and Ben Franklin in the American colonies; critics like Denis Diderot and the great Voltaire in France; as well as the dramatist Gotthold Lessing in Germany. In one form or another, nearly all in this group promoted the idea of a simple and shared "natural religion" of the human race. It consisted of belief in a creator God who made the world and then left it to its own natural laws, a moral code given to guide the conduct of human beings, and the promise of an afterlife if they did what was good and avoided evil. To the Deists, this elegantly simple creed was the faith of the very first human beings—the common philosophy of all races long before the churches of later centuries entered the scene with their superstitious miracles, foolish sacraments, and power-hungry priests. The best hope of humanity was to try to recover this original faith and live by it in peace and serenity as a universal brotherhood of all people—Christian, Jew, Muslim, Hindu, Chinese, and all others—under their one creator God.

In addition to its commendable work in promoting tolerance, this Deist notion of an original, natural religion of humanity opened the door to a new way of explaining the many forms of religion as they presented themselves to missionaries, theologians, explorers, and others in all their many conflicts and confusions. Whatever the different beliefs of the various Christian sects—whatever the rituals of American Indians, ancestral rites of the Chinese, or teachings of Hindu sages—all of these could ultimately be traced back to the natural religion of the first human beings and then followed forward as it was gradually transformed and dispersed into its modern forms and distortions, largely through the corrupting influence of magicians, churches, bishops, and theologians.

When they asked where natural religion itself came from, Deists tended to differ among themselves. Some said it came from the use of reason, the gift that separated human beings from the animal kingdom; others traced it to the fear and ignorance of humanity in its savage state. They did not differ, however, in their fundamental conviction, which asserted that religion could *not* be explained in the way that the priests and theologians declared, as a set of truths given directly by God to one church—their own—and coldly denied to all others. Religion for the Deists had to be explained without recourse to supernatural revelation. It was to be as open as any other sphere of human activity to a theory that might explain why it existed, what was its purpose, and how it had come to be.[5]

Modern Theories

It was in part this Deist point of view that Max Müller and others like him inherited when they addressed their fellow Victorian audiences in the middle and later years of the nineteenth century. They believed, first, that it was possible to explain not just aspects of religion but *all* of religion; second, they were confident that they could do so through an investigation that was mainly historical. By sustained and diligent inquiry, they would reach far back in time to discover the earliest religious ideas and practices of the human race; that accomplished, it was a natural next step to trace their development onward and upward to the present day. Müller and his associates believed not just that they could do such a thing but also that in their time it could be done better than the Deists ever imagined, largely because of the great advances that had been made in the study of archaeology, history, language, mythology, and the newly created disciplines of ethnology and anthropology.[6] Müller himself was a keen student of mythology and one of Europe's foremost names in the field of comparative philology, or language study; the Hindu Vedas, which he had edited, were then thought to be the oldest religious documents of the human race. Archaeologists in the early years of the century had made significant new discoveries about earlier stages of human civilization; historians had pioneered new critical methods for studying ancient texts; students of folklore were gathering information on the customs and tales of Europe's peasants; and the first anthropologists had begun to draw upon reports from those who had observed societies of apparently primitive people still surviving in the modern world. In addition, there was now the very successful model of the natural sciences to work from. Instead of just guessing about the origins and development of religion, as many Deists had done, inquirers could systematically assemble facts of ritual, belief, or custom from a wide sample of the world's religions in order to draw out certain general principles—the scientific "laws of development," as they were then called—that would explain how such things arose and what purposes they served.

By the middle decades of the 1800s, then, scholars felt that both the methods and materials were on hand to abandon unfounded pronouncements about the beginnings of religion and formulate, instead, systematic theories of origin that could claim the authority of science. Not only in Müller's lectures but in other writings of the time as well, we can notice an optimism, energy, and confidence about the research that was being undertaken. The aim of these writers was not to offer just another guess or set of speculations but to frame well-founded theories. Like their counterparts in the physical sciences, they would work from a solid foundation of facts and formulate generalizations that could be carefully tested, revised, and improved. To all appearances, this scientific method had the further advantage that it could be applied in full independence of one's personal religious commitments. Müller was a deeply devout, almost sentimental Christian, who believed that the truth of his faith had nothing to fear from science and, in fact, would shine brighter if it were explained in the context of other religions. Conversely, as we shall soon see, E. B. Tylor, Müller's contemporary and critic, took an opposing view, believing that his scientific inquiries gave support to his personal stance of agnostic religious skepticism. Both, however, believed that a theory of religion could be developed from a common ground of objective facts which would, in every case, have to provide both the evidentiary support and the final test of truth. Both also believed that they could reach theories that were comprehensive and general in nature. Such was the confidence they had in both their science and the body of facts at their disposal that they felt no embarrassment in claiming to explain the entire phenomenon of religion—not just this ritual or that belief, not just religion in one place or time, but the worldwide story of its origin, development, and diversity! In stating this bold ambition, they laid out the issues that the major theorists of our own century—those whose names figure most prominently in this book—would later have to address.[7]

When we look back on it from the present, this hope of forming a single theory of all religions astonishes us by its naive overconfidence. Thoughtful observers today are inclined to be far more modest. Impressive books have been written just to explain one belief of one religion or to compare a single feature—a specific custom or ritual—of one religion with something similar in another. Nonetheless, the hope of one day discovering some broad pattern or general principle that explains all or even most religious behavior has not been given up easily. As we shall see in some of the chapters to come, several important theorists of the twentieth century have been inspired by this very same ideal, and for understandable reasons. Physicists have not given up on Einstein's "unified field" theory, even though finding it has proved far more difficult than any of them ever imagined. In the same way, religionists, despite the difficulties, have also been inspired by the scientific ideal of a general theory that could draw many different phenomena into one coherent, widely illuminating pattern. Moreover, explanations need not be valid to be of value. In religion as in other fields of inquiry, a suggestive and original theory can, even in failure, stimulate new inquiry or reformulate problems in such a way as to promote fruitful new understandings. Thus, even if most of what they have said were to be found in error, the theorists who appear in these pages would still deserve our time and attention, for their ideas and interpretations have often filtered beyond the sphere of religion alone to affect our literature, philosophy, history, politics, art, psychology, and, indeed, almost every realm of modern thought.

It is interesting in this connection to notice how well hidden are the origins and first advocates of ideas and notions now regarded as belonging to the stock of common knowledge. How many people who casually refer to religion as a superstitious medieval "belief in spirits" realize that they are essentially repeating a version of E. B. Tylor's famous theory of animism as he explained it in *Primitive Culture*, a work now over a hundred years old? Would they today recognize the name of either the author or his once revered book? Who among those who argue that science replaces religion can recall the fame of James Frazer at the turn of the century, when he placed this thesis at the center of his monumental *Golden Bough?* How many general readers with a curiosity about religion would recognize the unusual name and provocative theory of Mircea Eliade, even though his influence on the study of religion in America over the last four decades has been quite remarkably widespread? How many are aware of the role that the anthropologist E. E. Evans-Pritchard's work has played in recent philosophical debates over rationality and relativism? The views associated with the great radical thinkers of our time, especially Marx and Freud, tend to be better known, of course, but all too often in ways that are vague, fragmentary, or distorted. In consequence, a great deal of debate *about* such theories goes along without any clear and precise grasp of the assumptions, evidence, and logic to be found *in* them. One service this discussion can render is to help readers relatively new to this subject avoid making mistakes such as these.

Seven Theories

The following chapters consider seven of the more important theories of religion that have been put forward since the idea of a scientific approach to religion first caught the imagination of serious scholars in the century before our own. In each case the theory is presented first by discussing the life and background of its major spokesman, then by treating its key ideas as presented in certain central texts, and finally by noticing its distinctive features in comparison with other theories and recording the main objections raised by its critics.

Principle of Selection

From a number of theories that might have been chosen for its purpose, this book selects seven that have exercised a shaping influence not only on religion but on the whole intellectual culture of our century. The spokesmen representative of each are (1) E. B. Tylor and James Frazer, (2) Sigmund Freud, (3) Émile Durkheim, (4) Karl Marx, (5) Mircea Eliade (6) E. E. Evans-Pritchard, and (7) Clifford Geertz. Knowledgeable observers will notice at once that several highly regarded names—such as the great German sociologist Max Weber, the Swiss psychologist Carl Jung, and even Max Müller himself—fall outside this group. Omissions as large as these are not easy to justify and, indeed, another author might well have chosen differently. But the choices do have a rationale. Important as he was in promoting the idea of a science of religion, Max Müller has been left aside because his own theory, which found religion to originate in nature worship, was for the most part already rejected in his own time and had only limited influence thereafter. That, of course, cannot be said of Max Weber, who as a thinker is as profound and important as any of those who do appear in these chapters. But here another principle has come into play. In this book for nonspecialists, an effort has been made to present classic theories in what might be called their "purest" or least complicated form. The originality and importance of Weber, however, are to be found in just the opposite—in his extraordinary ability to see complexity and his skill in joining several perspectives to achieve rich explanatory combinations. Consideration of his work thus seems better left for another study or another day. Émile Durkheim, by contrast, *is* to be found in these pages, for in contrast to Weber, his single-mindedly sociological theory puts that approach on display in unmistakably clear and distinct outline. Again, the influential French philosopher Lucien Lévy-Bruhl, who is noticed briefly in Chapter 6, is a theorist who some would say deserves admission here. But Lévy-Bruhl too is a complex figure, whose views changed significantly over time; moreover, since the major issues he took up were also considered by E. E. Evans-Pritchard, who had the further benefit of grounding his views in actual fieldwork among tribal peoples, the latter seems for our purposes the better of the two to select. The same is true to a degree in the case of Carl Jung. It is well known that Jung took a subtle, sympathetic, and textured approach to religion and that he made extensive use of religious materials in his psychological research, but for just that reason he offers a somewhat less rigorously consistent example of a psychologically functional interpretation than we find in Freud, and his influence on the field, though great, was less extensive. So here again, Freud has seemed the better choice. Clarity, in short, has been chosen over complexity; the theories selected offer the sharpest image of their type.

Definition of Terms

Before we begin, some comment is needed on the two terms that are most basic to the discussions that follow: "religion" and "theory." Most people, even if they are coming to this subject for the first time, have some idea of what "religion" is. They are likely to think of belief in a God, supernatural spirits, or an afterlife. Or they are likely to name one of the great world religions, such as Hinduism, Christianity, Buddhism, or Islam. They probably also have some general idea of what a "theory" is. Having heard the term most often in the context of science, they think of it as a kind of explanation—an attempt to "account for" something that is not at first understood, usually by offering an answer to the common question "Why?" Most of us readily admit that we do not understand the theory of relativity, but we do recognize that it somehow "accounts for" the connection between matter and energy in a way that no one had imagined before. At the start of things, there is no need for us to go beyond everyday notions such as these. Whatever their limitations, ordinary understandings of general terms like "religion" and "theory" are indispensable for a book such as this—not only as starting points but as guideposts while we proceed. At the same time, we should also notice that few of the theorists we shall consider are content to stay with these intuitions of common sense once they have worked their way seriously into the issues. Some, for example, find that "belief in a God or gods" is far too specific, far too "theological" a definition to use for people—like some Buddhists—who worship no God, or for groups—like some Jews—who think of their faith chiefly as a matter of activities rather than ideas. To accommodate such instances, which clearly belong to the sphere of religion, a theorist might follow the path chosen by Durkheim and Eliade, who prefer a concept like "the sacred" as the defining essential of religion. They note that the Buddhist who does not believe in God does, after all, have a sense of the sacred. So they find this abstract term more suitable for considering the entire span and story of religion in the world rather than traditions of just one place, time, or type. Again, some theorists strongly prefer *substantive* definitions, which closely resemble the commonsense approach. They define religion in terms of the conceptual *content,* or the *ideas,* that religious people commit to and find important. Other theorists think this approach just too restrictive and offer instead a more *functional* definition. They leave the content—the ideas—of religion off to the side and define it solely in terms of how it *operates* in human life. They want to know what a religion does for an individual person psychologically or for a group socially. Less concerned with the actual substance of people's beliefs or practices, they are inclined to describe religion, whatever its specific content, as that which provides support for a group or brings a sense of comfort or wellbeing to an individual. As we proceed, it will be wise to keep in mind that the business of defining religion is closely linked to the enterprise of explaining it, and that the matter of definitions is considerably more difficult than common sense, at a first look, would lead us to believe.

The same can be said for "theory." On first sight, the idea of an "explanation" of religion is not hard to understand. But again, the more deeply one moves into the actual labor of explaining, the more complex it seems to become. Two brief illustrations may be enough to show the problem. First, a theorist who proposes to explain religion by showing its "origin" can mean by this word any of several things: its *prehistorical* origin—how, at the dawn of history, the first human beings might have acquired a religion; its *psychological or social* origin—how, at all times in human history, it arises in response to certain group or individual needs; its *intellectual* origin—how, at one time or all times, certain perceived truths about the world have led certain people to believe certain religious claims; or its *historical* origin—how at a certain known time and place, a specific situation in the natural world, a certain prophetic personality, or a special sequence of events, has created a religion and given it a distinctive character or shape. Both in describing and in evaluating theories, it is important to know what kind of "origin" of religion they advance and, no less, what connection one kind of origin may have with the other kinds.

The second illustration of complexity is one already alluded to above. Theories of religion, no less than definitions, may also be either functional or substantive in character. Theorists who advocate substantive approaches tend to explain religion intellectually, in terms of the ideas that motivate, move, and inspire people. They stress conscious human intention, emotion, and agency. People are religious, they say, because certain ideas strike them as true and valuable; therefore people feel that these ideas ought to be followed in the framing of their lives. Theorists who stress this role of human thought and feeling are sometimes described as "interpretive" rather than "explanatory" in their approach. Religions, they contend, are adopted by persons; they are about things that "have meaning" to human selves; accordingly, interpretations—which take account of human intent—best explain the phenomenon. Interpretive theorists reject "explanations" because they are only about "things," not persons. Explanations in their view are unsuitable because they appeal to impersonal processes rather than humanly meaningful purposes. Functional theorists, by contrast, strongly disagree. They think that though explanations certainly are good for things—for physical objects and natural processes—they are just as useful in understanding people. Functional theorists strive to look beneath or behind the conscious thoughts of religious people to find something deeper and hidden. They contend that there are underlying social structures or unnoticed psychological distresses which form the real roots of religious behavior. Whether they are individual, social, or even biological, these compelling forces—and *not* the ideas that religious people themselves imagine to be governing their actions—are the real causes of religion wherever we find it. We shall be able to trace the differences between explainers and interpreters in some detail later on in our discussion.[8] For the moment, however, they can serve as fair warning that with theories of religion no less than with definitions, the seemingly simple often masks the deceptively complex.

In the chapters that follow, it will be worth attending carefully to both the definitions and explanations of our theorists as well as the links that, in each case, connect the one with the other. Along the way, it should become apparent how and why each is moved beyond the obvious to the unnoticed, beyond the surface to the substrate, in his attempt to understand religion. It should also be clear that these theories have been placed in a sequence, both chronological and conceptual, that is meant to show a pattern. After starting with the classic intellectualist theory of Tylor and Frazer, we move next to explanatory approaches, tracing the lines of psychological, social, and economic functionalism through Freud, Durkheim, and Marx. We then turn to Eliade, who marks a protest against the more extreme form of the explanatory approach (often called "reductionism"), and finish with the more recent theories of Evans-Pritchard and Geertz, both of which may be seen as attempts to overcome the interpretive-explanatory divide. The conclusion then offers some brief comparisons.

Notes

1. F. Max Müller, *Lectures on the Science of Religion* (New York: Charles Scribner and Company, 1872), p. 11; it was also published under the title *Introduction to the Science of Religion*. On Müller's interesting life, see Nirad Chaudhuri, *Scholar Extraordinary: The Life of Professor the Rt. Hon. Friedrich Max Müller* (London: Chatto & Windus, 1974).

2. On these ancient precursors of the modern theory of religion, see Eric J. Sharpe, *Comparative Religion: A History* (New York: Charles Scribner's Sons, 1975), pp. 1–7.

3. Sharpe, *Comparative Religion*, pp. 7–13.

4. On the connection between the wars of religion in Europe and the effort to explain religion comparatively, without theological judgments, see J. Samuel Preus, *Explaining Religion: Criticism and Theory from Bodin to Freud* (New Haven, CT: Yale University Press, 1987), pp. 3–20.

5. On early Deism and later skepticism during the Enlightenment, see the discussions of Herbert of Cherbury and David Hume in Preus, *Explaining Religion*, pp. 23–39, 84–103.

6. On the rise of anthropology in the mid-Victorian years, see, among others, Richard M. Dorson, *The British Folklorists: A History* (Chicago: University of Chicago Press, 1968); Paul Bohannan, *Social Anthropology* (New York: Holt, Rinehart & Winston, 1969), pp. 311–15; J. W. Burrow, *Evolution and Society* (Cambridge, England: Cambridge University Press, 1970); and George W. Stocking, Jr., *Victorian Anthropology* (New York: The Free Press, 1987).

7. On these early efforts to develop theories of religion with the help of anthropological and other research, see Brian Morris, *Anthropological Studies of Religion* (Cambridge, England: Cambridge University Press, 1987), pp. 91–105.

8. The most important, and provocative, analyses of this division are to be found in two collections of trenchant essays by Robert A. Segal: *Religion and the Social*

Sciences: Essays on the Confrontation (Atlanta: Scholars Press, 1989); and *Explaining and Interpreting Religion: Essays on the Issue* (New York: Peter Lang Publishing, 1992).

Suggestions for Further Reading

Chaudhuri, Nirad C. *Scholar Extraordinary: The Life of Professor the Rt. Hon. Friedrich Max Müller*. London: Chatto & Windus, 1974. A detailed study of the life and some consideration of the theories of Friedrich Max Müller.

Eliade, Mircea, Editor in Chief. *The Macmillan Encyclopedia of Religion*. New York: Macmillan, 1987. At present the most useful and comprehensive English-language reference work on religion.

Evans-Pritchard, E. E. *Theories of Primitive Religion*. Oxford, England: Clarendon Press, 1965. A brief and penetrating analysis of certain classic approaches to the explanation of religion.

Harrison, Peter. *"Religion" and the Religions in the English Enlightenment*. Cambridge, England: Cambridge University Press, 1990. An informative historical study which shows how the thinkers and ideas of the Enlightenment in England contributed to the rise of the scientific study of religion.

Masuzawa, Tomoko. *In Search of Dreamtime: The Quest for the Origin of Religion*. Chicago: University of Chicago Press, 1993. An original but difficult book that examines the presuppositions behind the keen interest of earlier, evolutionary theorists in the historical origin of religion.

Morris, Brian. *Anthropological Studies of Religion*. Cambridge, England: Cambridge University Press, 1987. A comprehensive survey of scientific theories of religion in the nineteenth and twentieth centuries.

Preus, J. Samuel. *Explaining Religion: Criticism and Theory from Bodin to Freud*. New Haven: Yale University Press, 1987. A recent study, much-praised by current theorists, that follows the history of thinking about religion over most of the last three centuries.

Segal, Robert A. *Religion and the Social Sciences: Essays on the Confrontation*. Brown Studies in Religion, no. 8. Atlanta, Georgia: Scholars Press, 1989. Trenchant essays by a keenly analytical younger theorist who sees an inescapable conflict between the theories of those who personally sympathize with religion and the critical explanatory methods of the social sciences.

Sharpe, Eric J. *Comparative Religion: A History*. New York: Charles Scribner's Sons, 1975. A wide-ranging overview of theories and theorists of religion. Helpful both as an introduction to the field and for short accounts of the lives and thought of leading figures in the field.

1

Animism and Magic:
E. B. Tylor and J. G. Frazer

Are the forces which govern the world conscious and personal, or
unconscious and impersonal? Religion, as a conciliation of the
superhuman powers, assumes the former. . . . it stands in
fundamental antagonism to magic as well as to science [which hold
that] the course of nature is determined, not by the passions or caprice
of personal beings, but by the operation of immutable laws acting
mechanically.

James Frazer, *The Golden Bough*[1]

Our survey begins with not one but two theorists whose writings are related
and whose ideas closely resemble each other. The first is Edward Burnett
Tylor (1832–1917), a self-educated Englishman who never attended a university but, through his travels and independent study, arrived at the theory
of animism, which in his view held the key to the origin of religion. The
second is James George Frazer (1854–1941), a shy, scholarly Scotsman
who, unlike Tylor, spent virtually all of his life in a book-lined apartment
at Cambridge University. Frazer is often associated with what is sometimes
called the "magic" theory of religion, rather than with Tylor's animism, but
in fact he was a disciple of Tylor, who readily took over his mentor's main
ideas and methods while adding certain new touches of his own. As we
shall see in our discussion, the two theories are so closely related that we
can more helpfully consider them as differing versions—an earlier and later
form—of the same general point of view. Tylor is perhaps the more original
thinker, while Frazer enjoys the greater fame and influence.

E. B. Tylor

E. B. Tylor's first interest was not religion but the study of human culture,
or social organization. Some, in fact, consider him the founder of cultural,

or social, anthropology as that science is now practiced in Britain and North America.[2] He was born in 1832 to a family of prosperous Quakers who owned a London brass factory.[3] The Quakers originally were an extreme, almost fanatical group of English Protestants who dressed in plain, unfashionable clothes and lived by the inspiration of a personal "inner light." By the 1800s, however, most had discarded their unusual dress, earned social respect, and moved all the way over to very liberal, even nonreligious views. This perspective is clearly present in Tylor's writings, which show throughout a strong distaste for all forms of traditional Christian faith and practice, especially Roman Catholicism.[4]

Because both of Tylor's parents died when he was a young man, he began preparations to help in management of the family business, only to discover his own health failing when he showed signs of developing tuberculosis. Advised to spend time in a warmer climate, he chose travel to Central America and left home in 1855, at the young age of twenty-three. This American experience proved decisive in his life, for it kindled his keen interest in the study of unfamiliar cultures. As he traveled, he took careful notes on the customs and beliefs of the people he saw, publishing the results of his work on his return to England in a book entitled *Anahuac: Or Mexico and the Mexicans, Ancient and Modern* (1861).[5] On his journeys, Tylor also met a fellow Quaker, the archaeologist Henry Christy, who sparked his enthusiasm as well for prehistoric studies. Though he did not travel again, Tylor began to study the customs and beliefs of all peoples who lived in "primitive" conditions, whether from prehistoric ages (insofar as they could be known from archaeological finds) or from tribal communities of the present day. Soon he published a second book, *Researches into the Early History of Mankind and the Development of Civilization* (1865).[6] And six years later, after much more work on these subjects, he published *Primitive Culture* (1871), a large two-volume study that became the masterwork of his career and a landmark in the study of human civilization. This important book not only appealed to a wide audience of general readers but also cast a spell over a number of brilliant younger men who were to become Tylor's enthusiastic disciples. Through their further outstanding work, the system and study of folklore and the newly developing science of anthropology made great strides in the later years of the nineteenth century.[7] Though it was not the only such book, *Primitive Culture* served as a virtual bible for all those who were inspired by what some called "Mr. Tylor's science."

Tylor too continued to work, and in 1884 was appointed by Oxford University to be its first reader in the new field of anthropology. Later on he became its first professor in the discipline, enjoying a long career that extended all the way to World War I. Even so, none of his later writing matched the importance of *Primitive Culture*.[8] Since this influential book presents his theory of animism in definitive form, it is the natural centerpiece for our examination of Tylor's views.

Primitive Culture

BACKGROUND

The significance of Tylor's work is best appreciated within its historical and religious context. *Primitive Culture* was published in Victorian Britain at a time when thoughtfully religious people were wrestling with more than a few disturbing challenges to their faith. Since the early years of the century, a number of philosophers, historians, and naturalists in the field of geology found themselves drawn to the idea of very long-term development both in nature and human society. To some, the earth and human life were beginning to look far older than the mere 6000 years that theologians had assigned to them from their readings in the biblical book of Genesis. The young Tylor was well acquainted with these discussions and was strongly disposed to think in similar terms.[9] Then, in 1859, Charles Darwin published his famous *Origin of Species,* perhaps the most important single book in science or any other field during the entire nineteenth century. The theory of evolution by natural selection that he presented struck many as shockingly contrary to the scriptures but irresistibly persuasive nonetheless. It was followed in 1871 by *The Descent of Man,* a work just as controversial because of its startling thesis about the animal origins of the human race. After the *Origin* the controversy over "evolution" was on almost everyone's lips, and the idea of development took an even stronger hold on Tylor's thought. Moreover, while these disputes raged, other thinkers were raising further troublesome questions about some of the most basic elements of Christian religious belief, including the historical accuracy of the Bible, the reality of miracles, and the divinity of Jesus Christ. Thus, when *Primitive Culture* appeared, with its new theory on the origin of *all* religious belief systems including the Christian one, it seemed to send yet another tremor of doubt through an already unsettled populace.

Tylor also drew upon new trends in research. He placed a pioneering emphasis on "ethnography" and "ethnology." These were the labels he and his associates gave to a distinctive new kind of study: the description (ethno-*graphy:* from the Greek *grapho,* "to write") and scientific analysis (ethno-*logy:* from the Greek *logos,* "study"), of an individual society, culture, or racial group (from the Greek *ethnos,* a "nation" or "people") in all of its many component parts. They also used the term "anthropology," the scientific study of mankind (from the Greek "*anthropos*, "man"). In addition, as a personally nonreligious man, Tylor refused to settle any question by an appeal to the divine authority of the church or the Bible.

Prior to Tylor's day and still during much of his career, people of traditional views insisted that the origin, at least of the Christian religion, had to be understood as something miraculous in character, primarily because it had been revealed as such by God in the scriptures and affirmed in church traditions. Over against this orthodox view, Christian scholars of more liberal inclinations pursued a more naturalistic understanding of things, but still in a manner quite supportive of traditional religious beliefs. They were led by Friedrich Max Müller, the personable and eloquent German whom we met in our opening pages.[10]

Müller and Tylor shared the view that appeals to the supernatural should be left out of their discussions, but they disagreed strongly on the value of Tylor's ethnological research. Müller felt that the key to religion, myth, and other aspects of culture lay in language. He and other students of comparative philology (the forerunner of today's linguistics) had shown that the forms of speech in India and most of Europe belonged to a group of languages that originated with a single ancient people known as Aryans.[11] By comparing word parallels across these languages, they tried to show that the thought patterns of all these "Indo-European" Aryans were largely the same, and that, in this large portion of the human race, religion began when people reacted to the great and powerful workings of nature. In awesome natural processes like the sunrise and sunset, these ancient Aryans experienced a dim "perception of the infinite," the sense of a single divinity behind the world. Unfortunately, when they expressed this feeling in their prayers and poems, their speech betrayed them. They personified things. The Greeks, for example, belong to the Aryan family; for them the word "Apollo" once simply meant "sun" and "Daphne," the "dawn." Over time these simple original meanings came to be forgotten; at the same time, because the words were nouns with either masculine or feminine gender and because they were used with verbs expressing activity, the names for these natural objects came gradually to suggest personal beings. As Müller put it in a clever wordplay of his own, the *nomina* (Latin for "names") became *numina* (Latin for "gods"). Instead of recalling that every day the dawn fades as the sun rises, people began to tell fanciful tales of the goddess Daphne dying in the arms of the god Apollo. Through this strange process, which Müller called a "disease of language," words meant to describe nature and hint at the infinite power behind it degenerated into silly stories of many different gods, along with their misdeeds and often comical misadventures. Instead of framing a pure, natural religion drawn from an inspired and beautiful perception of the infinite, people succumbed to the absurd stories of mythology.

Tylor, who had little training in languages, thought a few of Müller's ideas made sense and even incorporated them into his own. But he strongly disagreed with Müller's method of building a theory almost entirely on little more than language habits and word derivations. One needed much more than mere verbal misunderstandings of events like the sunrise to explain the beginnings of the complex systems of belief and ritual that go under the name of religion—or even the tales of mythology, for that matter.[12] One purpose of *Primitive Culture,* accordingly, was to present Tylor's decidedly different approach. Even without knowing the language, he felt, it was far better to study a given culture in *all* of its component parts—to explore the actual deeds, habits, ideas, and customs that language *describes*—than to make far-fetched guesses based only on the analogies and origins of certain words. Ethnology was clearly better than etymology.

AIMS AND ASSUMPTIONS

It was against this backdrop—of evolutionary ideas at odds with the Bible and ethnologists opposed to philology—that Tylor introduced his book, announcing it in quite grand fashion as an attempt to pursue a new "science of culture." The proper subject of such an inquiry, he claimed, is not just language, but the whole network of elements that go into the making of what is commonly called human civilization. Ethnology assumes that any organized community or culture must be understood as a whole—as a complex system made up of knowledge and beliefs, of art and morals, tools and technology, language, laws, customs, legends, myths, and other components, all of which fit themselves into a singular whole. Ethnology further requires that these complex systems be explored scientifically. It tries to find patterns, or laws, of human culture and expects these laws to be "as definite as those which govern the motion of waves" and "the growth of plants and animals."[13] Like the chemist or biologist, the ethnologist gathers facts, classifies and compares them, and searches for underlying principles to explain what has been found. Tylor was convinced, moreover, that when this work is properly done, and when the whole span of the human past is placed under observation, two great laws of culture come clearly into view. They are (1) the principle of psychic unity, or uniformity, within the human race and (2) the pattern of intellectual evolution, or improvement, over time.

With regard to the psychic unity of the race, Tylor maintained that throughout the world many things done or said by human beings at different times and places quite obviously resemble each other. Though it may be true that some of these likenesses have come from "diffusion"—from one people managing to teach another its good ideas—it is more often the case that different people discover the same ideas and invent the same customs quite independently. In other words, the similarities are not coincidental; they demonstrate the fundamental uniformity of the human mind. Unlike the "racialists" of his day, who saw fixed and unalterable differences separating various groups within the human race, Tylor and his associates contended that all human beings are in essence the same, especially with regard to their basic mental capacity.[14] When in different cultures we observe very similar things, they may be presumed to be products of a single, universal rationality. With respect to logic—that is, the capacity to follow certain formal and necessary procedures of reasoning—humans of all places and times are the same.[15] For Tylor, as one observer has put it, "all the world is a single country."[16] But if this is true (and here the second principle plays its role), then whenever variations *do* occur, they cannot be evidence of a difference in kind, only of a difference in degree, or a change in the level of development. When two societies are seen to diverge, it is because one must be higher and the other lower on the scale of cultural evolution. Tylor thought evidence of these grades of development could be found everywhere. Because in all cultures each generation learns from the last, he believed he could trace through human history a long pattern of social and intellectual improvement, from the first savages, who hunted and gathered their food, through the cultures of the ancient world and the Middle Ages, which were based on farming, up to the modern era of trade, science, and industry. In history, each generation improves upon the last by standing on its shoulders and starting where the earlier has left off. In brief, Tylor believed firmly that the story of civilization told the tale of "the ascent of man."

The Doctrine of "Survivals"

Having his assumptions, Tylor proceeds to the evidence. We cannot speak of progress, he says, without noticing in some cultures certain things that do not look progressive at all. If a London physician prescribes surgery for an ailment while a doctor in a rural village advises bloodletting, we can hardly say that all of modern English medicine is progressive. We must account also for what is backward. Tylor chooses to do so by outlining his much-discussed "doctrine of survivals."[17] He notes that not all cultures and not all things in any one culture evolve at the same pace. Some practices, proper at a given time, linger long after the march of progress has passed them by. Among these are curious pastimes, quaint customs, folklore, folk medicine, and assorted superstitions associated with almost every conceivable sphere of human endeavor. For example, while no serious modern hunter would still use a bow and arrow to kill game, the skills of archery are still with us; now a sport or hobby, archery "survives" from a bygone age when gathering food was the central task of life. Again, nothing is more common than for people everywhere to give a blessing after a sneeze; it seems trivial. Yet this was once a serious gesture, associated with the belief that at that very moment a spirit, or demon, had come out of the body. Today the blessing survives, but as a meaningless custom whose original intent has been long forgotten.[18] In many countries, people urge, strangely, that one should never try to save a drowning person. Though to a modern view such advice may seem cruel and selfish, it was in earlier cultures perfectly rational, for it was everywhere held that the river or sea, deprived of its almost captured victim, would take revenge on the very person who made the rescue![19] Tylor observes that the record of human history is filled with superstitions such as these, which perfectly illustrate the fact that while the stream of social evolution is real and its current is strong, a trail of cultural "leftovers" always floats in its wake.

If the principle of evolution shows why survivals exist, then it is the companion principle of uniformity, says Tylor, which enables us to understand and explain them. Since—regardless of race, language, or nationality—all human beings reason the same, we can always enter the minds of people in other cultures, even though the level of their knowledge may have been very different from our own. Modern primitives, like ancient peoples, know less than we do and fail to test their opinions sufficiently, but Tylor is certain they still think with the same mental mechanism as ours. So even amid great differences, the uniformity of mind unites the human race.

Aspects of Human Culture

For Tylor the connection between basic rational thinking and social evolution is apparent in all aspects of a culture if we only take time to look at them closely enough. He furnishes as a prime example the use of magic, which is common everywhere among primitive peoples. Magic is based upon the association of ideas, a tendency which "lies at the very foundation of human reason."[20] If somehow in thought people can connect one idea with another, then their logic moves them to conclude that the same connection must also exist in reality. Primitive people believe that, even at a distance, they can hurt or heal others just by acting on a fingernail, a lock of hair, a piece of clothing, or anything else that has been in contact with their persons. Or they think that a symbolic resemblance matters. Some tribal peoples imagine that because certain diseases tint the skin yellow and because gold is of the same color, jaundice in the body can be cured with a golden ring. Others who practice primitive agriculture have been known to torture human victims brutally in the belief that their tears of pain will bring showers of rain to the fields. To us such actions may seem stupid or cruel; to believers in magic, they are rational efforts to influence the world.

Tylor finds the same pattern of rationality in two of humanity's most basic and significant accomplishments: the development of language and discovery of mathematics. In each case, the process starts very simply, with single words that mimic the sounds of nature and with counting systems based on fingers and toes. Then, through the centuries, these concepts are slowly built up to produce the very complicated systems of speech and number that today we master even in childhood and apply with ease in everyday affairs. Over the long span of history, Tylor explains, this process has required countless trials and ended in many errors, but through them all the line of progress makes itself visible. Even mythology, that storehouse of seemingly irrational ideas and often comical stories, is in fact governed by a similar pattern of rational thinking. Myths arise from, among other things, the natural tendency to "clothe every idea in a concrete shape, and whether created by primitives of the remote past or those of modern times, they tend to follow orderly laws of development."[21] Myths originate in the logical association of ideas. They account for the facts of nature and life with the aid of analogies and comparisons, as when the Samoans recall the ancient battle of the plantains and bananas to explain why the winners now grow upright while the losers hang down their heads. In the same vein, a myth may connect suitable imaginary events to the lives of legendary or historical figures; it may grow logically out of a play on words; or it may try, through stories, to teach a moral lesson. In some cases—and here Tylor includes an idea of Müller's—myths arise under the influence of language, which has gender, and out of the natural inclination to make analogies between human activities and processes in nature.[22] If the noise of a storm sounds like an angry human outburst and rainfall suggests tears of sorrow, it is easy to see how, in myth, the great forces of the natural world lend themselves routinely to tales in which their activities are made to look just like those of animals and human beings. Thus earthquakes are attributed by the Scandinavians to the underground writhings of their god Loki, by the Greeks to the struggles of Prometheus, and by Caribbean peoples to the dancing of Mother Earth.[23] Though partly works of the imagination, these personifications are just as clearly exercises in rational thought; they are meant to be real explanations of how things happen. When primitives animate the sun, moon, or stars, they honestly think of these objects as having personal characteristics.

The Origin of Religion

Tylor's comments on myth are important, for in his eyes they mark the path of inquiry that must also be followed in searching for the origin of religion. He recognizes, of course, that we cannot explain something unless we know what it is; so religion must first be defined. He recognizes further that we cannot casually follow the natural impulse to describe religion simply as belief in God, though that is what his mostly Christian readers might want to do. That approach would exclude a large portion of the human race— people who are plainly religious but believe in more, and other, gods than Christians and Jews. He therefore proposes, as a more suitable place to start, his own minimal definition: religion is "belief in spiritual beings." [24] This formula, which others, following Tylor, have adopted as well, has the merit of being simple, straightforward, and suitably wide in scope. For though we can find other similarities, Tylor feels the one characteristic shared by all religions, great or small, ancient or modern, is the belief in spirits who think, act, and feel like human persons. The essence of religion, like mythology, seems to be animism (from the Latin *anima,* meaning spirit)—the belief in living, personal powers behind all things. Animism further is a very old form of thought, which is found throughout the entire history of the human race. So, Tylor suggests, if we truly wish to explain religion, the question we must answer is this: How and why did the human race first come to believe that such things as spiritual beings actually exist?

Stating this question is easy; answering it is another matter. Devout people will want to say that they believe in a spiritual being, such as God, because that being has actually spoken to them, supernaturally, through the Bible or the Quran or some other scripture. For Tylor, however, as for Müller, appeals to divine revelation are not acceptable. Such statements may be pleasing as personal confessions, but they are not science. He insists that any account of how a human being, or the whole human race, came to believe in spiritual beings must appeal only to natural causes, only to considerations of the kind that scientists and historians would use in explaining an occurrence of any sort, nonreligious as well as religious. We must presume, he says, that early peoples acquired their first religious ideas through the same reasoning mechanisms they employed in all other aspects of their lives. Like us, they undoubtedly observed the world at work and then tried to explain it.

What observations, then, did these primitives make? And what explanations did they choose? Tylor at this point peers backward, deep into prehistoric times, to reconstruct the thoughts of the very first human beings:

It seems as though thinking men, as yet at a low level of culture, were deeply impressed by two groups of biological problems. In the first place, what is it that makes a difference between a living body and a dead one; what causes waking, sleep, trance, disease, death? In the second place, what are those human shapes which appear in dreams and visions? Looking at these two groups of phenomena, the ancient savage philosophers probably made their first step by the obvious inference that every man has two things belonging to him, namely, a life and a phantom as being its image or second self; both, also, are perceived to be things separable from the body. . . . The second step would seem also easy for savages to make, seeing how extremely difficult civilized men have found it to unmake. It is merely to combine the life and the phantom. . . . the result is that well-known conception . . . the personal soul, or spirit.[25]

From their vivid encounters with both death and dreams, in other words, early peoples reasoned first to a simple theory of their own lives: every human being is animated by a soul, or spiritual principle. They thought of this soul as "a thin, unsubstantial human image, in its nature a sort of vapour, film, or shadow; the cause of life and thought in the individual it animates."[26] From this premise, they then reasoned, as we all do, by analogy and extension. If the concept of a soul explains the movements, activities, and changes of the human person, why should it not also be applied more widely to explain the rest of the natural world? Why should not plants and trees, the rivers, winds, and animals, even the stars and planets also be moved by souls? Further, since souls are separable from the objects they animate, why may there not also be, behind the visible scene of nature, beings who do not even need to be connected to physical objects—why not spirits, pure and simple? If there are souls in humans, could there not actually be such powerful beings as demons and angels who have no necessary attachment to normal physical objects, though they certainly can enter and "possess" them if they wish? Last, and above all, could there not perhaps be certain supreme spirits, the beings we call gods?

Through this natural, almost childlike chain of reasoning, says Tylor, early humans arrived at their first religious beliefs. Like their myths, their religious teachings arose from a rational effort to explain how nature worked as it did. And from this perspective, all seemed quite clear: as souls animate persons, so spirits must animate the world.

Tylor further argues that the value of this animistic theory to primitive peoples is apparent from the great variety of early beliefs and customs it can readily explain. Doctrines of a future life provide an example. In Oriental cultures there is widespread belief in reincarnation, while in religions of the

Western world, like Christianity and Islam, there are the doctrines of resurrection and immortality of the soul. All of these can be understood, in animist terms, as ways of extending the life of the soul beyond the time of
death. Being separable from the flesh, the soul has an afterlife and destiny
of its own. Animism also explains why sacred objects and trinkets—things
called "fetishes"—are important to primitives. Such people are not "idol-
worshippers," as narrow-minded Christian missionaries used to describe
them. They do not worship sticks and stones; they adore the "anima" within,
the spirit which—not wholly unlike the god of Christians themselves—gives
the wood of the stick or substance of the stone its life and power. Knowing the nature of animism, we can also make sense of tribal medicine. When
a man shakes uncontrollably with fever, he knows that he does not make
himself do this; he believes he is "possessed" by a demon within. To be
cured, he needs not a medicine but an exorcism. The evil spirit must be
driven out of his body.

Throughout most of the entire second volume of *Primitive Culture,* Tylor
provides detailed demonstrations to show just how far-reaching was the doctrine of animism in the earlier centuries of human civilization. He describes
it as a system that spread worldwide, becoming the first "general philosophy
of man and nature" ever devised.[27] Moreover, as it was absorbed by a tribe
or clan or culture, it spread into every aspect of daily life. If one asks why,
across almost all cultures, the gods have human personalities, the answer is
that they are spirits modeled on the souls of human persons.[28] If we want to
know why gifts are given to the dead at primitive funerals and why the
services, especially for great and powerful men, sometimes even include
human sacrifice, animism gives the answers. The gifts provide support for
the soul in its new residence beyond the grave; the sacrifices furnish the
king or prince with the souls of servants to wait upon him in the realm of
death, just as they did in life.[29] Why do the Indians of America talk to
animals as they would to each other? Because, like themselves, animals are
owners of souls. Why does the water move, or the tree grow? Because
nature spirits inhabit them.[30] Why does the medicine man fast or use drugs?
To qualify himself "for intercourse with the . . . ghosts, from whom he is
to obtain direction in his craft."[31]

In this systematic, sequential fashion, with hundreds of examples at his
disposal, Tylor proceeds through the whole range of primitive life, thought,
and custom. At each point he shows how the doctrine of animism makes
sense of ideas and behaviors that otherwise would strike us as nothing more
than irrational and incomprehensible nonsense.

The Growth of Religious Thought

Tylor further explains that once these spiritual ideas acquired their grip on the minds of ancient peoples, they did not remain in a fixed form. Like everything else in history, animism also follows a pattern of growth and development. At first people think of individual spirits as small and specific, associated with each tree, river, or animal they happen to see. Later on, their power begins to widen. Gradually, in tribal thought, the spirit of one tree grows in power to become the spirit of the forest or of trees in general. Over time, that same spirit also comes to be thought of as more and more separable from the object it controls; it acquires its own identity and character. At this stage, when people worship a goddess of the forest, they recognize that the woodlands are her home, but they know she can also leave this home if she wishes. Among the very earliest Greeks, for example, Poseidon was at first simply the spirit of the "divine sea"; later he acquired his trident, beard, and distinctive character, so that by the time of the poet Homer, he had become a mighty and personal deity who could leave the sea and travel swiftly to Mount Olympus when Zeus assembled the gods in council.

Interestingly, Tylor approaches this later growth of a belief in the personal gods of mythology much the way Max Müller does, though he refuses to see it as arising from some unfortunate "disease of language." In the animistic view, the more complex polytheism that we see among the Greeks belongs to an age of cultural progress rather than decline. In ancient Greece, from about the time of Homer forward, a new era of civilization—Tylor calls it the "barbaric" stage—takes over from the earlier "savage" stage. In the savage era, people hunted, gathered, lived in simple villages, and never got beyond their first simple ideas of spirits. With the coming of the barbaric age, we find agriculture, cities, and literacy—all the main elements of the great civilizations built by the Babylonians, Greeks and Romans, the Aztecs, Hindus, and Chinese. In these "higher" cultures, there are divisions of labor and complex structures of power and authority, and their religions show the same characteristics. We find the spirits of local trees and rivers on one level, while above them stand the much greater spirits of the wind, rain, and sun. The local spirit of the river can do nothing about it if the god of the sun should decide to bake dry the streams that feed him or the goddess of rain should choose to transform him into a raging flood. Just as a king and council of nobles rule their subjects, so the sun (or heaven) as king and the earth as queen rule the natural world with the wind, rain, and seasons as their powerful agents or advisers.

Such complex polytheistic systems are quite typical of the barbaric age. They reach their highest form, however, when they are organized in such a way that one god, one supreme being, stands at the top of the divine society. And gradually, by different paths, most civilizations do move to this last, highest stage of animism—belief in one supreme divinity.[32] Needless to say, Judaism and Christianity are the leading examples of the last stage. They form the logical end to the process of development that began centuries ago, in the dark mists of prehistory, when the man whom Tylor calls the first "savage philosopher" concluded that souls just like his own must animate all of the world around him.

The Decline of Animism and Progress of Thought

In one sense, Tylor declares, the story of animism is an encouraging one. Religion can be seen to have gradually evolved upward from the first primitive belief in the spirits of the trees and rocks to the later high plain of monotheism and ethics exhibited in the Judaism and Christianity of the present day. Higher civilization seems to correlate with "higher religions." But that is not the whole of the story. A clear-eyed look at animism and its history in the dry light of science actually suggests a less cheerful view. Whatever progress we find, says Tylor, has been severely limited, and for a simple reason. However great its spread and wide its appeal through history, we cannot forget that animism at bottom is a grand mistake. As any thoughtful modern inquirer knows, the world is *not* animated by invisible spirits. As any modern geologist can tell us, rocks do *not* have phantoms within them. As any botanist can explain, plants are *not* moved to grow by some secret anima in their stem. Science has shown that the real sun and sea owe nothing to the adventures of Apollo and Poseidon, that plants grow by the reactions of chemicals within their fibers, and that the wind and water are only names for a powerful flow of molecules governed by iron laws of cause and effect.

In its time, Tylor concedes, the animist explanation of things was reasonable enough. But the better methods of today's science show us that the reasoning of early peoples has always had its element of unreason as well. Though they can think rationally, one must also remember that primitives think rationally only as children do. Savages, Tylor reminds his readers, are

> exceedingly ignorant as regards both physical and mental knowledge; want of discipline makes their opinions crude and their action ineffective. . . . the tyranny of tradition at every step imposes upon them. . . . much of what they believe to be true, must be set down as false.[33]

It follows from this that whereas the course of reason once led people naturally toward the system of animism, in the modern era, the age of science, that same course of reason ought now to lead away from it. Intellectual progress in the present day must be measured by an opposite movement— the retreat of animist theory from all of those very realms of life it was once thought to explain. Gradually, but nonetheless certainly, Tylor concludes, the falsehoods of savage and barbaric peoples must withdraw before the spreading truth of the sciences. In sphere after sphere of nature, animist spirits and deities must now give way to modern science's impersonal causes and effects. In the modern era, religion's growth, like that of its close friends magic and myth, "has been checked by science, it is dying of weights and measures, of proportions and specimens."[34] Today we truly understand our world only to the degree that we can pull ourselves away from animism's powerful but misguided embrace. A few of its ethical principles may linger as still useful, but its gods must die and disappear.

In the end, then, Tylor's theory provides a mixed portrait of religion and its development. He argues that as an effort of early peoples to understand the world, as a response to its mysteries and uncertain events, animistic religion presents a natural parallel to science.[35] Both are inspired by the human search for understanding—the deep desire to know just how things work. But he insists that religion is also earlier, more primitive, less skilled than science. For him, belief in spiritual beings represents a natural stage in the evolution of human reason, but it is not the end stage, and it is certainly no longer the most rational response to the world now that the program and methods of empirical science have come our way. Like the other odd customs and superstitions people are unwilling to part with, religion is now a "survival." In that connection, the double mission of ethnology, "the reformer's science," requires not only that it point the way of progress but that it also take on "the harsher task" of clearing away the clutter of animism that still persists.[36] Destined to disappear, religion can only slow the progress of mind for those who persist, unwisely, in clinging to its comforts. In the final analysis, says Tylor, animist ideas belong properly to the childhood of the human race, not to its maturity. And having entered adulthood, we must put away childish things.

At the close of this chapter, we will have to examine and assess this theory, along with the judgment on the future of religion that follows from it. Before doing so, however, we must consider how these ideas were adopted and further developed by the younger scholar James Frazer, who was to become Tylor's most famous and influential disciple.

J. G. Frazer

Early in his career, while still a promising young student in classics at Cambridge University, James George Frazer became a "convert" to Tylor's ideas and methods. Thereafter, he began to devote immense effort to anthropological research, and, through the rest of his long life, he promoted his own amplified version of the animistic theory. The centerpiece of Frazer's many labors was *The Golden Bough* (1890–1915), a monumental study of primitive customs and beliefs. As we shall see in chapters to come, this important book has exercised a lasting influence on all subsequent thinking about religion. More than that, in the early years of our century it left a large imprint on almost every field of modern thought, from anthropology and history to literature, philosophy, sociology, and even natural science.[37]

Like Tylor, Frazer came from a Protestant Christian family, but his was not a home of liberal, affluent Quakers.[38] Born on New Year's Day, 1854, in Glasgow, Scotland, he was raised by stern and devout Scottish Presbyterian parents. His father's daily habit of reading the Bible in family worship left him steeped in its sacred stories and permanently affected by the beautiful imagery and the stately rhythms of its language. Of course, the truth of the Bible—as well as the Scotch Calvinist theology of his parents—was quite another matter. Frazer rejected both. Early in life he took the stance of an atheist, or at least an agnostic, in regard not only to Christian teachings but also to those of any other religious system. For him, religion was to be always an interest but never a creed. During the years of his early schooling, he much preferred to immerse himself in the non-Christian world of ancient Greek and Roman civilization. He studied classical languages intensively, winning numerous prizes in Latin and Greek at his high school and at Glasgow University and later earning a scholarship to Trinity College, Cambridge. Eventually he became a fellow of Trinity, where he was to marry a very protective spouse, remain childless, and live the quiet, private life of an English university don for the rest of his days. If ever there was a man who fit the description of an "ivory tower" scholar, it was James Frazer.

While at Cambridge, Frazer pursued his first interest, which was classical literature. He wrote on the philosopher Plato and began to translate the writings of Pausanias, an ancient Greek traveler from the second century A.D. who had compiled a rich record of Greek legends, folklore, and popular customs. These were to prove very useful in Frazer's later studies of primitive religion.

At just about the time he was starting his work on Pausanias, two unexpected encounters changed the course of Frazer's thought—as well as his career. While he was on a walking tour, a friend gave him a copy of *Primitive Culture*. As he began to read, he was attracted at once to Tylor's account of animism and his demonstration of its importance to primitive thought. Even more important, however, was the fact that Frazer found his eyes suddenly opened to the possibilities created by anthropological research and the use of the comparative method.[39] The second encounter was not with a book but a person. In 1883, the very same year that he came upon Tylor's work, Frazer also met William Robertson Smith (1846–1894), a brilliant and controversial Scottish biblical scholar, who soon became his mentor and very close friend.[40] Intellectually, Smith was a perfect soulmate. Like Frazer, he too was fascinated by the way in which anthropology, through its study of the habits of modern tribal societies, could shed light on an ancient subject, in his case the story of the ancient Israelites as told in the Bible. Ahead of his time, Smith actually traveled to Arabia to observe the customs of desert communities and apply them in his research. In particular, he felt that use of "totems" by these tribal peoples was extremely important. Totem use was a practice associated with the tribal custom of dividing into different clans, or kinship groups. Each of these clans commonly attached itself to a specific animal (or occasionally a plant), which it recognized as its totem and then accorded worship as a kind of divinity. Totemism was also linked to exogamy, the practice of marrying only "outside" the clan. If, within a large tribe, a man belonged, say, to the smaller clan of the bear, he was obliged to marry only a woman from another clan (say, of the eagle or deer) and not from his own totem group. In addition, because the totem was sacred, members of the clan were not allowed to kill or eat their chosen animal except (Smith supposed, though there was no evidence) on certain special occasions, when the rule might have been purposely broken, perhaps for some ceremonial totem animal sacrifice. In *The Religion of the Semites* (1890), his most important book, Smith drew on his observations in Arabia and on Tylor's concept of evolutionary survivals to argue that ancient Hebrew practices, especially their sacrifices, fit with uncanny precision into just this category of tribal totemism.

Frazer, for his part, was captivated by both the originality of Smith's ideas and the intellectual excitement that came through his personality in almost every scholarly conversation. In return, Smith, who at this very moment was editing the *Encyclopaedia Britannica*, wisely used his new position to encourage his friend. He asked Frazer to write for him the articles on the subjects of "totem" and "taboo." Frazer accepted, insisting, however, that Smith give him help. It was not long before the work Frazer did to prepare these articles won him over permanently to the anthropological perspective—and laid the groundwork for most of his later research. Soon the

two men were sharing research on primitive customs and beliefs, each rely-
ing on the other in almost equal measure.

The Golden Bough

As he began his turn to anthropology, Frazer did not leave his classical
studies behind. His aim was still to read the Greeks and Romans, but with
one eye also on anthropology, looking for traces of a much older, more
primitive world behind the cultivated poetry, drama, and philosophical writings of the classical authors. Strongly affected by Tylor's doctrine of survivals, he felt that classical civilization could be seen with new clarity once
one noticed the earlier primitive ideas and habits that persisted within it. He
was convinced that a blend of classics and anthropology, of the well worn
and the as yet untried, offered the prospect of a virtual revolution in understanding the ancient world. And it was this perspective that guided him in
the immense research project that was to become *The Golden Bough*. The
publication of this ever-expanding book occupied Frazer for most of his
adult years and became his definitive statement on the origin and nature of
religion. Over its life, *The Golden Bough* grew to three editions and twelve
thick volumes and required over twenty-five years of Frazer's long days in
his study to bring to completion. It was first published in two volumes in
1890. A second, three-volume edition appeared in 1900. New installments
were then added regularly until it eventually reached its full length in 1915.
By that time, what began as a book had ended as an encyclopedia. Fortu-
nately for us, in 1922 Frazer abridged *The Golden Bough* into one very long
single volume; in the discussion that follows, we shall take advantage of
this helpful shorter version.[41]

   The Golden Bough begins like a good mystery. It offers a riddle, some
tantalizing clues, and a striking description of long-forgotten scenes and
events. Frazer explains that along the Appian Way, the ancient road that
runs from Rome to the villages of central Italy, there is a small town named
Aricia; near it, in a wooded grove by a lake called Nemi, stands the ruin of
a temple dedicated by the Romans to Diana, goddess of the hunt, as well as
of both fertility and childbirth. In the happy days of the empire, this lakeside
shrine with its woodland was both a country resort and a place of pilgrimage. Citizens of Rome traveled often to the site, especially at midsummer,
to celebrate a yearly festival of fire. It was to all appearances a restful,
civilized, and lovely place. But the woods at the lakeshore also held a secret. The Roman poets told of a second god, Virbius, who was also worshipped at the temple. He was sometimes identified with the young Greek
hero Hippolytus, who, according to other myths, had been murdered by one

of the gods in a fit of anger, only to be restored to life by Diana, who then chose to hide him here at her temple. Virbius was represented by a very mysterious figure, a man who was understood actually to live in the woods and was said to be both a priest and a king. He took it as his duty to keep constant watch not only over Diana's temple but also over a sacred tree that grew in the forest—an oak with a distinctive yellow branch, or "golden bough." The man bore the title Rex Nemorenis, Lake Nemi's "King of the Wood." Though obviously a human being, this king was thought also to be a god; he was at once both the divine lover of the goddess Diana and the animating spirit of the sacred oak tree around which he stood guard.

Now strange as this King of the Wood himself may seem, the way in which he acquired his position was still stranger. It came by way of a murder. Legend held that this priest-king had taken over the wood by putting to death the previous one, and that he too would keep his power only as long as he remained vigilant and strong, ready in a moment to defend his very life against other would-be kings who might try to take his place and seize his power. To keep his life and rule, the king had constantly to walk the temple woods, sword in hand, and wait for the approach of any would-be assailant. Should his guard fail or his strength weaken, the intruder might at any moment break through, duel the king to his death, and tear away the golden bough, which then entitled the victor to both the sexual favors of the goddess Diana and the priestly rule of the woodland. To the victor also, however, went the same wearying burden of vigilant self-defense—the need to guard the oak without rest and to search the forest for the threatening form of any new man who might approach, ready to kill, and eager himself to become the next King of the Wood.

With an opening scene such as this, so haunted with mystery and hidden danger, curious readers find it hard to resist following Frazer into the long pages of his narrative. But the reason for all of this drama is not just Frazer's wish to tell an unusual story. His purpose is rather to set the stage for his study by providing us with a single, sharp contrast—one that discloses the outline of an earlier, more brutal state of humanity lying just below the surface of the cultures we like to think of as civilized. How, Frazer asks could there be a place as beautiful as the grove at Nemi, a temple and grounds so loved by visitors for its peace and healing renewal, yet at the same time so steeped in a heritage of savage brutality? How is it that a center given over to the comforts of religion could be the stage for a ritual murder? That is a riddle we should very much like to see explained. In searching for solutions, however, Frazer tells us that we will get nowhere if we keep only to the evidence available from the days of classical Greek and Roman civilization. The pastimes of cultivated Romans who visited Diana's temple offer no clues to explain the shadowy, foreboding personage of the King of the Wood. To account for such a figure, we must look elsewhere—into the deeper prehistoric past, when savage ancestors of the Romans walked the very same woods and shores centuries before Diana's temple was ever built. If it should be that among these much earlier peoples we can find an obscure custom or belief that continued down to Roman times, if we should discover one of Tylor's "survivals," then we might very well have a way to identify the King of the Wood and solve his deadly mystery. Doing so, however, requires a great deal of searching and comparing, for prehistoric peoples have left us no documents. The only thing we can do, says Frazer, is reach out everywhere into the folklore, legends, and practices of the most primitive peoples we know to see if among them there can be found any old patterns or traditions into which the Roman legends may fit. If only we can penetrate the system of primitive ideas that lies behind it, the dark riddle of the King of the Wood and his murder can perhaps be understood.[42] As Frazer explains it, however, that task is not a simple one, for when we look closely, it turns out that primitive thinking (and here he somewhat departs from Tylor) is in fact governed not by one but by two quite different systems of ideas: the one is magic, the other religion. Understanding both of these, and the connection between them, is the key that offers entry to the primitive mind.

Magic and Religion

Once introduced, the subjects of magic and religion become a central theme of *The Golden Bough,* and though Frazer does finally return to it, the mystery of the King of the Wood recedes into the background. *A Study in Magic and Religion* is, in fact, the subtitle given to the book in its second edition. To appreciate the crucial importance of both these enterprises to primitive peoples, says Frazer, we must notice a fundamental fact of early human life, whether lived in Diana's woodland or any other place on the globe. It centered on the struggle to survive. Hunters needed animals to kill; farmers needed sun and suitable rains for their crops. Whenever natural circumstances did not accommodate these needs, primitive peoples, being capable of thought, made every effort they could to understand the world and change it. The very first of these efforts took the form of magic. Frazer's full name for it is "sympathetic magic," since the primitive mind assumed that nature works by sympathies, or influences. In words that closely resemble Tylor's, he explains that "savages" (like Tylor, he preferred this word for prehistorical peoples) always suppose that when two things can in some way be mentally associated—when to the mind they appear "sympathetic"—they must also be physically associated in the outside world. Mental connections mirror physical ones. Going beyond Tylor, however, he finds in magic something more systematic, and even "scientific," than his mentor did. He points out that the main connections made by the sympathetic magician are basically of two types: imitative, the magic that connects things on the principle of similarity; and contagious, the magic of contact, which connects on the principle of attachment. In the one case, we might say "like affects like," in the other, "part affects part."[43] When Russian peasants pour water through a screen in a time of drought, they imagine that because the filtered falling water *looks* like a thundershower, sprinkling of this sort will actually force rain to fall from the sky. When a voodoo priest pushes a pin through the heart of a doll decorated with the fingernails and hair of his enemy, he imagines that merely by contact—by contagious transmission—he can bring death to his victim.

Frazer explains that evidence of this magical thinking can be multiplied in countless examples drawn from primitive life around the globe, and he himself supplies them in great number. When, as traders report, the Pawnee Indians touched the blood of a sacrificed maiden to their field tools, they did so because they firmly believed that, merely by contact, its lifegiving power would be transferred to their seeds of maize. When drought strikes certain villages of India, the people dress up a boy in nothing but leaves, name him the Rain King, and at each house sprinkle him with water, all in the belief that this ritual will bring the rains, making green plants to grow again. When the Indians of South America bury lighted sticks in the ground during an eclipse of the moon, they do so because they believe the darkening of its fire will also put out all fires on earth, unless some, at least, are hidden from its influence. In each of these cases, and many, many others that he cites, Frazer shows how simple peoples everywhere assume that nature operates on the principles of imitation and contact. Moreover, they think of these principles as constant, universal, and unbreakable—as firm and certain as any modern scientific law of cause and effect. In India, when the Brahmin priest makes his morning offering to the sun, he firmly believes it will not rise without his ritual. So too in ancient Egypt, the Pharaoh, who represented the sun, routinely made a solemn journey around the temple to ensure that the real sun would complete its daily journey as well. Magic is thus built on the assumption that once a proper ritual or action is completed, its natural effects *must* occur as prescribed. Moreover, the confidence placed in such rites shows that they form a kind of science for primitive peoples. They offer certainty about the natural world and control of its processes.

Frazer also goes beyond Tylor, who tends to speak of magical knowledge as its own reward, in emphasizing the social power that accrues to people who have knowledge of the magical art. It is not by accident, he observes, that in primitive cultures the person who can claim mastery of its techniques—whether called a magician, medicine man, or witch doctor—almost always holds a position of considerable prestige and power. Usually, in fact, the magician rises to the role of king, since he best knows how to control the natural world for the good of the tribe or for the evil of its enemies.[44] Evidence from around the globe supports the conclusion that among tribal peoples, nothing is more common than for the magician to be also the village chieftain or king.

The power that magic can confer on people in primitive societies ought not to blind us, says Frazer, to the fact that it is also faced with a quite fundamental problem. It may look like science, but it is a false science. Primitives can perhaps be deceived, but moderns are not. As every thinking person today certainly knows, the laws of imitation and contact do not apply to the real world. Magic cannot work because the primitive magician, for all his shrewd magical skill, is simply wrong. In point of fact, the real world does not work according to the pattern of sympathies and similarities he mistakenly applies to it. Over time, therefore, the more critical and thoughtful minds in primitive communities draw the reasonable conclusion that magic is, at bottom, nonsense. The magician can try to explain away failures or even take the blame himself, but the facts cry out loudly that it is the system, not the man, that is mistaken. The general recognition of that error is for Frazer a momentous development in the history of human thought, for as magic declines, it is religion that comes to fill its place.

Religion follows a path quite different from that of magic. Here we may recall that Tylor, after defining religion as belief in spiritual beings, found it generally to resemble magic, both being built upon the uncritical association of ideas. Frazer is perfectly content with Tylor's definition of religion, but he is more interested in the contrasts than the similarities it shows with magic. For him the interesting thing about religion is precisely its rejection of the principles of magic. Instead of magical laws of contact and imitation, religious people claim that the real powers behind the natural world are not principles at all; they are personalities—the supernatural beings we call the gods. Accordingly, when truly religious people want to control or change the course of nature, they do not normally use magical spells but rather prayers and pleadings addressed to their favorite god or goddess. Just as if they were dealing with another human person, they ask favors, plead for help, call down revenge, and make vows of love, loyalty, or obedience. These things are crucially important, for ultimately it is the personalities of the gods that control nature; it is their anger that can start a storm, their favor that can save a life, their sudden shift of attitude that can calm a

troubled sea. For Frazer, wherever there is belief in these supernatural beings and wherever there are human efforts to win their help by prayers or
rituals, human thought has moved out of the realm of magic and into that
of religion.

In addition, and though it may not seem so at first, this turn to religion
should be read as a sign of progress. Religion actually improves on magic
and marks an intellectual *advance* for the human race. Why? For the simple
reason that religious explanations are found to be better than magical ones
in describing the world as we actually experience it. Magic, we must recognize, asserts laws that are impersonal, constant, and universal. If the rain
ritual is done correctly, rain *must* actually come; the rules of imitation and
contact do not allow exceptions. Religion, on the other hand, is quite different. It never claims, in the first place, to have iron-clad principles of explanation. To the contrary, it confesses that the world is in the hands of the
gods, who control nature's forces for *their* interests, not ours. Moreover,
the gods are many, with different personalities and often competing aims
and agendas. We worship the gods, we pray and sacrifice to them in the
hope that they will bring rain, or give us children, or heal the sick, but we
cannot force them to do these things. Religion offers no guarantees. And
yet as Frazer sees it, this very uncertainty is in its way commendable. Is it
not a fact that most of nature's processes, great and small, *do* fall outside
our control? To offer prayers that sometimes are answered and sometimes
are not, to ask favors that are granted one day and denied the next—is not
such a view of the world, which places all things under the control of great
and powerful beings beyond ourselves, very close to the facts of our existence as we actually find them? Does it not actually fit far better than magic
to life as we actually encounter it, filled with both its surprise pleasures and
unexpected misfortunes? Like the gods, the world sometimes gives us what
we want—and sometimes it does not.[45]

Magic, Religion, and the Divinity of Kings

With the coming of religion, Frazer continues, there also appear certain
related changes in society. Gradually, the old magician-king gives way to
the new priest-king, whose power lies in the new religious type of thought—
specifically, in his ability to communicate with the gods or, just as often, in
the fact that he possesses a kind of divinity himself. Divine kings are as
natural to the age of religion as magician-kings were to the age of magic,
though we ought not to consider this transition between the two periods to
have been sharp or sudden.[46] Frazer reminds us that cultures evolve slowly
and often unevenly through time. Even as they were gradually turning over

the control of the natural processes from the principles of magic to the personalities of the gods, primitive peoples usually combined the two systems.
Though they may have come to believe in gods, they still reserved a place
for magic; in fact, they often used magic *on* the gods, trying, as it were, to
force them to act favorably on human wishes and prayers.[47] Frazer actually
finds magic and religion to have been mixed so often and in so many cultures around the world that, in the mountains of evidence he supplies, he
scarcely even tries to disentangle the two.

Examples of magic and religion in combination play a key role in some
of Frazer's most important discussions. Ritual prostitution is an instance.
Primitive people, he says, believe that if the sexual encounter reproduces
human life, a ritual act of intercourse performed in the house of the gods
will, by the law of imitation, actually *compel* the divine Sky Father and
Earth Mother to do the same. With that, the rains will come, and crops will
grow for another season.[48] Royal personages are seen in a similar light.
While many tribal societies think of their king, in religious terms, as a god,
they conceive of his powers and his relation to the tribe as magical. As a
deity, the king is regarded as the very center of the world. His mere words
become law. From his person an energy radiates outward in all directions,
so that any of his actions, or any change in his state of being, can affect the
whole balance of the natural order and the whole life of the tribe. At the
same time, it should be noted that this divine power is more magical than
personal in nature—so thoroughly magical, in fact, that even the king himself must bow to it. Frazer notes how some African peoples do not allow
the king to leave his house, because the mere movement of his body would
affect the weather. In ancient Ireland, kings were forbidden to be in a certain
town at sunrise or in another on Wednesdays or to sail their ships on certain
Mondays—all for fear of the effects of their magical powers on specific
places at specific times. The magical charge carried by the person of the
king also explains why monarchs are often surrounded by taboos—sacred
prohibitions meant as life preservers for souls. In some cases, the king may
not be allowed to touch certain persons or things because of the effect his
powers may have on them; in others, persons must avoid the king for just
the opposite reason—because of the ill effects *they* may have on *his* use of
his powers. Even into recent times, the person of the emperor of Japan, the
divine mikado, was so filled with magical power that his feet were not allowed to touch the ground.[49]

In more general terms, Frazer notes, primitive peoples often insist that
because the king is a god, measures must always be taken to preserve his
divine energy, transferring it to a new person whenever he shows signs of
sickness, injury, or age. Nothing was more startling to Victorian readers of

The Golden Bough than the evidence it furnished to show that when, in some tribal cultures, kings age or grow ill, they must be ritually put to death, so that their divine spirit can be conveyed in full strength to a new ruler.[50] Hardly less shocking were its demonstrations that to the primitive mind, such executions are not immoral acts of cruelty; they are sacred acts of magical necessity. This was true, moreover, even though the form of the ritual was subject to change. Since many kings did not relish the prospect of being executed, often a slave or captive, an animal, an image, or even a son was put forward as the king's substitute. Indeed, Frazer at one point suggests that the Jewish festival of Purim and the Christian remembrance of Christ's crucifixion at Passover both fall into the category of these royal substitutions. It is of interest, he notes, that both involve the sacrifice of a kind of "pretend" king and both show a similar intent—to preserve by magical transfer the power of the divine life.[51]

The Gods of Vegetation

Of all the places where magic and religion converge, perhaps none is for Frazer more common than the great, seasonal cults of vegetation and agriculture that are found so widely around the world. Worship of vegetation gods like Osiris, Tammuz, Attis, and Adonis was widespread not only in the ancient civilizations of Egypt, Greece, and Rome but almost everywhere that people began to practice the arts of agriculture. These agrarian cults were steeped in symbols of sexuality and the cycle of birth and death. Ancient Cyprus provides a typical instance. There the god Adonis was routinely paired with the goddess Aphrodite/Astarte, whose rituals included prostitution and a bizarre sexual law requiring all virgins to sleep with a complete stranger at the temple before their marriage.[52] Strange as it may seem, says Frazer, it was not perversion that inspired this practice but the sacred rules of imitative magic. The purpose of the rite was to compel the gods also to mate, so that all of nature could be reborn.

Rituals of death and rebirth served a similar purpose. In the cult of Attis, the myth that recounted the bloody death of the god had to be reenacted each year because it ensured the death of the crop at harvest time; then each spring the god was to be ritually reborn, so the plants could once again come to life and grow. As Frazer explains it, worshippers in these religions "thought that by performing certain magical rites they could aid the god who was the principle of life, in his struggle with the opposing principle of death. They imagined that they could recruit his failing energies and even raise him from the dead."[53] When the rites were performed, all of nature could be expected to benefit from the return of life and growth. In Egyptian traditions, the god Osiris clearly was a personification of the grain; the story of how, after death, his mangled body was scattered across the land offers a mythical counterpart to the process of planting, in which dead seeds are sown across the fields, later to be reborn and rise as growing plants. For nearly all who participate in these religious cults, the sacrifice of, say, some sacred animal identified with a deity, such as the bull of Dionysus, is a magical way of pushing the gods, and consequently the crops, forward in their natural cycle. Similarly, when among primitives an actual human king is sacrificed as a divinity, that horrible ritual runs quite parallel to myths like those of Attis and Osiris, where the magic of imitation is reinforced by the magic of contact. As in the myths, so in the ritual: the body of the victim may be torn apart or burnt, while the flesh and blood, or bones and ashes, are spread on the fields, releasing their magical power to fertilize the soil.[54]

In additional volumes of his study, Frazer brings forward still other primitive customs that fit this magical-religious pattern of thought, most notably those associated with the totem and the scapegoat. Robertson Smith, as we saw, first called Frazer's attention to the primitive practice of totemism, and this practice was the focus of pioneering new research at the very time the second edition of *The Golden Bough* was in preparation. Working among Australian aboriginal tribesmen, two field investigators, Baldwin Spencer and F. J. Gillen, made the remarkable discovery that on certain special occasions the sacred totem animal was indeed killed and eaten by its clan—just as Robertson Smith had earlier guessed![55] The aborigines called the ritual of eating the *intichiuma* ceremony. In it, says Frazer, we can see in perhaps their earliest form the rites of religious sacrifice and the concept of the dying god. By killing the totem, primitives protect against the decline of power in their animal god; by eating it, they take its divine energy into themselves.[56] A similar pattern is to be found in the custom of the tribal "scapegoat."[57] Anyone familiar with the Bible knows how the scapegoat was used by the Hebrews, who each year chose an animal for the specific purpose of being sent away from the community in a solemn ritual and left to wander until it died. Seen in the light of magical principles, this practice arises from the belief that sins or illnesses can somehow be physically driven out of the community by attaching them to an object like a stick or leaf and allowing them to be carried on the animal's back as it travels away. When placed in the context of totem practice and royal executions, the underlying purpose of the ritual becomes apparent: since the animal represents the divine, its banishment is another way of killing the tribal god.

Tree Spirits, Fire Festivals, and the Myth of Balder

In explaining the role played by magical-religious ideas in the worship of vegetation gods, Frazer draws most of his evidence from the ancient Mediterranean world. He was convinced, however, that these ideas and practices could be found in the European countries as well. To prove this point, he relied heavily on the work of a German student of folklore, Wilhelm Mannhardt (1831 1880), who had gathered evidence of the old customs, folklore, and mythology of European peasants into several important books.[58] Among these, Frazer made special note of certain traditions observed by the Celtic peoples of the British Isles and by the Nordic cultures of Scandinavia. In northern Europe, the worship of tree spirits was prevalent; perhaps because of its great size, the oak tree in particular was held sacred. Among the early Celts there were also dramatic fire festivals like the great Beltane ceremony, which was celebrated every spring and fall and called for human images to be thrown into its raging sacred flames.[59] In Norse tradition, again, there was the tragic myth of Balder, the beautiful young god killed by an arrow made of mistletoe, the only thing in all of nature that could do him harm.[60] As with Osiris in Egypt, Nordic mythology presented his death as an immense tragedy, and at the funeral, when Balder's body was burnt aboard his own ship in a huge fire at the ocean's edge, there was deep mourning in the assembly of the gods.

In general terms, these sagas and stories from the North provide still further evidence of magic and religion in close association. But for Frazer they also serve a second purpose; they begin at last to bring the long narrative of *The Golden Bough* to its end. With these stories in hand, he claims that the riddle which began his story can at last be solved, though even at this point the path to the solution is not a simple one. It follows a sequence of comparisons and connections too complicated to trace in detail, so we shall have to be content with a short summary sketch.

If we look closely at the myths and rituals of the North, Frazer explains, it is clear that Virbius, the king of Diana's woodland, and the Norse god Balder, who also may have been once a real person, are both human embodiments of the great tree spirit, the soul of the sacred oak. This is not surprising, for among primitives the spirit, or soul, of an object can always exist in external form.[61] The spirit of the tree need not remain in its trunk; it can also exist, outside its wooden body, in these human forms. Conversely, the souls of deities like Balder and Virbius are capable of traveling outside *their* quite human bodies as well; when they do, they lodge, naturally enough as tree spirits, in the evergreen mistletoe, which grows on the trunk of the oak even in the coldest winter. In this telltale clue, says Frazer, we have at last an explanation for the golden bough said to grow from the tree at Nemi; it is simply a poetic name for the mistletoe, which turns a definite shade of yellow when cut from its tree. Further, the action we find in the Nordic myth, the shooting of the arrow at Balder, closely parallels that of the Roman tale, where the bough is broken by the assailant and in the moment of challenge probably hurled (just like Balder's arrow) at the King of the Wood. Both stories thus seem to be describing the same kind of act: an assault on the god in which his own soul (in the form of the mistletoe) is seized from him and turned against his body to secure his death. The god is killed in order magically to take from him his divine power.

If these parallels are valid, then at this point anthropology can step in to make the final connection. It seems clear to Frazer that the tales of both Balder and Virbius alike must have originated in real events: the prehistoric murder of a tribal king in order to transfer his divine powers as commanded by the laws of early magic and religion. It is nothing less than the sacrificial murders of real human kings from the deep past that lie behind the mortal figures of Balder and Lake Nemi's King of the Wood. The midsummer festivals of fire which the Romans so innocently enjoyed at Diana's temple only confirm the connection. It is no accident that these rites bear a striking resemblance to the midsummer fire rituals found also in Scandinavia. In both there is the common fact of a fire ceremony held at precisely the same time of year—and fueled probably by the sacred wood of fallen oaks. In addition, there are, especially in the northern rites, those curious hints of a victim in the fire: the ritual burning of Balder's body and those human images thrown into the flames of the Irish Beltane fires. Such clues tell us that however innocent on their surface, these ceremonies too are survivals recalling the hideous sacrifice of human beings envisioned as dying gods. Frazer intimates that in the earliest centuries of human life together, there were countless occasions when fires such as these were solemnly lit to welcome the bodies of those unfortunate kings (or their unhappy substitutes) who were human predecessors of Balder and Virbius—gods who had to be slain so that the powers of nature would not weaken but be renewed.

From all of this, Frazer concludes, it should be indisputably clear that the earliest humans lived their lives by a system of ideas that was rational enough for them but fearfully distant from our own. Behind the rites of Diana's temple and the Roman legend of the King of the Wood lies the grim ordeal of human sacrifice, the ceremonial murder of a man thought to be a god.[62] Barbaric to us, such actions were nonetheless rational in the ages that knew them, for the laws of nature were seen to require nothing less than this ultimate sacrifice. Better to kill the one than risk the death of all. To the primitive mind, it was the voice not of revolution but of religion and reason that first uttered the cry: "The king is dead; long live the [new] king."[63]

Conclusion

Looking back on it when he had finished, Frazer described his book as a "voyage of discovery," a journey backward in time to explore the mind of prehistoric humanity.[64] A long voyage it certainly was! Though he rarely left his study, his investigations had taken him—in thought at least—to nearly every place, time, and culture known to the human race. No corner of undiscovered humanity could escape the global reach of his discussions. He gathered information, seemingly, from everyone and everywhere, and he had the great good fortune of being himself at the right place and time to do so. Writing in Cambridge during the golden last decades of the British empire, he was ideally positioned to gather stories from missionaries and soldiers, from traders and diplomats, from travelers, scholars, and explorers who passed on personal observations from every odd and lonely corner of the world. Through their letters, reports, and responses to Frazer's own questionnaire, these sources—some reliable, others less so—provided him with all that he could need and, indeed, more even than he could want.[65]

This great fund of information which Frazer had at his disposal gave him great confidence in the scientific merits of his theory and, with it, his account of the origin of religion. In his view, worship of the gods had arisen, as Tylor first suggested, in the earliest human attempts to explain the world, and it was driven by the human desire to control the power of nature—to avoid its hazards and win its favors. Magic was the first such attempt, and it failed. As it declined, belief in the gods arose, combined with it, and over the centuries moved more and more fully into its place. Religion put its hopes in prayers and pleadings. But in the end, it too has been found wanting; its claims about the gods have been found to hold no more truth than the laws of magic. Accordingly, says Frazer, just as the age of magic was replaced by that of religion, so too the present era of belief in the gods, one or many, must yield to the third and next era of human thought—the age of science, which is now upon us. Like magic, religion must be assigned to the category of Tylor's survivals. Though it clings to life among backward peoples, as a kind of intellectual fossil, its time has passed. In its place has come science, a way of thought now very much alive, which offers knowledge of the world that is both rational and faithful to facts. Like a new and better magic, science abandons the belief in supernatural beings and once again tries to explain the world by appealing to general and impersonal principles. In the present age, however, these are no longer the secret sympathies of imitation and contact but the valid principles of physical cause and effect. As religion fades, science inevitably assumes its place, for it is the rationality of the present, and it knows the true laws of nature. For Frazer, it is magic without the mistakes.[66]

Analysis

If we stand back to observe the theories of Tylor and Frazer in broad outline, several key themes come clearly into view:

1. Science and Anthropology

In terms of their method, Tylor and Frazer both regard themselves as *scientific* theorists of religion. They assume from the outset that any explanation of religion which appeals to claims of miraculous events or to some supernatural revelation must be ruled out. One thing they will not allow is a theory which might claim, for example, that the reason the ancient Hebrews followed the Ten Commandments is because they were actually revealed by God. Only natural explanations, theories acceptable to religious and nonreligious people alike, can be seriously considered. Accordingly, scientific study requires the wide collection of facts, followed by comparison and classification; only after that can one formulate a general theory that accounts for all the instances. Both men feel they can do this best through their new sciences of ethnology and anthropology, which gather samples of behavior from every culture in the world and thus seem ideally suited to the purpose of framing something so broad as a theory of religion.[67] Not surprisingly, both *Primitive Culture* and *The Golden Bough* are very large books, their pages crowded and bursting with examples, instances, parallels, and variations, all meant to support the broad generalizations that are central to the theories they advance.

2. Evolution and Origins

Tylor and Frazer both are committed to explaining religion primarily in terms of its prehistorical origin, its beginning in ages long past and its gradual evolution to present form in the centuries thereafter. They believe that the way to explain religion is to discover how it began, to observe it in its earliest, simplest form, and then to follow its path from its beginnings to the present day. Further, they are convinced that, broadly speaking, this origin is something we *can* actually discover, though not in any single event.[68] Religion, they say, arose in a set of circumstances faced by all prehistoric peoples, who responded to them in ways that, though mistaken, were the best their reason could manage, given the limitations of their knowledge. Further, having arisen in the past, religion has seen its status, along with its claims of truth and usefulness, change significantly over the long process of its intellectual evolution. Through their own hard efforts, Tylor and Frazer contend, human beings have slowly improved themselves by creating ever more civilized communities, by learning more about both the extent and limits of their knowledge, and by treating each other with gradually greater measures of decency, knowledge, and compassion. To be sure, religion—an agent of progress insofar as it once took the mind of humanity a step beyond magic—has played its role in this great evolutionary drama, but only for a time. With the arrival of science, that role now is ended.

3. Intellectualism and Individualism

Theorists today often refer to Tylor and Frazer as advocates of an "intellectualist" approach to religion.[69] By this they mean that both men think of religion as first of all a matter of beliefs, of ideas that people develop to account for what they find in the world. Religion is not seen as in the first instance about group needs, structures, or activities. On the contrary, it is thought to originate in the mind of the individual "savage philosopher," as Tylor calls him, the lone prehistoric thinker who tries to solve the riddles of life and then passes on his interests and ideas to others. Religion becomes communal or social only when an idea seen to be valid by one person comes gradually to be shared by others. Religious groups, accordingly, are in the first instance always viewed as collections of individuals who happen to share the same beliefs.

Critique

In the prime years of their influence, which came in the last decades of the Victorian era, Tylor and Frazer won many disciples within anthropology and even more admirers outside of it—among them people who enjoyed the fascinating application of their ideas to literature, art, history, philosophy, and even popular opinion. To those who read them at the time, these two talented authors seemed capable of shedding new light on almost every feature of religion or society one might want to address. Even so, there were a few, like Max Müller, who had serious doubts about how far one could really go with the methods of anthropology and the principles of intellectual evolutionism. As the years have passed, not only have the ranks of the skeptics grown; the severity of their criticisms has increased as well. Ironically, the most serious doubts now surround precisely those things we noticed above as the key elements of the intellectualist program. They include the following:

1. Anthropological Method

Though both Tylor and Frazer were pioneers in using anthropological data, their methods in going about this task have not worn well over time. Professional anthropologists in particular fairly cringe at the way in which these Victorian anthropologists bring together supposedly similar customs of different peoples in different times and places without the slightest regard for their original social context.[70] It is this method, for example, that allows Frazer to associate Celtic fire festivals with Scandinavian ones, and then, because his argument needs it, to assume conveniently that a practice found only in the former (tossing human images into the fires) must, at some point, have also occurred in the latter. All the while, he also overlooks the fact that while the Nordic fires occur in midsummer, as in the festival of Diana, the Celtic festival occurs only in the spring and fall. After a close look at such loosely made connections, we find ourselves asking what, apart from the mere coincidence that there is fire in each, allows Frazer to connect these festivals at all. Similar stretchings occur throughout the argument of *The Golden Bough,* though less often in the pages of *Primitive Culture.*

2. Evolutionism

The often casual approach to evidence which we find in both theories creates further problems in connection with the doctrine of intellectual evolution, which both Tylor and Frazer assume as an absolutely central element of their thinking. When Tylor finds an example of religious monotheism, he assumes that it reflects a stage of thought later than polytheism. Yet the evidence brought forward frequently does not show such a sequence because it is largely "timeless" in character. Often it is impossible to tell whether, say, belief in one high god developed in earlier or later centuries of a people's history, or perhaps somewhere in between. When Frazer finds a report of purely magical practices, for example, he naturally assumes that these are rooted in a historical era that comes before the age of religion. But how does he know this? The evidence usually cannot tell him. Most of the time, as we have seen, his examples show magic and religion existing together, as if both arose in the long single span of history that was half magical and half religious at the same time. It is not surprising that Tylor and Frazer both found it difficult to respond when other scholars of the time, most notably critics like Andrew Lang and Wilhelm Schmidt, pointed out the uncomfortable fact that monotheism, supposedly the "higher" form of religion, was more common in the simpler cultures of people who hunted and gathered food than in the later, advanced communities of those who farmed and kept herds of domestic animals.[71]

3. The Individual and the Social

Finally, as we shall see in the chapters immediately following, strong doubts have been raised about the intellectualist individualism that Tylor and Frazer endorse. Is it really true that religious behavior arises only, or chiefly, from intellectual motives, as the work of solitary thinkers seeking explanations for life's great riddles and mysteries? Is it really true that the social and ritual elements of religion are purely secondary—always dependent upon the intellectual factor, which is supposedly more fundamental? Moreover, if the origin of religion lies in ages and peoples far beyond the reach of the historical record and must be creatively reconstructed from legends and folkways, how can we ever prove such speculations? They involve so much guesswork as to seem beyond either proof or disproof. It was this issue that led a theorist we shall meet later, E. E. Evans-Pritchard, to say that most explanations of the sort given by Tylor and Frazer are "just so stories"—imaginative reconstructions of what *might have happened,* but nothing more.[72]

However all of this stands, there is little doubt that, historically considered, the intellectualist theories of Tylor and Frazer are of great importance. As we shall see in our later chapters, their work has in many ways served as the starting point for most other theorists both in their time and in ours. Their theories of animism and magic have come to represent a theoretical stance that rival thinkers have felt free to reject, endorse, or revise, but never to ignore.

Notes

1. Abridged ed., p. 51; see n. 40 below.

2. Paul Bohannan, *Social Anthropology* (New York: Holt, Rinehart & Winston, 1969), pp. 311–15, for example, considers Tylor a scholar of major importance, whose work is of lasting value to the field. For a less enthusiastic opinion, however, see Mary Douglas, *Purity and Danger* (Harmondsworth, England: Penguin Books, [1966] 1970), p. 24.

3. The only full-length biography of Tylor is R. R. Marett, *Tylor* (London: Chapman and Hall, 1936). Robert Ranulf Marett was one of Tylor's disciples and an

important theorist of religion in his own right. There is a short appreciation of Tylor's life and work prepared in honor of his seventy-fifth birthday by Andrew Lang, who regarded himself as more an associate and peer of Tylor than a follower; see "Edward Burnett Tylor," in *Anthropological Essays Presented to Edward Burnett Tylor* (Oxford: Clarendon Press, 1907), pp. 1–15. See also the entry by Eric Sharpe, under "Tylor, E. B.," in *The Macmillan Encyclopedia of Religion.*

4. J. W. Burrow, *Evolution and Society* (Cambridge, England: Cambridge University Press, 1970), pp. 234–35; see, for a particularly vivid example, *Primitive Culture: Researches into the Development of Mythology, Philosophy, Religion, Language, Art, and Custom*, 2 vols., 4th ed., rev. (London: John Murray, [1871], 1903), 2: 450.

5. London: Longman, Green, Longman, and Roberts.

6. Third ed., rev., New York: Henry Holt & Company, n.d.

7. For Tylor's associates, disciples, and influence on the study of folklore, see Richard M. Dorson, *The British Folklorists: A History* (Chicago: University of Chicago Press, 1968); on Tylor's work in particular, see pp. 167–97. For his contribution to anthropology, see Paul Bohannan, *Social Anthropology* (New York: Holt Rinehart & Winston, 1969), pp. 311–15.

8. His handbook *Anthropology* (1881), however, was widely read, and he was an active participant in the spirited debates that arose within folkloric and anthropological studies right up to his death in 1917. For an appreciation of the wide range of Tylor's lifelong interests, see Marett, *Tylor*, pp. 120–214.

9. On the influence of early evolutionary ideas on Tylor's thought, see George W. Stocking, Jr., *Victorian Anthropology*, pp. 46–109, and Robert A. Segal, "Victorian Anthropology," *Journal of the American Academy of Religion* 58, no. 3 (Fall 1990): 469–77.

10. On Müller and his theories, see Nirad C. Chaudhuri, *Scholar Extraordinary: The Life of Professor the Rt. Hon. Friedrich Max Müller* (London: Chatto & Windus, 1974); Johannes Voigt, *Max Müller: The Man and His Ideas* (Calcutta: Firma K. L. Mukhopadhyay, 1967); G. W. Trompf, *Friedrich Max Müller As a Theorist of Comparative Religion* (Bombay: Shakuntala Publishing House, 1978); and Ronald Neufeldt, *F. Max Müller and the Rg-Veda: A Study of its Role in His Work and Thought* (Calcutta: Minerva Associates, 1980).

11. Müller developed his views over a period of more than four decades from the late 1850s to the end of the century. Among his most important works were the influential essay "Comparative Mythology," in the *Oxford Magazine* (1856), *Lectures on the Origin and Growth of Religion: As Illustrated by the Religions of India* (1878), and the Gifford Lectures, published as *Natural Religion* (1881). Müller's subsequent series of Gifford lectures, entitled *Physical Religion* (1890), *Anthropological Religion* (1892), and *Theosophy, or Psychological Religion* (1893), develop in more detail the general themes of natural religion—deity, morality, and immortality—which are laid out in the two earlier works. Articles that Müller published to the end of the century echo or offer variations of themes developed in the books.

12. On the differences between Tylor and Müller, see my "Max Müller, E. B. Tylor, and the 'Intellectualist' Origins of the Science of Religion," *International Journal of Comparative Religion*, 1, no. 2 (June 1995): 69–83.

13. E. B. Tylor, *Primitive Culture*, 1: 2.

14. On racialist anthropology among the Victorians, see Segal, "Victorian Anthropology," p. 472.

15. On Tylor's doctrine of the "psychic unity" of the race, see J. Samuel Preus, *Explaining Religion: Criticism and Theory from Bodin to Freud* (New Haven, CT: Yale University Press, 1987), p. 138: and Burrow, *Evolution and Society*, p. 248.

16. Stocking, *Victorian Anthropology*, p. 162.

17. On the general doctrine of "survivals," see Margaret T. Hogden, *The Doctrine of Survivals: A Chapter in the History of Scientific Method in the Study of Man* (London: Allenson, 1936). On Tylor's use of the concept and the way in which it tended to close off discussion of the continuing role such survivals play in the living society that embraces them, see the comments of Bronislaw Malinowski in *A Scientific Theory of Culture* (Chapel Hill, NC: The University of North Carolina Press, 1944), p. 31. Burrow, *Evolution and Society*, p. 240, takes a similar view, pointing out that the key question Tylor leaves unanswered is "why the survivals have survived."

18. Tylor, *Primitive Culture*, 1: 97–102.

19. *Primitive Culture*, 1: 108–11.

20. *Primitive Culture*, 1: 115–16; on the association of ideas, see Burrow, *Evolution and Society*, pp. 248–51.

21. *Primitive Culture*, 1: 408.

22. Though here Tylor's views closely converge with Müller's in other respects, their concepts of myth and religion are noticeably different. While the latter sees mythology as a "disease of language" and quite different in character from religion, the former sees both as arising from "rational" thinking about events and experiences in the world; see my "Max Müller, E. B. Tylor, and the 'Intellectualist' Origins," pp. 69–83.

23. *Primitive Culture*, 1: 327.

24. *Primitive Culture*, 1: 424.

25. *Primitive Culture*, 1: 429

26. *Primitive Culture*, 1: 429.

27. *Primitive Culture*, 2: 356.

28. *Primitive Culture*, 2: 247.

29. *Primitive Culture*, 1: 459–66.

30. *Primitive Culture*, 2: 209.

31. *Primitive Culture*, 1: 414.

32. *Primitive Culture*, 2: 335–36.

33. E. B. Tylor, "The Religion of Savages," *Fortnightly Review* 6 (August 15, 1866): 86.

34. *Primitive Culture*, 1: 317.

35. This is perhaps the best place to note the important work of the contemporary anthropologist of Africa Robin Horton. His approach, which places an emphasis on the close parallel between primitive religious thought and modern scientific theories, is often called "Neo-Tylorian," though it departs from Tylor's dismissal of religious thinking as an outmoded survival. The major essays from Horton's thirty-year career as both a fieldworking anthropologist and quite original theorist of religion have been

published in Robin Horton, *Patterns of Thought in Africa and the West: Essays on Magic, Religion, and Science* (Cambridge, England: Cambridge University Press, 1993).

36. On this "harsher task" Tylor assigns to ethnology, see Stocking, *Victorian Anthropology*, p. 194.

37. For Frazer's influence on historical studies and his role in the development of anthropology, see Eric Sharpe, *Comparative Religion: A History* (New York: Charles Scribner's Sons, 1975), pp. 87–96; Brian Morris, *Anthropological Studies of Religion* (Cambridge, England: Cambridge University Press, 1987), pp. 103–106; and Robert Ackerman, *The Myth and Ritual School: J. G. Frazer and the Cambridge Ritualists* (New York: Garland Publishing, Inc., 1991). On the relevance of his work to issues in philosophy and science, especially questions of epistemology, see Ludwig Wittgenstein, *Remarks on Frazer's Golden Bough*, ed. Rush Rhees, tr. A. C. Miles, (Nottinghamshire, England: Brynmill, 1979). The two most important studies of Frazer's great influence on literature in the twentieth century are John B. Vickery, *The Literary Impact of The Golden Bough* (Princeton, NJ: Princeton University Press, 1973), and the collection of essays in Robert Fraser, ed., *Sir James Frazer and the Literary Imagination: Essays in Affinity and Influence* (New York: St. Martin's Press, 1990). An interesting study of *The Golden Bough* as *itself* a work of literature more than science is Stanley Edgar Hyman, *The Tangled Bank: Darwin, Marx, Frazer & Freud as Imaginative Writers* (New York: Athenaeum, 1974), pp. 233–91.

38. There is an excellent recent biography of Frazer by Robert Ackerman, *J. G. Frazer: His Life and Work* (Cambridge, England: Cambridge University Press, 1987); see also *The Macmillan Encyclopedia of Religion*, under "Frazer, James, G."

39. Robert Fraser, *The Making of the Golden Bough: The Origins and Growth of an Argument* (New York: St. Martin's Press, 1990), p. 14. This study is especially helpful in discovering the sources, influences, and lines of thought that went originally into *The Golden Bough* as well as the revisions and amplifications that followed in the editions after the first.

40. On the encounter with Roberston Smith and his influence on Frazer, see Ackerman, *J. G. Frazer*, pp. 53–69, and Robert Alun Jones, "Robertson Smith and James Frazer on Religion: Two Traditions in British Social Anthropology," in George W. Stocking, Jr., ed., *Functionalism Historicized: Essays on British Social Anthropology*, History of Anthropology, vol. 2 (Madison, WI: University of Wisconsin Press, 1984), pp. 31–58.

41. James George Frazer, *The Golden Bough: A Study in Magic and Religion*, abridged edition (hereafter cited as *Golden Bough*), (New York: The Macmillan Company, 1924). It needs to be pointed out that over the years of its composition, Frazer changed his views on a number of important issues considered in *The Golden Bough*. Myth proved an especially troublesome topic, as did totemism. On the latter, he wavered from one theory to another and had to accommodate new information that kept coming in from ethnographic field studies. On the differences between *The Golden Bough*'s three editions, see Ackerman, *J. G. Frazer*, pp. 95–100, 164–79, 236–57, and Fraser, *The Making of the Golden Bough*, pp. 117–55; 156–202.

42. Frazer, *Golden Bough*, pp. 2–3.

43. Frazer also calls imitative magic "homeopathic." On the forms of magic see *Golden Bough*, pp. 11–48.

44. Frazer, *Golden Bough*, pp. 83–91.

45. *Golden Bough*, p. 58; on this "improvement" through religion, see Jones, "Robertson Smith and James Frazer on Religion," in Stocking, ed., *Functionalism Historicized*, p. 39, where this development is described as "the birth of humility" in human thought.

46. Frazer, *Golden Bough*, pp. 83–109.

47. Frazer, *Golden Bough*, p. 324.

48. For an example, see *Golden Bough*, p. 135.

49. *Golden Bough*, p. 168.

50. *Golden Bough*, pp. 264–83.

51. On this thesis, which was developed chiefly in the second edition, see Ackerman, *J. G. Frazer*, pp. 167–69.

52. *Golden Bough*, pp. 329–35.

53. *Golden Bough*, p. 324.

54. *Golden Bough*, p. 379.

55. On the work of Spencer and Gillen, see Ackerman, *J. G. Frazer*, pp. 154–57; also chapter 3 of the present volume, where the research of Émile Durkheim is considered.

56. *Golden Bough*, p. 494.

57. *Golden Bough*, pp. 562–87.

58. These were *Die Korndämonen (Spirits of the Corn)* (1868); *Der Baumkultus der Germanen (The Tree-Worship of the Germans)* (1875); and *Antike Wald- und Feldkulte (The Ancient Worship of Forest and Field)* (1875–77). On Mannhardt's influence on British anthropology and the work of Frazer, see Sharpe, *Comparative Religion: A History*, pp. 50–51.

59. *Golden Bough*, pp. 617–22.

60. *Golden Bough*, pp. 607–609.

61. *Golden Bough*, p. 667.

62. For a more recent analysis of human sacrifice in religion, see René Girard, *Violence and the Sacred*, tr. Patrick Gregory (Baltimore: Johns Hopkins University Press, 1977) and *The Scapegoat*, tr. Yvonne Freccero (Baltimore: Johns Hopkins University Press, 1986).

63. *Golden Bough*, p. 714.

64. *Golden Bough*, p. 714.

65. For examples of Frazer's correspondence and methods of research, see Fraser, *The Making of the Golden Bough*, pp. 75–85, and throughout. On Frazer's "questionnaire" and the critical comment that he did not rely on it nearly as much as on the work of other scholars, see the two articles by Edmund Leach, "Golden Bough or Gilded Twig," *Daedalus* 90 (1961): 371–99, especially p. 384, n. 4, and "On the 'Founding Fathers': Frazer and Malinowski," *Encounter* 25 (1965): 24–36. Other criticisms of Frazer's method, which are considered further below, can be found in Matthew Hodgart, "In the Shade of the Golden Bough," *Twentieth Century* 157

(1955): 111–19, and Marvin Harris, *The Rise of Anthropological Theory* (New York: Crowell, 1968), pp. 204–205, 562.

66. *Golden Bough*, p. 712.

67. On the contributions, for good and ill, of Tylor and Frazer to the formative ideas and methods of anthropology, see Robert Lowie, *The History of Ethnological Theory* (New York: Rinehart & Company, 1937), pp. 68–85, 101–104; also Harris, *Rise of Anthropological Theory*, pp. 148–66, 204–205.

68. On the scholarly search for the origins of religion, see the recent study by Tomoko Masuzawa, *In Search of Dreamtime: The Quest for the Origin of Religion* (Chicago: University of Chicago Press, 1993).

69. On the intellectualism of Tylor and Frazer, see my "Max Müller, E. B. Tylor, and the 'Intellectualist' Origins," pp. 69–83; for an assessment of recent attempts to restate the Tylorian position, see Gillian Ross, "Neo-Tylorianism: A Reassessment," *Man*, n.s. 6, no. 1 (March 1971): 105–16.

70. These criticisms have come from many quarters of modern anthropology, and they are the main reason why Frazer's views, especially, have been almost universally discarded. There is more respect for Tylor. For an appreciation of his work and a criticism of the doctrine of "survivals," see Burrow, *Evolution and Society*, pp. 244–45. For a particularly stringent criticism of Frazer, see the two articles by Edmund Leach cited in n. 65 above.

71. On the important work of Lang and Schmidt, see Sharpe, *Comparative Religion*, pp. 58–65, 182–84.

72. Evans-Pritchard, *Theories of Primitive Religion* (Oxford, England: Clarendon Press, 1965), p. 25.

Suggestions for Further Reading

Ackerman, Robert. *J. G. Frazer: His Life and Work.* Cambridge, England: Cambridge University Press, 1987. The definitive intellectual biography of Frazer.

Burrow, J. W. *Evolution and Society.* Cambridge, England: Cambridge University Press, 1970. A close study of E. B. Tylor and other early Victorian anthropological thinkers who argued for a pattern of evolutionary growth in both society and religion.

Dorson, Richard M. *The British Folklorists: A History.* Chicago: University of Chicago Press, 1968. Still the best study of the circle of learned amateurs whose work provided a context for the researches of Tylor and Frazer and helped lay the foundations for modern scientific anthropology.

Fraser, Robert. *The Making of the Golden Bough: The Origins and Growth of an Argument.* New York: St. Martin's Press, 1990. Published on the centennial anniversary of the first printing of *The Golden Bough* in 1890, this study examines ideas and influences that found their way into its pages as well as the changes that occurred over the long interval of its composition.

Fraser, Robert, ed. *Sir James Frazer and the Literary Imagination: Essays in Affinity and Influence.* New York: St. Martin's Press, 1990. A collection of essays also published on the centennial anniversary of *The Golden Bough*, it explores

Frazer's wide impact on modern literature and other spheres of intellectual life.

Frazer, James George. *Folklore in the Old Testament: Studies in Comparative Religion, Legend, and Law.* 3 vols. London: The Macmillan Company, 1918.

Frazer, James George. *The Golden Bough: A Study in Magic and Religion.* 3rd edition. 12 vols. London: The Macmillan Company, 1911–1915.

Frazer, James George. *Totemism and Exogamy: A Treatise on Certain Early Forms of Superstition and Society.* 4 vols. London: The Macmillan Company, 1910.

Horton, Robin. *Patterns of Thought in Africa and the West: Essays on Magic, Religion, and Science.* Cambridge, England: Cambridge University Press, 1993. A collection of illuminating essays by the most well known current neo-Tylorian theorist.

Hyman, Stanley Edgar. *The Tangled Bank: Darwin, Marx, Frazer & Freud as Imaginative Writers.* New York: Athenaeum, 1974. An interesting study of *The Golden Bough* as a contribution to literature rather than science.

Lang, Andrew. "Edward Burnett Tylor." In *Anthropological Essays Presented to Edward Burnett Tylor,* edited by Andrew Lang. Oxford, England: Clarendon Press, 1907, pp. 1–15. A short appreciation of Tylor's life and work by a brilliant contemporary of Tylor, who also wrote extensively on the matter of explaining religion.

Leach, Edmund. "Golden Bough or Gilded Twig." *Daedalus* 90 (1961): 371–99. A severe critique of Frazer by a leading contemporary British anthropologist.

Marett, R. R. *Tylor.* London: Chapman and Hall, 1936. Though now dated, the only available biography of Tylor. Marett was one of Tylor's disciples and an important theorist of religion in his own right.

Stocking, George W., Jr. *Victorian Anthropology.* New York: Free Press, 1987. A perceptive and detailed study of the early British anthropologists in their nineteenth-century social and intellectual context.

Tylor, E. B. *Anahuac: Or Mexico and the Mexicans, Ancient and Modern.* London: Longman, Green, Longman, and Roberts, 1861.

Tylor, E. B. *Anthropology: An Introduction to the Study of Man and Civilization.* New York: D. Appleton and Company, [1881] 1898.

Tylor, E. B. *Primitive Culture: Researches into the Development of Mythology, Philosophy, Religion, Language, Art, and Custom.* 4th ed., rev. 2 vols. London: John Murray, [1871] 1903.

Tylor, E. B. *Researches into the Early History of Mankind and the Development of Civilization.* 3rd. ed., rev. New York: Henry Holt & Company, [1865] n.d.

Vickery, John B. *The Literary Impact of* The Golden Bough. Princeton: Princeton University Press, 1973. A study of the surprisingly wide and deep influence which Frazer's book had on some of the greatest writers of the early twentieth century, including, among others, T. S. Eliot and James Joyce.

2

Religion and Personality: Sigmund Freud

Religion would thus be the universal obsessional neurosis of humanity.
Freud, *The Future of an Illusion*[1]

Few thinkers in modern times have stirred more fierce debate than Sigmund Freud (1856–1939), the psychologist from Vienna, Austria, who at the turn of our century shocked not only the field of medicine but society at large with his startling new analyses of the human personality. To this day, almost anyone who hears the name "Freud" associates it at once with two things: psychological therapy and sex. That impression is not inaccurate as far as it goes, but it really does not go very far. Freud was a most unusual man, driven by ceaseless curiosity, towering ambition, and a remarkably wide range of intellectual interests. His original profession was medicine, especially brain research. But the more he traveled on this path of specialized study, the more it branched into new and different directions. His neurological research soon widened into a more general interest in mental illness and other puzzles of the mind. And before long he had proposed a provocative new theory of the human personality. From this platform, he moved confidently ahead, searching out the psychological dimension in almost every aspect of human life, from seemingly insignificant things like dreams, jokes, and personal quirks to the deep, complex emotions that steer personal relationships and shape social customs. Wherever he turned, he seemed able to find yet another application of his ideas. They illuminated questions about the nature of the family and social life; they offered clues to the explanation of mythology, folklore, and history; and they suggested new interpretations of drama, literature, and art. To Freud and his followers, it sometimes seemed as if he had found an explanatory golden key. Analysis of the psyche opened a door on the innermost motives of human thought and action, from the stresses of the individual personality to the great forces that drive and shape civilizations. It could uncover the smallest secret of a single, troubled self and at the same time offer a new perspective on the great endeavors of human history, among them society, morals, philosophy, and—not least—religion.

Background: Freud's Life and Work

Freud was born in 1856 in Moravia, a part of central Europe which then belonged to the sprawling Austro-Hungarian empire.[2] His family was Jewish, and his father, a widowed merchant, already had two grown sons when he chose to remarry. Freud was the first child born to his father's much younger second wife; he thus grew up in a complex extended family. His playmates as a child were his own nephew and a niece, Pauline, a girl whom he liked to torment but to whom he was also attracted. Looking back later on his childhood, Freud found this experience to be evidence of ambivalence, a state of divided emotion, which appears as a key theme in his writings, especially when he considers religion. Human beings, he believed, are often driven by contradictory feelings of both love and aggression directed toward the same object or person.

While still a boy, Freud moved with his family to the capital of the empire, Vienna, where he was to live and work almost all of his years. As a Jew, he found it impossible to develop any real love for this predominantly Catholic city, but his family did become comfortable in it. For almost his entire life, in fact, he would remain there, raising his own children to adulthood and leaving only in the year before his death, when the coming of the Nazis to Austria forced him to take refuge in England. Freud's parents were conscious of their Jewish identity, observing Passover and giving the children some synagogue instruction, but in other respects they were religiously indifferent. They did not follow Jewish dietary laws, and they adapted to Christian holidays, such as Christmas.

In high school Freud was a gifted student who took courses in Greek, Latin, and Hebrew and finished at the top of his class. Alongside German, his native language, he became fluent in both French and English, then went on to teach himself Spanish and Italian. In 1873, when he was seventeen, he became a medical student at the University of Vienna, where he began research in anatomy and physiology. After graduating as a doctor of medicine in 1881, he began working in the Vienna General Hospital, where he continued his brain research. A few years later, he married Martha Bernays, who became a housewife, a mother to their six children, and a companion throughout their long married life.[3]

During his earlier years of medical work, Freud encountered Josef Breuer,

a man who had done careful case studies of mental illness and soon became
a close friend. In addition, in 1885 he visited Paris to study nervous disorders with Jean-Martin Charcot, a famous French physician. This visit became a turning point, for it sparked Freud's permanent interest in the psychological study of the mind rather than purely physiological research on
the brain. After Paris, Freud returned to Vienna, continued his work with
the mentally ill, and published his first book, *Studies on Hysteria* (1895),
which was written with his friend Breuer. Significantly for Freud's later
work, the two authors described in this study a process of *repression,* by
which troubled people seem to force themselves to forget painful experiences in their lives. Freud also reported success in treating neurosis—that
is, the irrational behavior of these troubled people—by using hypnotism or
simply by engaging them in discussions of their illnesses.[4] With one patient
in particular, a woman he called Anna O., he claimed success in curing her
of hysteria by working back through word associations to an event which
was the cause of her problem. This use of a conversational approach was a
key step. Out of it Freud would develop a way of investigating—and treating—the human mind which he put at the center of all his work. He chose
to call it "psychoanalysis."

As Freud envisioned it, the clinical practice of psychoanalysis consisted
mainly of listening to a patient, who at regular appointments was encouraged
to feel comfortable saying whatever came to mind, in whatever way it came,
without any logical sequence or story line. Patients were to speak simply by
"free association" of ideas and memories. To many people (in Freud's day
and ours), such a technique may seem little more than a waste of a good
physician's time. But Freud felt differently; he found in psychoanalytic conversation an unexpected avenue into the most hidden part of his patients'
personalities. He began also to analyze himself, making special note of the
things that came up when he was dreaming, and he asked his patients to do
the same. Working in this vein with patients over a full five years of practice
and research, Freud listened, read, reflected, and then drew conclusions that
were put into a work entitled *The Interpretation of Dreams* (1900). It was
this epoch-making book, published on the very edge of the new century,
which launched the great "Freudian revolution" in modern thought. Among
other things, this work outlined for the first time Freud's remarkable concept
of "the unconscious"—a notion we will examine more closely in a moment.

Though severely criticized by the medical establishment, Freud's work
nonetheless attracted a small circle of interested followers. In 1902 he
formed with these first associates and disciples a professional organization
that became the Vienna Psychological Society. Included in this circle, or
connected with its members, were several men who became famous along-

side Freud: Otto Rank, Karl Abraham, Alfred Adler, Carl Jung, Ernest Jones, and others. Several journals were established, and psychoanalysis found itself gradually transformed from a method and a few creative ideas to a path-breaking new field of scholarly investigation.[5]

During this same interval and through the hardships of World War I, new ventures in psychoanalytical theory began to flow steadily from Freud's pen. In several extremely productive years just after the turn of the century, he sought to explore the wider implications of psychoanalytic thought, publishing such works as *The Psychopathology of Everyday Life* (1901) and *Three Essays on the Theory of Sexuality* (1905). A number of journal articles appeared in the decade before the war, including one on religion and neurosis and several others on primitive religion.[6] These latter efforts became the book *Totem and Taboo* (1913). In the following years, while fighting raged elsewhere in Europe, he wrote further articles on the topics of the unconscious, the basic human drives, and repression while also completing his *Introductory Lectures on Psychoanalysis* (1916–1917). As peace returned and his struggle to draw notice continued, he added new works, among them *Beyond the Pleasure Principle* (1920), *The Ego and the Id* (1923), and *The Question of Lay Analysis* (1926). All along, he energetically promoted the field of psychoanalytical study by continuing to see patients, corresponding with colleagues in his inner circle, arranging scholarly congresses, and supporting two academic journals which published new work in the field.

In the last two decades of his life, Freud added to his more specifically psychoanalytical studies several controversial works on general subjects related to society, science, and religion. These included *The Future of an Illusion* (1927) and *Moses and Monotheism* (1938), two books which, along with the earlier *Totem and Taboo*, express his main ideas on religion. We will consider them shortly.

Freudian Theory: Psychoanalysis and the Unconscious

We can best understand Freud by beginning where he himself does—with the discoveries he reports in *The Interpretation of Dreams* (1900).[7] In this important book he begins by observing that human dreams have always attracted curiosity, figuring widely in myth, literature, folklore, and magic. Tylor, as we saw, thought that it was the experience of dreams which led primitive people to believe in souls. Freud accepts these claims, but makes it clear that he is prepared to say more. He insists that dreams are more significant than mere curiosity or even theories of the soul would ever lead us to guess. Among other things, dreams show just how much more there is to the activity of the human mind than what appears on the surface of ordinary life. Everyone, Freud tells us, has at least some grasp of everyday conscious thought; when we speak to a friend, write a check, play a game, or read a book, we not only use our minds but know that we are doing so. Further, we all recognize that beneath our surface awareness lie other ideas and concepts that seem best described as "pre-conscious." These are memories, ideas, or intentions that we are not aware of at the moment but can easily recall when asked—things like the ages of our parents, what was served for dinner yesterday, or where we intend to go on the weekend. Though not in a given moment aware of such things, the mind can easily retrieve them when needed. In the experience of dreams, however, Freud contends that we come upon something quite unlike either the conscious or pre-conscious level of mental activity. We draw upon another layer, a different region, of mind that is deep, hidden, huge, and strangely powerful. This is the realm of the unconscious. Like the underside of an iceberg, this deep sector of the self, though unrecognized, is enormously important. It is the source, first, of our most basic physical urges, our desires for food and sexual activity. Second, bundled together with these drives is a quite extraordinary assemblage of ideas, impressions, and emotions associated with everything a person has ever experienced or done or wished to do, from the first days of life up to the most recent minute. If we want an image of it, we might call this realm of the unconscious the mind's mysterious cellar, a dark storehouse necessary for life upstairs, but filled down below with a jumble of half-formed urges that blend with images, impressions, and trace memories of past experience. Up above, the conscious mind is unaware of these things, but they do exist, and they exercise a powerful indirect influence on all that we think and do.

When he first wrote of it, Freud recognized, of course, that his idea of an unconscious mind was not entirely new. He noted that great poets and philosophers had suggested such an entity long before him, but their writings were intuitive, not scientific. Though they perceived something mysterious that was deep in the self and sensed its power, they had no way of explaining why such a thing should exist or how it might work. Psychoanalysis, he felt, was very different. It possessed a rational method of finding out the contents of this hidden realm and explaining what purpose it serves. Freud claimed that basic biological drives, for example, are found there because they cannot be anywhere else; they are by nature without consciousness.[8] Images and emotions, on the other hand, sink down into it from the conscious mind up above. In fact, they can be understood to come into the unconscious in two ways. Either they drift in quietly as a kind of faint transcript of past experience, or they are forced down, as it were, for quite specific and unusual reasons. In the second instance they have traveled down into hiding because of a complex sequence of events that has first taken place up on the plane of conscious thought and action. Freud asserted the opinion that they have been forced there by repression, the remarkable process he and Breuer managed to identify in their intense conversations with distressed patients.[9] Most of these people possessed a common characteristic. Some earlier event or circumstance in their lives produced an emotional response so powerful that it could not be expressed openly; it was therefore repressed, or pushed down into the unconscious and out of mental view. On the surface, said Freud, an event repressed is an event forgotten, but, in fact, it has not disappeared. Unconsciously it remains very much in the mind, only to work itself back out in quite puzzling ways. Repressed thoughts and emotions release themselves in forms of action no rational person would engage in: pointless movements, unfounded fears, irrational attachments, obsessive personal rituals, and other strange behaviors Freud described with his term "neurotic." Victims of such neuroses, he insisted, could not be treated with medicines, but they could be helped by psychoanalysis. A skilled therapist, he observed, can bring the repressed thought up into consciousness, allow all of the neurotic emotions to be properly released, and through this process bring the behavior to a level of awareness that allows it to be controlled.

In first framing these central concepts of repression and the unconscious, Freud relied heavily on his early encounters with neurotic people, some of whom were suffering from serious personality disorders. But the evidence he drew from dreams, which, of course, everyone experiences, suggested to him that *all* human activity—normal as well as abnormal—could be shown to be powerfully affected by the unconscious.[10] Dreams indicated that to a degree, all persons are neurotic. Freud chose to describe dreams as "wish fulfillments." They are states of mind created by the fact that we feel certain powerful drives—such as the craving for a sexual encounter—which are rooted in the needs of the body.[11] These drives naturally have no sense of time; they want satisfaction immediately. And though we might like to accommodate them exactly as felt, the facts of normal life usually make this impossible. In most waking hours, when the conscious mind is in control, they must be repressed—driven down into the unconscious. And yet so powerful are these urges and emotions that, as soon as we sleep, as soon as our consciousness fades, they begin to "leak out" in the form of dreams—just as the mentally disturbed person's repressions leak out in the form of strange, neurotic behavior. For the psychoanalyst, then, the interpretation of a dream achieves a purpose similar to that of an audience with a neurotic person; both offer pathways into the secret corridors of the unconscious.[12]

Nor is this all. Freud came to believe that many things we do even in waking life are ruled by the hidden energies of the unconscious. In further books like *The Psychopathology of Everyday Life* (1901) and *Wit and Its Relation to the Unconscious* (1905), he sought to show that such routine happenings as jokes, slips of the tongue (the well-known "Freudian slip"), absentmindedness, memory lapses, doodling, and even bodily quirks and gestures all originate in the unconscious. Widening the circle still further, he pointed to the power of the unconscious in the achievements of great artists, dramatists, and writers. In the light of psychoanalysis, the works of Leonardo da Vinci, Michelangelo, Dostoyevsky, Sophocles, and Shakespeare all could be seen as shaped by forces rising up from the unconscious.[13]

According to Freud, then, it is no accident that the familiar stories found in mythology and folklore and the recurring themes of art, literature, and religion bear a strong resemblance to the subjects and images that keep returning in human dreams. All testify to the secret, subterranean power of the unconscious.

The Personality in Conflict

In his writings, Freud traces so many different things to the unconscious that one may wonder whether the idea is pushed to an unbalanced extreme. But he insists not. The unconscious, in his view, is central to thought because it serves as the crucial link between what is physical and what is mental in the human person. After all, there are no pure spirits in the human race. Every personality must be rooted in a physical body, which is driven by certain basic biological instincts, or drives. Hunger is instinctive and so is the sex drive; these physical impulses preserve both the self and the species, the human individual and the race. Both operate on the "pleasure principle." We feel a need, and we feel pleasure when it is satisfied. It is an element of our very nature as physical beings that we seek pleasure and turn away from whatever fails to provide it.

In themselves, then, the physical drives are simple things. They represent the instinct for pleasure. Strains and tensions arise, however, because these drives are of different kinds: they can and do come into conflict whenever they collide with each other or whenever they meet the unchangeable set of facts that make up the outside world. If I see an apple when hungry, I eat it and satisfy the pleasure principle in doing so. But should another person, also hungry, be holding the apple, then I face a conflict. The facts of the situation force me to repress my drive. Since the risk of losing the apple altogether is too great, I must, regretfully, agree to share it. In the face of reality or the claims of other drives, we cannot escape the fact that some drives on some occasions must be repressed. And such repressions feed the unconscious.

Freud struggled long and hard to determine just what were the most basic human drives and to describe how they operated. At first he thought there were only the "ego instinct," represented by hunger, and the *libido* (the Latin word for "desire"), which represented sexuality. Later on he spoke of both of these as forms of one drive he called *eros* (the Greek for "love") and suggested an opposite drive, aggression, as the other. Later still, and without discarding the idea of aggression, he settled upon eros as the drive to continue life and *thanatos* (the Greek for "death") as the drive to end it.[14]

Whatever the labels, the fundamental thing about the drives is the idea of conflict, of struggle that takes place both within the family of drives themselves and between the drives and the outside world. This idea of an unavoidable competition at the center of the self is what led Freud to come up with perhaps the best known of all his concepts—the threefold division of the human personality into the ego (Latin for "I"), the superego (Latin for the "I above"), and the id (Latin for "it").[15] In this scheme, the id is considered the earliest and most basic of the three elements. Rooted in the early, animal stage of human evolution, it is unconscious and unaware of itself; it is where the raw, physical drives of the body come to a form of mental expression in wishes—to eat, to kill, or to engage in sex. At the other extreme, the top of the personality so to speak, lies the superego. It represents a collection of influences which, from the moment of birth, begin to be imposed on the personality by the outside world. These are the attitudes and expectations of our society, as framed first by the family and then by larger groups, such as the tribe, the city, or the nation. Finally, suspended in a position between the demands of society and the desires of the body, we find the third element of the self—the ego, or "reality principle." The ego might best be called the "choosing center" of the human person. Its troublesome task is to perform a continual balancing act within. It must, on the one hand, satisfy the desires of the id and, on the other, be ready to curb or deny them whenever they clash with the hard facts of the physical world (like the fact that fire burns), or the social restraints imposed by the superego.[16]

As some have noticed, this sketch of the mind bears an interesting resemblance to that of Plato, the Greek philosopher who explained the self on the analogy of a charioteer trying to control the wayward horses of reason and passion. Freud, too, suggests that the personality is the scene of a continuing struggle to balance out powerful contending forces. There are the physical drives; there is the immovable outer world; there is the weight of society's demands; and there is the difficult task, which falls heavily upon the ego, of finding a way to accommodate and balance all contenders. "Action by the ego," Freud writes, "is as it should be if it satisfies simultaneously the demands of the id, of the superego, and of reality—that is to say, if it can reconcile their demands with one another." [17]

Infantile Sexuality and the Oedipus Complex

Freud's most fascinating application of this conflict model of the personality appears in his now famous theories of infantile sexuality and the Oedipus complex. As most know, Freudian theory places great importance on childhood, especially the earliest years of life—from birth to age six. If he had merely claimed that this is the age when much of what he calls the superego is formed—that is, the age when parents plant the rules of reality, family, and society in the child's mind—Freud would have pleased many and disturbed no one. That only confirms common sense. What he actually puts forward, however, is a stunning idea that many people found not just wrong but perverted. He boldly insists that early childhood, no less than adult life, is strongly shaped by the sexual desires of the id. In his *Three Essays on the Theory of Sexuality* (1905), he argues that from the moment of birth onward, physical, sexual urges govern much of the behavior of an infant child. In the first eighteen months of life, there is an oral phase, in which sexual pleasure comes along with nourishment from sucking at a mother's breast; from that time up to age three, there is an anal phase, when pleasure comes from control of excretion; from age three onward, the genital organs assume importance. This phallic stage (from the Greek *phallos,* meaning "penis"), which includes masturbation and sexual fantasies, reaches to the age of six, at which point a nonsexual stage of latency sets in. This phase lasts until the early teens and the arrival of full adult sexual capacities.

As a person passes through this development, the earlier sexual stages do not completely disappear; they are instead overlaid by the new ones. Accordingly, cases of abnormal behavior are best understood as fixations, as the failure to move on to the next level of growth, or in other cases as regressions, in which people move backward into earlier stages. A person obsessed with ordering the trivial details of life, for example, might be described as suffering a fixation in the anal stage, when behavior is excessively control-oriented, and could conceivably even regress to the infantile oral stage. This view of human development turns out to be especially important when Freud turns to religion, for one of his main concerns is to find the place of religious belief in the sequence of normal emotional growth. Does it belong to an adult stage of the personality's development or to an earlier phase? A great deal, obviously, hinges on the answer to this question. Moreover, when Freud discusses the history of human civilizations, he likes very much to use the analogy of individual growth, as if he were talking about an individual person. This comparison enjoyed wide acceptance in Freud's day, and a version of it was captured in the famous aphorism of his contemporary, the German biologist-philosopher Ernst Haeckel: "Ontogeny recapitulates phylogeny." (The development of the individual reenacts the evolution of the species.) Haeckel, of course, sees the individual as the mirror of the group, while Freud finds the reflection to go the other way. The important thing to notice, however, is that anyone who accepts Freud's pattern will be inclined to take one view of religion if it is seen as belonging to the childhood of the human race and quite another if it is taken as a mark of adulthood, of civilization in its maturity.

Probably no one needs to be told that infantile sexuality—and its link to religion—is on clearest display in what Freud calls the Oedipus complex. This well-known term comes from the celebrated tragedy (which Freud translated as a schoolboy) by Sophocles, the great dramatist of ancient Greece. It tells the story of King Oedipus, a proud, good man whose fate it was quite unknowingly to kill his father and then marry his own mother. In a way that is remarkably parallel to the story of Oedipus, Freud tells us, children in the phallic stage (between ages three and six) experience the desire to displace one of their parents and become the lover of the other. The boy, discovering the pleasure given him by his penis, wants to become the sexual partner of his mother, thereby taking the place of his father, whom in a sense he "hates" as his rival. Sensing these feelings, the mother, with supporting threats from the father, discourages her son from touching his sexual organ; there is even the threat it could be cut off. The son, in turn, is genuinely frightened, and surmising from girls' lack of a penis that such a thing could actually happen to him, experiences a castration complex—"the severest trauma of his young life."[18] The son therefore finds that he must submit to his father, give up hope of possessing his mother, and get his satisfaction from sexual fantasies instead. Still, he never entirely gives up his desire for his mother or ends his jealous rivalry with his father. Young girls experience similar emotions but along a different path. They envy the male penis, imagine they have the same organ, and at first seek a similar encounter with the mother, only later to accept their feminine role and acknowledge the rightful authority of their father.

Even after the contemporary sexual revolution, Freud's account of the

Oedipus complex still comes to many people as something of a shock. They find it inconceivable that the innocence of childhood could be shaded by such powerful drives and dark emotions. But Freud is convinced of it. Even more, he feels that the Oedipus complex is actually "the central experience of the years of childhood, the greatest problem of early life, and the main source of later inadequacy."[19] Indeed, oedipal conflicts are a problem for society as well as the individual. If this deep incestuous urge were to be acted upon, it would be exceedingly damaging to the entire family unit, which is crucial to the child's own survival. If carried out, in other words, the urge toward incest would ultimately be destructive of both the self and society, just as it certainly was for King Oedipus in the play. It follows, then, that already in the earliest phase of life, a struggle arises in the child between the drive for sex and the need of a family. In their very first years, all human beings begin to discover that unless they find a balance, unless they can control their colliding desires, there can be neither a family nor society and hence no framework of security for the self. Restraints must be placed on some of our urges, for without them we cannot have a civilization, and without civilization we cannot survive.

Later Developments and Writings

In his mature years, Freud developed and refined his theories, looking always for new dimensions and wider applications of his core ideas: the unconscious, the Oedipus complex, neurosis, and the three-part framework of human personality. In *Beyond the Pleasure Principle* (1920), he revised his earlier understanding of the basic drives, which to him centered on sex and self-preservation—the two urges that create and sustain life—by adding a different but equally basic drive that sought to do just the opposite. This "death instinct" (thanatos) was the backward urge to restore the world to its primal state, to the time when there was no life at all. Such a concept, he felt, was the only thing that could account for the many instances of such behaviors as masochism and sadism, in which people avoid pleasure and actually seek pain. In *Group Psychology and the Analysis of the Ego* (1921), he expanded the concept of the *libido,* or sexual desire, to include the broader idea of diffused emotional attachment, such as is found in a family. Then he applied it to explain how an organized community like a church depends on personal attachments to a leader; in Christianity, for example, devotion to the person of Christ and one's fellow believers is what gives this huge, varied community of people a sense of binding solidarity.

    With the outbreak of World War I, Freud began to reflect at length on the themes of death, human weakness, and the limits of civilization. In the difficult years between the two world wars, his commitment to psychoanalysis remained strong, and he placed great faith in the progress of science. Still, a general sense of melancholy, of pessimism about the plight of humanity began to come forward. We find this attitude especially in *Civilization and Its Discontents* (1930), where he explores the unhappy conflict between our instinctive personal desires, most notably the power of human aggression, and the strong restraints that society must place upon them if humanity is to survive.

Freud and Religion

Once he had developed the basic ideas of psychoanalysis, Freud found religion a most promising subject of study.[20] In childhood, of course, he had gained a basic acquaintance with the teachings of Judaism. Although his family was largely non-religious, he knew well the stories and writings of the Hebrew Bible.[21] He also developed a useful working knowledge of Christianity, drawn partly from the facts of life in staunchly Catholic Vienna and partly from his own wide reading in the history and literature of Western civilization. Further, religious ideas, imagery, and parallels figured prominently in the neuroses of some of his first patients. His personal stance, however, was one of complete rejection of religious belief. The biographer who knew him best tells us bluntly that "he went through life from beginning to end a natural atheist."[22] Freud found no reason to believe in God and therefore saw no value or purpose in the rituals of religious life.

In light of this background, it is not surprising that Freud's approach to religion, like that of Tylor and Frazer, is quite the opposite of that taken by people who are themselves religious. In most cases religious believers say that they believe as they do because God has spoken to them through the Bible, because a divinity has touched their hearts, or because what their church or synagogue teaches is the truth. Freud, by contrast, is quite sure that religious ideas do not come from a God or gods, for gods do not exist; nor do such beliefs come from the sort of sound thinking about the world that normally leads to truth. Like Tylor and Frazer, Freud is certain that religious beliefs are erroneous; they are superstitions. At the same time, he notes that they are interesting superstitions, which raise important questions about human nature: Why, if they are so obviously false, do so many people persist in holding these beliefs, and with such deep conviction? If religion is not rational, how do people acquire it? And why do they keep it? Tylor shows almost no interest in these questions, and Frazer, though he does somewhat explore the attractions of magic, largely ignores them as well. Freud, however, does consider them—and with good reason. In psychoanalysis he claims to have found the answers.

In an early article published under the title "Obsessive Actions and Religious Practices" (1907), we can find a first clue to Freud's approach. In it he observes that there is a close resemblance between the activities of religious people and the behaviors of his neurotic patients. Both, for example, place great emphasis on doing things in a patterned, ceremonial fashion; both also feel guilty unless they follow the rules of their rituals to perfection. In both cases too, the ceremonies are associated with the repression of basic instincts: psychological neuroses usually arise from repression of the sex drive; religion demands repression of selfishness, control of the ego-instinct. Thus, just as sexual repression results in an individual obsessional neurosis, religion, which is practiced widely in the human race, seems to be "a universal obsessional neurosis." [23] This comparison suggests a theme that is fundamental to almost everything Freud writes on religion. In his view, religious behavior always resembles mental illness; accordingly, the concepts most suited to explaining it are those that have been developed by psychoanalysis.

All three of the books Freud devotes to religion take this basic approach, but they do so in distinctive ways. As it happens, all three are also fairly brief. So instead of choosing just one, we can give some consideration to each of them, all the while noticing the pattern of psychoanalytic explanation that is common throughout.

Totem and Taboo

Totem and Taboo (1913) is a book Freud regarded as one of his best. It presents a psychological interpretation of the life of primitive peoples. It employs the concepts of psychoanalysis, but, like other books of the time, is also influenced by evolutionary thinking—not just Darwin's theory of biological evolution but the general ideas of intellectual and social evolution as well. In it, Freud accepts the opinion of his age that it is not just our physical selves which are products of evolution; he also adopts the idea, shared by Tylor and Frazer, that we have also evolved intellectually and observes that our social institutions, like our animal species, have traced an unsteady but still upward line of progress. Consequently, he argues, just as we find clues to the personality of individual adults in their earlier character as children, so we find in the character of past cultures important clues to the nature of civilization in the present. This past, moreover, includes not just our civilized ancestors like the Greeks and Romans but—now that Darwin has shown the connection—even prehistoric cultures and peoples, those communities of humans who first descended from their animal ancestors.

With these premises in hand, Freud turns next to two practices of primitive peoples which strike modern minds as especially strange: the use of animal "totems" and the custom of "taboo." Tylor, Frazer, and other anthropologists were fascinated by these customs, as we have noticed.[24] In the first case, a tribe or clan chooses to associate itself with a specific animal (or plant), which serves as its sacred object, its "totem." In the second, some person or thing is called "taboo" if a tribe wants to declare it "off limits" or forbidden. According to the oldest and strongest known taboos, most early societies seem to have strictly prohibited two things. First, there could be no incest; marriage must always be "exogamous," that is, outside the immediate family or clan. Among primitives there is almost always what Freud calls a "horror of incest." Second, there could be no killing or eating of the totem animal; except on certain rare ceremonial occasions, when this rule was solemnly broken, eating the "totem" was also "taboo." Third—and here Freud goes beyond other theorists—there could be no point in making taboos, in publicly disallowing these things, unless somehow, at some time, people actually *wanted* to do them. Evidently, these are crimes that people did try to commit. But if so, why make them crimes in the first place? Why make everyone miserable by creating rules that no one really wanted to keep?

Here in specific form we meet the kind of question that does not appear in the works of theorists like Tylor and Frazer. From their intellectualist standpoint, human religious behavior is a conscious endeavor; it represents an effort to use reason to understand the world while, at the same time, it demonstrates a failure to reason correctly. Religious people try to be rational but do not succeed; their rites of "taboo" and rituals of totemism cannot achieve what they suppose. But then the question remains: If it is a mistake to believe in totems and taboos, why should anyone continue to do so? Freud finds the answer in the unconscious. He claims that experience with neurotic patients shows the personalities of both disturbed and normal people alike to be strongly marked by ambivalence—by the clash of powerful opposing desires. They want to do certain things, and at the same time they do not. Obsessively neurotic people, for example, will sometimes feel extreme grief when a loved one, a father or mother, dies. Yet on probing the unconscious, we often find that it is not love but guilt and hate that actually cause their emotion. We discover, says Freud, that the neurotic person unconsciously *wants* the parent to die, yet—once the death has occurred—goes on to feel intense guilt for having harbored such a terrible wish. To cope with the stress, the neurotic may even project onto the dead person certain negative characteristics, so that the death wish will seem justified. Now, remarkably enough, tribal peoples show just this trait, thinking of their dead ancestors as demons, or "wicked spirits," who deserve their hate. In their use of magic, too, they imagine that the world is just an extension of their own selves. By thinking about the sound of thunder and imitating it, they suppose they can make real rain.

More than anything else in primitive cultures, it is the practices of totemism and taboo that present us with a particularly striking display of psychic ambivalence—one which opens a window on the power of human emotions in the very earliest age of humanity. After all, says Freud, if Darwin is right about our descent from the apes, we should think of the first human beings as living, like their animal ancestors, in "primal hordes"—extended families of women and children dominated by one powerful male. Within these groups there would have been loyalty, affection, and security against danger; for the young males, however, there was also something else—frustration and envy. Though they feared and respected their father, they also sexually desired the females, all of whom were his wives. Torn between their need for the security of the horde and their suppressed sexual urges, they were at length driven to a fateful act. In a fearsome turn of events, which undoubtedly occurred many times in different hordes, the sons banded together, murdered their father and consumed his body (since they were cannibals), even as they proceeded to take possession of his wives. At first this primeval murder in the horde brought a sense of joy and liberation, but grave second thoughts soon followed. The sons were overcome with guilt and remorse. Wanting desperately to restore the master they had killed, they found in the totem animal a "father substitute" and symbol; they agreed to worship it, and before it they then swore the oldest of all taboos: "Thou shalt not kill the totem." Over time, this rule was generalized to the entire clan and became the universal commandment against all murder. "Thou shalt not kill" thus undoubtedly became the first moral rule of the human race.

The same powerful feelings of remorse led quickly to the second taboo—the commandment against incest. Regretting their act and recognizing at once that seizing the father's wives would only create new conflict among themselves, the sons agreed to a second commandment: "Thou shalt not take thy father's wives." In order to live together, the sons had to agree to find any new wives only "outside the clan." Freud suggests that these prehistoric agreements of the brothers may, in fact, have been the real events that lay behind the mythical "social contract" which philosophers have often presented as the foundation of human society.

The case of the first taboo is more complicated than the second, and to explain it Freud draws on the work of William Roberston Smith, the very same man who influenced Frazer and first suggested the idea of the primitive "totem sacrifice."[25] Though normally the totem's life was sacred, the newer Australian research had shown that there were certain sacred occasions on which the pattern was reversed. The totem animal then *was* killed and consumed by all in a ritual feast. From the standpoint of psychoanalysis, says Freud, this too is highly significant. The totem sacrifice makes sense only as a deeply emotional ceremony in which the community reenacts the primeval murder of the first father, who, through death, has now become its god. In the ritual, the sons publicly reaffirm their love for him and—quite unconsciously—also release the hate caused by the sexual renunciation they now endure.

The totem sacrifice thus confirms that the original murder of the father—a crime committed, fittingly, in the childhood of the human race—is nothing less than the acting out in history of the powerful, double human emotions that converge in every male's infancy to form the Oedipus complex. The brothers' assault upon their father is in essence the crime of Oedipus enacted thousands of years before Sophocles ever wrote his play! Out of jealous desire for their father's wives—a desire for their own mothers—the first sons committed a murder which was followed by a great ritual of remorse and affection. To the human race, these extraordinary events have left a legacy of profound emotional ambivalence. On the level of conscious activity, the members of the tribe identify the animal in the totem sacrifice with their dead father and, by projection, give him the status of divinity; they confess that they are all children and offer him their worship by eating the totem flesh and chaining their sexual desire. On the deeper plane of the unconscious, however, they express quite the opposite emotions, for the ritual by its very nature recreates their original deed of rebellious murder and cannibalism, thereby releasing the frustration and hate that arise from the ongoing denial of their oedipal urges.

Seen in this light, moreover, a modern sacrament like the Christian communion shows its true character. Like the ancient totem ritual, it reenacts, and seeks to reverse, the original crime of humanity.[26] In the communion, the flesh and blood of Christ, God's son (symbolizing the eldest brother, leader of the rebellion), are eaten in remembrance of his crucifixion, a death suffered as punishment for the "original sin" of the primeval rebellion. On behalf of his brothers, Christ atones for their prehistoric crime. Yet the atonement is also reenactment. Since, in Christian theology, the father and son are one, the sacrament of the son's death is symbolically in the same moment the sacrament of the father's murder. Thus the communion secretly recalls oedipal hate as well as love.

Freud, of course, recognizes that a long process of evolution stands between the totem rites of early cannibals and the communion meal of Christianity. He suggests that, over time, the totem animal was reduced to a simple sacrificial gift. Its place was taken by others, first by animal-human deities, later by the gods of polytheism, and finally by the father God of Christianity. But these are details. Freud's main concern, like Frazer's, but now from the standpoint of emotions rather than intellect, is to show the striking connection between present-day religion and the dark ceremonies of the primitive past. If we want to find the origin of religion, he insists, we need look no further than these grim events and deep psychological tensions. The birth of belief is to be found in the Oedipus complex, in the powerful, divided emotions that led humanity to its first great crime, then turned a murdered father into a god and promised sexual renunciation as a way to serve him. In Freud's own words, "Totemic religion arose from the filial sense of guilt, in an attempt to allay that feeling and appease the father by deferred obedience to him. All later religions are seen to be attempts at solving the same problem." [27]

For Freud, then, the murder in the prehistoric herd is an event of momentous importance in the history of human social life. In the powerful emotions it produced, we find the origin of religion. In the incest taboo—the agreement to protect the clan in its aftermath—we can see the origin of morality and the social contract. Taken together, totem and taboo thus form the very foundation of all that later comes to be called civilization.

The Future of an Illusion

Totem and Taboo met with approval from Freud's associates in psychoanalysis—and with outrage from just about everyone else. Christian critics found the book particularly insulting. For his part, Freud ignored most of the debate and turned to other interests. Not until fourteen years later did he return to the subject of religion in *The Future of an Illusion* (1927), a book he chose to describe as a continuation of the earlier study. In it he notes that while *Totem and Taboo* looks backward into the prehistoric past, *The Future of an Illusion* considers religion in the present and looks ahead. It centers not on an event hidden in prehistoric times but on the "manifest motives" of religion in all places and times. In addition, the second book puts a focus less on rituals than on ideas and beliefs—particularly belief in God.

Freud begins *The Future of an Illusion* with certain facts recognized by almost everyone. Human life has arisen, or evolved, out of the natural world, an arena that is not necessarily friendly to our enterprises. Though it has produced our species, nature constantly threatens also to destroy us, whether through predators, disasters, disease, or physical decline. For protection, therefore, we have from the first joined into clans and communities, thereby creating what we call civilization. Through it we gain security, but at a price. As the events recounted in *Totem and Taboo* show us, society can survive only if we bend our personal desires to its rules and restraints. We cannot just kill when anger seizes us, take what we do not own, or satisfy sexual desires as we want. We must restrain our instincts, compensating ourselves (though never enough) with other satisfactions we can hope to find in, say, the joys of art and leisure or the ties of family, community, and nation. Yet even with these sacrifices and comforts, civilization cannot fully protect us. In the face of disease and death, we are all ultimately helpless. In the battle between nature and culture, nature's laws of decay and death will always finally win.

Freud next observes that none of us finds this unhappy truth easy to accept; it runs counter to all we treasure most. We would rather face things as we did in the sunnier days of our childhood. Then there was always a father to reassure us against the dangers of the storm and the darkness of the night. Then there was always a voice of strength to say that all would be well in the end. As adults, in fact, we all continue to crave that childhood security, though in reality we can no longer have it. Or can we? The voice of religion, says Freud, makes us think that indeed we can. Following the childhood pattern, religious belief projects onto the external world a God, who through his power dispels the terrors of nature, gives us comfort in the face of death, and rewards us for accepting the moral restrictions imposed by civilization. Religious belief claims that "over each one of us there watches a benevolent providence which . . . will not suffer us to become a plaything of the over-mighty and pitiless forces of nature." [28] In the eyes of such faith, even death loses its sting, for we can be certain that our immortal spirits will one day be released from our bodies and live on with God. In denying our desires, therefore, we can be sure we are not just helping society; we are obeying the eternal laws of a just and righteous Lord.

The best word we can use to describe such beliefs, Freud contends, is "illusion." By this he means something quite specific. An illusion for him is a belief whose main characteristic is that we very much want it to be true. My belief that I am destined for greatness would be a case in point. It could turn out someday to be true, but that is not why I hold it. I hold it because I strongly *wish* it to be true. An illusion is not the same as a delusion, which is something I may also want to be true but which everyone else knows is not, and perhaps never could be so. If I were to claim that I will one day be 8 feet tall (which, being now fully grown, I most certainly will not), I would be holding to a delusion. Rather shrewdly, Freud claims that he is not here calling belief in God as Father a delusion; in fact, he insists otherwise: "To assess the truth-value of religious doctrines does not lie within the scope of the present enquiry. It is enough for us that we have recognized them as being, in their psychological nature, illusions."[29]

Religious teachings, therefore, are not truths revealed by God, nor are they logical conclusions based on scientifically confirmed evidence. They are, on the contrary, ideas whose main feature is that we dearly want them to be true. They are "fulfillments of the oldest, strongest and most urgent wishes of mankind. The secret of their strength lies in the strength of those wishes."[30]

We should notice here that, though it may be helpful for some, for Freud himself this distinction between "illusion" and "delusion" comes to very little. In his view, it hardly makes a difference which term we use, because even if they cannot be absolutely proved to be such, religious beliefs are in the end delusions; they are teachings we have no right to believe because they cannot pass the test of the scientific method, which is the only way we have of reliably telling us what is true and what is not. It is the habit of believers to draw on nothing more than personal feelings and intuitions, and these are notorious for being often mistaken. Hence, we ought never to put our trust in religion, even if its teachings can be shown to have provided certain services for humanity in the past. Freud concedes that, at times, religious beliefs may have been of some small assistance in the growth of civilization. Certainly the early totem made a contribution through its role in the denunciation of murder and incest, and later religion did its part when these and similar crimes were discouraged by presenting them as offenses deserving of punishment in Hell. But civilization is now mature and established. We would no more want to build today's society on such superstition and repression than we would want to force grown men and women to obey the rules of behavior we lay down for children.

Religious teachings should be seen in this same light—as beliefs and rules suitable to the childhood of the human race. In the earlier history of humanity, "the times of its ignorance and intellectual weakness,"[31] religion was inescapable, like an episode of neurosis that individuals pass through in their childhood. However, when there is a failure to overcome the traumas and repressions of earlier life and the neurosis persists into adulthood, then psychoanalysis knows that the personality is in disorder. The same is true for the growth of civilization. Religion that persists into the present age of human history can only be a sign of illness; to begin to leave it behind is the first signal of health. In Freud's words:

Religion would thus be the universal obsessional neurosis of humanity; like the obsessional neuroses of children, it arose out of the Oedipus Complex, out of the relation to the father. If this view is right, it is to be supposed that a turning-away from religion is bound to occur with the fatal inevitability of a process of growth, and that we find ourselves at this very juncture in the middle of that phase of development.[32]

Echoing Tylor, Freud concludes it is best "to view religious teachings . . . as neurotic relics, and we may now argue that the time has probably come, as it does in an analytic treatment, for replacing the effects of repression by the results of the rational operation of the intellect."[33] In short, as humanity grows into adult life, it must discard religion and replace it with forms of thought suitable to maturity. Mature people, Freud maintains, allow their lives to be guided by reason and by science, not by superstition and faith.

An interesting feature of *The Future of an Illusion* is its dialogue format. Freud routinely stops along the way of his discussion to answer the objections of an imaginary critic who takes the side of religion. Among other things, this critic insists that it is wrong to talk of religion as arising merely from our emotional needs, that religion ought to be believed on the basis of tradition, and—perhaps most important—that if religion is discarded as the ground for morals, society will collapse into violence and chaos. These criticisms are, of course, designed to strengthen Freud's case, and in each instance he offers a skillful and persuasive reply. In one of these objections, Freud is asked why he seems to have changed his theme since *Totem and Taboo*. That book was also about the origin of religion, but its subject was totemism and the father-son relationship; this one talks mainly about human helplessness. Has the theory now changed? Freud's answer to this question is instructive if not quite convincing. He explains that *Totem and Taboo* explored only one element, though it was deeply concealed, of what goes into religion. That was the two-sided feeling of both love for and fear of the father, who ruled the primeval horde. The present book, he says, explores "the other, less deeply concealed part"—the realization of adults that in the face of nature's crushing power, they will always be as weak as children and in need of a loving Father to defend them. Freud does not address the puzzling fact that while God is presented in the first book as a figure about whom human beings have very mixed emotions, in the second He is the Father who only loves—and is only loved in return. Still, whatever the motives, the result in Freud's eyes is always the same. The God whom people call upon in prayer is not a being who belongs to reality; he is an image, an illusion projected outward from the self and onto the external world out of the deep need to overcome our guilt or allay our fears.

Moses and Monotheism

Freud's interest in religion did not end with *The Future of an Illusion*, even though it is perhaps the most important statement of his views. At the very end of his career, while struggling with the cancer that eventually took his life and finding himself driven from Vienna by the Nazi takeover of Austria, he returned to the subject for one final effort—writing this time on Judaism, his own religious tradition. In a series of essays undertaken between 1934 and 1938, he focused his attention on the figure of Moses, examining his foundational role in Jewish life and thought. These essays were then brought together in a single volume and published in the year of his death under the title *Moses and Monotheism.*[34]

As in *Totem and Taboo*, so in this quite unusual book, Freud puts forward a set of startling new claims about certain events in religious history—in particular Jewish history—and tries to show how the concepts and comparisons drawn from psychoanalysis can help to explain them. In the Bible, he observes, we learn that Moses is the great Hebrew prophet who inspired the people of Israel by his leadership and shaped their lives by giving them the law of God. True enough perhaps, but how do we know, Freud asks, that Moses was really a Hebrew? A close look at the texts gives reason to believe that he was actually an Egyptian prince, a ruler and follower of the radical Pharaoh Akhenaton, who tried to replace the many gods of ancient Egypt with a strict devotion to one and only one deity—the sun god Aten.[35] Unlike the other cults, the worship of Aten employed neither images nor superstitious rituals; it stressed a purely spiritual god of love and goodness, who was also revered as the strong guardian of an eternal moral law. When Akhenaton died, his new religion failed in Egypt, but not entirely. One of those who kept it alive was this same man Moses, who adopted the Hebrew slaves as his people, united them behind the new faith, and with great courage led them out of their captivity. Initially those who followed Moses prospered under his leadership. Later on, however, buffeted by their misfortunes in the desert, Moses' chosen people rebelled against his leadership, renounced his god, and put him to death. His monotheistic religion was then overlaid by a new cult dedicated to a violent, volcano-deity named Yahweh, the god whom Israelites worshipped as they fought their bloody battles to win the Land of Promise. Later, in writing their scriptures, Jewish scribes attached the name of Moses also to the founder of this second faith, but this sleight of hand could not disguise the differences between the new religion and the earlier monotheism of the original Moses, their first and true spiritual leader. The new faith replaced the pure spirituality and morals of the old with the rituals, superstitions, and bloody animal sacrifices we find in

Israel during the age of the great Hebrew kings. Degraded as it appears to us, says Freud, the new religion managed almost completely to push out the old, leaving behind little more than a faint memory of the original Moses and his faith.[36]

Yet that is not where the story ends. Centuries later in the life of the community, and against all probability, the people of Israel found themselves face to face with the great monotheistic prophets, men seized with the mission to recover and revive the old faith of the tribe. These prophets— Amos, Isaiah, and others—denounced the religion of sacrifices; they demanded worship of the one universal God announced by the first Moses, and they called again for obedience to his stern moral law. Their words thus marked a decisive turn that affected not just Jewish history but the entire world. For it was out of the soil of this revived Jewish monotheism that Christianity would one day rise to become a great world religion. From the time of the Hebrew prophets forward, faith in the awesome, righteous God of Moses took its place as the immovable center of both Jewish and Christian belief.

There is, of course, no question that this quite extraordinary retelling of Hebrew history as Freud sees it rests on a number of adventurous connections and eye-opening historical conjectures that would trouble both the historian and the biblical scholar. It is not easy to find in the Bible any clear proof that Moses was an Egyptian, that he was murdered, that two persons were given his name, or that the early Hebrews ever had two different religions. To Freud, however, all these problems are hardly a concern. Much more interesting to him is the mystery of how, over many centuries, a true monotheism was somehow born, apparently died, and then came back to life. How can it be, he asks, that the faith of the original Moses virtually disappeared from the life of his people, only to revive centuries later in dramatic fashion and win back the hearts and minds of the entire Jewish community? Theologians may be at a loss to answer such a question, but psychoanalysis certainly is not. Freud asks us to suppose once again that a parallel can be found between what happens psychologically to an individual person over the course of a life and what happens in history, over a much longer time, to an entire community of people like the Jews.[37] And he restates his view that religion is best conceived along the lines of a neurosis. Those premises in place, he proceeds to the following ingenious argument.

Psychoanalytic theory has clearly demonstrated that cases of personal neurosis follow a familiar pattern. They start, often in early childhood, with a traumatic, disturbing event that is pushed out of memory for a time. There follows a period of "latency," when nothing shows; all seems normal. Then at a later point—often at the onset of puberty or in early adulthood—the irrational behavior which is the sign of neurosis suddenly makes its appearance. We find that there is a "return of the repressed." Now if these stages are indeed identifiable, Freud suggests that we can compare them with the sequences discovered in the history of Judaism. And as we do, he adds, let us recall as well the points made in the earlier books about ambivalent emotions, tribal murder, and religion as childlike desire for the figure of a father. Do they not fit with an almost uncanny accuracy? The message of monotheism spoke to the Jews' natural human longing for a divine father. The powerful personality of Moses, whom the people may even have identified with his God, recalled the imposing figure of the first father in the primeval horde. His death in a desert rebellion was more than a mere historical accident; it can be read as a reenactment of the primeval murder of the great father, an event no less traumatic for the Jews than the first murder was for the sons and brothers in the prehistoric human community. Fittingly, once the murder had been committed, the community, in an act of collective repression, sought to relieve its guilt by striving to erase the entire memory of Moses—both the monotheism and the murder—from community life, thus allowing the crude Yahweh religion of the second Moses to take its place. For the true Mosaic religion, this was the period of its latency, a long period when it lay submerged and almost forgotten in the communal Hebrew mind. And yet the law of neurosis is clear: Whatever is repressed must return. After centuries in eclipse, the pure and ancient creed of the founder made its powerful return in the oracles of the prophets. Henceforth, pure monotheism, the religion of loving devotion to the Creator and Lord of the Covenant, became again the faith all Jews, who on those terms rightfully and to the present day claim the honor of being his chosen people.

Significantly, Freud adds, even the role of Christianity as Judaism's successor comes into clearer focus once we read its history through the eyes of psychoanalysis. It is clear from the discussion in *Totem and Taboo* that the revolt in the primeval horde had a two-sided emotional outcome: love and fear. Judaism recalls the urge to idealize the Father, to make him into a loving God and repress the guilt left behind by his murder. Christianity feels the same mix of affection and guilt but responds by declaring the need for atonement. As framed by its chief thinker, the Jewish rabbi Paul, Christian theology centers not on God the Father but on Christ the Son and his death—in other words, on God who, in the form of the firstborn Son, goes to his death to atone for the original sin committed by the first sons in the prehistoric horde.

Never modest in his claims, Freud here offers a psychoanalytic portrait of both Jewish and Christian monotheism that few theologians or historians would dare attempt. Along the same bold lines of analogy laid out in his earlier works, he argues that the appeal of these—and all—religions lies not in the truth of their teachings about a god or a savior, their claims about miracles or a chosen people, or their hopes of a life after death. These doctrines are empty because they lie beyond any chance of proof. The concepts of psychoanalytic science, however, are very different. And they show in ever so interesting ways that the real power of religions is to be found beyond their doctrines, in the deep psychological needs they fill and the unconscious emotions they express.

Analysis

1. Psychology and Religion

In commenting on the twentieth century, the great English poet W. H. Auden once said, "We are all Freudians now." This remark pays tribute to the enormous influence that Freud's ideas have had on all spheres of thought in our time. The field of religion is no exception. Freud's analysis of the hidden forces within the human personality has compelled not just those concerned with the theory of religion but almost everyone associated with its practice—theologians, clergy, counselors, and teachers—to look beneath the surface of accepted doctrines and discover the deep, unnoticed elements of personality that shape human religious faith and are in turn shaped by it. Interestingly, though Freud himself takes a decidedly negative view of religious behavior, other leaders in psychoanalysis—and even entire schools of thought in contemporary psychology—have been eager to adapt his insights to their own much more sympathetic views. Among others, perhaps the most notable figure in this tradition has been the Swiss psychologist Carl Jung (1875–1961), one of the most important men in the circle of Freud's earliest associates.[38] For Jung, religion draws on a deep fund of images and ideas that belong collectively to the human race and find expression in mythology, folklore, philosophy, and literature. Religion like these other endeavors, draws on the resources of this "collective unconscious" not as a form of neurosis but as the healthy expression of true and deep humanity. Others, such as contemporary ego psychologists and object relation theorists, have followed a similar path, developing an entire field of studies in religion and personality and producing a rich literature of theory and therapy. It seems to matter little on this account whether analysts share Freud's distaste for belief or Jung's approval; both perspectives have contributed greatly to the contemporary understanding of religion.

2. Freud's Explanation of Religion

The importance of Freud's theory of religion is closely connected to the context in which he wrote. His views actually follow a line of thought developed early in the 1800s by Ludwig Feuerbach, a German philosopher who gained fame in his day for a book called *The Essence of Christianity* (1841). In this controversial study, he claimed that all of religion is just a psychological device by which we attach our own hopes, virtues, and ideals to an imaginary supernatural being we call "God" and in the process only diminish ourselves. Feuerbach, whom we shall meet again in this book because his work made a strong impact on Karl Marx, might well be called the first modern thinker to offer a purely "projectionist" explanation of religion. That is to say, he explains religion by showing not what truth or rationality believers find in their ideas but rather what is the psychological mechanism that creates religious beliefs, *regardless* of whether they are true or false, rational or irrational. Though briefly popular, Feuerbach was not able to keep his following, and his theory faded from view. Karl Marx developed it further, as we shall see, but he too was largely ignored in his age. By Freud's day, however, the time for just such a functional projectionist theory was again ripe. And that was largely because of the work of Tylor and Frazer. As we saw in our last chapter, both of these thinkers conclude that religion is something primarily "intellectual"; it is a system of ideas once sincerely believed and now known to be mistaken and absurd. But again, assuming all of this to be so, we must still try to explain how and why the human race has held so firmly to this great collection of superstition and error through history and into the scientific present. Why, if it is so absurd, do people insist upon religion? In the eyes of some, that is the puzzle that Freud, who knew well the work of these English anthropological writers, brilliantly managed to solve. On his view, if we want to know why religion persists even when it has been discredited by science or better philosophy, we need only turn to psychoanalysis, which tells us quite clearly that the real and ultimate source of religion's appeal is not the rational mind but the unconscious. Religion arises from emotions and conflicts that originate early in childhood and lie deep beneath the rational, normal surface of the personality. It is best seen as an obsessional neurosis. Accordingly, we can no more suppose that believers would give up their faith because it has been proved irrational than that a neurotic would give up continuous handwashing because someone has pointed out that his hands are already quite clean. The normal causes we see on the surface of things are not the real causes of the behavior.

Freud is quite prepared to push this functional account of religion as far as it can possibly go. He does not just say that, *among other things*, religion seems to have certain psychological functions. He asserts that religion arises *only* in response to deep emotional conflicts and weaknesses; he insists that these are in fact its true and fundamental causes and, consequently, that once psychoanalysis has scientifically resolved such problems, we can expect the illusion of religion quite naturally to disappear from the human scene.[39] Freud thus presents us with a particularly vivid instance of an explanatory strategy that has had great influence in the twentieth century—the approach theorists today describe as functionalist *reductionism*. In what he sees as a radical unmasking of the real truth about religion, Freud claims not just to explain it but to explain it away. In his view, religion in its entirety can be "reduced" to little more than a by-product of psychological distress, to a collection of ideas and beliefs that, once their surface appearance has been penetrated, turn out to be illusory wish fulfillments generated by the unconscious.

We do need to add here that Freud is not always consistent in his judgments; in some places he seems not quite so exclusively committed to this psychological reductionism as in others.[40] But in the main, he furnishes us with a particularly clear and outspoken version of the reductionist approach, which strongly insists that religion is never a reality on its own terms; it is always an appearance, an expression of something else. It is not a genuine agent in human behavior or thought because its fundamental character is always passive; its nature is to reflect other realities—more powerful and more basic—that underlie it. Outspoken and influential as he has been, moreover, Freud is by no means alone in pursuing this particularly aggressive functionalist strategy. As we shall see in the chapters that immediately follow, the same kind of approach is evident in the work of two other theorists whose views on religion have been of major importance to twentieth-century thought. We find versions of it both in the sociology of Émile Durkheim, Freud's French contemporary, and in the economic materialism of Karl Marx.

Critique

Any appraisal of Freud requires comment not only on his theory of religion but also on the larger framework of psychoanalytic science that serves as its support. We have space here to raise just a few pertinent questions about the first, then to note an ongoing, serious debate about the merits of the second.

1. The Problem of Theistic and Nontheistic Religions

The first thing to observe is that Freud's is not so much a theory of religion in general as it is a theory of Judeo-Christian, or at least monotheistic, religion in particular. In all three of the works we have examined, the ideas of the Oedipus complex and the need for a father image are so central to the discussion that it is hard to see how the arguments could be applied to any form of religion that is not monotheistic. Though he does mention them in a few places, religions that affirm many gods, that propose mother gods, or that articulate a faith in divine powers which are not personal in character fall almost entirely outside the reach of Freud's thinking. Since he chooses not to consider such religions, we cannot say for certain how Freud would have explained them had he made the attempt. But even if we were to try, on his behalf, to extend his explanations to cover them, it is not easy to see how this could be done. Much of his theory seems constructed specifically to account for those religions that affirm one, and only one, all-powerful Father God. Others just do not fit.

2. The Problems of Analogy and History

Even if we could find a way past the problem of monotheism, Freudian theory presents other difficulties. Most notably, there is the troubling matter of his reasoning by analogy. For example, as we have seen in *Totem and Taboo* and *Moses and Monotheism,* the argument of both books turns on an extended comparison between the psychological growth of an individual and the historical development of a large social group. The one takes place over a period of years, or sequence of decades, that comprise the life of a single individual; the other takes place over the course of centuries in the history of an entire community or even civilization. But in that case, what ground do we have, logically, to assume any real similarity or clear connection between these two very different things? It may well be true that from childhood onward a neurotic person passes through stages of early trauma, defense, latency, outbreak of neurosis, and return of the repressed. But outside of pure coincidence and Freud's ingenuity, what grounds do we have to think that such a thing as the entire history of the Jews conforms to the pattern of development found in a single disturbed human personality?

Again, by what logic do we conclude, as Freud does in *Totem and Taboo,* that the Christian rite of communion is somehow created from the hidden communal memory of an oedipal murder that took place thousands of years earlier in the first animal-like hordes of humans? We can perhaps understand how an early trauma could stay with one person for the rest of his or her life. But how can an ancient murder be "remembered" by the whole human race? Freud, of course, feels that there are such collective memories, but that is mainly because he relies on a version of evolutionary theory, put forward by the French scientist Lamarck, which holds that an experience acquired during one's life can be biologically inherited by descendants. Unfortunately, in the decades after Darwin, this version of evolution came under severe challenge from those who saw far better grounds for concluding that natural selection was the key to the evolutionary process. It is troubling to discover that Freud, who so often advertised his solemn commitment to science, rested his analyses of religion so heavily on a form of evolutionism that other important scientists of his day had given good reasons to reject.

A further point also needs notice here. Even if we were to grant everything Freud says about human individuals in his analogical arguments, very large historical questions remain about their cultural side. From almost their first encounters with *Moses and Monotheism,* scholars have found in the biblical and archaeological evidence little support for Freud's highly imaginative reconstruction of the early history of the Jews. If anything, anthropologists have been even more skeptical about Freud's conjectures on the original human hordes and the murder of the first fathers. The plain fact is that most of these events are simply lost in the fog of prehistory; reconstructing them requires a great deal of pure guesswork. It is not a matter of uncertainty, as if some evidence supports Freud and the rest does not; it is really a matter of ignorance and inaccessibility. About such matters we often have little evidence of any kind to support a theory of the sort Freud advances.

3. The Problem of Circularity

As we saw in his very first essay on religion and at the core of the argument in *The Future of an Illusion,* Freud argues that religion is very similar to a neurosis. Just as neurotic people believe and do irrational things, so religious people also believe and do irrational things. The kind of obsessional neurosis discovered by psychoanalysis appears mainly in individual persons. The kind of obsessional neurosis seen in religion afflicts entire cultures; it is universal. Here again, however, we must inquire about Freud's curious uses of analogy, for context is crucial in explaining behavior. As a number even of critics friendly to Freud have pointed out, a nun who spends hours at devotions moving her prayer beads and a neurotic who spends hours counting the buttons on his shirt are both engaged in the same form of behavior, but only one is mentally disturbed. For nuns it is normal, not neurotic, to pray. Freud chooses to find unconscious motives for such action only because *from the start* he has assumed that prayer is an abnormal behavior.

But of course he cannot do that without claiming that it arises not from rational motives but from irrational ones located in the unconscious—the very thing he sets out to prove. In brief, some of Freud's discussions wear the look of arguments that are decidedly circular.

Furthermore, the idea of projection itself is open to some question. The mere fact that people project things from their minds out onto the world is hardly proof that they are engaged in neurotic wish fulfillment. The symbols of science and mathematics belong, strictly speaking, to numerical and conceptual systems that we project upon the world not out of neurosis but simply because they help us describe and understand it better. The obvious fact that every day these "projections" of ourselves are successfully applied to real life shows that they do, in fact, reflect something of the character of the world as we experience it. But if that is true for the conceptions of mathematics and natural science, there is no reason why, in principle at least, we cannot also allow that certain religious projections might also be true and might originate not from neurosis but from a reasonable and appropriate understanding of the real world as we perceive it.

4. Psychoanalysis as Science

We must finish this brief critique by raising finally the troublesome issue of psychoanalysis itself as a form of science. Freud was trained in the natural sciences; he began his career with research on the physiology of the brain. When he turned to psychoanalysis, he stressed from the beginning, and in absolute terms, that its methods were those of science. Psychoanalysis was to be built on in-depth consultations with patients, on the careful framing and testing of hypotheses, on the search for general theories, and on the exchange of criticism in scholarly journals. In *The Future of an Illusion* Freud proudly compared the slow, steady progress of sciences like psychoanalysis with the backward dogmatism of religion. And today, certainly, the wide acceptance of psychoanalysis rests mainly on the common view that it is a *science* of the mind.

It is just this accepted view, however, that in recent decades has come under severe scientific attack. Over the last twenty years especially, critics in many quarters have subjected the entire enterprise of psychoanalysis—from Freud onward—to a rigorous and searching reassessment. Their common verdict, which is not friendly, can be summarized in two sentences: Whatever his talents, Freud was not a scientist. And whatever its claims, psychoanalysis is not a science. The weightiest charges against the discipline have been leveled by an American philosopher of science, Adolf Grünbaum, who argues that psychoanalysts regularly assume the very things they hope to prove in their work with patients, that their techniques for gathering evidence are scientifically unsound, and that when usable evidence is, in fact, brought forward, it does not support the elaborate Freudian conclusions conventionally drawn from it. Grünbaum does not say that the field is unscientific in principle, but he does state that it has yet to establish truly scientific methods for testing its claims.[41] Others, looking on from a different perspective, have joined in these criticisms, noticing that the principles which form the core of the science—Freud's theories of the personality and neurosis—are constructed out of vague comparisons and misleading inferences, most of which cannot be either proved or disproved because, again, there is simply no scientific way even to test them.[42] Still other observers have turned a severely critical eye upon Freud himself, only to find someone quite different from the man his disciples presented to the world as a pioneering scientist, the spokesman for truth in a world of Victorian repression. They point out that while his talents of imagination and persuasion were certainly quite formidable, Freud was also a shrewd promoter of his own interests as well as a man willing to bend evidence, ignore valid criticism, and even misuse people when such actions served the purpose of his program.[43]

In the light of these criticisms, it must be said that the scientific future of psychoanalysis does not look especially promising. Freud's theory of religion is unlikely to fare better—unless (and that is always a possibility) it is refitted to a new frame and placed on a less uncertain footing. At the same time, it should be duly noted that psychoanalysis is only one strand of modern psychology. Clearly, psychological research as a whole will continue to bear significantly on the ways and means of explaining religion.

Notes

1. *The Future of an Illusion*, in *The Standard Edition of the Complete Psychological Works of Sigmund Freud*, ed. James Strachey with Anna Freud (London: Hogarth Press, 1961), 21: 43.

2. The classic older biography of Freud, written by an Englishman who belonged to the circle of his original followers, is Ernest Jones, *The Life and Work of Sigmund Freud*, 3 vols. (New York: Basic Books, 1953–1957). An authoritative recent biography is Peter Gay, *Freud: A Life for Our Time* (New York: W. W. Norton, 1988). There are also numerous thematic and shorter biographical studies, including important studies such as Paul Roazen, *Freud and His Followers* (New York: Alfred A. Knopf, 1975) and Philip Rieff's widely appreciated intellectual biography, *Freud: The Mind of the Moralist*, 3rd ed. (Chicago: University of Chicago Press, 1979).

3. The letters of Freud to Martha Bernays during their courtship offer a fascinating portrait of his personality and attitudes as a young man. See *The Letters of Sigmund Freud, 1873–1939*, ed. Ernst Freud (London: Hogarth Press, 1970).

4. There have been a number of detailed studies of these and other early cases,

which were central to the development of Freud's main ideas and his entire program of research. See for example, Muriel Gardner, ed. *The Wolf-Man* (New York: Basic Books, 1971), which includes the memoirs of the patient, Freud's own case history, and additional comments; Patrick Mahony, *Freud and the Rat-Man* (New Haven, CT: Yale University Press, 1971); and more controversially, Jeffrey Moussaieff Masson, *The Assault on Truth: Freud's Suppression of the Seduction Theory* (New York: Farrar, Straus, and Giroux, 1984), which analyzes, very critically, Freud's handling of one of his first patients, Emma Eckstein, who began analysis with him early in the 1890s.

5. On these early developments, see Vincent Brome, *Freud and His Early Circle* (New York: William Morrow & Company, Inc., 1968); Linda Donn, *Freud and Jung: Years of Friendship, Years of Loss* (New York: Charles Scribner's Sons, 1988); and Phillis Grosskurth, *The Secret Ring: Freud's Inner Circle and the Politics of Psychoanalysis* (Reading, MA: Addison-Wesley Pub. Co., 1991).

6. "Obsessive Actions and Religious Practices," in *Standard Edition*, 9: 116–27.

7. Much in this book was based on self-analysis, especially Freud's interpretations of his own dream experiences. See Gerald Levin, *Sigmund Freud* (Boston: Twayne Publishers, 1975), p. 28.

8. See Alasdair C. MacIntyre, *The Unconscious: A Conceptual Analysis* (London: Routledge & Kegan Paul, 1958), p. 33; for a full account and careful appraisal of this crucial Freudian concept, see especially pp. 29–38.

9. Much has been written on Freud's concept of repression. A good brief account of this idea and its place in Freud's thought can be found in Rieff, *Freud: The Mind of the Moralist*, pp. 37–44, 314–20; for a close contemporary analysis of the concept in Freud and more current psychoanalytic theory, see W. D. Hart, "Models of Repression," in *Philosophical Essays on Freud*, ed. Richard Wollheim and James Hopkins (New York: Cambridge University Press, 1982), pp. 180–202.

10. This evidence came especially from Freud's own dreams; see above, n. 7.

11. Although Freud recognized drives other than sex, such as hunger, and conceded that they might be just as strong and even more basic, it seems clear that in developing his notions of both repression and the unconscious and in his dream interpretations, the restraint of sexual desires figures most prominently—an anticipation, perhaps, of the oedipal hypothesis he would develop later on. See MacIntyre, *The Unconscious*, p. 29. It must be noted, however, that in later works, like *Civilization and Its Discontents*, he gave ever greater emphasis to the drive of aggression, even to the point of regarding it as at least the equal of the sex drive.

12. A more recent reassessment of the concept of the unconscious is Patricia Herzog, *Conscious and Unconscious: Freud's Dynamic Distinction Reconsidered* (Madison, CT: International Universities Press, 1991).

13. Freud's study *Leonardo da Vinci and a Memory of His Childhood* (1910) and his articles on "The Moses of Michelangelo" (1914) and "Dostoyevsky and Parricide" (1928) continue to fascinate historians of art and literature. On his great love for literature, especially English novels, see Levin, *Freud*, p. 32.

14. The evolution of Freud's thinking on these issues can be found in essays he wrote between approximately 1910 and the early 1920s and in works like *Beyond the Pleasure Principle* (1920) and *The Ego and the Id* (1923).

15. Freud first presented this formulation in *The Ego and the Id* in 1923.

16. For recent philosophical discussions of the concepts of the ego and id, see Brian O'Shaughnessy, "The Id and the Thinking Process," and Richard Wollheim, "The Bodily Ego," in Wollheim, *Philosophical Essays*, pp. 106–23, 124–38.

17. See Freud, *An Outline of Psychoanalysis*, in *Standard Edition*, 23: 146.

18. Freud, *An Outline of Psychoanalysis*, in *Standard Edition*, 23: 190.

19. Freud, *An Outline of Psychoanalysis*, in *Standard Edition*, 23: 191.

20. Among a number of instructive works on Freud's Jewish background and his religious opinions, see Howard Littleton Philp, *Freud and Religious Belief* (New York: Pitman, 1956), G. Zillboorg, *Freud and Religion: A Restatement of an Old Controversy* (Westminster, MD: Newman Press, 1958); Earl A. Grollman, *Judaism in Sigmund Freud's World* (New York: Appleton-Century, 1965); Hans Küng, *Freud and the Problem of God* (New Haven, CT: Yale University Press, 1979); Edwin R. Wallace IV, "Freud and Religion," in Werner Muensterberger et al., eds., *The Psychoanalytic Study of Society*, vol. 10 (Hillsdale, NJ: The Analytic Press, 1984), pp. 113–61; and Peter Gay, *A Godless Jew: Freud, Atheism, and the Making of Psychoanalysis* (New Haven, CT: Yale University Press, 1987). Wallace and Gay also provide substantial recent bibliographies.

21. David Bakan, *Sigmund Freud and the Jewish Mystical Tradition* (Princeton, NJ: D. Van Nostrand Company, Inc., 1958), attempts the very bold thesis that psychoanalysis arose out of Freud's acquaintance with Jewish mysticism. While that position is extreme, it does suggest that Freud's debt to Jewish traditions runs deeper than some have supposed.

22. Jones, *Life and Work of Freud*, 3: 351.

23. Freud, "Obsessive Actions and Religious Practices" (1907), in *Standard Edition*, 9: 126; this famous phrase, which heads this chapter, appears again in *The Future of an Illusion*.

24. See chapter 1, pp. 21–22, 25–26, 31–32, 38, 40. Frazer's studies of totemism led to a typically comprehensive work, *Totemism and Exogamy: A Treatise on Certain Early Forms of Superstition and Society*, 4 vols. (London: Macmillan and Co., 1910).

25. *Totem and Taboo*, in *Standard Edition*, 13: 132–42.

26. *Totem and Taboo*, in *Standard Edition*, 13: 153–55.

27. *Totem and Taboo*, in *Standard Edition*, 13: 145.

28. Freud, *The Future of an Illusion*, in *Standard Edition*, 21: 19.

29. *The Future of an Illusion*, in *Standard Edition*, 21: 33.

30. *The Future of an Illusion*, in *Standard Edition*, 21: 30.

31. *The Future of an Illusion*, in *Standard Edition*, 21: 43.

32. *The Future of an Illusion*, in *Standard Edition*, 21: 43.

33. *The Future of an Illusion*, in *Standard Edition*, 21: 44.

34. In *Standard Edition*, 23: 3–137.

35. Freud, *Moses and Monotheism*, in *Standard Edition*, 23: 20–30.

36. Freud, *Moses and Monotheism*, in *Standard Edition*, 23: 49–50.

37. Freud, *Moses and Monotheism*, in *Standard Edition*, 23: 72–80.

38. On the association and conflicts between the two men, see Linda Donn, *Freud and Jung: Years of Friendship, Years of Loss* (New York: Charles Scribner's Sons, 1988).

39. For example, in *The Future of an Illusion*, in *Standard Edition*, 21: 44.

40. See Wallace, "Freud and Religion," pp. 113–14, 138–48.

41. See his important work, *The Foundations of Psychoanalysis* (Berkeley, CA: University of California Press, 1984) and his later book, *Validation in the Clinical Theory of Psychoanalysis: A Study in the Philosophy of Psychoanalysis* (Madison, CT: International Universities Press, 1993).

42. See especially Malcolm Macmillan, *Freud Evaluated: The Completed Arc* (New York: North Holland, 1991). An earlier investigation of Freudian thought, which points in the direction of these more recent criticisms, is Roazen, *Freud and His Followers*.

43. On Freud's literary talents, especially in the area of expository nonfiction, see Patrick J. Mahony, *Freud as a Writer* (New Haven, CT: Yale University Press, 1987). The scientific criticisms, along with appreciations, of Freud are put with special force in Frank Sulloway, *Freud, Biologist of the Mind: Beyond the Psychoanalytic Legend* (New York: Basic Books, 1979); see also Masson, *The Assault upon Truth: Freud's Suppression of the Seduction Theory;* Frederick C. Crews, *Skeptical Engagements* (New York: Oxford University Press, 1986); Paul Roazen, *Encountering Freud: The Politics and Histories of Psychoanalysis* (New Brunswick, NJ: Transaction Publishers, 1990); and John Kerr, *A Most Dangerous Method: The Story of Jung, Freud, and Sabina Spielrein* (New York: Alfred A. Knopf, 1993). For summaries of these criticisms and the heated debates they have elicited, see Paul Robinson, *Freud and His Critics* (Berkeley, CA: University of California Press, 1993), and Frederick C. Crews, "The Unknown Freud," *New York Review of Books* 40, no. 19 (November 18, 1993): 55–66.

Suggestions for Further Reading

Crews, Frederick C. "The Unknown Freud." *New York Review of Books* 40, no. 19 (November 18, 1993): 55–66. Questionings by a formerly Freudian literary theorist who has since become a stern critic of psychoanalysis, its history, and its methods.

Freud, Sigmund. *The Standard Edition of the Complete Psychological Works of Sigmund Freud.* Translated under the editorship of James Strachey, in collaboration with Anna Freud. London: Hogarth Press, 1953. The definitive collection of Freud's works in English. Individual works are available in many reprints and editions.

Gay, Peter. *Freud: A Life for Our Times.* New York: W. W. Norton, 1988. The most substantial and authoritative recent biography by a distinguished intellectual historian.

Gay, Peter. *A Godless Jew: Freud, Atheism, and the Making of Psychoanalysis.* New Haven: Yale University Press, 1987. A brief, insightful assessment of Freud's perspective on religion.

Grünbaum, Adolf. *The Foundations of Psychoanalysis.* Berkeley: University of California Press, 1984.

Grünbaum, Adolf. *Validation in the Clinical Theory of Psychoanalysis: A Study in the Philosophy of Psychoanalysis.* Madison, Connecticut: International Universities Press, 1993. Two important, compelling studies by the philosopher who is the leading current critic of psychoanalysis as a science.

Herzog, Patricia. *Conscious and Unconscious: Freud's Dynamic Distinction Reconsidered.* Madison, Connecticut: International Universities Press, 1991. An informative recent examination of the central concepts in Freudian thought.

Jones, Ernest. *The Life and Work of Sigmund Freud.* 3 vols. New York: Basic Books, 1953–1957. Until recently the definitive biography of Freud, written by an English admirer who belonged to the circle of his original associates and followers.

Kerr, John. *A Most Dangerous Method: The Story of Jung, Freud, and Sabina Spielrein.* New York: Alfred A. Knopf, 1993. Raises questions, both moral and scientific, about certain aims and agendas of Freud, Jung, and one of their early associates.

Küng, Hans. *Freud and the Problem of God.* New Haven: Yale University Press, 1979. A thoughtful analysis of Freud's theological opinions by a distinguished modern Catholic theologian.

MacIntyre, Alasdair C. *The Unconscious: A Conceptual Analysis.* London: Routledge & Kegan Paul, 1958. Now somewhat dated, but valuable as a clear, brief, and instructive study of the idea that gave birth to psychoanalysis. Written by an influential English analytical philosopher.

Masson, Jeffrey Moussaieff. *The Assault upon Truth: Freud's Suppression of the Seduction Theory.* New York: Farrar, Straus, and Giroux, 1984. A controversial exposé of Freud's methods which attempts to show how he mishandled one of his early patients in psychoanalysis.

Neu, Jerome, ed. *The Cambridge Companion to Freud.* New York: Cambridge University Press, 1991. Instructive essays on Freud by various scholars currently writing on his life and thought.

Rieff, Philip. *Freud: The Mind of the Moralist.* 3rd ed. Chicago: University of Chicago Press, 1979. A widely read and much appreciated study of Freud's ideas in their biographical and cultural context.

Roazen, Paul. *Encountering Freud: The Politics and Histories of Psychoanalysis.* New Brunswick, New Jersey: Transaction Publishers, 1990. An exploration of the controversies surrounding the aims of both Freud and his new field of study.

Roazen, Paul. *Freud and His Followers.* New York: Alfred A. Knopf, 1975. An instructive study of the first Freudians and their intellectual agenda.

Robinson, Paul. *Freud and His Critics.* Berkeley: University of California Press, 1993. Summarizes and evaluates issues in the current heated debate over Freud and the validity of psychoanalysis as a science.

Sulloway, Frank. *Freud, Biologist of the Mind: Beyond the Psychoanalytic Legend.* New York: Basic Books, 1979. A comprehensive study by a scholar who, since this book, has gradually grown more critical of Freud's science.

3

Society as Sacred:
Émile Durkheim

The idea of society is the soul of religion.

Durkheim, *The Elementary Forms of the Religious Life*[1]

In the very years during which Freud put forward his controversial views in Vienna, an equally original thinker in France, Émile Durkheim, set to work on a theory of religion that was just as revolutionary, though in quite a different way. If Freud is the first name that people associate with modern psychology, then that of Durkheim—though less widely known—should be one of the first that comes to mind at the mention of sociology. Durkheim championed the central importance of society—of social structures, relationships, and institutions—in understanding human thought and behavior. His distinct perspective consists in his determination to see almost every major enterprise of human life—our laws and morality, labor and recreation, family and personality, science, art, and above all religion—through the lens of their social dimension. Without a society to give them birth and shape them, he claimed, none of these things could exist.

At a first glance, of course, a theorist who sounds this social theme hardly seems revolutionary. In the present climate of thought, few discussions of any kind take place without some reference to the "social environment." Hardly a day passes without some comment on "social decay," "social engineering," "social reform," or "social context." Less than a century ago, however, such language would have been almost as rare as it is common now. "Society" was a word mostly associated with upper-class manners and the dinner parties of the wealthy. The leading systems of thought were quite individualistic, with a tendency to see any social arrangement—from a single family to a village, a church, or an entire nation—as little more than a collection of separate persons who happened to be brought together by a common location and shared interests. Durkheim's view was decidedly different. He went so far as to say that social facts are more fundamental than individual ones—that they are, in their way, as real as physical objects, and that individuals are more often than not *mis*understood when the powerful imprint of society upon them is ignored or insufficiently noticed. Human beings, after all, are never just individuals; they always *belong* to something—to parents or relatives, a town or city, a race, a political party, an ethnic tradition, or some other group. In Durkheim's view, it is futile to think that we can really comprehend what a person is by appealing only to biological instinct, individual psychology, or isolated self-interest. We must explain individuals in and through society, and we account for society in social terms.

In accord with this social premise, Durkheim insisted, very much like Freud, that his subject required nothing less than a new scientific discipline to investigate it. This field he chose to call "sociology," even though he was not the first to use the word and was not himself very fond of it. Simply put, sociology was to be the science of society. In a significant measure it is because of Durkheim's strong advocacy and guiding influence that social science holds such a prominent place in modern life, whether we appeal to it in matters of government, economics, education, or in any other forum of public discussion, from the university lecture room to the television talk show. Today, our instinctively social view of the world is an index of just how thoroughly successful Durkheim's revolution in thought has turned out to be.[2]

Durkheim actually presents us with two parallels to Freud.[3] Not only did both men feel the need to promote special fields of study—psychology in the one case, and sociology in the other—but both also found that their new perspectives led them unavoidably back to the very old question of religious behavior and belief. Like Freud, Durkheim too was driven to ask: What is religion? Why has it been so important and central in human affairs? What does it do for both the individual and society? Freud, as we saw, thought he could not explain the individual personality without also accounting for the appeal of religion. Durkheim felt precisely the same about society. In the course of trying to understand "the social" in all of its hidden and powerful dimensions, he found himself drawn steadily and repeatedly to "the religious." For Durkheim, religion and society are inseparable and—to each other—virtually indispensable.

Life and Career

Durkheim was born in 1858 in the town of Epinal, near Strasbourg in northeastern France.[4] His father was a rabbi, and as a young boy he was also

strongly affected by a schoolteacher who was Roman Catholic. These influences may have contributed something to his general interest in religious
endeavors, but they did not make him personally a believer. By the time he
was a young man, he had become an avowed agnostic.

In high school, Durkheim was a brilliant student, and at the age of
twenty-one (after failing on his first two attempts), he was admitted to the
demanding École Normale Supérieure, one of France's finest centers of
learning, where he studied both history and philosophy. His experience there
was not a completely happy one, in part because he did not like the rigid
way in which the programs of study were designed. Yet his response at the
time, which offers a clue to his temperament, was not to withdraw or com-
plain. He had too keen an appreciation for social order and structure to
abandon an institution just because he was personally unsuited to its rules.
After finishing his program and writing the two dissertations required of all
students at the École Normale, he began teaching at secondary schools in
the vicinity of Paris. He also took a year to study in Germany with the noted
psychologist Wilhelm Wundt. In 1887 he married Louise Dreyfus, a woman
who devoted herself lifelong to his career and their two children. In the same
year he became a professor at the University of Bordeaux, which created a
new chair of social science and education specifically for his sociological research.[5]

Over the next fifteen years, while working at Bordeaux, Durkheim dili-
gently pursued his sociological inquiries and developed his ideas. His first
major book was *The Division of Labor,* published in 1893. It was followed
in 1895 by *The Rules of Sociological Method,* a theoretical work which
stirred a great deal of debate. He also published an important study, *Suicide*
(1897), which looked for the public, social factors behind what others of his
day commonly regarded as a strictly private act of despair. At about the
same time, he established with other scholars *L'Année sociologique,* a new
academic journal which published articles and reviewed other writings from
a sociological perspective. This journal, which became famous throughout
France and the world, did as much as any of Durkheim's own books to
promote the discipline of sociology. Other talented scholars were drawn to
contribute their work to its pages and in the process developed Durkheim's
perspective into an identifiable "school of thought." Not surprisingly, on the
strength of these impressive achievements (and with the help of some political maneuvering in the government), Durkheim was named a professor at
the University of Paris. At the age of forty-four, he could boast the supreme
achievement of a French academic career.

At Paris, Durkheim passed through years of triumph and later of tragedy.
Already in Bordeaux his interests had begun to turn strongly toward an ex-

ploration of religion's role in social life, but after his move, new commitments and tasks slowed the progress of his research. Nonetheless, he kept to his plan and a decade later published *The Elementary Forms of the Religious Life* (1912), his best-known and most important book. Durkheim's chief claim to importance as a theorist of religion—and his great influence on other thinkers—rests largely on this impressive study, which we shall examine closely in this chapter. As its date reveals, however, *The Elementary Forms* appeared just two years before Europe was shaken by World War I. This enormous catastrophe fell hardest on Belgium and France, where much of the fighting took place, and it did not fail also to leave its mark on Durkheim's personal life, as it did on the lives of so many others. Though he believed that scholars should preserve their scientific objectivity by avoiding comment on current affairs, he made an exception during the war, speaking out fiercely for the cause of France against Germany. Then, early in 1916, he learned that his only son, André, himself a promising young scholar, had been killed on a military campaign in Serbia. Broken by grief, Durkheim struggled to work and write, only to suffer a debilitating stroke some months later. His own death came just over a year thereafter, in 1917, at the relatively young age of fifty-nine.

Ideas and Influences

Durkheim's great interest in society was not some sudden creation of his own. As he would have been the first to point out, a sequence of French thinkers before him had shown similar interests, and his ideas could be seen as a development of theirs.[6] One of his two dissertations had been written on the Baron de Montesquieu, the French philosopher of the eighteenth century who carefully observed and analyzed European culture and political institutions. Montesquieu's work showed that social structures could be examined in a critical scientific fashion. Durkheim also read the writings of the Comte de Saint-Simon, a socialist thinker of the early 1800s who believed that all private property should be given over to the state. And he was even more impressed by the most famous French thinker of the early nineteenth century, August Comte (1798–1857), who proposed, somewhat like Tylor and Frazer, a grand evolutionary pattern of civilization. In this scheme, earlier stages of human thinking, governed first by theology and then by the abstract ideas of philosophers, are eventually surpassed by the current age of "positive," or scientific, thought, in which close study only of observable facts provides the key to all knowledge. During this present epoch of science, a new "religion of humanity" replaces the discredited religions and philosophies of the past. From Comte, Durkheim took an appreciation of the human need for communal ties and a deep commitment to scientific analysis of social phenomena, even though he committed himself only in a quite vague and general way to the notion of evolutionary social progress.

In addition to these earlier figures, we must not forget two of the most celebrated scholars in France during Durkheim's youth: the great biblical critic Ernest Renan, who took a keenly social interest in both ancient Judaism and early Christianity; and an extraordinarily gifted classical historian who was one of Durkheim's own, greatly admired university teachers at the École Normale. This was Numa Denys Fustel de Coulanges, whose influential book *The Ancient City* (1864) was to become a classic study of social life in the ancient world. In this fascinating work, Coulanges presented his readers with a close social analysis of the Greek and Roman city-states, showing not only how ordinary life was governed by deeply cherished traditions and rooted in conservative moral values but also how thoroughly these traditions and values were saturated with the beliefs of classical polytheistic religion.

Durkheim built naturally upon the ideas of these thinkers in framing his own perspective.[7] But the circumstances of modern French life contributed something as well. As most would know, by the later 1800s France and Europe had passed through two great revolutions. One was economic: the industrial revolution; the other was political: the French Revolution and its several successors. In Durkheim's estimate, the joint impact of these two momentous developments permanently changed the pattern of life in Western civilization. Europe had long relied for stability on its agriculture, its well-defined social classes, its property-owning aristocracies and monarchies, and the intimate community ties of its villages and towns, along with the overarching truths, traditions, and structures of the Christian church. In the aftermath of the twin revolutions, these fixtures of Western culture found themselves shaken as never before and altered in such a way as never again to be the same. Around and within them, there began to grow up a truly new and different kind of civilization, which saw its people moving to factories and cities, its wealth moving from titled lords to enterprising merchants, its power shifting from the old privileged classes to radical movements or popular causes, and its religion everywhere facing disputes, indifference, or open disbelief. In specific terms, Durkheim noticed especially the following four trends, or patterns:

1. In place of Europe's traditional social system, laced together as it was by ties of family, community, and religious faith, a new "contractual"

order was emerging, in which private concerns and money-related interests seemed to predominate.

2. In the realm of morals and behavior, the sacred values once sanctioned by the church were now challenged by newer ideals, which stressed reason over religious faith and a desire for a happiness in this life over any hope of Heaven (or fear of Hell) in the life to come.

3. In the sphere of politics, the emergence of the democratic masses at the bottom of society and a powerful central state at the top had changed the nature of social control. Individuals were finding themselves disconnected from their old moral teachers—the family, village, and church—and were left to find what guidance they could from political parties, mass movements, and the state.

4. In the area of personal affairs, this new freedom of individuals released from their old frameworks presented great opportunity *and* great risk. With it came the chance of greater prosperity and self-realization but also the serious threat of loneliness and personal isolation.

Sociology and "the Social"

Looking over these momentous changes, Durkheim felt that there was only one way to approach them—scientifically. Only a fully scientific sociology could help people comprehend the tremors of an entire world that was moving beneath their feet. Accordingly, he laid down for his scholarly investigations two fixed and fundamental principles: (1) that the nature of society is the most suitable and promising subject for systematic investigation, especially at the present moment in history, and (2) that all such "social facts" should be investigated by the most purely objective scientific methods attainable.

The Nature of Society

In *The Division of Labor,* Durkheim's first major book, he shows how easily one can go wrong by ignoring the first of these principles. Social life, he explains, has shaped the most fundamental features of human culture, but that is not how previous thinkers tended to see it. If they considered it at all, they did so as a kind of afterthought. When they looked at the past, they proposed ideas like the famous "social contract," which held that society began when two individual persons first made an agreement to cooperate. One said "I will do this if you will do that." The other agreed, and so society was born. Such stories offer an interesting exercise in imaginative fiction, says Durkheim, but the real history of humanity was never so. Even in prehistoric times, individuals were always born *first* into groups—into families, clans, tribes, nations—and raised in that context. Their languages, habits, beliefs, and emotional responses—even the very concept they had of their individual selves—always came from a social framework which was there to shape them from the first moment they appeared in the world. Ancient contracts, for example, always had to be sworn with a sacred religious oath, which showed that such agreements were not just a matter of convenience between the two parties involved but were to be enforced by the gods, for all of the community had an interest in the outcome. So too with the concept of private property. It too is thought to have developed individually. Conventional thinking holds that the idea of a person's right to own an object or piece of ground arose because these things could be seen as extensions of the individual self. But again, Durkheim claims the facts of history show otherwise. The first possessions were not individual but communal in character, starting with the sacred ground that early peoples regarded as belonging not to the priest or any other single person but to the whole tribe. These *common* holdings provided the earliest ideas of property and ownership. Only out of the notion of *public* rights to things owned or possessed by all—things sacred to the whole clan—did cultures ever develop the idea of something that could be privately possessed by one person alone or by some apart.

Social solidarity, then, has always been primary. Out of an underlying sense of the group have come such basic structures of life as moral obligation and ownership of personal property. That having been said, Durkheim observes that the main difference between ancient and modern societies pertains to the ways in which they try to achieve their unity. Study of legal codes, for example, shows that early communities tend to rely on "mechanical solidarity." Good behavior is secured by punishments (often severe) for anyone who breaks the moral code of the group. This is external enforcement. In more modern times, on the other hand, a different pattern of "organic solidarity" tends to take over. Because there is the division of labor, because different people can do different things, the sense of moral commitment develops in another way. It comes not from the threat of punishment but from the need that each person acquires for the work of the others. Here enforcement must become internal. A wrong done by any one person must be seen as damaging to the others on whom that person depends. Ancient societies also have a broad and strong "collective conscience"; in them, there is uniform agreement as to what is right and what is wrong in almost all matters of human conduct. Modern societies, by contrast, are marked by moral individualism; they still need a foundation, a common moral basis, but because they allow for more individual diversity and personal freedom, their collective conscience is smaller in scope. It is limited to a few commands and obligations rather than many.

This last fact is especially significant because Durkheim believes firmly that morality, the obligation of each to others and all to the standards of the group, is inseparable from religion. Further, as we shall shortly see, both religion and morals are inseparable from a social framework. We cannot have either without a social context, and as that changes, so must they. When, as has happened especially in Western civilization, a society gives up the collective conscience it had in more primitive times and through division of labor replaces it with a morally individualistic system like that of the present, we should not be surprised to see that religion and morals have changed right along with the rest of the social order.[8]

The Scientific Study of Society

The second of Durkheim's two principles of inquiry is developed in *The Rules of Sociological Method* (1895), where he explains how sociology must be pursued as an objective, independent science.[9] In France, many people knew the perceptive analyses of society carried out by Montesquieu, Alexis de Tocqueville, and August Comte; these were admirable and insightful narratives in the style of traditional historical study. When Durkheim, in contrast, insisted that his "science" of society was really quite another thing, reasonable people naturally wondered: What kind of other thing? How can there be a science of an abstraction like the social order, of something we really cannot see or touch in the way a chemist or botanist can observe the visible, solid objects of nature? Durkheim's answer was to think of society in a manner similar to that of Tylor and the British anthropologists when they spoke of "culture" but then to go even further. He insisted that social facts, no less than stones or seashells, are real things, as solid in their way as physical objects are in theirs. A society is not just a passing thought in someone's head; it is an accumulated body of facts—of language, laws, customs, ideas, values, traditions, techniques, and products—all of which are connected to one another and exist in a manner quite "external" to individual human minds. They are in the world before we individuals arrive; the moment we are born, they impose themselves on us; as we grow through childhood, they mold us; in adulthood, they animate and guide us; and, just as surely, in death they survive us. Moreover, it stands to reason that if there indeed are such real and independent social facts surrounding us, then there ought to be a distinct scientific discipline devoted to the study of them.

We do not imagine that we can explain a living organism only through physics or chemistry; we also need biology. In the same way, we cannot explain society if we look only to biology and psychology or even economics. Society requires sociology; other disciplines are not sufficient.

None of this means for Durkheim that the actual methods of sociological study will be dramatically different from those of other sciences. The key to any science, physical or social, is the gathering of evidence, followed by comparison, classification into groups, and finally the framing of general principles, or "laws," which can in some way be tested for their validity. In this connection, sociology not only does what other sciences do but in some ways hopes even to do it better. For example, Durkheim takes care to separate himself from the well-known comparative method as it was practiced by Tylor, Frazer, and the other Victorian British anthropologists. We have seen how, in their searches for significant patterns, they preferred to travel globally, choosing customs or ideas at will and placing them into a general category, such as "imitative magic," with little or no attention to context. Such determined gathering of facts from the remotest ends and ages of the world does make for large, impressive books like *The Golden Bough,* but in Durkheim's view it is not science. It rests everything on surface similarities and very little on substance. Sociology is much more cautious. It knows that comparisons can be made, and general laws laid down, only when two societies are very closely examined and can be seen to fit clearly into a common type.

Though we cannot here follow his account of sociology's methods in detail, we can briefly take note of at least some of the categories Durkheim puts into play in his approach to religion. Among other things, he believes that we can determine, for any society, what is *normal* behavior and, consequently, what is also *pathological,* or abnormal, behavior.[10] This is certainly not a matter of absolute values, of what is good or evil at all times and places. The normal is always determined from within a group, never from outside of it. Suicide, for example, is more "normal" for some societies, like Japan, than for others. Polygamy is more normal for primitive societies than for modern ones. We must always judge the normal from within the social. In addition, whether normal or not, the category of *function* in a society is for Durkheim also extremely important in explaining behavior. And it must be kept separate from the idea of cause. The *cause* of an inner-city religious revival might be the spellbinding sermons of a storefront preacher, but the revival's social *function* may be something that goes entirely unnoticed by those who join it.[11] From the sociologist's standpoint, the preacher's success can be traced not to the number of sinners brought to conversion but to something wholly unnoticed by those who are kneeling in prayer: the event as a whole has restored a sense of community, of shared identity and purpose, to a neighborhood of otherwise poor, isolated, even disillusioned individuals.

A good illustration of these categories can be found in Durkheim's famous study *Suicide* (1895), which was published not long after the *Rules*. After examining and closely comparing the suicide rates in the major countries of Europe, he noticed that the figures were highest in Protestant countries, lowest in Catholic ones, and fell in between for countries of mixed religious population.[12] In light of these ratios, it is possible to say that a certain kind of suicide, which Durkheim labels "egoistic," is more normal—that is, more typical—for Protestant countries than Catholic ones. We cannot account for this circumstance, he says, directly from the differing religious belief systems because both groups think suicide is wrong. Sociologically, however, there are certain definite and interesting differences. Protestant societies offer the individual greater freedom of thought and life; in them, people are "on their own" before God. Catholics, by contrast, belong to a more strongly integrated social community, where priests mediate between God and the believer and ties within the parish are strong. It would seem, therefore, that the rate of suicide in a community is closely correlated, in a negative way, to the degree of its social integration. The tighter the social ties, the lower the rate of suicide. In addition, the distinction between cause and function is also relevant. The specific causes of individual suicides vary in each person's case, but functionally, egoistic suicide in general can be read as the natural consequence of loosened social ties and constraints. A similar pattern seems to hold for another kind of suicide—Durkheim called it "anomic" (from the Greek *anomia:* "lawlessness") to suggest a feeling of dislocation and aimlessness—which tends to occur most in times of great economic and social instability. To the trained sociologist, then, the phenomenon of suicide appears in a light very different from that which strikes the eye of the ordinary observer.

Politics, Education, and Morals

Durkheim felt that his sociological perspective offered special insight into the nature of political systems, education, morals, and especially religion. In the sphere of political philosophy he gave lectures on socialism and communism, describing both as responses to the unsettlement of modern life but rejecting their ideas of class struggle and their theories of a powerful state.[13] In other lectures, especially *Professional Ethics and Civic Morals* (published after his death) he recognized that the state must have certain extensive powers, which can even be good for the lives of individuals. At the same

time he stressed the importance also of what he called "secondary," interme-
diate groups, such as local brotherhoods and professional associations, to
help protect the rights and well-being of individuals lest national governments become too strong. A key task of the state is the promotion of moral
values, which is why it must also play a central role in a society's system
of education. Durkheim addressed this subject often, writing, among other
works, a two-volume history of education in France.[14] As he describes it,
the purpose of schools is not just to give technical training in certain skills
but also to pass along the values of self-discipline and community welfare
and to promote them over the selfish personal interests of individuals. Such
instruction in moral values is not a luxury or an option; it is vital to the
health and harmonious operation of any society. These opinions, which have
had considerable influence on modern French educational theory, are at least
partly responsible for the wry observation that, on any given day, the minis-
ter of education in Paris knows precisely which page of their textbooks all
the children of France are reading. Against this backdrop, it is not surprising
to find that alongside his treatments of both politics and education, Durkheim also makes the analysis of moral theory and legal traditions a key part
of his program.[15]

The question of morals, as we have already noticed, is in Durkheim's
view impossible to answer without at some point turning also to the question
of religion. This he had done in the earlier years of his career indirectly,
through essays, articles, and reviews of the work of others. But he reserved
his complete and definitive discussion of religion for his last and most important book, *The Elementary Forms of Religious Life*. It was published in
1912, after more than ten years of research and reflection. Since it presents
the heart of Durkheim's theory of religion, we must here consider its arguments in some detail.

The Elementary Forms of the Religious Life

Perhaps the two most important things to notice about this lengthy, pioneering book are its title and the way it begins. *The Elementary Forms* (1912) is
concerned to find certain fundamentals—the "basic elements," as a nuclear
physicist might say—out of which all of religion has been formed. And it
starts off in a way a nuclear physicist might well approve—by apparently
setting aside all the usual and customary ways of thinking about its subject.
We may recall that Tylor and Frazer, and Freud as well, were largely content with the conventional idea that religion is belief in supernatural beings,
such as a God or gods. Durkheim is not. From the start he claims that

primitive peoples normally do not really think of two different worlds, one supernatural and the other natural, in the way that religious people living in developed cultures do. Moderns are heavily influenced by the assumptions and natural laws of science; primitive people are not. They see all events— miraculous and ordinary—as basically of the same kind. In addition, the concept of the gods itself is a problem, since not all religious people believe in divine beings even if they do believe in the supernatural. Certain Buddhists, for example, deny that there are gods, while other people routinely observe rituals that have nothing to do with spirits or deities. It is obvious to Durkheim, then, that the subject needs a new definition, and clearing away the old view is a necessary first step. But where do we go after that?

Durkheim next observes that the thing which seems truly characteristic of religious beliefs and rituals is not the element of the supernatural but the concept of *the sacred,* which is actually quite different. Wherever we look, people who are religious do divide the things of their world into two separate arenas, but they are not the natural and supernatural. Rather, they are the realms of the sacred and the profane. Sacred things are always set apart as superior, powerful, forbidden to normal contact, and deserving of great respect. Profane things are the opposite; they belong to the ordinary, uneventful, and practical routine of everyday life. The overwhelming concern of religion is with the first of these two sets of things. In Durkheim's own words, "religion is a unified system of beliefs and practices relative to *sacred things,* that is to say, things set apart and forbidden."[16] If we then ask what is the purpose of these sacred things, that is answered in a second part of Durkheim's definition; these practices "unite into one moral community called a church, all those who adhere to them."[17] The key words here are "community" and "church." Sacred things always involve large concerns: the interests and welfare of an entire group of people, not just one or a few. Profane things, on the other hand, are little matters; they reflect the day-to-day business of each individual—the smaller, private activities and endeavors of the immediate family and personal life.

Though it is tempting to do so, Durkheim warns us not to make the mistake of thinking that this division between sacred and profane is a moral one—that the sacred is good and the profane evil. That line of separation actually runs *through* the division between the sacred and the profane. The sacred can be either good or evil, but the one thing it can never be is profane; the profane can be either good or evil, but the one thing it can never be is sacred. The sacred arises especially in connection with whatever may concern the community; the profane is more naturally the realm of private and personal concerns.

This stress on the sacred as something communal leads Durkheim to another disagreement with his predecessors, which centers on the puzzling question of magic. In Frazer's opinion, as we saw, magic and religion are cut from the same cloth; they try to do the same thing but in different ways. Both try to explain the way the world works, so that it can be controlled for human benefit. The human race first followed the rules of magic, and when they failed, it turned to religion as a better form of thought. With this, too, Durkheim disagrees. For him, religion does not come along to replace magic when it fails, because the two are not concerned with the same thing. Magic is an exclusively private matter, which has little or nothing to do with the sacred and its concerns. The magician, like a doctor, heals my sickness or puts a spell on your enemy; but this is a purely personal issue. I may not even know that my magician is also helping you, because each of us is going to him to satisfy separate and largely private needs. None of this is the case, however, with the much greater matter of religion. Religious rituals and beliefs come into play whenever group concerns are foremost in the mind; the sacred functions as the focal point of the claims that affect the entire community. Accordingly, magic and religion can exist quite comfortably side by side; the one is the place for the personal, the other the sphere of the social. A magician, as Durkheim puts it, has clients but no congregation. "There is no church of magic."[18]

   These two points of disagreement—on the definition of religion and the nature of magic—lead on to the third and most important of Durkheim's quarrels with other theorists. In his view, they have all misunderstood what it is about religion that really needs to be explained.

Previous Theories: Naturism, Animism

Durkheim contends that a close look at the leading theories of the day will show a common theme throughout: all claim that religion is simply a natural instinct of the human race; it is assumed that in all cultures people have devised their systems of belief as quite logical responses to the world as they encounter it. The most prominent of these theories are the naturism of Friedrich Max Müller, whom we met in our introduction, and the animism of E. B. Tylor.[19] Müller holds that people came to believe in gods by trying to describe the great objects and events of nature—things like the sun, sky, and storms. Tylor, as we have seen, holds that belief in gods developed out of the idea of the soul.[20] Now in framing these views, Durkheim observes, both of these thinkers have been exceedingly ambitious. They have assumed that human society has gone through a long process of evolution, and they have then tried to travel backward in time to imagine what the ideas and emotions of the very first human beings would have been. But this is really an impossible enterprise. If we truly want to be scientific about religion, we cannot rely on guesses about how people thought at the dawn of history. We must try to look instead for "the ever-present causes" on which religion rests, the things that at all times and places push people to believe and behave in religious ways. Instead of making a grand guess about the distant past, Durkheim proposes that we look firsthand at a real example of religion in action. And for this purpose, what better method could there be than to locate the simplest society we know of and rely on someone who has actually observed it? A religion linked to the simplest social system that exists might well be regarded as "the most elementary religion we can possibly know."[21] And if we can explain this religion, we have a start on explaining all religion. We will have in hand religion's "elementary forms."

Australian Tribal Religion: Totemism

It was Durkheim's further conviction that on just this point—finding a specimen of a truly simple civilization—recent researches provided a remarkable breakthrough. We have already noted how in the years just before and after the turn of the century, Frazer took an interest in the work of Baldwin Spencer and F. J. Gillen, two field anthropologists who had been able to observe closely certain primitive aborigine tribes in the remote hinterlands of Australia. Their work—along with that of the German fieldworker Carl von Strehlow and others who had made similar observations—furnished a detailed portrait of social life in these extremely simple communities.[22] And quite remarkably, it had also shown that the religion of these peoples was none other than totemism, the very same thing that, as we have seen, so captivated Robertson Smith, Frazer, Freud, and other early anthropological inquirers.

Durkheim was no less fascinated than the others by this new Australian research, but he was also convinced that none of these earlier theorists had grasped its full importance. None had really appreciated how fundamental to primitive culture totemism really is. All recognized, for instance, that tribal peoples divide themselves into different clans, each of which is identified with a separate totem animal, plant, or other object. And all noticed that the totem itself, whether it be the bear or the crow, the kangaroo or the tea tree, is considered sacred to the clan that claims it. But none had detected the genuinely important thing: how totemism impressively illustrates the concepts of the sacred and the profane.

In each of these primitive societies, Durkheim observes, animals other than the totem, which are profane, can ordinarily be killed and eaten by the clan; the totem animal cannot. Because it is sacred, it is absolutely forbidden to the clan—except on those select occasions when, as a part of specially designated ceremonies, it is ritually sacrificed and eaten. In addition, the clan itself is regarded as sacred because it is considered to be one with its totem. And perhaps most important, the emblem, or logo, of the totem animal is always extremely important; it is not just sacred but the very model, the perfect example, of a sacred thing. When the clan gathers together for its ceremonies, it is always the totem symbol, carved into a piece of wood or rock, that holds center stage. The totem is supremely sacred and communicates its sacred character to all around it.

Totem beliefs, moreover, are so fundamental to the life of these simple societies that everything of importance is ultimately shaped by them. One can hardly find anything more basic than the very categories of human thought and experience; among the aborigines, these are provided by totemism. For example, totemic concepts govern their most basic perceptions of nature, so that not only groups of people but the entire world of natural objects is divided into categories based on totem clans, or clusters of clans, called phratries. One tribe, for example, places the sun in the clan of the white cockatoo, while the moon and stars are assigned to the clan of its black counterpart.[23] In addition, natural objects are placed in a hierarchy of power, which could only have been devised on the basis of the levels of authority which primitives experience first in the structures of the family and clan. The concepts of the totem and the clan thus find their way into every significant aspect of tribal life. There are even cases of individual totems—those which a clan member can choose as a sort of personal friend—and sexual totems, which group people by gender. Both of these undoubtedly derive from more basic and general clan totems and offer further proof of their central importance.

In casting about for explanations of totemism, earlier theorists have followed their own quite predictable paths. Tylor, as we might have guessed, insists that the custom arises out of animism; others have thought that it derives from nature worship; and still others, like Frazer, have claimed that it is magical, or that it may have no connection at all to either religion or magic. Where all of these theories go wrong is, for Durkheim, not hard to see. Each attempts to trace totemism to *something else* that is supposedly earlier and more fundamental. But this is a crucial mistake. Finding a form of religion older than totemism is quite impossible, for the simple reason that *there is none*. Totemism, which appears in the very simplest societies, is itself the simplest, most basic, and original form of religion; all other forms can only grow out of *it*. Totemism is not a product, not a derivative of some more basic form of religion; it is itself the source from which all other kinds of religious worship—whether it be of spirits, gods, animals, planets, or stars—ultimately arise.

It is true that at first glance totemism seems to be merely another of the usual religious types: a kind of animal or plant worship and nothing more. But Durkheim insists that when we look at it in detail, it turns out to be something considerably different. Followers of totem cults do not actually adore the crow, the frog, or the white cockatoo; they commit to the worship "of an anonymous and impersonal force, found in each of these beings but not to be confounded with any of them. No one possesses it entirely and all participate in it." If we want, we can of course speak loosely of a "god" adored in the totem cult, but "it is an impersonal god, without name or history, immanent in the world and diffused in an innumerable multitude of things." [24] Durkheim prefers that we speak more accurately of something called "the totemic principle," which stands at the center of all of the clan's beliefs and rituals. Behind the totem is an impersonal force that possesses enormous power, both physical and moral, over the life of the clan. People respect it; they feel a moral obligation to observe its ceremonies; and through it they feel tightly bound to each other in deep and abiding loyalty.

Here we can see why Durkheim thinks it misleading, at least at the outset, for theorists to define religion as belief in gods or supernatural beings. In his view, before we ever get to belief in gods, there is always this first and more basic thing, the sense of a hidden, impersonal, and powerful force—the totemic principle—that is the original focus of the clan's worship. It is significant, moreover, that the evidence we find for this totemic principle is by no means limited to Australia. Under different names, Durkheim claims to find it as well in other tribal societies. Among the Melanesians, there is the similar concept of *mana;* and among various American Indian tribes, we find the same principle described in such words as *wakan, manitou,* and *orenda,* all of which convey the same idea of an all-pervading, impersonal force, a dominating power, which is the real center of clan or tribe worship. [25] It follows, then, that if we want to account for religion, we must explain more than surface beliefs in the gods or spirits that people routinely worship; we need to explain this more fundamental reality. We must show what this worship of "the totemic principle" really is.

Society and the Totem

The totem is in the first instance a symbol. But a symbol of what? One answer, we can now see, is the totemic principle, the hidden force worshipped by the clan. At the same time—and here Durkheim makes his pivotal turn—the totem is also the concrete, visible image of the clan. It is its flag, its banner or logo, its very self in a symbol, just as one might say that the American eagle, "Old Glory," or "Uncle Sam" is a visible emblem of the United States. But if the totem "is at once the symbol of the god and of the society, is that not because the god and the society are only one?" "The god of the clan, the totemic principle, can therefore be nothing else than the clan itself, personified and represented to the imagination under the visible form of the animal or vegetable which serves as totem."[26] The totem, in brief, is simultaneously the symbol of both the god *and* the clan, because both the god and the clan are really the same thing! In succinct form, devotion to a god or gods is how primitive peoples express and reinforce their devotion to the clan.

It is true, of course, that in their rituals of worship, which are always communal, the members of these aborigine clans themselves think they are worshipping some divinity, some animal or plant, "out there" in the world, who can control the rain or make them prosper. But what is really happening is something else, something that can best be grasped in terms of social function.[27] Society needs the commitment of the individual. It "cannot exist," Durkheim observes, "except in and through individual consciousness"; that is why the totem principle must somehow always "penetrate and organize itself within us."[28] Moreover, we can know exactly when and how this occurs. It happens on those awe-inspiring ceremonial occasions when the whole community assembles for its general rites of the clan or tribe. In these great and unforgettable ceremonies, the worshippers seal their commitment to the clan. In their moments of great excitement, in the wild emotional ecstasies of chanting and dancing, individuals manage to lose themselves in the heaving mass of the crowd; they allow their private—that is, profane—selves to sink into the great single self of the clan. In the middle of such throbbing assemblies, individuals acquire sentiments and undertake actions they would never be capable of embracing on their own. They leave behind what is most distinctively their own and merge their identities joyfully into the common single self of the clan. In such ceremonies, they leave the everyday, the humdrum, the selfish; they move instead into the domain of what is great and general. They enter the solemn sphere of the sacred.

Durkheim vividly describes the sentiments that "bubble up" in the excitement of these group ceremonies. They are ritual times, filled with energy, enthusiasm, joy, selfless commitment, and complete security. "It is in the midst of these effervescent social environments and out of this effervescence itself that the religious idea seems to be born."[29] At such moments the profane is left behind; only the sacred exists.

The Implications of Totemism

Once Durkheim has made his key point—the idea that worship of the totem is nothing less than worship of society itself, he feels that all other pieces in the puzzle of Australian society and religion fall quite naturally into their appropriate places. The role of the totem symbol, for example, now seems clear. Carved in wood or stone, it is a concrete object which conveys to each person the fact that the clan, which claims the loyalty of all, is not just something imagined; it is a real thing, which imposes itself on everyone's life and thoughts. The totem symbol also conveys the idea that society, like itself, is something fixed and permanent; it remains as a focus of inspiration long after the excitement of the religious ceremonies is over. If we ask why animals and plants should be the most common totems, that too is clear. The clan does not want as its symbol something distant and vague; it needs an object that is specific, concrete, and near at hand, something closely tied to its daily experience. If we ask how such primitive societies developed their systems of thought, their ways of ordering and classifying the world, that can be seen clearly as well.[30] The aim of totemism is to notice the interconnectedness of things, the intricate web of ties that bind each person to the next in the clan, the clan as a whole to the natural world, and different parts of the natural world to each other. This urge to embrace and connect all things is so strong, in fact, that it enables primitive totemism, simple as it is, to lay the groundwork for the intricately connected systems of language, logic, and science which develop in later stages of civilization.

Properly understood, the totemic principle can account for all the rest of religion as well. Belief in souls, or spirits, is a case in point. Totemism shows how such beliefs have developed. The idea of the soul is really just the totemic principle implanted in each individual. Since the clan exists only because individuals think about it in their minds, it is only natural for its members to think of the totemic principle as somehow spreading itself into each one of them. As it distributes itself throughout the clan, the fragment of it which each individual comes to possess becomes his or her separate soul; it is "the clan within."[31]

This "social" idea of the soul is quite enlightening, Durkheim adds, when we think of the age-old religious (and philosophical) problem of its relation to the body. If the soul is, in effect, the clan idealized and implanted within the self, then in that capacity its task is to represent to the individual society's demands and ideals. The soul is the conscience of the self, the voice of the clan within, informing each of his or her personal obligation to the group. The body, on the other hand, naturally asserts its own self-centered desires, which can and often do clash sharply with the demands and restraints of social life. No wonder, then, that religion has always been suspicious of the desires of the flesh! They satisfy the individual and are profane; religion asserts the claims of the social and is therefore sacred.

The doctrine of the immortality of the soul is also a natural development from totemism. To speak of the soul as immortal is for totem peoples only another way of saying that while individuals die, the clan lives on. Ancestral spirits appear as fragments from the clan's past that have survived into the present. Interestingly, these spirits often associate themselves with living members of the clan in a way that gives each person a kind of double soul: "one which is within us, or rather, which is us; the other [in the form of the ancestral spirit], which is above us, and whose function it is to control and assist the first one" in doing its duty to the clan.[32] Over time, these guardian spirits begin to grow in power and prestige. They become more important; their sphere of influence widens; and they acquire "mythical personalities of a superior order." In short, as the concept of the soul and its immortality gradually arises out of the worship of the totemic principle, so, over time, the worship of the gods emerges in its turn from the immortality of ancestral souls.

With the emergence of the gods from original totemism, Durkheim comes at last to the realm of religion as it has been more traditionally understood. Even in Australia, he admits, clan religion has developed to the point where it has numerous gods, most of whom are associated not with the smaller clan ceremonies but with the larger tribal rites of initiation, which make young men and women full members of adult society. The best way to understand these greater gods, in fact, is to think of them as personifications of these wider tribal units. And the same is true for that other well-known feature of primitive religion which is on exhibit in Australia: the belief in a high god who rules over all. Modern scholars have been fascinated to find among early peoples a belief such as this, which is so strikingly similar to the Jewish and Christian faith in a creator and moral ruler of the world. But in Australia, says Durkheim, the idea of such a god is just a natural extension of the same thinking that accounts for tribal gods. As contacts increased among tribes that lived in a certain region, and as they exchanged ideas, they began to suppose that there was one ancestor of special importance whom they all shared. That ancestor was the high god. His status is grand, but he comes into being like all other gods—as a further extension of the original totemic principle. For whatever the level we observe, the process that gives rise to belief in the gods has left us clear traces of its operation. The gods grow out of the totemic principle as it filters gradually through the clan, first into souls, next to ancestors who become clan spirits, and finally beyond them to the higher and highest of gods.[33]

Totemism and Ritual

The last part of the *Elementary Forms* turns from the matter of beliefs to take up the other side of Australian religion: its ritual performances. Here we must note Durkheim's earlier observation that religious sentiments and emotions first arise not in private moments but in the great group ceremonials of the clan. It follows from this that the beliefs found in totemism are not the most important thing about it. Rituals are. In Durkheim's view, the "cult" (from the Latin *cultus:* "worship"), which consists of emotional group ceremonies held on certain set occasions, is the very core of the clan's life together.[34] Whenever they occur and however they are performed, these cultic acts of worship are the most important things the people of the clan ever undertake. They are sacred; all else is profane. Their purpose is always to promote consciousness of the clan, to make people feel a part of it, and to keep it in every way separate from the profane.

In totem practice, the cult breaks into two main forms, negative and positive, while a third type, called "piacular" (from the Latin *piaculum:* "atonement") plays a role of its own alongside the first two. The rituals of the negative cult have one main task: keeping the sacred always quite separate from the profane.[35] They consist chiefly of prohibitions, or taboos. Taboos of location protect certain sacred places, usually rocks or caves. They are the source of the belief, common in later religions, that a temple or church stands on holy ground or encloses a sacred space. The sacred and the profane must also be kept from colliding in time. The negative cult therefore sets aside certain holy days for sacred festivals; one of the most common taboos on such days is the prohibition of any routine activities from profane life. Normal work and play are prohibited; only rest or sacred activity is permitted, just as more developed religions like Judaism and Christianity require on the Sabbath or Sunday. If such rules have often seemed inconvenient and annoying, no one should be surprised, for that is what they are supposed to be. Their role is to press upon everyone the need to deny the self, or even endure pain, for the sake of the group. Indeed, Durkheim continues, that is precisely why almost all religions point with pride to certain people—"ascetics" as they are commonly called—who make a point of extreme self-denial. Invariably such people are highly respected. Their excessive pain and self-restraint, their refusal to enjoy sex, good food, or other luxuries, is meant to serve as an ideal for everyone. They are models of what, to a lesser degree, is required of everyone for the good of the clan.[36] Without sacrifice of self, the clan can neither prosper nor survive.

Normally, then, the sacred is off limits, and the point of the negative cult is to keep it so. When the time and place are right, however, and the clan does move into the realm of the sacred, the means for doing so are then provided by the rituals Durkheim describes as belonging to the positive cult. For Australians, the central rite is the *intichiuma,* the ceremony which, as we may recall, Robertson Smith, Frazer, and Freud found so uncannily similar to the Christian communion meal. At the beginning of every rainy season, men of the clan start a sequence of ceremonies to promote the growth of their totem. They begin with rituals done over certain sacred stones; a period of keen religious excitement comes next; then amid a solemn ritual the totem creature itself is seized, killed, and eaten in a sacred meal. Why is this done? asks Durkheim. It is, as Robertson Smith correctly saw, the earliest form of the rite of sacrifice, which has assumed such a central place in so many later religions. In worshipping the totem, each person publicly celebrates its existence and declares that he or she will be loyal to it; in return, by eating the totem, each receives back from the god an infusion of divine power and a renewal of the divine life in the soul. Durkheim describes it, ingeniously, as a sacred exchange. In the *intichiuma* rite, the worshippers give life to their god, and the god returns it to them.

On the level of appearances, there can of course be little doubt that the Australian *intichiuma* is a strictly religious ritual—a transaction between the people of the clan and their god. Underneath, however, and in reality, it is none other than the social renewal of the life of the clan. Beneath the surface of theology lies the substrate of sociology. Durkheim explains it thus:

> If the sacred principle is nothing more nor less than society transfigured and personified, it should be possible to interpret the ritual in lay and social terms. And, as a matter of fact, social life, just like the ritual, moves in a circle. On the one hand, the individual gets from society the best part of himself, all that gives him a distinct character and a special place among other beings, his intellectual and moral culture. . . . But, on the other hand, society exists and lives only in and through individuals. If the idea of society were extinguished in individual minds and the beliefs, traditions and aspirations of the group were no longer felt and shared by the individuals, society would die. We can say of it what we just said of the divinity: it is real only in so far as it has a place in human consciousness, and this place is whatever one we may give it. We now see the real reason why the gods cannot do without their worshippers any more than these can do without their gods; it is because society, of which the gods are only a symbolic expression, cannot do without individuals any more than these can do without society.[37]

In this important paragraph, we can see as clearly as anywhere else in *The Elementary Forms* the thesis that stands at the heart of Durkheim's theory. Religious beliefs and rituals are in the last analysis *symbolic expressions of social realities.*[38] Worship of the totem is really a statement of loyalty to the clan. Eating the totem is really an affirmation and reinforcement of the group, a symbolic way for each member to say that the clan always matters more than the individual selves it comprises.

Totem rituals thus put us in a position to explain religious practice in the same way that totem ideas can explain religious belief. The concept of society once again furnishes the key. The function of religious rituals, which are more fundamental than beliefs, is to provide occasions where individuals renew their commitment to the community, reminding themselves in the most solemn fashion that they depend on the clan, just as it depends on them. Feast days and festivals exist to put society, the community's, back in the foreground of people's minds, and to push personal, self-oriented concerns back into a secondary place, where they belong.

Other rituals besides the *intichiuma* ceremony are included in the positive cult. There are, for instance, imitative rituals of the sort which Frazer classified as a type of magic. In the rites of certain clans, people mimic the cries of their totem birds, thinking that this will make them reproduce and thrive. In other cases, there are what Durkheim calls "representative" rites, or rituals of remembrance, in which one clan member simply recites the myth of a great ancestor to a group of listeners, apparently just to provide entertainment and instruction. But even so, the underlying motive is social. Telling the story of an ancestor, after all, is a way of binding the past members of the community to those alive in the present. And people come to believe that certain rituals can make the totem magically reproduce precisely *because of* the power those ceremonies have already demonstrated in bringing together the members of the clan. It is the social force of rituals which leads to the thought that they have physical force as well.

Piacular Rites

In addition to both the positive and negative cult there are finally certain important rituals Durkheim calls piacular,[39] These are the clan's rites of atonement and mourning, which always take place after a death or some other tragic event. Tylor thought that primitive peoples held such rituals in order to make peace with the spirits of the dead, who were angry that their life had ended. But once again, Durkheim provides a social reason. In cultures where funeral mourners weep loudly and beat themselves in despair, these acts are not just spontaneous outbursts. They are quite formal gestures, required by custom from all clan members, even those who hardly knew the dead person. And why? Because when someone dies, it is not just the immediate family that has been weakened; the whole clan has lost a member, a portion of its strength. At such a time, it needs, through the cult, to regroup, revive, and reaffirm itself. In the earliest ages, the rites performed—processions, wailings, breast-beatings—were not even directed to any spirits or gods. Belief in these supernatural beings actually developed later in time and only *as a result* of the ritual, just to give people a better mental image as a focus for their action. Originally, there were no gods to command a ritual; there was only the ritual, which over time itself created the gods.

Piacular rites, finally, show the double-sided power of the sacred, which can be dim and demonic as well as bright and divine. Just as the positive cult is a celebration of the clan in the full vigor of its joy and confidence, it falls to the piacular cult to carry it through its darker passages—the moments of grief, catastrophe, fear, or uncertainty that can descend on a community at any place or time. An example of Durkheim's point can here be supplied from recent history. Few Americans who were living in November 1963, when President John F. Kennedy was assassinated, can ever forget the overwhelming emotional impact on the nation of the elegant, somber funeral procession that moved through the streets of the capital and was followed by the heartbreaking rites of burial at Arlington National Cemetery. For those in every town and state who watched on television, it could well have seemed that an entire nation was a single, grieving family. Durkheim's concept of a piacular rite well explains why this should have been so. Whatever the mood of society, the rites of religion will invariably reflect and reinforce it.

Conclusion

Durkheim contends that if his analysis is correct, there is a great deal to be learned from the primitive peoples of Australia. In the totemism of their tribes and clans, one finds on clear display all of the truly "elementary forms" of the religious life: a separation between the sacred and the profane; ideas of souls and spirits; the beginnings of mythical beings and great gods; and a full assortment of rituals, including those of prohibition (taboo), celebration, imitation, remembrance, and sorrow. With these building blocks in hand, it becomes possible to construct a theory that can be applied throughout history and across cultures to explain religious behavior of any kind wherever we may find it. Durkheim's theory holds that no matter where we look for the determining causes of religion—all religions—those causes invariably turn out to be social. Though harder to detect in the great and dominant religions of the world, they are as unmistakably present in these complex traditions as they are in the simplest totemism. East or West, ancient or modern, beliefs and rituals always express a society's needs—its constant call upon all members to think first of the group, to sense its importance, feel its power, and sacrifice personal pleasures for its permanent well-being. Religion's role, accordingly, is not to make claims about "the outside world," not to teach what it thinks are truths about the creation of the world, the existence of a god, or a life after death. On all of these subjects, which people once thought proper for faith, it has had to yield to science, a more valid system of thought which, in fact, religion helped to create. Religion's true purpose is not intellectual but social. It serves as the carrier of social sentiments, providing symbols and rituals that enable people to express the deep emotions which anchor them to their community. Insofar as it does this, religion, or some substitute for it, will always be with us. For then it stands on its true home ground, preserving and protecting the very "soul of society."

Analysis

In following Durkheim's approach to religion, we have naturally had to pass over certain details, but the main outlines of his theory should now be fairly clear. From almost the moment it appeared, *The Elementary Forms* stirred excitement, especially in France, where Durkheim had associates and disciples who were already disposed to look at religion through sociological lenses. Even beyond France, however, Durkheim's originality was widely recognized. In Britain, the study of anthropology was shaped by his influence, as was the new field of social psychology in the United States, where such noteworthy spokesmen as G. H. Mead and C. H. Cooley adapted his ideas to their programs of research.[40] Durkheim's strong imprint can also be seen in such leading studies of religion as W. Lloyd Warner's *The Family of God* (1959), which explores the power of Christian symbolism in American communities, and contemporary sociologist Robert Bellah's analysis of religion and society in both the United States and Japan. Clearly, among those who work in the social sciences, Durkheim's thought continues to win new admirers and open fresh lines of inquiry.

Why all of this recognition? The answer to that question lies partly in the fact that Durkheim, like Freud, is a very wide-ranging thinker. He finds in sociology a new way of understanding almost every aspect of human behavior—not only religion, but science, philosophy, history, ethics, education, politics, and psychology as well. In addition, where religion in particular is concerned, his analyses open the way to a variety of new insights and applications. Among these, at least four deserve notice here.

1. Society and Religion

As we have seen throughout this discussion, the core of Durkheim's view lies in his claim that "religion is something eminently social."[41] He insists that although as individuals all of us make choices in our lives, we make them within a social framework that is a "given" for us from the day of birth. "We speak a language that we did not make; we use instruments that we did not invent; we invoke rights that we did not found; a treasury of knowledge is transmitted to each generation that it did not gather itself."[42] Religion is in all cultures the most prized part of that social treasury. It serves society by providing from infancy onward the ideas, rituals, and sentiments that guide the life of every person within it. In the present circumstance, discussions of "social influence" on religion, and vice versa, are so routine as to seem like common sense; everyone speaks in such terms. But to see how distinctive this perspective is, we need only remind ourselves of how Tylor wrote on religion only half a century before Durkheim. When he considers primitive religion, he speaks only of a single "savage philosopher," thinking his way all alone to the ideas of the soul and the gods. Similarly for Freud. Though he does grasp the importance of family and society, his focus, too, is primarily on the personality of the individual. Durkheim's view, however, is decidedly different. He is not the first or only thinker of his age to have glimpsed the power of "the social" in human life, but he is unique in understanding its full importance and in pushing it to the forefront of study.

2. Scientific Method

Durkheim takes great pride in being scientific. Like earlier theorists, he wants to gather data, compare it, classify it, and make generalizations, or laws, to explain it. In a limited way, he also embraces social evolution. He assumes human societies do evolve from the elementary to the complex. And he agrees that the best place to start is with cultures that are simple— with so-called primitive peoples. He does not, of course, like the idea of some broad scheme of human progress. He rejected this view for the most part when he met it in the philosophy of Comte. He also rejects Frazer's version, which presents the portrait of humanity marching steadily upward through the ages of magic, religion, and science. Against the British anthropologists, he insists that we must not use the comparative method to pick out customs and beliefs casually from around the world and then arrange them, out of their contexts, into some predetermined scheme of historical progress. That will not work. What he says we must do—and here *The Elementary Forms* serves as a model—is center on a single society, examine it carefully, and attend to details. Only *after* that close work has been done may theorists begin to make very limited comparisons with other societies, and even then, only if they are societies *of the same type*.[43] True science, he insists, works slowly—from a few specimens carefully examined, not from many gathered in haste.

In the years after World War I, this important point of Durkheim's method was taken very much to heart in the field of anthropology, especially in Britain and America. In England, it was promoted especially by the social theorist A. R. Radcliffe-Brown and by the field anthropologist Bronislaw Malinowski, who wrote on the religion and other features of primitive cultures in the South Pacific.[44] This principle of investigating one and only one society in depth before going on to comparisons is now widely approved in social science. It seems to have put an end permanently to the grand ambitions of Tylor, Frazer, and their associates from the older, Victorian era of anthropology.

3. Ritual and Belief

Durkheim also parts from the ways of Tylor and Frazer on the question of the relation between religious ritual and belief. Their "intellectualist" approach holds that beliefs and ideas about the world are the primary elements in the religious life. Religion's practices—its customs and rituals—are seen as secondary; they follow from the beliefs and depend upon them. On this view, as noted, the practice of those primitive peoples who bury servants along with their kings arises out of the prior belief that, in the afterlife, the king's soul will need the souls of servants to assist him. The belief comes logically before the ritual; the idea can be said to cause the practice.[45] In Durkheim's thinking, just the opposite view is put forward. For him the rituals of religion have priority; it is they that are always basic and actually create the beliefs that accompany them. If there is anything "eternal" about religion, he says, it is that a society always needs rites—ceremonial activities of renewal and rededication. Through them, people are reminded that the group always matters more than any of its single members. Beliefs, by contrast, are not so eternal. While the social function of religious rituals has always remained constant, the intellectual content of religious beliefs has always been changeable. Beliefs are the "speculative side" of religion. They may serve to separate the Christian from the Jew and the Hindu, but in reality the particular ideas they assert make little difference. Ideas always change from religion to religion and even from age to age in the same religion. But the need for ceremonies always remains; they are the true source of social unity, and in every society they are the real ties that bind. They disclose the true meaning of religion.

4. Functional Explanation

The matter of ritual takes us to the heart of Durkheim's theory: the functional explanation of religion. Durkheim, like Freud, sees himself as presenting not just a different theory but a theory different in *kind* from those that came before him. In explaining religion, he thinks he can go beneath the surface of things. Tylor and Frazer try to explain religion as it appears; they take more or less at face value the beliefs that religious people hold and then ask how those beliefs explain their lives and deeds. In this intellectualist approach, ideas and beliefs—Durkheim's speculative side of religion—are the key to explaining other cultures. For the follower of Tylor, a primitive ritual makes sense once we know that the Indian rainmaker believes an imitation of thunder can create a storm and send showers on his fields. The principle of imitative magic may be absurd to us, but not to him; so it explains *why* he acts as strangely as he does. Like Freud, however, Durkheim wants to ask another question. If we agree that these beliefs are absurd, then why do people hold them? If such ideas are silly superstitions, they nonetheless do not die easily. Why do they survive?

For Durkheim, the answer to this riddle can be found only in one place: not in the content of the beliefs, not in what they claim about gods or the world, but in their *function*—in what they *do,* socially, for those who live by them. The true nature of religion is to be found not on its surface but underneath.[46] As the case of Australian totemism clearly shows, religion's key value lies in the ceremonies through which it inspires and renews the allegiance of individuals to the group. These rituals then create, almost as an afterthought, the need for some sort of symbolism that takes the form of ideas about ancestral souls and gods. Moreover, if a society truly needs such rites to survive and flourish, it follows that there can never be a community without either a religion or something similar to fill its place. So, even when the ideas of religion are thought by some to be false and absurd, religious behavior can remain very much alive in the society it helps to support. Religious ideas can be questioned, but religious rituals, or something very much like them, must endure. Society cannot exist without ceremony; hence the persistence of religion.

Critique

Needless to say, Durkheim's aggressively social approach presents us with a most original and intriguing theory of religion. Unlike Tylorian animism, it claims to show how the roots of religious behavior run much deeper than the purely intellectual need to understand how the world works. And unlike Freudian personality theory, it appreciates in all its wide scope the powerful shaping influence that social structures exert when people declare some things sacred and others profane. Yet compelling as it appears in these respects, Durkheim's ambitiously sociological theory displays certain noticeable limitations in others. The very first reviewers of *The Elementary Forms* were quick to notice some of these difficulties, and more recent critics have not hesitated to multiply the complaints. The criticisms tend to cluster about three main issues: Durkheim's assumptions about the nature of religion, his Australian evidence, and his "reductionist" conclusions. We take them here in turn.

1. Assumptions

With Durkheim, as with our other theorists, a great deal depends on what the Greek thinker Archimedes called his *pou sto,* the place "where I stand" at the start of the argument. Consider, in this connection, the definition of religion laid out in the opening pages of *The Elementary Forms.* Religion, we are told, is rooted in the basic distinction all societies make between the sacred and the profane. The main concern of religious rites is with the first, that is, with the sacred, which is to be kept separate from the profane. Further, the sacred is always tied up with the great social events of the clan, while the profane is the realm of private affairs. This root conception serves as the foundation on which the full framework of Durkheim's imposing theory is then erected. If we look at it very closely, however, surely the pivotal role of this definition in the theory creates something of a problem. If, already at the start of the discussion, Durkheim envisions the sacred as the social, is it not quite easy—rather too easy—to reach the conclusion that religion is nothing more than the expression of social needs? The inquiry would seem to begin at the very place where Durkheim wants to finish. The sacred is the social, he writes, and the religious is the sacred; therefore, the religious is the social.[47] To be sure, Durkheim is not the only theorist whose reasoning tends toward a certain circularity; we have seen something of the same in Freud, and others too are inclined to offer definitions that most easily accommodate the theory they hope to defend. But Durkheim's way of starting the analysis very near the place where it ought to end is, logically, a cause for some concern.

This problem becomes even more troubling when we recall Durkheim's own rather summary dismissal of other definitions. He tells us, for instance, that we may not define religion as belief in the realm of the supernatural because primitive peoples of the world, who are clearly religious, have no such concept. For them, all events are the same; there is no supernatural realm separate from the natural; there is only the sacred and social, which they separate from the profane and personal. But more than a few scholars both in Durkheim's day and since then have insisted—with evidence—that this is just not so. Primitive peoples may not have exactly *our* concept of the supernatural, but they *do* hold ideas about mystical or extraordinary kinds of events which are quite similar to our modern conceptions. At the same time, interestingly enough, many of them *do not* in all cases manage to separate the sacred from the profane, especially in the absolute way that Durkheim says they must.[48] Considerations such as these, which tend to count in favor of more traditional notions of religion and against Durkheim's conception, could perhaps be dismissed if the questions of the supernatural and the sacred were minor matters. Unfortunately, they are not. Durkheim's choice of definitions is quite central to his entire strategy of explanation. It does not meet us at the fringes of the theory, where adjustments could be made without loss. It stands out in front and at the center.

2. Evidence

Durkheim contends that the great merit of his study, unlike those of earlier theorists, is his determination to study only one type of culture, the aborigine communities of Australia, and explain religion in that context. He relies on the widely acclaimed ethnographical reports of Spencer and Gillen, along with those of other firsthand observers, and he rests his theory squarely on the evidence they provide. The scientific value of such an approach is clear and undisputed—but so is its potential weakness. Should reason arise to question the value of these reports, or Durkheim's readings of them, what would be left of his theory, linked as closely as it is to this Australian evidence? Significantly, several of the very first critics to comment on *The Elementary Forms* made this point in forcible terms. One, a sociologist named Gaston Richard, who had earlier worked with Durkheim, carefully examined the Australian reports and showed how, in a number of places, the evidence could be read to prove quite the opposite of what Durkheim concludes. Richard also claimed, rather persuasively, that most of Durkheim's theory had been assembled before he ever looked at the Australian reports.[49] Other critics now question whether even the Australian reports themselves were completely accurate.[50] Perhaps the harshest words on this subject were to come from Arnold van Gennep, the famed Dutch anthropologist of Africa. In a strongly worded review written soon after *The Elementary Forms* appeared, he wrote, "In ten years the whole of his analysis of the Australian material will be completely rejected." He then added that it was based on "the most unsound group of ethnographical facts I have ever encountered."[51] These words have proved very nearly prophetic. Today, much of the evidence and most of the interpretation of totemism that Durkheim makes a part of his theory have come to be quite widely rejected.[52]

3. Reductionism

Just as psychological functionalism is the cornerstone of Freudian theory, sociological functionalism is the key to Durkheim's explanatory method. In a certain sense, of course, the value of such an approach seems beyond question. Who can really doubt that, beneath the surface of things, religious beliefs and rituals often accomplish social purposes that believers themselves may be quite unaware of? Who would wish to deny that for devout Catholics, a requiem mass, which on its face is a plea to God to save the souls of the dead from Hell, is, underneath that surface, also a powerful ritual of group solidarity and renewal? Such socially functional readings of religion seem so natural and appropriate that no one is any longer likely to dispute them.

But even if all agree in a general way that religion and society are thus functionally related or even inseparable, we must still ask just how this relationship really works. In discussing this matter, Durkheim almost always claims that society determines, while religion is the thing that is determined. Society controls; religion reflects. In each Australian instance he considers, Durkheim insists that society powerfully shapes religious ritual and belief, while religious beliefs never seem able to do the reverse. In each instance we are reminded that social structure is always the reality, while religion is merely an appearance. It seems at least reasonable to ask why this should have to be so. It is one thing to say that *alongside* its other claims and purposes, religion *also* has a social function; it is quite another to say that religion has *only* a social function. As we saw in the case of Freud, "reductionism" is the theoretical term for this particularly aggressive form of functionalist explanation. Freud explains religion as "nothing but" a surface appearance, a set of neurotic symptoms produced by an underlying psychological trauma. Durkheim's agenda is similar; he accounts for religion as nothing but the surface foam—his own word actually is "effervescence"—given off by an underlying social reality. He differs from Freud, of course, in that he is much more reluctant to pass a negative judgment on religion from this perspective. Freud sees religion as a sign of disease, a symptom of psychic aberration. Durkheim is not so sure; even when its beliefs are mistaken, he thinks it may, for some societies, still be a hallmark of social health.

Despite that difference, Durkheim's theory, like Freud's, fits the mold of an aggressively reductionist functionalism; his aim is to "reduce" religion to something other than what it appears to be. Although functionalist explanations have proven their merits through the years, the question of such reductionist versions of functionalism is a different matter—one that leaves present-day theorists sharply divided. Some applaud such approaches, finding in reductionist theories the very model of a strong scientific method.[53] Others find them one-sided and fundamentally misleading.[54] In that connection, it should not come as a surprise that most actual religious believers find the reductionist theories of both Freud and Durkheim generally unacceptable. In the eyes of religious faith, these approaches, though they may offer insight into *aspects* of belief, simply misunderstand what religion at bottom is all about. Even at that, however, the views of Freud and Durkheim are probably less offensive to religious ears than those expressed, well before theirs, in one of the most militant and aggressive of all reductionist theories: that of the German socialist philosopher Karl Marx. His unsparing and combative account of religion is the one we consider next.

Notes

1. Émile Durkheim, *The Elementary Forms of the Religious Life*, tr. Joseph Ward Swain (New York: The Macmillan Company, 1915), p. 419.

2. Durkheim was, of course, not the only contributor to the "sociological revolution" in modern thinking. On the matter of Durkheim's influence, see Albert Salomon, "Some Aspects of the Legacy of Durkheim," in Kurt H. Wolff, ed., *Essays on Sociology and Philosophy: Durkheim, et al. with Appraisals of His Life and Thought* (New York: Harper Torchbooks, [1960] 1964), pp. 247–66; also helpful, in the same volume, is Roscoe C. Hinkle, Jr., "Durkheim in American Sociology," pp. 267–95.

3. On the similarities between Freud and Durkheim, see Stjepan G. Mestrovic, *Émile Durkheim and the Reformation of Sociology* (Totowa, NJ: Rowman & Littlefield, 1988), pp. 99–102.

4. The authoritative recent biography of Durkheim is Steven Lukes, *Émile Durkheim, His Life and Work: A Historical and Critical Study* (New York: Harper & Row, 1972). Helpful brief introductions include Anthony Giddens, *Émile Durkheim* (New York: Viking Press, 1978); Kenneth Thompson, *Émile Durkheim* (London: Tavistock Publications, Ltd., 1982); and Robert Alun Jones, *Émile Durkheim* (Beverly Hills, CA: Sage Publications, 1986). Especially good introductions to Durk-

heim's thought are Dominick LaCapra, *Émile Durkheim: Sociologist and Philosopher* (Ithaca, NY: Cornell University Press, 1972), and Robert Nisbet, *The Sociology of Émile Durkheim* (New York: Oxford University Press, 1974). An excellent study in depth is W. S. F. Pickering, *Durkheim's Sociology of Religion: Themes and Theories* (London: Routledge & Kegan Paul, 1984).

5. On the cultural and intellectual milieu of France during the years of Durkheim's career, see the fascinating piece by Henri Peyre, "Durkheim: The Man, His Time, and His Intellectual Background," in Wolff, ed., *Émile Durkheim*, pp. 3–31; also Robert N. Bellah, "Introduction," in Bellah, ed., *Émile Durkheim: Morality and Society: Selected Writings* (Chicago: University of Chicago Press, 1973), pp. ix–lv.

6. For Durkheim's own appreciation of the French sociological tradition in which he stood, see his "Sociology in France in the Nineteenth Century," tr. by Mark Traugott, in Bellah, ed., *Émile Durkheim: Morality and Society*, pp. 3–22.

7. On the importance of these thinkers to the development of Durkheim's thought, see Nisbet, *Sociology of Durkheim*, pp. 24–30.

8. Informative analyses of the theories Durkheim developed in this important early work can be found in Giddens, *Durkheim*, pp. 26–38; Lukes, *Durkheim*, pp. 137–78; Nisbet, *Sociology of Durkheim*, pp. 73–104; and Robert K. Merton, "Durkheim's *Division of Labor in Society*," in Robert A. Nisbet, *Émile Durkheim: With Selected Essays* (Englewood Cliffs, NJ: Prentice-Hall, 1965), pp. 105–12.

9. A thorough study of the *Rules*, exploring its argument, origins, and reception, is Mike Gane, *On Durkheim's Rules of Sociological Method* (London: Routledge, 1988).

10. On this distinction, see Gane, *Durkheim's Rules*, pp. 15–17.

11. A still useful analysis of Durkheim's view of causation is Charles Elmer Gehlke, *Émile Durkheim's Contribution to Sociological Theory* (New York: AMS Press, [1915] 1968), pp. 58–92. Though Durkheim uses the term "function" in the way described here, the question of whether his sociology is "functionalist" in the sense of belonging to one of the schools of modern sociology that were given this name is a complicated one. For a discussion that sees Durkheimian explanation as decidedly functionalist, see Harry Alpert, "Durkheim's Functional Theory of Ritual," in Nisbet, *Émile Durkheim: With Selected Essays*, pp. 137–41; for a discussion of those senses in which Durkheim can or and cannot be called a functionalist, see Albert Pierce, "Durkheim and Functionalism," in Wolff, ed., *Essays on Sociology and Philosophy*, pp. 154–69.

12. For discussions of Durkheim's theory of suicide see Lukes *Émile Durkheim* pp. 191–225; La Capra, *Émile Durkheim*, pp. 144–86, and Hanan C. Selvin, "Durkheim's *Suicide*: Further Thoughts on a Methodological Classic," in Nisbet, *Émile Durkheim: With Selected Essays*, pp. 113–36.

13. On Durkheim as a political theorist, see Steve Fenton, *Durkheim and Modern Sociology* (Cambridge, England: Cambridge University Press, 1984), pp. 81–115; Giddens, *Émile Durkheim*, pp. 54–68; Thompson, *Émile Durkheim*, pp. 145–60; Nisbet, *Sociology of Durkheim*, pp. 128–55.

14. It was not published in its entirety until 1938; see Lukes, *Émile Durkheim*, pp. 379–91.

15. See Ernest Wallwork, *Durkheim: Morality and Milieu* (Cambridge, MA: Harvard University Press, 1972); Nisbet, *Sociology of Durkheim*, pp. 187–208; Robert Reiner, "Crime, Law and Deviance: The Durkheim Legacy," in Fenton, *Durkheim and Modern Sociology*, pp. 175–201; and Morris Ginsberg, "Durkheim's Ethical Theory," in Nisbet, *Émile Durkheim: With Selected Essays*, pp. 142–52.

16. Durkheim, *Elementary Forms*, p. 47. On the importance of this distinction, see Nisbet, *Sociology of Durkheim*, pp. 172–76.

17. Durkheim, *Elementary Forms*, p. 47.

18. Durkheim, *Elementary Forms*, p. 44. Durkheim does not address an issue that would seem problematic for this view of magic; namely, that in the accounts Frazer and Tylor provide, it often has a decidedly communal rather than just personal dimension. Magical rites are often performed not just to heal individuals of sickness or cast out a demon, but to protect entire communities from harm or to ensure favorable weather for fields and crops that belong to all.

19. Durkheim, *Elementary Forms*, pp. 71–86.

20. Durkheim, *Elementary Forms*, pp. 48–70.

21. Durkheim, *Elementary Forms*, p. 168.

22. Though Durkheim pays most attention to the work of Spencer and Gillen, he does give credit to several of these less well known figures who did similar research; see *Elementary Forms*, pp. 88–93, and 91, n. 1. On his debt to the English and American "anthropological school," see Lukes, *Émile Durkheim*, pp. 450–53.

23. For this discussion see Durkheim, *Elementary Forms*, pp. 144–48.

24. Durkheim, *Elementary Forms*, p. 188.

25. On the totemic principle see LaCapra, *Émile Durkheim*, pp. 261–65.

26. Durkheim, *Elementary Forms*, p. 206; on this crucial linkage between the clan, the totem, and the totem symbol, with each as sacred, see Giddens, *Émile Durkheim*, p. 94.

27. See Alpert, "Durkheim's Functional Theory of Ritual," in Nisbet, *Émile Durkheim: With Selected Essays*, pp. 137–41.

28. Durkheim, *Elementary Forms*, p. 209.

29. Durkheim, *Elementary Forms*, pp. 218–19.

30. On this see Nisbet, *Émile Durkheim: With Selected Essays*, pp. 78–80.

31. Durkheim, *Elementary Forms*, p. 249.

32. Durkheim, *Elementary Forms*, pp. 280–81.

33. Kenneth Thompson, *Émile Durkheim*, pp. 138–39, cites the controversial work of Guy Swanson, *The Birth of the Gods: The Origin of Primitive Beliefs* (Ann Arbor, MI: University of Michigan Press, 1960) as a recent attempt to develop this theme of Durkheim by showing, with the help of statistical analysis, a correlation between certain types of society and the presence of belief in a high god. For a close analysis of Swanson, see Ian Hamnett, "Durkheim and the Study of Religion," in Fenton, *Durkheim and Modern Sociology*, pp. 208–11.

34. On the importance of the cult and ritual to Durkheim's theory, see Nisbet, *Sociology of Durkheim*, pp. 176–84.

35. Durkheim, *Elementary Forms*, pp. 299–309.

36. Durkheim, *Elementary Forms*, pp. 309–14.

37. Durkheim, *Elementary Forms*, p. 347.

38. On this "causal" action of society in the creation of religion, see Lukes, *Émile Durkheim*, pp. 462–477, and Hamnett, "Durkheim and the Study of Religion," in Fenton, *Durkheim and Modern Sociology*, pp. 207–208.

39. Durkheim defines his use of this term in *Elementary Forms*, p. 389.

40. On Durkheim's influence in the United States, see Roscoe C. Hinkle, "Durkheim in American Sociology," in Wolff, ed., *Essays on Sociology & Philosophy*, pp. 267–95; see also Nisbet, *Sociology of Durkheim*, pp. 55–61, 110–13, 210–11.

41. Durkheim, *Elementary Forms*, p. 10.

42. Durkheim, *Elementary Forms*, p. 212.

43. Durkheim, *Elementary Forms*, p. 92; on this, see especially the comments by Nisbet, *The Sociology of Émile Durkheim*, pp. 69–72.

44. On these later anthropological theorists, see Eric Sharpe, *Comparative Religion: A History* (New York: Charles Scribner's Sons, 1975), pp. 175–76, 188.

45. On Frazer's intellectualism and the "ritualist school" which in England followed him and reacted against his work, see Robert Ackerman, *The Myth and Ritual School: J. G. Frazer and the Cambridge Ritualists* (New York: Garland Publishing, 1991).

46. A careful discussion of causal, interpretive, and functional levels of explanation in Durkheim's work can be found in Lukes, *Émile Durkheim*, pp. 462–77.

47. See Thompson, *Émile Durkheim*, p. 136.

48. E. E. Evans-Pritchard, *Theories of Primitive Religion*, p. 65.

49. "Dogmatic Atheism in the Sociology of Religion," in W. S. F. Pickering, ed., *Durkheim on Religion*, tr. by Jacqueline Redding (London: Routledge & Kegan Paul, 1975), pp. 228–76; first published in *Revue d'histoire et de philosophie religieuse* (1923).

50. W. E. H. Stanner, "Reflections on Durkheim and aboriginal Religion," in Pickering, ed., *Durkheim on Religion*, pp. 277–303.

51. Arnold van Gennep, review of *The Elementary Forms of the Religious Life*, in Pickering, ed., *Durkheim on Religion*, pp. 205–208; first published in *Mercure de France* (1913).

52. See in particular Stanner, "Reflections on Durkheim and aboriginal Religion," and A. A. Goldenweiser, review of *The Elementary Forms of the Religious Life*, both in Pickering, ed., *Durkheim on Religion*, pp. 277–303, 209–27. Goldenweiser's article was first published in *American Anthropologist* (1915).

53. See, for example, the writings of Donald Wiebe, especially "The Failure of Nerve in the Academic Study of Religion," *Studies in Religion* 13 (1984): 401–22; also the following works of Robert Segal: "In Defense of Reductionism," *Journal of the American Academy of Religion* 51 (March 1983): 97–124; *Religion and the Social Sciences: Essays on the Confrontation* (Atlanta: Scholars Press, 1989); and *Explaining and Interpreting Religion: Essays on the Issue*, Toronto Studies in Religion (New York: Peter Lang, 1992).

54. Daniel L. Pals, "Is Religion a *Sui Generis* Phenomenon?" *Journal of the American Academy of Religion* 55, 2 (1987): 260–82.

Suggestions for Further Reading

Bellah, Robert N., ed. *Émile Durkheim: Morality and Society: Selected Writings.* Chicago: University of Chicago Press, 1973. An instructive selection of Durkheim's more important shorter writings, chosen and introduced by a leading American sociologist of religion.

Durkheim, Émile. *The Elementary Forms of the Religious Life.* Translated by Joseph Ward Swain. New York: The Macmillan Company, [1912] 1915.

Durkheim, Émile. *The Division of Labor in Society.* Translated by G. Simpson. Glencoe, Ill.: The Free Press, [1893] 1964.

Durkheim, Émile. *The Rules of Sociological Method.* Translated by S. A. Solovay and J. H. Mueller. Chicago: University of Chicago Press, [1895] 1938.

Durkheim, Émile. *Suicide: A Study in Sociology.* Translated by J. A. Spaulding and G. Simpson. London: Routledge & Kegan Paul, [1897] 1951.

Fenton, Steve, ed. *Durkheim and Modern Sociology.* Cambridge, England: Cambridge University Press, 1984. Essays by recognized authorities who assess Durkheim's role and influence in the development of contemporary sociological research.

Giddens, Anthony. *Émile Durkheim.* New York: Viking Press, 1978. An insightful, brief study by a leading contemporary sociological theorist.

Jones, Robert Alun. *Émile Durkheim.* Beverly Hills, Calif.: Sage Publications, 1986. An illuminating short study by a scholar familiar with Robertson Smith, Frazer, and other early interpreters of religion.

LaCapra, Dominick. *Émile Durkheim: Sociologist and Philosopher.* Ithaca, N.Y.: Cornell University Press, 1972. A substantial account of the full range of Durkheim's thought.

Lukes, Steven. *Émile Durkheim, His Life and Work: A Historical and Critical Study.* New York: Harper & Row, 1972. The definitive recent examination of Durkheim's life and thought.

Mestrovic, Stjepan G. *Émile Durkheim and the Reformation of Sociology.* Totowa, N.J.: Rowman & Littlefield, 1988. An assessment of Durkheim's role in creating the modern field of sociological inquiry.

Nisbet, Robert A. *Émile Durkheim: With Selected Essays.* Englewood Cliffs, N.J.: Prentice-Hall, 1965. A critical assessment with illuminating contributions from other authors on Durkheim's most important books and leading theories.

Nisbet, Robert. *The Sociology of Émile Durkheim.* New York: Oxford University Press, 1974. Excellent on the historical context of Durkheim's work and on the social thinkers, especially in France, who preceded Durkheim and influenced his thought.

Pickering, W. S. F., ed. *Durkheim on Religion.* Translated by Jacqueline Redding. London: Routledge & Kegan Paul, 1975. Presents selections from Durkheim's original works on religion along with selected reviews by other scholars, including some of the very earliest assessments of *The Elementary Forms.*

Pickering, W. S. F. *Durkheim's Sociology of Religion: Themes and Theories.* London: Routledge & Kegan Paul, 1984. An excellent in-depth study of Durkheim on religion.

Wolff, Kurt H., ed. *Essays on Sociology and Philosophy: Durkheim, et al., with Appraisals of His Life and Thought.* New York: Harper Torchbooks, [1960] 1964. Illuminating essays by different authors on the origin, character, and influence of Durkheim's thought.

4

Religion as Alienation:
Karl Marx

"Marx discovered . . . the simple fact . . . that mankind must first of
all eat, drink, have shelter and clothing, before it can pursue politics,
science, art, religion."
            Friedrich Engels, "Speech at the Graveside of Karl Marx" [1]

If the order of this book were strictly chronological, the theorist we take up
in this chapter would have appeared at the beginning, not here in the middle.
Karl Marx (1818–1883), the German social philosopher and guiding spirit
of the movement that has come to be known as communism, had lived much
of his life before the other figures in our survey had even begun their work.
His major writings were completed well before Tylor published *Primitive
Culture* in 1871, while Frazer's *Golden Bough* did not appear until nearly
twelve years after Marx's death in 1883. It would be still another twenty
years before Freud and Durkheim developed their leading ideas. Nonetheless, it makes sense to consider Marx here and not earlier in our survey. For
though he wrote in the middle years of the nineteenth century, his ideas
gained little notice in his day beyond a small circle of his own radical associates—and the suspicious eyes of public authorities. Only late in his life,
after he published *Das Kapital* [2] (in English, *Capital*), the first volume of
his huge critical study of economics, did people in the mainstream of
thought begin to pay close attention to his views. From that point on, however, his influence did begin to grow enormously, as anyone now alive certainly knows. In Russia, he won a convert in Vladimir Lenin, the major
force behind the Russian Revolution of 1917, which destroyed an empire
and shocked the world. Later, in the 1940s, the same shock went through
China when another Marxist, Mao Tse-tung, led an army of poor peasants
to an equally shattering victory. As similar revolts unfolded around the
world in lesser lands, intellectuals in both Europe and America found themselves forced to grapple with Marx's explosive and all-embracing vision of

society. Some have been strongly attracted, others thoroughly repelled. In the present circumstance, even after communist systems have begun to collapse, all would readily agree on at least one thing: Marx's own century could ignore him, but ours cannot.[3]

About Marx, two things must be noticed from the very start. First, as the shaper of communism, he presents us less with a theory of religion than a total system of thought that itself resembles a religion. Though some have said the same even of Freud's psychoanalysis, the impact of the Marxist creed around the world has been far greater. For a time in our century, Marxist thought in one form or other was the ruling philosophy of governments in many parts of the world, though—since the great collapse of communism in Europe and the Soviet Union—only a few outposts remain. Marx's writings are as sacred to some communists as is the Bible to the most sincere and devout of Christians. Communism offers a system of doctrines with authorized interpretations. It has its own ceremonies, sacred places, and sacred persons. It has missionaries, who in the space of one century have won (and now lost) millions of converts; and it has conducted persecutions more brutal even than those of the Middle Ages or Wars of Religion. Communism, in fact, claims to present not just a broad theory of politics, society, and economics but a compelling total vision of human life, complete with a philosophical stance on humanity's place in the natural world, an explanation of all that is past in history, and a prophecy of what is still to come.[4]

Second, because Marx's philosophy is so far-reaching, what he offers as a "theory" of traditional religion makes up a rather small—and not necessarily central—part of his thinking. In this respect, he is quite unlike Durkheim or Freud or our other theorists. The views he held were clear and outspoken, as we shall shortly see; they have also had tremendous influence in the modern world, especially in officially communist societies. But among all of Marx's voluminous writings, it is significant that not one addresses specifically or in systematic fashion the subject of religion. Though he touches on it often enough in his many books, letters, and articles on other subjects, he almost always does so in indirect fashion, commenting here on religion in general, there on churches, sacraments, or clergy, and at other places on this belief or that practice. Consequently, this chapter calls for a strategy slightly different from that which we followed in the others. Instead of tracing the argument of a single book, as we could do with figures like Tylor and Durkheim, we will have to reconstruct Marx's view of religion mainly from certain early philosophical and social writings, where he addresses the subject most explicitly, and from occasional comments he makes in later books on politics and economics.[5] With that exception out of the way, we can still keep to our pattern. We shall look first at Marx's life and intellectual background, next at the overall framework of his thinking, and then at his view of religion. After that, we can devote our remaining space to analysis and criticism.

Background: Marx's Life, Activities, and Writings

Karl Marx was born on May 5, 1818, the second of eight children in the family of Heinrich Marx, a Jewish lawyer who lived in the small and beautiful Rhineland city of Trier.[6] During this time, when Germany was not yet a single nation, Trier was under the control of Prussia, the most powerful of many separate German states ruled mainly by Christian noble families. Marx's grandfathers on both sides were rabbis, but because of Prussia's anti-Jewish laws, his father had converted to Christianity, in name at least, shortly before Marx was born. The father's gentle personality contrasted sharply with that of his son, who was intellectually gifted but also stubborn, blunt, and fiercely independent; he rarely showed emotion. Though his high school record was unspectacular, Marx found an informal mentor in a cultivated Prussian state official and family friend, Baron von Westphalen, who kindled his early interest in literary classics. Marx later married the baron's daughter Jenny, with whom he was to have six children.[7]

For a year Marx studied philosophy and law at the University of Bonn, where he did his share of drinking and dueling. He was able to avoid military service on grounds of bad health. He did not become a truly serious student until he transferred to the University of Berlin, where he adapted at once to its thriving cultural life. The university was a great center of learning in a large city, which was itself a gathering place for scholars, government officials, and serious intellectuals, some with very radical ideas. Berlin and most other German universities were at the time dominated by the towering figure of one man, the philosopher Georg Wilhelm Friedrich von Hegel (1770–1831). Hegel's system of thought is extremely important for understanding Marx, but it is not easy to explain in simple terms. We will need to return to it later on. Here we can say, in a word, that Hegel was an idealist, a thinker who solved the age-old philosophers' question of matter and mind by deciding that mental things—ideas, or concepts—are fundamental to the world, while material things are always secondary; they are the physical expressions of an underlying universal spirit, or absolute idea. Any thinker who wished to be taken seriously in Germany had to respond in some fashion to this idealist system. Marx did so by placing himself in a circle of thinkers—known as the Young Hegelians—who were not just disciples but also critics of their master.[8] Also known as Hegelians of the left wing, they claimed that though Hegel was right to see the problem of matter and mind as fundamental, his solution was precisely the reverse of the truth. Matter is primary, while mind—the realm of concepts and ideas so important to thinkers—is, in fact, just the reflection, like the color red in an apple, of a world that is fundamentally material in nature. Marx defended this view with vigor. In 1841 he completed a doctoral dissertation devoted— significantly—to two decidedly "materialist" ancient Greek philosophers, Democritus and Epicurus.

This general principle, that what is fundamentally real about the world can be found in material forces rather than mental concepts, became the philosophical anchor for all of Marx's later thinking. In particular, it underlies two themes that took center stage as his thought developed: (1) the conviction that economic realities determine human behavior and (2) the thesis that human history is the story of class struggle, the scene of a perpetual conflict in every society between those who own things, usually the rich, and those who must work to survive, usually the poor.

Marx had hoped for a career as a university professor, but his association with the Young Hegelians and his own increasingly radical ideas made that impossible. He turned, therefore, to journalism, first writing for a German political newspaper, then moving to Paris, where he read the works of French social and economic thinkers and began to develop his own theories in depth. This early period was, in fact, the key phase of his career as a thinker. Over an interval of about seven years, from 1843 to 1850, during which he lived first in Paris, then in Brussels, and briefly back in Germany, Marx wrote a cluster of his most important political essays and philosophical treatises. Among these were *On the Jewish Question* (1843), *Toward the Critique of Hegel's Philosophy of Right: Introduction* (1843), *Economic and Philosophic Manuscripts* (1844), *The Holy Family: Or a Critique of all Critiques,* and others.[9] In these writings he formulated his overarching materialist view of human nature and destiny. In them he also framed his key ideas on history and society, on economics and politics, on law, morals, philosophy, and religion. As for the general perspective he adopted, we can take a clue from the motto on the masthead of one of the newspapers he edited: "The reckless criticism of all that exists."[10]

What Marx wrote in this period was truly decisive for the rest of his life, but he did not do it entirely on his own. For at just this key moment he met and began a lifelong friendship with Friedrich Engels, the son of a German factory owner. Living in England, where he observed the depressing lives of factory workers, Engels, on his own, had developed materialist economic and social views that closely resembled those of Marx. In 1845, Marx and Engels found their way to something that rarely happens among intellectuals: a nearly perfect collaboration.[11] They were men of like minds, but with very different talents. Marx, the more original thinker, served as the philosopher and oracle, a man often obscure but also profound. Engels was the interpreter and communicator, always able to express ideas in ways that were clear, direct, and persuasive. Over the years, they visited factories together; they shared results of their studies; they criticized each other's ideas; they joined in writing for their common cause; and they combined to support and advise new political parties. Together in 1848 they wrote the celebrated *Communist Manifesto.*[12] Consequently, it is not really Marx alone, but Marx and Engels jointly who are the fathers of "Marxism" as we know it today. Together they promoted their message of materialism, class struggle, communism, and revolution in a way that neither could have managed as effectively on his own.

Though ordinary people knew little about them, the "revolutionary" ideas of Marx and Engels were no secret to authorities. When, in 1848, revolutions began to break out across Europe, Marx came under immediate suspicion. Having already been forced out of Paris and over to Brussels, he was soon arrested and expelled from Belgium. Returning to Germany to take part in the revolution that was beginning there, he was again arrested but had the good fortune to be acquitted of all charges in court. In 1849 he left the European continent for London. There he chose to live for the rest of his life—in exile but emphatically not in retirement. Despite grinding poverty and a family on the edge of starvation, he worked tirelessly on further studies in politics and economics. Returning regularly to a favorite chair in the reading room of the British Museum (where today a plaque marks his place), he wrote two works on French revolutionary politics, two more on political economy, and several others on economic history and theory.[13] *Capital* (1867) was of course the most important of these studies. In it Marx assembles a wealth of factual data, subjects it to social analysis, and adds his acute insight into political and social structures—all in order to show how the facts of economic activity support his materialist view of history and point the way to a revolutionary communist future.

During this time Marx also tried to remain active in what he regarded as the ongoing class struggle, the battle of workers against their capitalist oppressors. He gave advice and assistance to socialist parties in France and Germany. He was a leader in organizing the Workingmen's International Association (more simply, "the International"), whose aim was to represent the common interests of the workers, regardless of their national home. All the while he continued his writing. *Capital* was only the first of three volumes on that subject. He continued work on two others, which were in manuscript but not complete, and which were to be part of the great project he envisioned under the general title *Economics*. His work habits were strange. Some days he would be drunk or asleep while on others he would work fanatically through the night and into the day despite a house full of noisy children. He was fortunate to have almost limitless energy, and when he wished, he could apply it with a mental discipline made of iron. Only during the last ten years of his life did his energies abate, as illness began to take its toll. A timely inheritance and some financial help from Engels had at least taken his family out of poverty. But though he continued to read and correspond with friends, all of his major writing was by then behind him. His wife, Jenny, died in 1881, and two years later he followed. With Engels at the graveside, he was buried in London—largely unmourned and unnoticed in the land where he lived, studied, and wrote for the last thirty years of his life.

Marxism: Economics and the Theory of Class Struggle

Few thinkers have ever presented their main thesis in words as blunt or as disturbing as those of Marx and Engels in the *Communist Manifesto:*

> The history of all hitherto existing society is the history of class struggles.
>   Freeman and slave, patrician and plebeian, lord and serf, guild-master and journeyman, in a word, oppressor and oppressed, stood in constant opposition to one another, carried on an uninterrupted, now hidden, now open fight, a fight that each time ended, either in a revolutionary re-constitution of society at large, or in the common ruin of the contending classes.[14]

The message of these ringing sentences is unmistakably clear. If we wish to understand what humanity and its history are all about, we must recognize what is truly fundamental. And what is fundamental is the following: From their first emergence on earth human beings have been motivated not by grand ideas but by very basic material concerns, the elementary needs of survival. This is the first fact in the materialist view of history. Everyone needs food, clothing, and shelter. Once these needs are met, others, like the drive for sex, join them. Reproduction then leads to families and communities, which create still other material desires and demands. These can be met only by developing what Marx calls a "mode of production."[15] The necessities and even comforts of life must in some way be produced—by hunting and gathering foods, by fishing, growing grain, or entering on some other labor. Moreover, because various people are involved in these activities in different ways, they sooner or later fall into a division of labor; different people do different things. Marx calls the ties or connections among those who divide their labor in this fashion "relations of production." I may be a boat maker; you may make nets to fish with. In the earliest, simplest form of society, the kind which Marx calls primitive communist, both the boat and the net are commonly owned by everyone in the village, where each shares all things as need may arise.[16]

For Marx this original tribal communism was in a sense the most natural of human organizations. It allowed people to enjoy variety in their lives by participating in a healthy mix of meaningful work and refreshing leisure. They belonged to the group but also knew the worth of their separate selves. A fateful turn occurred, however, once the notion of private property was introduced, and its effects are most markedly evident in the stage of history known as classical civilization. Here, Marx explains, the relations of production are greatly changed. The maker of the boat claims it as his own property, as does the maker of the net. They can deal with each other only by exchanging what they have made—that is, by selling the products of their labor. And before long, by talent, crime, or good fortune, some acquire more and better private property while others are left with virtually nothing. In addition, as the mode of production changes from hunting and gathering to the growing of grain, those who happen to hold property find themselves in a position of tremendous advantage. They own not just products but also the very means of production—the land on which crops are grown. Since others do not, the landowners are masters; the rest must fall in as their dependents, assistants, or even slaves. Private property and agriculture—two hallmarks of early civilization—thus help to create the central crisis of all humanity: the separation of classes by power and wealth, and with it the beginnings of permanent social conflict.[17] Later still, in the medieval era, the mode of production remains largely the same. It is agricultural, and the structure of class conflict continues unaltered. The feudal lord and serf simply replace the ancient master and slave. Even among craftsmen, the master artisan and his lowly apprentice reenact the old conflict between the Roman patrician and plebeian.

In the final, modern stage of development, this age-old conflict of classes persists, but it acquires a new intensity and a darker coloring. Modern capitalism introduces a new mode of production: trade and manufacturing; and with it comes also a profound change in the relations of production. Owner and worker are still with us, but now the conflict between them is far more intense. By introducing commercial activity and the profit motive on a large scale, capitalism produces great wealth for some, for those whom Marx calls the bourgeoisie, or "middle class." (By this term Marx means what today we would call the affluent upper middle class, the owners and managers of corporations.) Meanwhile workers, those whom Marx calls "the proletariat," are left with almost nothing; they must sell their precious daily labor to the owner-managers in return for wages on which they simply subsist. This bad situation is made even worse because capitalism has also become industrial. It has given birth to the factory, the place where workers spend long, exhausting hours at machines that make objects in huge quantities and bring a fabulous return of wealth—of course only to their owners. The spread of this industrial capitalism thus raises the conflict between classes to a fever pitch, ushering in its last and most desperate phase—a period of proletarian misery so great that workers find their only hope in revolution. They lash out, bitterly, in an attempt to overthrow by force the entire social and economic order that oppresses them. Violence in this situation is to be expected, for the rich will never give up what they have unless it is taken by force. Confrontation is, in fact, unavoidable, for it is driven by deep historical forces that no one group, nation, or class can resist.[18]

In such a world, it is quite clear that communism has a double mission. Part of its job is education: it must explain these realities to people who cannot see them. The other part is action: it calls proletarians everywhere to prepare for revolution. With the commanding voice of an ancient Hebrew prophet, the Communist party denounces the state and the ruling class. It urges workers to organize, to swim with history's powerful current, to add their weight to its waves, and to throw themselves forward till the day comes for them to crash down upon the edifice of capitalism, shattering its frame and very foundation. Only then, only after this stormy surge of destruction, will the paradisal age of genuine freedom and peace at last return to the social order of humanity. To achieve perfection, there will first have to be a phase of transition, a preliminary interval governed by what Marx calls the "dictatorship of the proletariat." The poor, once powerless, will be truly in control. Their rule will then gradually give way to a second and final episode of history, in which true human harmony at last arrives, the time when neither classes nor private property will any longer exist.[19]

Materialism, Alienation, and the Dialectic of History

In outlining his great scheme, Marx did not himself invent the concept of social classes or even social struggle; he did feel, however, that he had discovered *the connection* between the social class divisions and certain stages of economic development, and he believed that he alone had seen how, in the future, this struggle would lead to revolution and the end of classes altogether. But if so, where did he get these ideas? How did he reach the unusual notion of human history moving toward a happy future, but only after passing through a sequence of oppositions marked by ever more bitter and violent episodes of struggle?

To answer this question we must recall Marx's early years in Berlin and, once more, the influence of Hegel. We have already noticed Hegel's idealism; he found material objects to be secondary things. He spoke of ultimate reality as "the absolute spirit," or "absolute idea"—what religious people call God. In his system, this "absolute" is a being that constantly strives to become ever more aware, more conscious, of itself. It does so by pouring itself into material forms and events, just as, let us say, the mind of an architect might express itself in a beautiful building. But because the actual never fully captures the ideal (as every dissatisfied architect knows), the material form is always inadequate, or, in Hegel's language, "alien" to spirit. Try as it may, material reality never quite measures up to the absolute. So, each time an event occurs in the material world (Hegel called it a "thesis"), spirit generates an opposed event (an "antithesis"), which tries to correct it. The tension between these two is then resolved by yet a third event (the "synthesis"), which blends elements of both, only to serve as the new thesis for yet another sequence of opposition and resolution. Again, we should think of an architect who designs each new building as an improvement on earlier efforts and does so by always combining the best elements of the previous two attempts. For Hegel, all that happens in the world arises in the form of this great alternating sequence, which he calls the "dialectic"—the "give and take"—of spirit in nature and history. In it, the absolute alienates itself, unsatisfactorily, in one material form, then responds with another, and finally combines and surpasses them both with still another. In addition, Hegel thought of this alternation as happening not in little ways but in very large social patterns. In his scheme, an entire culture, such as the civilization of classical Greece or that of Renaissance Europe, can serve as a great, single expression of the absolute—a thesis which, after an interval calls forth as its antithesis an opposing culture. In time, these two then merge into a third, richer and still higher form of civilization, which can be called the synthesis. Thus the entire world unfolds through a great and varied process of alternating movements and subtle interweavings that tie nature, history, and spirit into a grand and unitary whole.

We noted above that Marx rejected Hegel's idealism. But he did not reject either the concept of alienation or the idea that history moves along by a vast process of conflict.[20] On the contrary, he folded both of these ideas into his materialism and put them at the very center of his own view of the human story. History, he says, is indeed a great scene of conflict, and Hegel is right to see "alienation" at the core of it. But he fails to see just how deeply alienation and historical progress are rooted not in ideas but in the basic material realities of life. Like the theologians with their Creator God, when Hegel speaks of alienation, he thinks chiefly of how the physical world never lives up to the perfection of its spiritual source, the absolute idea, or mind. But in fact, Marx counters, things are just the other way around. It is concrete, actual, working human beings who create their own alienation, and precisely by attributing to others—including the realm of ideas—the very things that properly belong to themselves. That is the *real* alienation and the true source of human unhappiness. In religion, God is always being given the credit, the worship, that properly belongs to human beings. In philosophy, Hegel gives his absolute spirit all the praise for what human sweat and toil actually accomplish. Even in politics he makes this mistake; he sees government—the modern nation state—as a great and recent expression of the absolute spirit, with the naturally conservative conclusion that human beings must resign their individual interests and desires to those of a king or some ruling elite. But why do people choose in the first place to give all this glory to God and all this power to kings? Not because there really is a God or because there are people deserving to be called royal, but because something is fundamentally wrong with human thinking—because at the very core of our being, we suffer from *self*-alienation, a deep sense of inner separation from our natural human character as it ought to be.[21]

If we truly want to understand alienation, Marx continues, we must notice how singularly important the everyday economic fact of labor is to everyone that lives. Labor is the free activity of human beings as they generate and support their social lives over against the world of nature. It ought to be rich, creative, varied, and satisfying—an expression of the whole personality. But unfortunately, it is not. It has, in fact, become something apart, something alien to ourselves, partly because of the evil notion of private property. As we noticed with the boatman and the net maker, alienation begins once I think of the product of my labor as an object apart, as something other than the natural expression of my personality for the benefit of a community. From that moment I am alienated from the object of my production; it is something I can sell and another person can buy. I am also alienated from my own self; rather than expressing my unique talents, my weaving of nets is just the making of a commodity, something I can use to barter or buy other commodities. The net maker is also further alienated from what Marx calls the "species-life" of humanity: dealing in a mere product, I have nothing meaningfully human to show for my work. And finally, of course, I am alienated from other individual people because my personality, the thing that is essentially human about me, no longer engages yours; we just trade the objects each of us has made.[22] In these multiple forms of alienation we find the real misery of the human condition. And only when it is somehow overcome can real human happiness eventually be recovered.

Exploitation of Labor: Capitalism and Surplus Value

The cure for this corrosive alienation cannot be applied without first finding the cause. And here it is plain that however bad in itself, alienation has been made cruelly worse by the coming of modern industrial capitalism. Marx tries to provide an explanation for all of this in the many pages of *Capital*. Though no short summary of this long book can be fair to it, we can at least notice what Marx says in it about labor and value. He explains that the value of something I make or want to buy is created by the amount of work that goes into it. If it takes a day to make a pair of shoes and twenty days to make a precision clock, the value, or cost, of the clock will be twenty times that of the shoes. The shoemaker who wants to buy a clock will have to make at least twenty pairs in order to buy or barter for one. This sort of example offers a fairly close approximation of how, in the past, economics actually tended to work—by even exchange of value for value.

Unfortunately, Marx continues, capitalism and property ownership are all about *profit* rather than the equal exchange of value; they are about trading and investing to come out ahead rather than coming out even. And if we ask, "Where does this profit come from?" there can be only one answer. In capitalism the very thing about the clock or shoes which gives them their worth—the quantity of human labor they carry within them—is being *under*valued. Of this sober truth there is abundant evidence almost anywhere one looks. While workers must put into goods at least enough value to earn wages that will support their families, modern machinery allows them to do this in the mere fraction of a day. But they actually work a *full* day, or even (in the London Marx knew) much more than a full day.[23] In addition, entire families often worked for as many as ten, twelve, or more hours at machines; yet they were extremely poor. What was happening? Each day, Marx claims, each of these workers was creating an enormous amount of *surplus value* for the capitalist factory owner.[24] After working a short time to earn their wages, they continued to create value—surplus value—all of which was taken directly from them and sold for profit by the factory owner. Surplus value, in other words, is quite simply that which is left over after the workers' wages (which they need to pay for rent, clothing, and food) are subtracted from the much greater value they daily produce in their work. In each of the farms and factories of Marx's Europe, therefore, one owner who possessed fields or operated a plant was each day harvesting the surplus value created by hundreds or thousands of workers, taking it as his profit and using it to build a country estate complete with servants, foxes, and hounds. All the while, his workers were squeezed into cramped, dirty apartments in the city center, befriended by boredom, disease, and virtual starvation.

Regrettably, Marx asserts, this unjust circumstance is not just a matter of personal greed. Even if he did not like foxes and hounds, the owner's hand would still be forced by the brutal competition of the capitalist market. To keep his company alive, he *must* take most of the surplus funds it generates in order to invest in new, bigger factories that will exploit still more workers, so another factory owner does not begin to undersell and ruin him. Since he must keep his costs down to compete, every capitalist tries to use better and bigger machines; and he tries to center everything in one bigger and better company—into a trust or monopoly—so as to produce and sell his products at ever lower prices. The effect of these actions on the worker is not hard to notice. His life becomes ever more dismal as his position weakens in the brutally competitive marketplace. As population grows and factories become more efficient, workers find that they themselves are a surplus; there is always a "reserve" of unemployed proletarians reminding those who do have jobs that they can be replaced—and more cheaply—at any moment.

To make matters worse, even the excess of workers is not the most serious problem. The fierce rule of competition in capitalism, the drive to get greater production from workers, leads eventually to a strange new dilemma—the "overproduction of capital." Workers and machines make more products than can actually be sold. Owners in that unfortunate circumstance then have no choice but to reverse their path and reduce production, thereby bringing on periods of economic crisis marked by layoffs, business downturns, and crippling unemployment. After such depressions, economies do revive, but only to start the grim cycle of growth and decline all over again. It is hardly a surprise to learn that over time, this numbing, vicious cycle drives the proletariat finally to desperation. Here is how Marx describes the circumstance:

> Within the capitalist system . . . all means for the development of production transform themselves into means of domination over, and exploitation of, the producers; they mutilate the laborer into a fragment of a man, degrade him to

the level of an appendage of a machine, destroy every remnant of charm in his work and turn it into a hated toil; they estrange from him the intellectual potentialities of the labor-process . . . they distort the conditions under which he works, subject during the labor-process to a despotism the more hateful for its meanness; they transform his life-time into working-time, and drag his wife and child beneath the wheels of the Juggernaut of capital.[25]

In this way, the excesses and misfortunes of economic life fuel the fires of social conflict and lead capitalism finally to its own self-destruction. Amid their awful degradation and economic misery, says Marx, the proletarians discover something: They "have nothing to lose but their chains." Out of their fury, and with all the weight of history on their side, the workers are finally driven to plan, to organize, and in the end to act against the entire capitalist system. When the time is right, they can be expected to revolt. In that moment, the great day of reckoning for the capitalist world will at last have arrived.

Base and Superstructure

For Marx, then, the central drama of history is the struggle of classes, a conflict controlled from below by the hard realities of economic life. In a world of private property, some—usually the rich—own the means of production, while others—overwhelmingly the poor—do not. But even so, economics is not all of existence. What about the types of activity that form the other dimensions of our social life? What about politics and law? What about morality, the arts, literature, and various other intellectual endeavors? And what about religion? Where do all of these fit in?

Marx has much to say on each of these topics, and his starting point for all of them is to make a distinction between what he calls the "base" of society and its "superstructure."[26] Through all of history, he insists, economic facts have formed the foundation of social life; they are the base that generates the division of labor, the struggle of classes, and human alienation. By contrast, certain other spheres of activity, the things that are so visible in daily life, belong to the superstructure. They not only arise from the economic base but are in significant ways shaped by it. They are created by the deep, hidden energies and emotions of the class struggle. The institutions we associate with cultural life—family, government, the arts, most of philosophy, ethics, and religion—must be understood as structures whose main role is to contain or provide a controlled release for the deep, bitter tensions that arise from the clash between the powerful and powerless.

Consider the case of government. The role of the state is not hard to understand. Marx says it exists in all ages to represent the wishes of the ruling class, the dominant group. In a capitalist society built on the principle of private property, it therefore passes strict laws against theft, so that the mother of a starving child can be jailed for stealing a loaf of bread even from a factory owner so wealthy that he has enough food to feed a village. Government creates and pays a police force to make sure that the laws are enforced; thieves must be caught and brought to trial. And it establishes a judiciary to make certain that those laws are upheld; the accused must be convicted and sentenced for her offense. Disintegration, the breakdown of law, is a constant threat to any society that, like the capitalist order, is made up of just a few oppressors and so many who are oppressed. So the presence of a strong state, one that will impose laws and crush any threat of deviation, is absolutely essential.

Although the state uses force to achieve control, other authorities in the cultural superstructure achieve the same end by using persuasion. In each age of the past, ethical leaders—theologians, philosophers, and moral teachers—have helped to control the poor simply by preaching to them, by telling them what is right and what is wrong. The particular virtues they promote depend, naturally, on the kind of society they live in, for "the ideas of the ruling class are in every epoch the ruling ideas."[27] In the Middle Ages, when farming was the chief means of production, all lands were owned by bishops of the church or by feudal lords, who defended their property with armies of vassals and serfs sworn to their service. Should we be surprised, then, that the moral code of the day stressed devotion to the church, along with warrior virtues such as obedience, honor, and loyalty to one's feudal master? In modern industrial society, capitalist owners need a huge pool of movable workers, people with few ties beyond their immediate family and no claim to social privilege or status. Should we be shocked, then, that in the present era the moral watchwords are individual freedom and social equality? Modern philosophers and theologians promote these new moral values because they serve the new economy. Like their medieval counterparts, they claim that the morals they preach are eternal truths, that they belong to a fixed order of nature, when, in fact, they are determined by the economic realities of their own specific place and time. Nor are the creative arts really much different. For all their talk of individualism and originality, writers and artists depend on the accepted ideas of the age for their success, so even when they seem to protest, they in reality give unwitting, silent approval to society under the oppressors' control.[28]

For historical support of these views, Marx often turns to the recent revolutions in modern Europe: the English Civil War of the 1600s and especially the revolutions in France, which he studied all of his life and discussed in no less than three separate works.[29] On the surface, these great conflicts seem to be purely matters of politics and religion; the underlying realities, however, look considerably different. In seventeenth-century England, says Marx, it is capitalism that leads the London merchants and middle-class gentry to challenge the political authority of the king, whose power lay with established landowners. It is capitalism that leads the rising middle class to adopt a new form of religion, Protestantism, which is much better suited to its interests in trade, investment, and individual enterprise. And, we might add, it is capitalism that leads artists like Rembrandt and Frans Hals to paint portraits of Dutch townsmen and their families instead of the saints and kings whom we find in the mosaics and frescoes of medieval churches. In France of 1789 it is the rising middle class (the urban bourgeoisie) of professionals and bureaucrats who engineer the overthrow of the king and lead the attack on the church in the name of human rights. Once the upheaval subsides, economic interests again prevail as the same middle class unites to hold back the revolutionary aspirations of the impoverished masses. In each case we can see that the superstructure of politics and religion is really controlled by the economic base and the dynamics of class warfare.

Marx has a special word for all of the intellectual activity that makes up this superstructure: The endeavors of artists, politicians, and theologians all amount to "ideology."[30] Such people produce systems of ideas and creative works of art which in *their* minds seem to spring from the desire for truth or love of beauty. But in reality these products are mere expressions of class interest; they reflect the hidden social need to justify things as they stand, the natural inclination of those who benefit from injustice to show why the circumstance that creates it should remain unchanged. The thinkers are always the servants of the rulers.

Critique of Religion

Mention of such things as ideology and superstructure brings us at last to the sphere of religion, where by now Marx's basic view should hardly come as a surprise. There are, in truth, few subjects on which he is as brief or as blunt. Religion, he says, is pure illusion. Worse, it is an illusion with most definitely evil consequences. It is the most extreme example of ideology, of a belief system whose chief purpose is simply to provide reasons—excuses, really—for keeping things in society just the way the oppressors like them. As a matter of fact, religion is so fully determined by economics that it is pointless to consider any of its doctrines or beliefs on their own merits. These doctrines differ from one religion to the next, to be sure, but because religion is always ideological, the specific form it takes in one society or another is in the end largely dependent on one thing: the shape of social life as determined by the material forces in control of it at any given place and time. Marx asserts that belief in a god or gods is an unhappy by-product of the class struggle, something that should not only be dismissed, but dismissed with scorn. In fact, no thinker considered in this book—not even Freud—discusses religion in quite the same mood of sarcastic contempt as that of Marx.

The settled hostility in this attitude undoubtedly has roots that go beyond mere intellectual disagreement. Marx's first steps toward a fierce rejection of religion were taken in his youth. Early on, he made clear in absolute terms that he was an atheist. Whether the reasons for this original stance were social, intellectual, purely personal, or some combination of several such factors is hard to know. He may well have resented his father's weakness in converting to Christianity just to save his law practice, and certainly he had no love for the anti-Semitic, militantly Christian ethos of the Prussian state. Yet his absolute repudiation of belief ran deeper than his denial of Christianity. In the preface to his doctoral dissertation, he took as his own the motto of the Greek hero Prometheus, "I hate all the gods," adding as his reason that they "do not recognize man's self-consciousness as the highest divinity." [31]

A simple rejection of religion is one thing, of course; a full intellectual campaign to unmask its falsehood is quite another. Marx did not begin to develop an explanatory account—what he called a "critique"—of religion until the decade of the 1840s, which was, as already noted, the decisive period in his thinking and the time when he read the important writings of Ludwig Feuerbach, a man closely associated with the Young Hegelians in Berlin. [32] Feuerbach, like the others, was at first a disciple of Hegel, but later he reversed course to become a stern critic of idealism. In 1841, he created a sensation with an attack on orthodox religion called *The Essence of Christianity.* The furious debate over this book was still going strong when he astonished German opinion with two other works that proceeded to launch a parallel attack on the almost equally sacred system of Hegel. [33] Predictably, Feuerbach at once became a cult hero to the more radical students in the German universities.

Though Feuerbach too wrote in the difficult philosophical language of his day, which spoke of "consciousness" and "alienation," his basic point was not hard to grasp. Both Hegel and Christian theology, he said, make the same error. Both talk about some alien being—about God or the absolute—when what they are really talking about is humanity and nothing more. Christian theologians notice all of the personal qualities we most dearly admire—ideals like goodness, beauty, truthfulness, wisdom, love, stead-fastness, and strength of character—then proceed to strip them from their human owners and project them onto the screen of heaven, where they are worshipped—now in a form separate from ourselves—under the name of a supernatural being called God. Hegel does the same thing. He notices abstract ideas like freedom, reason, and goodness, then feels he must "objectify" them by claiming they are really expressions of the absolute, of some ultimate spirit that supposedly operates as an invisible stage manager behind the scenes of the world. But this, too, is mistaken. Concepts like "rationality" and "freedom" merely describe features of our own natural human life. Christian theology and Hegelian philosophy are thus both guilty of "alienating" our consciousness. They take what is properly human and assign it, quite wrongly, to some alien being called the absolute or to God.

When he read these arguments of Feuerbach, Marx found himself completely convinced. In fact, they only expressed in detail the view that he had already begun to adopt. He hailed Feuerbach as "the true conqueror of the old philosophy of Hegel" and described his books as "the only writings since Hegel's . . . which contain a real theoretical revolution." [34] And in his own *Critique of Hegel's Philosophy of Right: Introduction,* written a year after Feuerbach's book, he followed him almost to the letter: "Man, who looked for a superman in the fantastic reality of heaven . . . found nothing there but the *reflexion* of himself." He then added: "The basis of irreligious criticism is: *Man makes religion,* religion does not make man." [35]

Persuasive as Feuerbach's arguments were, Marx saw two places where they could be made still better. First, if we ask *why* human beings refuse to take credit for their own accomplishments, if we ask why they insist on calling themselves miserable sinners and offer instead all praise and glory to God, Feuerbach really has no answer beyond an empty generality. He tends to say, in effect, that is just the way people are; it is human nature to be alienated—unhappy with ourselves yet pleased with God. This will not do for Marx. There is a real answer to the question of alienation, he insists, and it fairly leaps out at us the moment we look at things from a materialist *and* economic perspective.

Marx insists that we must notice a striking parallel between religious and socioeconomic activity. Both are marked by alienation. Religion takes qualities—moral ideals—out of our natural human life and gives them, unnaturally, to an imaginary and alien being we call God. Capitalist economies take another expression of our natural humanity—our productive labor—and transform it just as unnaturally into a material object, something that is bought, sold, and owned by others. In the one case, we hand over a part of our selves—our virtue and sense of self-worth—to a wholly imaginary being. In the other, we just as readily deliver our labor for nothing more than wages to get other things money will buy. As religion robs us of our human merits and gives them to God, so the capitalist economy robs us of our labor, our true self-expression, and gives it, as a mere commodity, into the hands of the those—the rich—who are able to buy it. Nor is this unhappy combination just a coincidence. Religion, remember, is part of the super-structure of society. Economic realities form its base. The alienation we see in religion is, in actuality, just the *expression* of our more basic unhappi-ness, which is always economic. The alienation evident in religion is there-fore to be seen as a reflection, a mirror image of the real and underlying alienation of humanity, which is economic and material rather than spiritual.

In these terms, of course, it is easy to understand why, for many people, religion has such a powerful and lasting appeal. Better than anything else in the social superstructure, it addresses the emotional needs of an alienated, unhappy humanity. Here is how Marx puts it in the famous lines that, de-pending on the reader, are now among the most widely hated or admired in all of his writing:

> *Religious* distress is at the same time the *expression* of real [economic] distress and the *protest* against real distress. Religion is the sigh of the oppressed creature, the heart of a heartless world, just as it is the spirit of a spiritless situation. It is the *opium* of the people.
>
> The abolition of religion as the *illusory* happiness of the people is required for their *real* happiness. The demand to give up the illusion about its condition is the *demand to give up a condition which needs illusions.*[36]

We do not know how much Marx understood about opium use in his day, but he certainly knew that it was a hallucinogenic and narcotic substance; it eased pain even as it created fantasies. And that, for him, is precisely the role of religion in the life of the poor. Through it, the pain people suffer in a world of cruel exploitation is eased by the fantasy of a supernatural world where all sorrows cease, all oppression disappears. Are the poor without jewels? No matter, the gates of Heaven are inlaid with pearl. Are the op-pressed without money? The very streets of Heaven are paved with gold. Are the poor jealous of the rich? They can read Jesus' parable of poor Laza-rus, who died and went to father Abraham, while the soul of the rich man who ignored him in life traveled directly to Hell at his death. To "fly away" one day and go home to live with God, as the old Negro spirituals declare, is to enjoy in the next life a well-deserved consolation for all of the suffer-ings endured in this one.

From Marx's standpoint, it is just this unreality, this leap into an imagi-nary world, which makes religion such a wickedly comforting business.

After all, if there is neither a God nor a supernatural world, being religious is no different from being addicted to a drug, like opium. It is pure escapism. Worse, in terms of the struggle against exploitation in the world, it is also fundamentally destructive. What energies will the poor ever put into changing their circumstance if they are perfectly content with the thought of the next life? How will they organize, plan their attack, and begin their revolt if their hope of heaven leaves them no more wish to change their life than the "sigh of protest" we find in otherworldly rituals and ceremonies? Religion shifts their gaze upward to God, when it should really be turned downward to the injustice of their material, physical situation.

It is in just this connection that Marx offers his other improvement on Feuerbach, whose major problem is that, like most thinkers, he prefers restricting himself merely to the life of the mind; he is a passive commentator on the human situation, one who quite rightly observes that human beings are alienated and therefore turn to religion. But mere observation is not enough. Feuerbach and other intellectuals must be awakened to the fact that the purpose of analyzing the problem of religion is not just to have a new subject for discussion; the purpose of analysis is to find an active strategy that will solve the problem. This emphasis on *action,* in contrast to the purely theoretical concerns of so many thinkers in his day (and ours), is a crucial point in Marx's communist program. As he puts it in the last of his famous *Theses on Feuerbach,* "The philosophers have only *interpreted* the world, in various ways; the point, however, is to *change* it."[37]

Escape, then, is the main thing religion offers the oppressed. For those who are not oppressed, for those lucky enough to control the means of production, it offers something far better. Religion provides the ideology, the system of ideas, which they can call upon to remind the poor that all social arrangements should stay just as they are. God wills that the owning rich and laboring poor remain where they are, which is just where they belong. Religion's role in history has been to offer a divine justification for the status quo, for life just as we find it. "The social principles of Christianity," Marx insists,

> justified the slavery of Antiquity, glorified the serfdom of the Middle Ages and equally know, when necessary, how to defend the oppression of the proletariat, although they make a pitiful face over it.
>
> The social principles of Christianity preach the necessity of a ruling and an oppressed class, and all they have for the latter is the pious wish [that] the former will be charitable. . . .
>
> The social principles of Christianity declare all vile acts of the oppressors against the oppressed to be either the just punishment of original sin and other sins or trials that the Lord in his infinite wisdom imposes on those redeemed.

The social principles of Christianity preach cowardice, self-contempt, abasement, submission, dejection.[38]

There is nothing half-hearted about Marx's verdict on religion, as these scathing words clearly show. For him, belief in God and in some heavenly salvation is not just an illusion; it is an illusion that paralyzes and imprisons. It paralyzes workers by drawing off into fantasy the very motives of anger and frustration they need to organize a revolt. Desire for heaven makes them content with earth. At the same time, religion also imprisons; it promotes oppression by presenting a system of belief which declares that poverty and misery are facts of life which ordinary people must simply accept and embrace.

It must be noted here that for all the force of Marx's original words and judgments on these matters, Marxism does exhibit variations in doctrine not unlike those found within a broad economic system like capitalism or a religion like Christianity. Engels, for example, and the later Marxist historian Karl Kautsky, in his *Foundations of Christianity* (1908), both saw that in certain respects the rise of Christianity in the ancient world could be seen as the expression of a proletarian revolutionary protest against privileged Roman oppressors. In recent decades of our own century, theologians in Latin America have drawn on Marxist categories and analyses to frame a powerful movement of protest against economic injustice known as "liberation theology."

While forms of Marxism that are more in sympathy with religion thus have come into existence, it unlikely that Marx himself would have thought much of them. He might have wondered why anyone should even try such salvage efforts, for his own final verdict is as much dismissive as it is contemptuous. In spite of his anger, it is significant that Marx does not try to make religion into communism's great public enemy, as religious people, conversely, often have done with communism. And that is because in his view of things, religion, for all its evil doings, really does not matter very much. Though it certainly aids the oppressors, there is no need to launch hysterical crusades against it, for it is just not that important. It is merely the symptom of a disease, not the disease itself. It belongs to society's superstructure, not to its base. And the base is the real field of battle for the oppressed. As Marx puts their plight in one of his characteristic reversals of phrase, "The call to abandon their illusions about their condition is a *call to abandon a condition which requires illusions*."[39]

He is fully confident that, in time, the attack on those conditions will succeed. And when it does, religion, like the state and everything else in the superstructure of oppression, will "wither away" on its own.

Analysis

Marx's explanation of religion has had great influence in our century, in part because it is not just another remote scholarly theory. It is tied to a philosophy of political action that, until recently, was embraced by nearly a third of the contemporary world, including not only nations as great as the Soviet Union and mainland China but many smaller ones as well. For countless people born in these cultures, Marxism and its relentless critique of religion are the only philosophy of life they have ever known. It is partly because of this political success, of course, that Marxism has had its equally great impact on modern intellectual life. During most of this century, Marxist thinkers and theorists have played a leading role in virtually every modern field of study outside the natural sciences. Forty years ago, more than a few serious intellectuals were convinced that communism had caught the flow of history's irreversible tide. To them, its ultimate triumph was assured. In the last astonishing decade, however, the world communist experiment has undergone an almost total collapse.[40] And the not surprising consequence is that, in the current moment, communism's own "ideology"—including its view of religion—stands in almost universal discredit. Of course, Marx himself might not have been as disturbed by all of this as we may suppose, for in his dialectical view of history, today's capitalist triumph can still be read as preface to *its* collapse amid the great proletarian revolution of a more distant future. Nonetheless, the almost blindly enthusiastic approval Marxist theory enjoyed in past decades has been replaced by an almost equally total rejection in the present.

Between these two extremes, objectivity about either Marx or his view of religion is difficult to achieve.[41] Perhaps the best that one can do, at least at the start, is to lay aside the issue of praise or blame and try simply to be descriptive. In that regard, at least two elements in Marx's theory that distinguish it from others deserve our notice: (1) his strategy of functional explanation, which ends in its own distinctive form of reductionism, and (2) his stress on the strong ties that link religion to economics.

1. Functional Explanation and Reductionism

Although he began writing more than half a century before either of them, Marx's general approach to religion is similar in form to the functional explanations we have observed in both Freud and Durkheim. What interests him is not so much the content of religious beliefs—not so much what people actually say is true about God, or Heaven, or the Bible, or any other sacred writing or divine being—as the role these beliefs play in the social struggle. He agrees with Tylor and Frazer that the main religious beliefs are, of course, absurd superstitions. But he also agrees with Freud and Durkheim that we still have to explain why people hold to them. Like them, he insists that we find the key to religion only when we discover what its *function* is, only when we discover what its beliefs do for people either socially or psychologically or both. Marx's stress on society puts his view in one respect closer to Durkheim than to Freud, for Freud's emphasis, as we saw, falls mainly on the *individual* rather than the group. On his view, the neurotic needs of the individual personality are the main cause of belief. Even so, the contrast is not a sharp one because Freud's theory also has social features, with the individual personality being shaped by the influences of the family and community.

At the same time, Marx and Freud are closer together—and farther from Durkheim—on another side of the issue. Since, for Durkheim, religion is in a very real sense simply the worship of society, he thinks it impossible to imagine human social life without *some* set of either religious rituals or their near equivalent. Marx and Freud, by contrast, believe no such thing. Both think religion expresses a false need for individual security, and they are perfectly happy to predict the disappearance of religion once the cause of its fantasies has been detected and removed. Freud thinks people would be much better off without the neurotic illusions of faith, but he seems to realize many will still cling to them. Marx goes further. He thinks people *cannot* be better off *until* they are without them—that is, until revolution has done away with the exploitation and misery that have created religion in the first place.

From this comparison, we can see that Marx's explanation is not just functionalist but aggressively reductionist as well. The tendency of his thinking throughout is to describe religion always as an effect, an expression, a symptom of something more real and substantial that lies underneath it. Even if he sometimes speaks of religious ideas as having some independence, his predominant emphasis is always the other way. His strategy is identical to that of Freud and Durkheim in that beneath the surface of religious beliefs and rituals, he is always seeking out the hidden cause of these things, which is to be found in something else. For Freud, that something is a neurotic psychological need; for Durkheim, it is society; for Marx, it is a reality beneath both of these—the material facts of the class struggle and alienation. Since these burdens form the reality behind the illusions of belief, we explain religion best only when we reduce it to the forces of economic life that have created it.

2. Economics and Religion

Whatever our judgment on Marx's reductionism, one thing is beyond debate. His emphasis on economic realities has now made it impossible to understand religious life anywhere without exploring its close ties to economic and social realities. In the century since his death, Marx's disciples have brought great insight to our understanding of relationships between the spiritual and material dimensions of life. They have cast a whole new light on the connections between economic needs, social classes, and religious beliefs, especially in the case of such pivotal events in history as the Protestant Reformation, the English Civil War, the French Revolution, and similar social upheavals of other times and places. In addition, they have produced provocative studies of the connections between religion and such subjects as modern imperialism, colonialism, and slavery.[42] In this respect, whatever happens to Marxist political regimes, Marx's materialist economic perspective will no doubt endure and continue to bear fruit wherever theorists address the role of religion in economic, social, and political affairs.

Critique

Marx's economic reductionism offers a wealth of insight into the ties that bind religion to social life. Insight, however, is not persuasion. Insofar as Marx gives us a theory of religion, how compelling is it? That question is an especially large one in this case, because Marx's judgment on religion is almost impossible to separate from the rest of his thought. We saw this to some degree also in the case of Freud, whose conclusions about religion rest heavily on his claims about psychology. In the same way, it is very hard to evaluate Marx's theory of religion without at the same time making judgments on his claims about economy, politics, and society. So, in the following, we start with some critical comments on the role of religion as Marx sees it but then move to his philosophy more generally taken.

1. Christianity and Religion

If we focus specifically on the theory of religion as explained above, two problem areas in Marxist thought require special notice. First, what Marx actually presents is not an account of religion in general but an analysis of Christianity—and of similar faiths that stress belief in God and an afterlife. In part, this may be due to the influence of Hegel, who saw Christianity as the highest form of religion and felt that whatever he said about Christianity applied automatically to all "lesser" religions as well. Feuerbach took this position, and Marx, as we saw, closely follows Feuerbach's analysis. But, more importantly, the main focus of Marx's thinking is not so much world civilization as the culture and economy of Western Europe, which is of course the historical homeland of Christianity.

It is chiefly Christianity that Marx has in mind when he explains religion as an opiumlike escape for the poor from economic misery and oppression. We can, of course, imagine a similarly Marxist explanation of, say, the Hindu doctrine of rebirth, which also offers people hope of a better next life, or the teachings of certain Buddhists who stress the joys of sheer nothingness over the miseries of the present world and life.[43] But Marx's thesis cannot be very well applied to certain primitive tribal religions, which have almost no meaningful doctrine of an afterlife, or to the religions of ancient Greece and Rome, which offered hope of an afterlife on terms just the opposite of Marx's: immortality for the great and powerful and a mere shadow existence for simple folk. Further, according to Marx, the phenomenon of alienation—which creates religion—came about only as human societies were introduced to the division of labor and private property. It would seem to follow that there was a time in human history before all of these things, when human beings needed no religion and, in fact, had none. It is possible that in some deep prehistoric age this was true, but there is no historical evidence to support such an idea. Nor is there any evidence available from any modern tribal peoples, whose form of life often comes close to Marx's idea of an original communism, which would show that they are without religion or even exhibit less of an inclination to it than anyone else.

2. Religion, Reduction, and the Superstructure

Whether Christian or not, religion in Marx's view is an ideology. Like the state, the arts, moral discourse, and certain other intellectual endeavors, it belongs to the superstructure of society, and it depends in a fundamental way on the economic base. Thus, if there is a change in economic life, a change in religion must follow. The problem with this position as stated is that Marx explicates it in an extremely elusive fashion. He insists that his own research is strictly scientific in nature, yet when he reduces religion to economics and the class struggle, he does so in terms so broad and variable that his theorems are exceedingly difficult to test in any systematically scientific fashion. For example, we could agree with Marx's view that the rise of capitalism at the end of the Middle Ages caused a shift away from Catholicism and toward Protestantism. But then, what about more specific, small-scale changes? Does the religious superstructure change with *them* as well?

When, in certain locations, we find evidence of capitalism earlier on, say in the medieval period, why are there no developments of a Protestant sort in the social superstructure to reflect *that* change as well? And why, after the rise of capitalism, do we find this new bourgeois economic system in some cities and countries that clearly did *not* become Protestant? Throughout the later Middle Ages and early modern era, certain of the Italian city-states moved toward capitalism, but they did not give up Catholicism. Why? Moreover, even in those countries where Protestantism did arise, can we be sure it was economics that changed the religion? Could it not be that the new religion actually changed the economics? Two decades after Marx's death, the great German social theorist Max Weber framed an intriguing argument for just this point. He claimed that it was the Protestant ethic which created the spirit of capitalism, rather than the opposite.[44] Weber's view, which in effect makes religion the base and economics the superstructure, has, of course, been challenged as well by later scholars. But if nothing else, it shows that few such historical connections are as clear or certain as Marx supposes them to be. Moreover, outside the realm of religion as well, there are countless specific cases in which ideas from the spheres of art, literature, and morals as well as from politics and law have changed or shaped economics in important ways, rather than the reverse, as Marx contends. Indeed, the whole formulation of the problem, which suggests that in these complex cultural interactions one element—economics—must always be the cause while all of the others are simply effects, is clearly simplistic. Religion fits into society as part of a tangled network of causes and effects which act and react on each other in complicated ways. To suggest, as Marx does, that economics is always the agent in these transactions and that ideologies are always its mere expressions is to take a stance that does not square easily with the record of either culture or economics as they have evolved even in the Western civilization Marx knows, let alone along the paths of development that may have been followed in other societies.

3. Marxist Political Theory: A Contradiction

A theory is only as strong as its assumptions. Since Marxist thinking reduces religion to economics, we cannot leave it without examining, at least briefly, the general theory of economy and society on which it rests. This is, to be sure, no simple task. In both communist and noncommunist countries, entire libraries are needed to hold all the interpretations and critiques of Marx and Marxism in its multiple variations. What we can do, however, is point to at least two central difficulties that bear strongly on the issue of religion and seem part of the very nature and fabric of Marxism. These are not just charges hurled by political enemies but apparently congenital disabilities that Marxists themselves, in candid moments, recognize the need to overcome.

The first is a fundamentally social and political problem, and to see it we must remember that Marx recommends his system not just as a theory but as a course of real action. The working class—the proletariat—is the great agent of revolution; it is the social group which, driven to desperation by its universal misery, must one day rise up to destroy bourgeois capitalism. Its leaders, whether they be the members of a communist party, self-styled revolutionary strongmen, or elected representatives, embody the singular, uniform interest of "the people" as a whole. They and they alone speak and act for the revolution. Moreover, because there can be only one such "collective will" of the people, there is no place for disagreement about its purposes. Though it is elected, there can be only one political party. Though they can do their work, there can be no such thing as "individual freedom" for artists, scientists, and intellectuals, since the only purpose in any of these pursuits is to serve the will of the proletariat. Though families exist, parents, too, must recognize that their children belong ultimately to the state. Religion, of course, cannot be tolerated because it saps revolutionary energies and demands an ultimate loyalty that should be given only to the cause of revolution.

If this is a fair portrait of Marx's revolutionary social program, then it is very hard to see how it could ever achieve the end of a perfectly classless, harmonious community which he sets for it. Marx seems to assume that the workers in all of their millions will, on any important social issue, have only *one* point of view—a stance determined fully by their miserable position as the oppressed class. But why should this necessarily be true? At the outbreak of World War I, some communist leaders expected that proletarians in each of the European nations involved would actually refuse to fight their fellow workers in enemy lands. But this obviously did not happen: French, German, and British workers discovered that the ties of language, nation, and culture were far stronger than any class loyalty that might have gone beyond national borders.

Second, and more dangerously, Marxist theory seems to assume that some smaller group—some elite, elected or otherwise—will, in fact, be making the important decisions in the name of the workers, but apparently *without any institution in the society that has a right to examine or question that claim*. If I as communist party leader say, "You must die because the cause of revolution demands it," the one question that no one—no artist, theologian, opposing politician, or ordinary citizen—really has a protected right to ask me is: "Who are *you* to speak for the cause of revolution?" Since I believe I speak for the party, the mere fact that someone questions me already suggests that she or he is an enemy of the revolution. I must respond to such challenging questions not with an answer or a persuasive argument but with force. The practical consequence of this impossible situation, borne out in almost every modern communist state, is the dark turn toward absolute rule by parties or dictators, along with the willing destruction of basic human rights. And why not? Marx himself was never swayed by appeals to human rights, for, as he pointed out in the case of the French Revolution, they are only bourgeois values—ideals imposed on all by the middle class, the group which, in modern Western nations, happens now to hold the power. In other ages, other masters did the teaching, but always it was power, the "might" of wealth, which determined the "right" of morals. Ironically, however, this unsparingly radical view of moral rights as relative has grave consequences for the very workers whose interests Marx supposedly has at heart. Since it places no independent moral restraints upon those people who, now in the name of the revolution, have acquired power and claim to speak on its behalf, it leaves ordinary people just as open as before to brutalization, though now under the new banner of revolution and their own (future) well-being. All of which is deeply troubling, to say the least. There seems to be a contradiction at the very heart of Marxist social theory, a paradox which some critics have quite perceptively described as the problem of "totalitarian democracy."[45]

4. Marxist Economic Theory: A Contradiction

Marx spent the latter portion of his life writing on economics in the several volumes of *Capital* and other books. He regarded this as extremely important work, providing the solid foundation in economic fact and theory for his doctrines of the class struggle and worker exploitation. In *Capital,* as we have seen, he argues that human labor creates the only real value to be found in products and that exploitation occurs when capitalists pay workers just enough to stay barely alive and then "steal" for themselves the remaining surplus value in the products the workers have made. To Marxist theoreticians, this analysis seems fundamentally correct. Others are not so sure.

   Writing just over a decade after Marx's death, Eugen Böhm-Bawerk, an Austrian economist, discovered in *Capital* what he regarded as a "massive contradiction" between its theories of value and the actual facts of capitalist life as we see it.[46] In simple terms, he argued as follows: Marx holds a labor theory of value; only workers (and never machines) create the value that goes into their products. If that is so, it should be the case that very labor-intensive industries will always create more value (that is, be more profitable) than others. They provide more surplus value for the owner to steal. The actual facts of capitalism, however, show that regardless of the industries we consider, their rate of return on investment—that is, their profit—is almost always just about the same. It makes no difference whether they have a few workers running many machines or many workers and few machines; the profit margin remains basically constant.[47] Toward the end of the first volume of *Capital,* Marx himself realized this problem and promised a solution later on. Ill health, however, prevented him from ever fully addressing the issue, though he did what he could and in later volumes actually moved away from his notion that value is defined entirely by the amount of human labor in products. Nonetheless, as Böhm-Bawerk observes, this labor theory of value is crucial to Marx's further, and related, theory of surplus value; the one cannot be given up without losing the other. But the theory of surplus value is nothing less than the pivot on which Marx's central claim of worker exploitation is made to turn. Without it, his fundamentally moral complaint against capitalism seems to dissolve in the air, with a catastrophic result for all that follows thereafter. So in sum, if Marx's theories of value must be given up (and it seems they must), it is hard to see what could remain of the rest of the whole grand framework of Marxist economic theory. The doctrine of exploitation, the thesis of class struggle, the claims about base and superstructure, and certainly also the theory of religion as a dire, dismal symptom of alienation—all of these become almost impossible either to defend or apply. If Böhm-Bawerk is right, it would seem that the massive contradiction he notices can hardly be dismissed as a side issue. On the contrary, his criticism suggests nothing so much as a scene of dominoes tumbling one after the other in quick succession once the table supporting them has been unexpectedly shaken. Later Marxists have worked hard to refute this critique or revise Marx, but without great success.

We thus end our encounter with Marx at a place apparently far removed from religion—in the details of economic theory. From the materialist perspective, however, any distance we claim to see between the two realms is mostly a matter of appearances and not reality. Marx, in fact, is certain of their connection. The key to religion, he confidently declares, is to be found in economics. He follows what is to him a clear and direct path from religious belief down through alienation and exploitation to the class struggle and from there to the root evils of private property and the theft of surplus value. If this explanatory road shows turns and twists similar to those followed by Durkheim and Freud, that should hardly surprise us. Like them, Marx is committed to the route of reductionism, though for him it ends at a different destination—with class struggle and economic alienation rather than the needs of society or the neurotic personality. In their differing ways, and sometimes taken together, all three of these ambitious reductionist theories have had an enormous impact on modern thought.[48] Their tide of influence on interpreters of religion can be said to have reached a crest in the decades of the 1960s and 1970s, and it has certainly not disappeared today. Yet while they still have much to say, they no longer have the last or only word—as our next chapter will show.

Notes

1. Friedrich Engels, "Speech at the Graveside of Karl Marx," in *Karl Marx and Frederick Engels: Selected Works,* tr. and ed. Marx-Engels-Lenin Institute, 2 vols. (Moscow 1951), 2: 153.

2. Marx's major work in economic theory, *Capital,* was published in 1867 as the first of three volumes to be printed by a German publisher in Hamburg; the initial edition was 1000 copies. Most of volume 3 and much of volume 2 had already been written before the first volume appeared. Marx continued his work on revisions of these volumes after 1867, but he never finished them. They were published after his death by his colleague Friedrich Engels. *Capital* was to be part of a much larger general study of economics. On this, see David McLellan, *The Thought of Karl Marx: An Introduction* (New York: Harper Torchbooks, 1971), pp. 84–85.

3. For an appraisal of Marxism from the long perspective of a century after his death, see Betty Matthews, ed. *Marx: A Hundred Years On* (London: Lawrence & Wishart, 1983); on the changing critical estimate of his system, see Paul Thomas, "Critical Reception: Marx Then and Now," in Terrell Carver, ed., *The Cambridge Companion to Marx* (Cambridge, England: Cambridge University Press, 1991), pp. 23–54.

4. On the religious dimension of Marxism, see, among the most recent studies, Alistair Kee, *Marx and the Failure of Liberation Theology* (London: SCM Press, 1990), pp. 88–127.

5. The most important of these early philosophical and social writings that lay out the premises and main contentions of the Marxist system can be found in Karl Marx, *The Early Texts,* ed. David McLellan (Oxford, England: Oxford University Press, 1971).

6. There are, of course, numerous biographical studies of Marx. Among those of recent decades, the most authoritative work in English is David McLellan, *Karl Marx: His Life and Thought* (New York: Harper & Row, Publishers, 1973). An earlier and classic intellectual biography that analyzes the development of Marx's thought in the context of the Europe of his day is Isaiah Berlin, *Karl Marx* (New York: Time Inc., [1939] 1963). For those wishing just a brief account, McLellan has also provided a shorter study, *Karl Marx,* Modern Masters Series (Harmondsworth, Middlesex, England: Penguin Books, 1976).

7. Marx had a seventh child with the family housekeeper, Helen Demuth. For a chart of family connections, see McLellan, *Life and Thought,* p. 466.

8. On this circle, see McLellan, *The Young Hegelians and Karl Marx* (London: Macmillan & Co., 1969).

9. Though written in the 1840s, *The Economic and Philosophic Manuscripts* were not published until 1932, long after Marx's death; they were not published in an English translation until 1959. See McLellan, *Karl Marx* (1976), pp. 29–36, 86–87.

10. Karl Marx, *A Correspondence of 1843*, in McLellan, *Early Texts*, p. 82.

11. For a brief biography of Engels and an assessment of his relationship to Marx, see David McLellan, *Friedrich Engels* (New York: Viking Press, 1977). The differences of character and personality between Engels and Marx have been noted by many authors. Among the more weighty analyses is a now dated but nonetheless searching philosophical appraisal of Marxism by Gordon Leff, *The Tyranny of Concepts: A Critique of Marxism* (London: Merlin Press, 1961). See, for example, p. 27, and other places, where Leff is critical of Engels for expanding on Marx in questionable ways.

12. Karl Marx and Friedrich Engels, *The Communist Manifesto*, in *Selected Works*, 2 vols. (Moscow: Foreign Languages Publishing House [1935] 1955).

13. These studies were *The Class Struggles in France* (1850); *The Eighteenth Brumaire of Louis Bonaparte* (1852); *Outlines of the Critique of Political Economy* (1857–1858), designed as an introduction to his study of economics and known from its shortened German title as *Grundrisse; Towards a Critique of Political Economy* (1859); *Theories of Surplus Value* (1862–1863); *Wages, Prices, and Profit* (1865); *Results of the Immediate Process of Production* (1865); and the three volumes of *Capital*.

14. Marx and Engels, *The Communist Manifesto*, in *Selected Works*, 1: 34.

15. A work that is especially helpful on such key concepts in Marxist theory as "mode of production" and "relations of production," is Terrell Carver, *A Marx Dictionary* (Totowa, NJ: Barnes & Noble Books, 1987).

16. On Marx's view of the modes of production and stages of society, see Friedrich Engels, ed., *Capital*, 3 vols. (New York: International Publishers, 1967) 1: 76–79. A clear and brief summary of these points is available in Julius Smulkstys, *Karl Marx* (New York: Twayne Publishers, Inc., 1974), pp. 37–40.

17. On Marx's concept of "class" and class struggle, see Carver, *Marx Dictionary*, pp. 57–64. McLellan, *The Thought of Marx*, p. 151, points out that Marx never really gives a systematic analysis of this concept, despite its centrality to his whole program. He was, of course, well aware that the concept of class was not a new idea, having been used extensively by the French thinker St. Simon whose works he read along with those of other French social theorists in the 1840s.

18. This final phase of conflict between capitalism and communism, between the bourgeoisie and the proletariat, is presented in sweeping summary form in *The Communist Manifesto*, in Marx and Engels, *Selected Works*, 1: 44, and elsewhere. But Marx touches on it as well in many places throughout his works.

19. For Marx and Engels's utopian description of this classless final society, without either private property or a division of labor, we need only notice the well-known passage in *The German Ideology*, 2nd ed. (Moscow: Progress Publishers, [1845–1846] 1968), p. 44, where they write, "In communist society . . . it is possi-

ble for me to do one thing today and another tomorrow, to hunt in the morning, fish in the afternoon, rear cattle in the evening, criticize after dinner, just as I have a mind, without ever becoming hunter, fisherman, shepherd, or critic."

20. Some interpreters of Marx, notably McLellan, *Karl Marx* (1976), p. xi, insist that though he may have taken over Hegel's notion of historical progress through conflict, he did *not* take over Hegel's elaborate dialectic of the *thesis, antithesis,* and *synthesis.*

21. Marx discusses the concept of alienation most fully in his *Economic and Philosophical Manuscripts,* in T. B. Bottomore, ed., *Karl Marx: Early Writings* (New York: McGraw-Hill Book Company, 1964), pp. 120–34.

22. Marx, *Economic and Philosophical Manuscripts,* in Bottomore, ed., *Karl Marx: Early Writings,* p. 129.

23. Marx had made some observations of the actual circumstances of workers both on the continent and in England, but on this matter he was greatly indebted to Engels, who knew in some detail the terrible conditions of workers in great English towns like Manchester, and he described their miseries with vivid and painful accuracy in *The Condition of the Working Class,* which was published in 1845. On this, see McLellan, *Engels,* pp. 40–41.

24. Marx's celebrated theory of "surplus value" has been much discussed by economists and later Marxist theorists, along with the associated "labor theory of value." A good introduction to these terms and their meaning can be found in Carver, *Marx Dictionary,* under "labour," pp. 93–101, and "value," pp. 135–45. For a recent sophisticated and rather more technical analysis of Marx's economic concepts, see N. Scott Arnold, *Marx's Radical Critique of Society: A Reconstruction and Critical Evaluation* (New York: Oxford University Press, 1990).

25. Marx, *Capital,* 1: 645.

26. On these terms, see Carver, *Marx Dictionary,* under "base and superstructure," pp. 43–45.

27. Marx and Engels, *The German Ideology,* Parts 1 and 3, ed. R. Pascal (New York: International Publishers, 1947), p. 39.

28. On Marx's view of the creative arts and literature, see Smulkstys, *Karl Marx,* especially chapter 5, "Art and Literature in Marx's Philosophy," and chapter 6, "The Literary Critic."

29. *The Class Struggles in France* (1850); *The Eighteenth Brumaire of Louis Bonaparte* (1852); *On the Civil War in France* (1871).

30. For the meaning of the term see, again, Carver, *Marx Dictionary,* under "ideology," pp. 89–92.

31. Karl Marx, "Doctoral Dissertation," in McLellan, *Early Texts,* p. 13; see also McLellan's comments in *Karl Marx* (1973), p. 37.

32. An excellent study of the relationship between the ideas of these two thinkers on religion is Van A. Harvey, "Ludwig Feuerbach and Karl Marx," in *Nineteenth Century Religious Thought in the West,* ed. Ninian Smart, 3 vols. (Cambridge, England: Cambridge University Press, 1985), 1: 291–328.

33. These were *Preliminary Theses on the Reformation of Philosophy* and *Principles of the Philosophy of the Future,* both published in 1843.

34. Karl Marx, "Preface," *Economic and Philosophical Manuscripts,* in Bottomore, ed., *Early Writings,* p. 64.

35. Karl Marx, "Contribution to the Critique of Hegel's Philosophy of Right: Introduction," in *Karl Marx and Friedrich Engels on Religion,* introduced by Reinhold Niebuhr (New York: Schocken Books, 1964), p. 41.

36. Marx, "Critique of Hegel's Philosophy of Right," in Niebuhr, *Marx and Engels on Religion,* p. 42.

37. Karl Marx, "Theses on Feuerbach," in Niebuhr, *Marx and Engels on Religion,* p. 72.

38. Karl Marx, "The Communism of the Paper *Rheinischer Beobachter,*" in Niebuhr, *Marx and Engels on Religion,* pp. 83–84.

39. Marx, "Critique of Hegel's Philosophy of Right," in Niebuhr, *Marx and Engels on Religion,* p. 42.

40. Among the many books that have recently appeared on this subject, see Zbigniew Brzezinski, *The Grand Failure: The Birth and Death of Communism in the Twentieth Century* (New York: Charles Scribner's Sons, 1989), which was one of the first.

41. One of the most thorough recent expositions of Marx on religion, accompanied by a penetrating analysis, can be found in Alistair Kee, *Marx and the Failure of Liberation Theology* (London: SCM Press, 1990), particularly chapters 1–5; for a study that goes beyond Marx to Marxist criticisms more broadly taken, see Delos B. McKown, *The Classical Marxist Critiques of Religion: Marx, Engels, Lenin, Kautsky* (The Hague: Martinus Nijhoff, 1975).

42. Lenin was among those who argued that imperialism and colonialism are late phases of capitalism, the result of the capitalist's constant search for new markets in which to sell goods as well as for new sources of cheap labor.

43. Marx did briefly address this in several articles written while serving as a correspondent for the *New York Daily Tribune;* see Trevor Ling, *Karl Marx and Religion in Europe and India* (New York: Harper & Row, 1980), pp. 68–80.

44. Max Weber, *The Protestant Ethic and the Spirit of Capitalism,* tr. Talcott Parsons (New York: Free Press, [1904–1905] 1930).

45. On this point, see R. N. Carew Hunt, *The Theory and Practice of Communism: An Introduction* (Harmondsworth, Middlesex, England: Pelican Books, [1950] 1963). An impressive study of this problem both in the French revolution and in other radical revolutionary movements in the West is J. L. Talmon, *The Origins of Totalitarian Democracy* (Boston: Beacon Press, 1952). The same point is made about Russian and other socialisms in the mid-twentieth century in Ivor Bulmer-Thomas, *The Socialist Tragedy* (London: Latimer House, 1949).

46. Eugen Böhm-Bawerk, "Unresolved Contradiction in the Marxian Economic System" [1896], in *Shorter Classics of Eugen Böhm-Bawerk,* tr. Alice Macdonald (South Holland, IL: Libertarian Press, 1962). See also Böhm-Bawerk, *Karl Marx and the Close of His System,* ed. Paul M. Sweezy (London: Merlin Press, [1896] 1974).

47. A brief, clear summary of Böhm-Bawerk's critique can be found in Arnold, *Marx's Radical Critique,* pp. 63–88.

48. See the highly praised study by J. Samuel Preus, *Explaining Religion: Criticism and Theory from Bodin to Freud* (New Haven, CT: Yale University Press, 1987), which argues that the most convincing scientific, naturalistic explanation of religion to date is to be found in a combination of the theories of Durkheim and Freud.

Suggestions for Further Reading

Arnold, N. Scott. *Marx's Radical Critique of Society: A Reconstruction and Critical Evaluation*. New York: Oxford University Press, 1990. A sophisticated, thorough, and detailed modern analysis of Marx's economic concepts and formulations.

Berlin, Isaiah. *Karl Marx*. New York: Time Inc., [1939] 1963. A classic intellectual biography which analyzes the development of Marx's thought in the context of European intellectual traditions.

Böhm-Bawerk, Eugen. *Karl Marx and the Close of His System*. Edited by Paul M. Sweezy. London, England: Merlin Press, [1896] 1974. Analyses by the foremost economic critic of Marxism.

Brzezinski, Zbigniew. *The Grand Failure: The Birth and Death of Communism in the Twentieth Century*. New York: Charles Scribner's Sons, 1989. One of the first appraisals of the collapse of communism, written by the former national security advisor for President Jimmy Carter.

Carver, Terrell, ed. *The Cambridge Companion to Marx*. Cambridge, England: Cambridge University Press, 1991. Instructive essays on the changing estimates of Marx, his political theories, views of science, economic analyses, and other topics.

Carver, Terrell. *A Marx Dictionary*. Totowa, New Jersey: Barnes & Noble Books, 1987. A useful reference work especially for key concepts in Marx's thought.

Gottlieb, Roger S. *Marxism, 1844–1990: Origins, Betrayal, Rebirth*. London: Routledge, Chapman, & Hall, Inc., 1992. An attempt by a sympathetic mind to rehabilitate Marxism in the aftermath of the Soviet collapse.

Kee, Alistair. *Marx and the Failure of Liberation Theology*. London: SCM Press, 1990. A wide-ranging recent critique of Marxism and the mostly Latin American theology which seeks to combine Marxist theory with Christian belief.

Leff, Gordon. *The Tyranny of Concepts: A Critique of Marxism*. London: Merlin Press, 1961. An older work, but still a searching philosophical analysis and criticism of Marxist ideology.

Marx, Karl, and Friedrich Engels. *Karl Marx and Friedrich Engels on Religion*. Introduced by Reinhold Niebuhr. New York: Schocken Books, 1964.

McKown, Delos B. *The Classical Marxist Critiques of Religion: Marx, Engels, Lenin, Kautsky*. The Hague: Martinus Nijhoff, 1975. An informative comparative study of differing critiques of religion among the major Marxist thinkers of the early twentieth century.

McLellan, David. *Friedrich Engels*. New York: Viking Press, 1977. A biography of Marx's collaborator and friend, with attention given to the relationship between the two men as well as their differences amid affinities.

McLellan, David. *Karl Marx*. Modern Masters Series. Harmondsworth, Middlesex, England: Penguin Books, 1976. A brief biographical account of Marx's career, controversies, and ideas.

McLellan, David. *Karl Marx: His Life and Thought*. New York: Harper & Row, 1973. The authoritative recent biography of Marx in English.

McLellan, David. *Marxism and Religion*. New York: Harper & Row, 1987. One of the best accounts of the subject in English, this analysis extends well beyond Marx and his earlier followers to Marxist thinkers and schools of the present day.

McLellan, David. *The Thought of Karl Marx: An Introduction*. New York: Harper Torchbooks, 1971. By the same author, a study focused on Marx's ideas, methods, and theory.

Plamenatz, John. *Karl Marx's Philosophy of Man*. Oxford, England: Clarendon Press, 1975. A profound, subtle, scholarly examination of the ideas and arguments at the core of Marx's thought.

Talmon, J. L. *The Origins of Totalitarian Democracy*. Boston: Beacon Press, 1952. An important study of absolutist style revolutionary movements during the French Revolution and afterward.

5

The Reality of the Sacred:
Mircea Eliade

"My duty is to show the grandeur, sometimes naive, sometimes
monstrous and tragic, of archaic modes of being."
                                    Mircea Eliade, *Journal III: 1970–1978* [1]

If we take the three of them together, one thing is quite clear about Freud,
Durkheim, and Marx. Each develops a broadly functional view of religion.
It is not enough, on their view, to show why it makes sense for a Hindu or
Muslim to accept the teachings of his or her faith as true; one must try to
show how these beliefs operate, or function, beyond the level of intellectual
assent, to satisfy other needs or conditions. Further, each theorist believes
that this functionalist approach can bring him to a reductionist conclusion.
None is content with the more modest claim that his strategy explains just
one part of religion, while other theories may well explain other parts. Each
insists that he has found what is basic and fundamental; hence, other theories
are not really needed. Each feels not just that he can explain religion but
that he can explain it away—that is, *reduce it* to something other than what
it appears.

Although these reductionist strategies have been widely influential in our
age, they certainly are not all that can be said on our subject. From the
beginning, there have been critics of such approaches, and in recent decades
they seem to have increased steadily in number. Among the voices of opposition, probably none has been more outspoken than Mircea Eliade, a truly
cross-cultural scholar who was born in Romania, spoke and wrote in several
European languages, read many others, and completed his career in the
United States. A man of wide learning who was also a talented writer of
fiction, Eliade devoted his life to the comparative study of religion, a field
which he, in keeping with European practice, preferred to call "the history
of religions." [2] As a young man he studied for a time in India, then carried
on further research at home in Romania and elsewhere in Europe. For a time

he held a university position in France. In the 1950s he moved to the United States, where, as a professor at the University of Chicago, he played a pivotal role promoting the study of religion in American universities. From the outset, Eliade developed his ideas in direct opposition to reductionist theories, which in his view seriously misunderstood the role of religion in human life. He advocated instead a humanistic approach, and throughout his long career as a scholar he held steadfastly to the thesis that religion must always be explained "on its own terms."[3] His theory thus deserves our attention not just on its own merits but because of the bold challenge it issues to all reductionist rivals.

Background

Mircea Eliade was born in Bucharest on March 9, 1907, the son of an officer in the Romanian army. As a boy he loved quiet places, science, stories, and writing. His autobiography reports how, at the age of eighteen, he celebrated with friends the appearance of his one-hundredth published article![4] Already at this young age, he was hired by a newspaper to write feature stories, opinion columns, and book reviews. Also among his recollections is a memorable incident from early childhood. He tells how one day at home, on entering an unused room of the house, he was startled by sunlight filtering through green curtains in a way that gave the entire space an unearthly emerald-golden glow. Dazzled and entranced, he felt as if he had been transported into an utterly different, transcendent world. Later, in words identical to those he used in his accounts of religious experience, he chose to describe his memory of this event as a profound "nostalgia"—a longing for a beautiful space of otherworldly perfection.[5] The theme of otherworldly ideals was to run through his education as well. At the University of Bucharest and in Italy, he studied the mystical Platonist thinkers of the Italian Renaissance. While doing this work, he discovered Hindu thought, with its stress on spiritual union with the Supreme Soul behind the world. And soon he was setting off for India to study with the noted sage and scholar Surendranath Dasgupta. Arriving late in the year of 1928, Eliade enrolled at the University of Calcutta and worked with Dasgupta in his home. On a somewhat less spiritual plane, he also began an affair with his mentor's daughter. An unpleasant separation from his teacher followed, and he moved on to train in yoga with a guru in the Himalayas.

Looking back in later years, Eliade declared that this stay in India had a decisive impact on his life. In particular, he says, he discovered three things: that life can be changed by what he called "sacramental" experience; that *symbols* are the key to any truly spiritual life; and, perhaps most important, that much could be learned from India's countryside, where there was a broad and powerful heritage of folk religion—a deeply felt form of spiritual life that had been in existence since time beyond memory. Simple peasants saw things sacred and eternal in the mystery of agriculture; they viewed the world as "an unbroken cycle of life, death, and rebirth." In addition, this "archaic religion," as Eliade came to call it, was a perspective on life that seemed to be shared across much of the world. It could be found to stretch from the villages of India to those of his own Romania, from Europe and Scandinavia to East Asia, the Americas, and other locales where primitive peoples tilled the soil as ancestors had taught them for generations. In India, he wrote, he first discovered "cosmic religious feeling."[6]

In 1931, after three years away, Eliade returned to Romania to complete his military service. He continued to write, and in 1933, at the young age of twenty-six, he became a national celebrity by publishing a prize-winning novel, *Maitreyi* (in English, *Bengal Night*), based on his romance with Dasgupta's daughter.[7] This decade was eventful in other respects as well. His doctoral dissertation, *Yoga: An Essay on the Origins of Indian Mystical Theology* (1936), was published in French, the first of several works on this subject. On receiving his degree, Eliade began teaching at Bucharest as an assistant to the influential philosopher Nae Ionesco, who was also a leading figure in a Romanian nationalist organization known as the Legion of the Archangel Michael. Some members of this group, whose violent, terrorist wing was known as the Iron Guard, saw their role in Romania as similar to that of the Nazi party in Germany, and they showed some sympathy for Hitler. Eliade had other friends as well in this circle, though for his part he seems to have preferred intellectual life, editing a journal, writing, and arranging discussions of current issues and movements in literature, philosophy, and art. About any other activities he was always reluctant to speak, describing himself as a largely nonpolitical person.[8]

During the years of World War II, Eliade was assigned by the Romanian government to a diplomatic post in Lisbon, Portugal. When the fighting ended, he chose not to return to Romania and took up residence in Paris, where he was given a chance to teach at the École des Hautes Études. There he completed research on two important books, which set the course for most of his later study and thought. *Patterns in Comparative Religion* (1949) explored the role of symbols in religion, while *The Myth of the Eternal Return* (1949) investigated the concepts of history and sacred time as well as the differences between archaic religion and modern thought. Both books were published in French. As his work progressed, Eliade drew further inspiration from Carl Jung, the great Swiss psychologist and Freud's former associate, whom he met in 1950 at Ascona, Switzerland, during a regular gathering of European intellectuals known as the Eranos Conference. Until Jung's death in 1960, Eliade visited him regularly, finding in him not just a supporter of his ideas on archaic religion but a kind of living exhibit of them as well. Of their discussions, he wrote, "I felt I was listening to a Chinese sage or an East European peasant, still rooted in Earth Mother yet close to Heaven at the same time."[9]

The 1950s brought the last important change in Eliade's scholarly career. After lecturing at the University of Chicago, he accepted a professorship in its Divinity School; in 1962, he became one of its Distinguished Service Professors.[10] His position at Chicago, where he remained for the rest of his life, enabled him to serve as mentor to a full generation of talented younger scholars who were inspired by his example, even when, as was common, they proceeded to disagree with his views. He chose to measure his own impact by citing a simple statistic. When he came to Chicago, there were three significant professorships in the history of religions in the United States; twenty years later, there were thirty, half of which were occupied by his students.[11] Beginning in India and ending in Chicago, Eliade's was a career—and life—in which he himself saw many opposites converge: East and West, tradition and modernity, mysticism and rationality, contemplation and criticism.[12] He continued his research and writing in retirement until his death of a stroke on April 22, 1986.

Eliade's Starting Point: Two Axioms

Before considering Eliade's theory in its particulars, we ought to notice the foundation on which it stands. Two ideas especially serve as its axioms, or cornerstones; they are fundamental to everything else. The first, which has come into view already, is his strong stand on reductionism. Eliade believes adamantly in the independence, or "autonomy," of religion, which for him cannot be explained as the mere by-product of some other reality. "A religious phenomenon," he insists,

> will only be recognized as such if it is grasped at its own level, that is to say, if it is studied *as* something religious. To try to grasp the essence of such a phenomenon by means of physiology, psychology, sociology, economics, linguistics, art, or any other study is false; it misses the one unique and irreducible element in it—the element of the sacred.[13]

In the language of the natural sciences, we might rephrase this to say that religion is not to be construed as a "dependent variable," the thing that always changes in any test or experiment. If anything, it must be taken as the constant, or as an independent variable; other aspects of life—social, psychological, economic—must be understood to depend upon *it*. As an element in human behavior, religion functions as a *cause* rather than an *effect*.

The second axiom applies to method. If religion is, in fact, something independent, something that cannot be explained purely through psychology or sociology, how, then, *should* we explain it? Eliade answers that we must combine two separate angles of vision. Because students of religion mostly study the past, their subject in one sense is simply history. Accordingly, like other historians, they gather and order facts, make generalizations, criticize them, and try to find causes or consequences. In this respect, their discipline certainly is the *history* of religions. At the same time, the study of religion cannot be *just* historical either. We understand religion only when we also apply what Eliade calls "phenomenology" (from the Greek *phenomenon,* "an appearance"): the comparative study of things in the form, or appearance, they present to us. Any science is partly phenomenology. We know the color red in the spectrum because its appearance differs from that of blue or violet. By the same measure, one way we know a religious form—a belief or a ritual—is by comparing it with others. Eliade thus emphatically endorses the famous words of the philosopher Goethe on language, which Max Müller, as we saw, had already adopted for the study of religion: "He who knows one knows none." Without comparison there can be no real science.[14]

It is true that historians are suspicious of comparisons, especially when they are used to find similarities. The skeptical mind of the scholar is always inclined to think that no two things are ever quite the same; every time, every place is different from the next. Eliade disagrees. He thinks that certain general forms, certain broad patterns of phenomena in religion, can be taken outside of their original time and place to be compared with others. Times and places may differ, he would say, but concepts are often the same. The mathematician Euclid was an ancient Greek, a man of his time; yet we can study his geometry as if he had taught it just yesterday. The man may be historical, but his theorems are timeless. The same would seem to apply to the concepts of religion. The worship of Zeus is in one sense tied to a single time and place in history; it is a belief and practice belonging to ancient Greek religion. But if we notice that, in the Greek stories of the gods, Zeus has a wife, that he lives on Mt. Olympus, and that he is more powerful than other divine beings, it is not hard to see in him certain typical features of the "sky god" as he appears in many different times and places around the world. Zeus may belong only to the Greeks, but the phenomenon of the sky god does not. And because such gods appear in many cultures, we can learn a great deal by tracing their patterns—by noticing which features they share with one another and which they do not.

These axioms in hand, we can now turn to the main elements of Eliade's program, although here, as we found with Marx and Freud, we will need help from more than one of his books. Eliade tends in all of his writings to explore the same major ideas and patterns, but in no one of them does he offer a sort of single, grand exhibit of his theory, as Frazer or Durkheim does. In addition, as a writer of fiction, he often seems to prefer the ways of the novelist even in his scholarly works; he gives long, winding commentaries rather than precise arguments. That being so, we can do best with his theory by keeping to a few central themes and examining each through the one book that explains it best. We shall explore in sequence each of the following:

1. Eliade's *concept of religion*. This is most clearly outlined in *The Sacred and the Profane* (1957), perhaps the best short introduction to his theory written for the general reader.

2. His *understanding of symbolism and myth*. This is best observed in *Patterns in Comparative Religion* (1949), the work that sets the agenda for most of his later works.

3. His *explanation of time and history* as seen by both archaic and modern cultures. These themes are discussed at length in *The Myth of the Eternal Return* (1949), perhaps the most original and challenging of all Eliade's books.

Eliade's Concept of Religion: *The Sacred and the Profane*

The Sacred and the Profane (1957) is a short introductory work which makes clear that in seeking to understand religion, the first move we make is probably the most important one. Eliade explains that the historian must step out of modern civilization, which, after all, accounts for only a small and recent fraction of all human beings who have ever lived, and enter the world of "archaic man." Archaic people are those who have lived in prehistoric times or who live today in tribal societies and rural folk cultures, places where work in the world of nature—hunting, fishing, and farming—is the daily routine. What we find everywhere among such peoples is a life lived on two decidedly different planes: that of the sacred and that of the profane. The profane is the realm of the everyday business—of things ordinary, random, and largely unimportant. The sacred is just the opposite. It is the sphere of the supernatural, of things extraordinary, memorable, and momentous. While the profane is vanishing and fragile, full of shadows, the sacred is eternal, full of substance and reality. The profane is the arena of human affairs, which are changeable and often chaotic; the sacred is the sphere of order and perfection, the home of the ancestors, heroes, and gods. Wherever we look among archaic peoples, religion starts from this fundamental separation.[15]

For readers with a good memory, the first impression made by these words is likely to be one of déjà vu. Eliade here seems to be repeating the very thing we heard from Durkheim concerning the sacred and the profane. Nor should that come as a surprise. Eliade was educated in the French intellectual tradition, where, largely because of Durkheim, this way of defining religion came to be widely accepted. A closer look, however, will show that, in fact, there is a difference. As we saw before, when Durkheim speaks of the sacred and profane, he is always thinking of *society* and its needs. The sacred for him is the social—that which matters to the clan; the profane is the opposite—that which matters only to the individual. For Durkheim, sacred symbols and rituals *seem* to speak of the supernatural, but all of that is just the surface appearance of things. The purpose of symbols is simply to make people aware of their social duties by symbolizing the clan as their totem god. When, by contrast, Eliade speaks of the sacred, this clan worship clearly is *not* what he has in mind. In his view, the concern of religion is with the supernatural, plain and simple; it centers on the sacred in and of itself, not on the sacred merely as a way of depicting the social. Though he uses Durkheim's language and agrees that the term covers more than just personal gods, Eliade's view of religion is closer to that of Tylor and Frazer, who conceive of it first and foremost as belief in a realm of supernatural beings.[16]

Instead of Durkheim, Eliade asks us to think of another scholar as his guide: the German theologian and historian of religion Rudolf Otto. In 1916 Otto published on this very subject a famous book entitled *The Idea of the Holy* (in German, *Das Heilige*), where he too uses the concept of the sacred but *not* as applying to society or social needs.[17] He writes instead about a distinct and dramatic kind of individual human experience. At one time or another in their lives, he writes, most people encounter something truly extraordinary and overwhelming. They feel gripped by a reality that is "wholly other" than themselves—something mysterious, awesome, powerful, and beautiful. That is an experience of "the holy," an encounter with the sacred. Using Latin terms, Otto calls it the *mysterium* which is both *tremendum et fascinans*, a mysterious something that both frightens and fascinates at the same time. Another name he gives it is the sense of "the numinous" (from the Latin *numen:* a "spirit" or "divine being"). When people have such an encounter, he says, they invariably feel that they themselves are nothing, no more than "dust and ashes" as the Bible puts it, while the sacred seems just the opposite: something overpoweringly great, substantial, sublime, and truly real. Otto believes this awe-inducing sense of the numinous is unique and irreducible. It is unlike any other encounter with things beautiful or terrible, though they may vaguely resemble it. In this thrilling experience that is unlike any other lies the emotional core of all that we call religion.

It is important to notice that Eliade's concept of the sacred bears a strong resemblance to Otto's. In an encounter with the sacred, he says, people feel in touch with something otherworldly in character; they feel they have brushed against a reality unlike all others they know, a dimension of existence that is alarmingly powerful, strangely different, surpassingly real and enduring.

> For primitives as for the man of all pre-modern societies, the *sacred* is equivalent to a *power,* and in the last analysis, to *reality*. The sacred is saturated with *being*. Sacred power means reality and at the same time enduringness and efficacity. . . . Thus it is easy to understand that religious man deeply desires *to be,* to participate in *reality,* to be saturated with power.[18]

Readers of Judeo-Christian or Muslim background naturally suppose that Eliade is referring here to one personal God, but his idea of the sacred is much wider than that. It could mean the realm of many gods, of the ancestors or immortals, or of what some Hindus call "Brahman," the Supreme Spirit beyond all personality. However the sacred is conceived, the role of religion is to promote encounters with it, to bring a person "out of his worldly Universe or historical situation, and project him into a Universe different in quality, an entirely different world, transcendent and holy."[19] Further, the sense of the sacred is not an occasional thing, found only among certain people or at certain times. In the secular societies of modern Western civilization, people display it in surprising, unconscious ways or through dreams, nostalgias, and works of the imagination. Yet however disguised, suppressed, or obscured, the intuition of the sacred remains a permanent feature of human thought and activity. No human being is without it. When eyes are open to notice it, it can be seen anywhere.

Among archaic peoples, Eliade continues, this idea of the sacred is more than just common; it is regarded as absolutely crucial to their existence, shaping virtually every aspect of their lives. They refer to it even when they think of something so basic as the time of day or the place where they live. When the ancient Greeks thought of their daily routine, they turned naturally to the myth of Phoebus Apollo, the god who each day drove the chariot of the sun across the sky. When they rose at dawn, they assumed that the light would be with them because Phoebus was just then harnessing his horses; they did their work while he traveled, knowing from him how much of the light had passed and how much still remained; and when, at the end of the journey, he rested his horses, they too could sleep and restore their strength for the next day's dawn. While to us such mythological tales are merely entertaining, to archaic peoples they mean a great deal more. They provide the very framework within which they think, the values which they admire, and the models—Eliade sometimes calls them "archetypes"—they choose to follow whenever they act. Such sacred patterns govern all sorts of archaic activity, from the grand and ceremonial to the ordinary and even trivial. In some ancient cultures, which had myths similar to the story of Phoebus, every chariot made for human use had to be built on the model of the chariot driven by the god of the sun. In others, similar rules applied. Among the early peoples in Scandinavia, for example, boats for day-to-day fishing and transport could not be made in just any way; they had to follow a sacred model, that of the ship on which the dead were placed for their funerals.[20] Such rules existed because archaic peoples insisted on the precept that the ways of the gods are best; divine models showed how life ought to be lived.

In *The Sacred and the Profane,* Eliade draws upon numerous examples from a wide range of cultures to show just how seriously such traditional peoples take the business of following the patterns set by the gods. The authority of the sacred controls all. When they set up their villages, for example, archaic clans do not choose just any convenient place to build. A village must be founded at a place where there has been a "hierophany" (from the Greek *hieros* and *phainein:* "sacred appearance"). Once it has been confirmed that this particular place has, in fact, been visited by the sacred, perhaps in the form of a god or ancestor, the location receives a ritual blessing that establishes it as the center point of a "world" (in Greek a *cosmos:* "place of order"). Around this center, the community can then be built in such a way as to show it has a definite divinely ordered structure; it is a sacred system. Because this constructed society extends outward from a ceremonial center point, it stands clearly separate from the disorder of the desert, forest, or open plain that normally surrounds it. Instead of a chaos, the village, built according to the blueprint given by the gods, is a cosmos; in a world of danger and disorder, it is a scene of security and design.

In many cultures, this sacred center is marked with a pole, pillar, or some other vertical object that plunges into the ground and rises up to the sky to join the three great regions of the universe: heaven, earth, and the underworld. That is because this point, which may also be marked by a tree or even a mountain, is regarded not just as the center of the village but as an *axis mundi* (in Latin: "centerpost" and "world"); it is the very axle, the central pillar, around which the whole world is seen to turn. If we remember the stories of the Bible, the tale of Jacob's ladder clearly fits into this pattern. The biblical patriarch Jacob, tired from his travels, chooses to sleep outdoors and lays down a stone as a pillow. During the night, he dreams of a ladder extending from the place where he sleeps all the way to heaven, while angels rise up and come down upon it. When he wakes, he is afraid, for he has here encountered the sacred. "How dreadful is this place!" he says, "This is none but the house of God, and this is the gate of heaven."[21] Significantly, he then sets his nightstone vertical, turning it from pillow to pillar, so that it will mirror the angelic ladder. For Jacob, this special place is the *axis mundi*, the spot where one finds the sacred pole that connects heaven to earth, the holy place where the separate worlds of the sacred and the profane are joined.

In medieval Christianity and early Islam, in ancient Babylon and modern Java, among the Indians of the American Northwest and the villages of Vedic India—almost everywhere we want to look—we find this recurring pattern, says Eliade. Life orients itself around a sacred center, a vertical "symbol of ascent" that links heaven to earth, the sacred to the profane. Around such sacred poles or atop sacred mountains, great temples have always been built. And from them also the surrounding world is divided into its different sectors, usually the four directions of the compass. Just as the universe itself starts from a center and spreads out to four horizons, so, in Bali and parts of Asia, villages must be built at a crossroads, so that they can reflect the four main sectors of the world. In some tribal cultures, the ceremonial house in the village center is supported by four columns, which represent the four main directions, while the roof of the house symbolizes the vault of heaven, and an opening squarely in the center allows prayers to rise, as if along the vertical sacred pole, directly to the gods.[22]

In all of these shapes and ceremonies, which, of course, vary in minor ways from one culture to the next, the role of divine patterns, or models, is plainly evident. Eliade explains that the archaic village, temple, or even house must be an *imago mundi*, a mirror image of the entire world as it was first fashioned by its divine makers. When such places are built, the process of construction is just as important as the structures themselves. Things must not only *be* a reflection of the sacred; they must *come into being* in a sacred manner as well. And that is, again, because human structures and activities must trace out the very process by which the gods brought the world itself into existence. Archaic peoples thus place great significance on "cosmo-

gonic" myths—their stories of how the world first came into being, whether
by divine command or by some struggle in which the gods overcome chaos
and defeat some evil monster. Whenever something new is begun—when a
new temple is built, a child is born, or new phase of life is entered—that
process must be a repetition of the creation, a reenactment of the original
deeds and struggles by which the gods brought the world into being. Eliade
offers a fascinating instance of this imitation of the gods from ancient India,
where, before building a house, an astronomer shows the masons exactly
where they must lay the first stone: "This spot is supposed to lie above the
snake that supports the world. The master mason sharpens a stake and drives
it into the ground . . . in order to fix the snake's head." There the foundation stone is laid, at the point now regarded as the exact center of the world.
The act of piercing the snake is profoundly sacred because it repeats the
very work of the gods Indra and Soma as described in the sacred texts.
These gods were the first to strike the snake, who "symbolizes chaos, the
formless, the unmanifested." By destroying it, they brought into existence
an orderly world, where once there was only a formless confusion.[23] So,
when the home is built, the work must exactly mirror the work of the gods.
Elsewhere, Eliade points to other examples of the same process. In many
myths, for instance, the dragon fills the role played by the snake in India;
he is the great ocean monster, the symbol of watery chaos, who rises from
the dark fluid depths and must be subdued by a hero or a god before an
ordered system of nature, as well as a human civilization, can come into existence.

In Eliade's view, this intense effort to imitate the gods is part of an even
deeper desire that archaic peoples have. They wish not only to mirror the
realm of the sacred but somehow actually to *be in* it, to live among the
gods. A full discussion of this issue must be deferred till we come to *The
Myth of the Eternal Return,* but for the moment we can simply note Eliade's
comment that all archaic peoples have a sense of a "fall," of a great tragic
loss, in human history. By this he does not mean only the fall of humanity
into sin as told in the biblical story of Adam and Eve, who disobeyed the
command of God and were punished accordingly. Archaic people know a
fall in the sense of a profound separation. They feel that from the first moment human beings become aware of their situation in the world, they are
seized by a feeling of absence, a sense of great distance from the place
where they ought to be and truly want to be—the realm of the sacred. Their
most characteristic attitude, in Eliade's words, is a deep "nostalgia for Paradise," a longing to be brought close to the gods, a desire to return to the
realm of the supernatural.

Archaic Religion: Symbol and Myth

It is one thing to sense or seek the realm of the sacred; it is quite another to find and describe it. Although archaic peoples, like any others, attempt to express their longings and beliefs, the very nature of the sacred, which is something utterly different from the profane, would seem to make this impossible. How can one describe that which is "wholly other" than anything in normal experience? The answer, Eliade explains, lies in *indirect* expression: The language of the sacred is to be found in symbols and in myth.

Symbols, we know, are rooted in the principle of likeness, or analogy. Certain things have a quality, a shape, a character that strikes us as similar to something else. In the realm of religious experience, certain things are seen to resemble or suggest the sacred; they give a clue to the supernatural. Myths are also symbolic, but in a slightly more complicated way; they are symbols put into a narrative form. A myth is not just one image or sign; it is a sequence of images put into the shape of a story. It tells a tale of the gods, of the ancestors or heroes, and their world of the supernatural. That seems clear enough. But just what is it that this indirect language actually tells us about the sacred? It is said to be something real, but what kind of reality is it? What are its qualities, its characteristics? These, of course, are questions that Eliade spent most of his life trying to answer in his many studies of symbolism and myth. Our plan, as noted, allows space to examine only the most important of these works, *Patterns in Comparative Religion,* which was first published in 1949, while Eliade was working in France.[24]

Patterns is a book designed to explain and explore religious symbols on a very wide scale. It examines the nature of symbolic thinking, showing what symbols are, how they work, and why archaic peoples, especially, make use of them. It also shows, with the help of many examples, just how systems of symbol and myth tend to follow certain constant, recurring patterns throughout the world. Eliade contends that regardless of what locations we choose or where we turn in history, certain common symbols, myths, and rituals keep turning up over and over again.

Now if we wish to see how symbols work, says Eliade, the first thing to notice is that just about anything can be one. Most of the things that make up ordinary life are profane; they are just themselves, nothing more. But at the right moment anything profane can be transformed into something more than itself—a marker or sign of that which is not profane, but sacred.[25] A tool, an animal, a river, a raging fire, a star or stone, a cave, a blossoming flower, or a human being—anything can become a sign of the sacred if people so discover or decide. Once recognized as such, moreover, all symbolic objects acquire a double character: though in one sense they remain what they always were, they also become something new, something other than themselves. In their shrine called the Kaaba, for example, Muslims revere a sacred black stone. Though on one level that object remains to this day just a stone, no faithful follower of Muhammad would ever recognize it as that. From the instant of hierophany—from the moment, that is, when Muslims saw it as something touched by the sacred—this profane object was transformed; it became no longer a mere stone but a holy object, an imposing package, we might say, that carries the sacred within. Eliade calls this infusion of the supernatural into natural objects the "dialectic of the sacred." Though concrete, limited in shape, and perhaps even movable from place to place, a sacred stone can—through another of its qualities, its solidity—convey to the eyes of a believer features of the sacred that are precisely the opposite of its limitations; it can suggest, as the sacred stone of the Kaaba does for Muslims, a God who is immovable and beyond change, the almighty, infinite, and absolute Creator of the world. In common logic, of course, such a combination of opposites strikes us as irrational. If the profane is truly opposed to the sacred, how can it *become* its precise opposite? How can the natural also be the supernatural? It can do so, says Eliade, because in such matters human reason is not in charge of the transaction.[26] Symbol and myth make their appeal to the imagination, which often thrives on the idea of contradiction. They grip the complete person, the emotions, the will, and even subconscious aspects of personality. And just as in the personality all sorts of colliding impulses are joined, just as in dreams and fantasies all sorts of illogical things can happen, so in religious experience opposites like the sacred and profane do converge. In an intuitive burst of discovery, the religious imagination sees things otherwise ordinary and profane as more than themselves and turns them into the sacred. The natural becomes supernatural.

It is interesting to notice that, like Max Müller, Eliade finds the main supplier of materials for symbolism and myth to be the world of nature. To the archaic mind, the physical world is a veritable storehouse of prospective images, clues, signs, and analogies. All that we see in the world is part of a grand framework which the gods brought into existence at the beginning of time, and everywhere in it, the sacred waits to shine through. In all of its beauty and ferocity, its complexity, mystery, and variety, the natural world is continually opening windows to disclose the different aspects of the supernatural—what Eliade calls "the modalities of the sacred." This, by the way, is what makes traditional cultures so rich in imaginative figures and symbols and their world so wonderfully alive with folklore and legend, with creation accounts, flood stories, and epic tales of heroes, monsters, and gods. As collections of symbols put in narrative form, all of these can be broadly associated with myth. They are tales of the sacred, stories that bring the supernatural world of divine life closer to the natural world of humanity.

Over the centuries, of course, human beings have generated countless new myths, symbols, and variations of both. No scholar could hope to find them all. Nor is it necessary to try. Eliade thinks a great deal can be learned just from the major symbolic patterns and systems, which are the only ones he chooses to trace out in detail. It will repay our effort to notice a few of them.

Sky Symbolism: Sky Gods and Others

One of the most common elements of archaic cultures is belief in sky gods, divinities whose character is suggested by the very nature of the wide heaven above the earth. The sky conveys a sense of transcendence, of a span raised high above us, something infinite, sovereign, and eternal—full of authority and reality. Fittingly, the sky god is often imagined in just this fashion. Like the god Iho among the Maoris, he is "raised up"; like Olorun among the African Yoruba tribes, he is "owner of the sky"; like the great god Ahura-Mazda in early Iran, he is the giver of all laws and enforcer of moral order in the world.[27] Because the heavens are high, these gods are, in fact, often portrayed as almost too elevated and distant, too far away to care about mere human beings. Australian myths tell the story of the withdrawal of the sky god, while in other primitive societies as well, the god of the sky seems so far beyond human reach that other religious conceptions must come in to replace him.[28] Often these new conceptions are gods of the rain and storm, deities who are more concrete and personal, more directly involved in human life because they specialize in one task. Here the early Hindu god Rudra is an example. Virile and violent, surging with life, he was for the villagers of ancient India the bringer of rain as well as the source of sexual energy. He and others like him had female partners or entered sacred marriages; they stood at the center of lavish ceremonies, which often included bloody sacrifices and orgies. Their imagery was powerful and their influence extremely widespread. In fact, says Eliade, in words that remind us of Frazer, "this structure made up of the rainy sky, bull, and Great Goddess was one of the elements that united all the protohistoric religions of Europe."[29]

It is not hard to guess why such a change from sky to storm gods may have taken place. Eliade explains that the appeal of rain and fertility gods was closely linked to one of the most important events in all of early civilization—the discovery of agriculture. Plowing the soil, planting seeds, and harvesting crops—all of these brought a new pattern of life, and with it an occasion for new hierophanies and different kinds of symbols. In an agrarian world, the great "fecundators," gods of storm and sex, conveyed the sacred with greater power and more vivid appearance than the distant god of the sky.[30]

"Son" gods, like Dionysos in Greece and Osiris in Egypt, also made their appearance in the age of agriculture. Like storm gods, they were dynamic, but not in quite the same way. Their role was rather to suffer and die. The so-called mystery religions, which were enormously popular in the ancient Mediterranean world, centered especially on these deities, which in name were vegetation gods but figured more prominently as dramatic, divine saviors. In these gods especially, Eliade discerns an important psychological aspect of religious symbols. They not only tell us about the world and the sacred but also show "the continuity between the structures of human existence and cosmic structures."[31] Their myths do not just reflect the cycles of life and death in nature; they reenact as well the great personal struggle that takes place in the life of each human individual: the drama of birth, life, and death as well as the hope of rebirth or redemption. No symbol, says Eliade, manages to bring divine life so near to human as the figure of the savior-god, the divinity who "even shared mankind's sufferings, died and rose from the dead to redeem them." Precisely because of his marked "humanity," this type of god plays a crucial role in the history of religion.[32]

Sun and Moon

Eliade points out that sun worship, which some earlier theorists (especially Max Müller) thought the center of all mythology, is in fact very rare.[33] Much more prominent and widespread are myths and symbols associated with the ever-changing moon. The moon, of course, moves through cycles; it grows, becomes full, and for a time completely disappears. Its phases connect readily to other events, such as the ebb and flow of the ocean tides, the coming and going of the rains, and, through these, to the growth of plants and the fertility of the earth. Since it always returns to its beginnings, the moon furnishes the archetypal image of ceaseless renewal. Eliade states that its dominant theme is "one of *rhythm* carried out by a succession of contraries, of 'becoming' through a succession of opposing modalities. It is a becoming . . . that cannot take place without drama."[34]

Lunar symbolism also shows a remarkable power of expansion; it keeps reaching out to make new connections. Besides waters and vegetation, the moon is often linked to death, the last phase of life; to the snake, which regenerates itself by shedding its skin; and to woman, whose power to renew life by giving birth arises from the "lunar" phases of the menstrual cycle. In fact, "the intuition of the moon as the measure of rhythms, as the source of energy, of life, and of rebirth, has woven a sort of web between the various levels of the universe, producing parallels, similarities, and unities among vastly differing kinds of phenomena."[35] Because of a long linkage that takes the form moon-rain-fertility-woman-serpent-death-periodic regeneration, a person can tap into the lunar network at any one of its points. A simple rain ritual, for instance, or a serpent charm worn on the wrist, can engage this entire system of cosmic associations, all of which play upon the fundamental theme of opposites that alternate and converge.

Like the "son" gods, the moon has both a cosmic and a personal dimen- sion. On the one level, it is treasured "in what it reveals of the sacred, that is, in the power centred in it, in the inexhaustible life and reality that it manifests."[36] On the other, it reminds us psychologically of the double na- ture of our human condition: rooted in the realm of the profane, the place of shadows and death, we nonetheless long for the sacred, the sphere of those things real and undying. In earlier ages, amid disease and death, the hopes of archaic peoples for their own personal renewal and immortality "gained confirmation from the fact of there being always a new moon."[37] The moon is in one sense a display of dualisms: light and dark, full and empty, old and new, birth and death, male and female. Yet by its alterna- tions and changes, it also suggests the *overcoming* of all dualisms, a key theme also in many symbolisms of the sacred. Eliade here points to myths of androgyny, which suggest that the first human beings, who lived close to the gods, were neither male nor female but a unity of both sexes.[38] This theme, moreover, is just one in a whole family of myths of reintegration. Common throughout the human race, these stories express a powerful hope for the end of all opposites, the dissolution of all separations, the return to the original unity of the sacred.[39]

Water and Stones

In addition to great symbols like those of the sky and moon, the world of archaic peoples is rich as well in lesser signs and images, which often link up with the more dominant ones. Water, for example, everywhere expresses the shapeless, unformed nature of things *before* they were ordered into a world by the gods. It starts the process of renewal. Neither the world nor the human self can be reborn until each has first returned to chaos by plung- ing into the watery depths, thence to emerge as a new creation.[40] In ritual initiations and in most rites of purification, water is the agent that cleanses and erases all, taking us back to the unformed, the primeval, the "clean slate," where a new beginning can be made.

The symbolism of stones, by contrast, suggests the opposite. Unlike water, the substance of stones is hard, rugged, and unchanging. To the primitive person, "rock shows . . . something that transcends the precariousness of his humanity; an absolute mode of being. Its strength, its motionlessness, its size . . . indicate the presence of something that fascinates, terrifies, attracts, and threatens, all at once."[41] If we put these words into the Latin *fascinans* and *tremendum,* we actually have here Otto's very words for the sacred. A normal stone would hardly attract our notice; a sacred stone generates awe and fear.

Other Symbols: Earth and Fertility; Vegetation and Agriculture

The symbolisms of life, growth, and fertility have played a very large role in the religion of archaic peoples, both before and after the dawn of agriculture. Of the many patterns Eliade considers at length in this category, we can notice just a few.

A very early image is that of the earth as sacred mother, the source of all living things. The sacred marriage of the divine sky father and earth mother is found in many mythologies, from the South Pacific to Africa, the Mediterranean, and the Americas. The sky fertilizes the earth with rain, and the earth produces grains and grass.[42] With the coming of agriculture and closer human involvement in cultivation of plants and grains, the earlier symbol of the earth as mother is often overlaid by that of the great goddess—once again, a more dynamic, emotional divinity who, like the "son" gods considered above, personally lives out the fate of the crops in her own life cycle of birth, sexual encounter, fertility, and death.[43]

More widespread than that of either the earth mother or the goddess, however, is the symbolism of trees. Sacred trees can be found "in the history of every religion, in popular tradition the world over, in primitive metaphysics and mysticism, to say nothing of iconography and popular art."[44] Some, like the cosmic tree Yggdrasil in Norse mythology, combine the symbolism of the *axis mundi,* the world's centerpost, with a second theme, the tree as the sacred source of life. As great vertical objects that are also alive, such trees represent "the very life of the entire world as it endlessly renews itself." Further, since trees live a long time, the life within them is considered inexhaustible; they become a focus of human hopes for immortality.[45] Frazer, we should remember, found the soul, the source of life, to be closely associated with both the mistletoe and tree worship in northern Europe. And in the many ancient myths of a tree of life, we read of a hero who must pass a test, much as Adam and Eve faced and failed the divine test of the fruit of the forbidden tree in the Garden of Eden. By defeating a dragon or resisting temptation, the great man wins the prize of immortality. Trees tell us that the sacred is the fount of all life, the one true reality, and to those who can pass the test, the giver of immortality.

Eliade reminds us that, to appreciate vegetation myths, we must recall how primitive people lived in ongoing fear that at some point the powers of the natural world would weaken and begin to run out.[46] For the archaic mind, all things—whether plant, animal, or human—are energized through "the same closed circuit of the substance of life," which passes from one level or creature to another.[47] When planted, the grains that die at harvest give their life to the next year's crop. When harvested, ground into flour, and baked, they transfer their life to humanity, for they then become the force of life in the bread that is eaten at meals. This tight connection shows why, in so many legends, we read of a murdered human being who is changed into a tree, or of plants that spring directly from the blood of a slain god or hero.[48] When the power of life leaves one living thing, it must move to another; when it runs down, it must be recharged. Always there is an ebb and flow, a fading and renewal. For archaic peoples, "the *real* is not only what *is* indefinitely the same, but also what *becomes* in organic but cyclic forms."[49] The sacred is not only durable like a stone; it is charged with life, like a plant. It is a power that perpetually renews things, not only in physical terms, as food renews the body, but spiritually as well. The personal, human message of vegetation symbolism is the promise of life eternal. As a plant is reborn after it dies, so a woman or man may be one day redeemed from death and reborn to immortality.[50] From this, Eliade notes, we can also see the importance of ritual activity in coming into contact with the sacred. Rites of initiation, purification, and redemption are activities which, by their very gestures and procedures, recreate the great origin of all renewals, the creation of the world itself, as it arises out of chaos and is given its form through the powerful commands or mighty struggles of the gods.

The Structure and Character of Symbols

From fertility and vegetation Eliade turns next to the symbolisms of space and of time. The first of these we have already noted above, and the second will come our way shortly. So we can pass over them here to observe something else. Though most of the discussion in *Patterns* is taken up with individual symbols and myths from around the world, Eliade takes time along the way to consider two broad features of all symbolic thinking. One is the structural, or systemlike, character of most symbolism and mythology; the other is the matter of ranking symbols—placing some above others in value.

Throughout his discussion, Eliade explains that symbols and myths rarely exist in isolation. It is their nature always to be part of larger symbol systems; they "connect up" with other images, or other myths, to form a pattern. The thought world of archaic peoples is thus filled with associations, linkages, and repetitions that keep extending the sense of the sacred, if possible, to almost every dimension of life—from the noblest occasions and ceremonies to the simplest daily task. A pair of examples may help to illustrate this process. In a first appearance of the sacred—an original hierophany—a religious person finds, let us say, a vision of the one true God in the sun, as did the Egyptian Pharaoh Akhenaton. (Freud, we may recall, thought Akhenaton was the religious genius who inspired Jewish monotheism.) Soon the round solar disk is declared the symbol of the divine. It is carved into walls, worn as jewelry, and required on flags at palace ceremonies. These gestures naturally expand the occasions for thinking about the sun; they "sacralize" places, people, and events quite beyond the occasion or place of the first sacred encounter.[51] In time, still more connections may be made. The sun is personified, and the stories of the sun and its adventures come to expression in myth. Akhenaton or his followers may claim that because it "defeats" the night, the sun is the lord of battle; or they may see in each morning's sunrise a sign of personal renewal and immortality. Because of its warmth, the sun can be tied to the return of vegetation each spring; it can be connected with plants, like the sunflower, or substances, like gold, that resemble its shape or possess its color. With each of these new connections, the sacred reaches out to capture a new aspect of life.[52]

Another vivid example of this systematic extension is the cycle of lunar myths and symbols noted above. From its center in the phases of the moon, this symbolic system continually spreads out its net to convey a sense of the sacred to many other dimensions of life: the waters and rains, fertility and woman, serpents and human redemption, even shells and spirals and bolts of lightning. There may be no formal rule of logic that compels people to connect lunar phases with spiral shells; yet intuitively and imaginatively, there is a plain "logic of symbols" that makes the connections. Symbols always lead naturally to other symbols and to myths in such a way as to create a framework, a world that is a complete, connected system, rather than a chaotic jumble.

In addition to noticing their systemic character, a second general issue Eliade alludes to is that of comparing symbols and myths. Are some symbols perhaps better in character than others? Can we rank myths on a scale of value? And if so, what standard would we use? In *Patterns*, Eliade does not address these questions as directly as one would like, but it is plain that he does, in fact, feel some images and myths to be superior to others.[53] The main standard he applies seems to be that of their scale or size. The "bigger" the symbol, the more complete and universal it is, the better it conveys the true nature of the sacred. Here again, a specific example may help. If the people of a primitive village encounter something supernatural in a nearby tree, that can be called a hierophany; the tree manifests the sacred. If, in the course of time, however, the council of elders should rethink this symbolism and decide that this sacred tree is in fact the cosmic tree, the center of the world, that too is a hierophany, but of a higher order. It is a better representation of the sacred because it is wider in extent, grander in scale than the original sacred tree. By means of the elders' decision, then, the first sighting of the sacred in the local tree is "revalorized" (as Eliade likes to say) into a far more impressive image of the sacred than it originally was. The new symbolism of the world tree surpasses the old symbol of the simple village hierophany.

Again, one type of hierophany is a *theo*phany (from the Greek *theos,* "deity"): the appearance of a god. A theophany can occur in something as simple as a stone. At the same time, drawing on his own tradition of Romanian Orthodoxy, Eliade points out that Christianity finds God to be incarnate in the man Jesus of Nazareth. This human theophany is superior to the stone theophany, not—as missionaries once would have said—because Christianity is true and other religions false, but because a human person, possessing intelligence and emotions, is by nature a richer, fuller being than an animal or stone. Thus, as a symbol, the figure of Christ, the God-man, captures more of the fullness and reality of the sacred. In addition, Christians make universal claims about the incarnation; they say that never has there been or will there be a theophany as final or as world-embracing. Christ is to other theophanies as the great cosmic tree is to the village tree—a wider, grander, and consequently better image of the divine. As the human form of the all-powerful Creator, he better conveys the full extent of the sacred than, say, the Greek god Pan, who is pictured only as god of the pastures and forests.

These concepts of replacement and "revalorization" of symbols play an important role in Eliade's theory. They show that he is interested in examining not just the timeless forms of religion but also their historical changes. In his view, human beings throughout time have been continually at work restating their perceptions of the sacred in original ways, fashioning new myths, discovering fresh symbols, and rearranging them into wider or different systems. Accordingly, the mission of the "history" of religions is first to discover symbols, myths, rituals, and their systems, then to trace them through the human past as they have been changed and interchanged from one age or place to the next. After that—and just as importantly—the more phenomenological side enters in. The historian seeks to compare and contrast these materials to determine their different levels and types of significance as carriers of the sacred. And he observes how, in different ages and places, symbols, myths, and rituals are perpetually subject to change. Through history, they are constantly being created, revised, discarded, and created again. Were he an evolutionary thinker, we might find Eliade claiming that all these changes are improvements, that each new myth or symbol is progressively better than the last. But this is not really his view. He believes the natural logic of symbols and myths pushes them always to become more universal, to shed the particulars of a single time and place and approximate ever more closely to a universal archetype, as when a local goddess acquires more and more of the features of the archetypal great goddess of fertility. But in the actual circumstances of human experience, symbols decay and degenerate as well. History presents occasions when cultures move counter to the logic of the sacred—say, by losing or corrupting a great world creation myth or by replacing more universal symbols with *less* universal ones, as when the smaller storm god replaces the earlier sovereign sky god. When that happens, certain new dimensions of the sacred may be discovered, but others are lost. Then again, while that is happening in one culture, in another located elsewhere the figure of the sky god might reappear.[54] The natural tendency of symbols and myths is to grow, to spread out their significance in new associations; but in different times and places there are also variations that "flow simply from differences in the mythological creativity of the various societies, or even from a chance of history."[55]

Throughout the ages, then, archaic and other peoples have enjoyed a certain freedom of imagination in selecting sacred symbols and myths. Eliade notes that there seems scarcely a single natural object that has not at some time or other become a symbol or figured in a myth. And yet, for all of this creativity, religious imagery has never been purely random or chaotic. The point of *Patterns* is to show just the opposite: that regardless of place, time, or culture, archaic peoples have shown a remarkable constancy in returning to the same types of symbol, the same themes in their myths, and the same universalizing logic in both. The closer we look at the historical specifics of religion, the more clearly we see its ever-recurring, ever-expanding patterns.

History and Sacred Time

It should be clear from all of this that to the scholar inquiring about the symbolism of the sacred, the human historical record is of key importance. It shows us how different people have recognized the sacred through, say, a holy mountain in China or a holy river like the Ganges in India. Archaic believers themselves, however, find their circumstance in history to be quite another matter. For them, the events of ordinary profane life, the daily round of labor and struggle, are things they desperately wish to escape. They would rather be *out* of history and in the perfect realm of the sacred. Eliade's term for this desire, as we noted earlier, is the "nostalgia for Paradise." It is a concept central to his theory. Though he refers to it in many places, he explains it best in the third of the three texts we have taken as our guides. This is *The Myth of the Eternal Return: Or, Cosmos and History,* which he first published along with *Patterns* in 1949.

Eliade considered this book one of his most significant, and even his critics have tended to agree.[56] In it, he sets out a strong thesis: that the one theme which dominates the thought of all archaic peoples is the drive to abolish history—all of history—and return to that point beyond time when the world began. The desire to go back to beginnings, he argues, is the deepest longing, the most insistent and heartfelt ache in the soul of all archaic peoples. A constant theme of archaic ritual and myth is the wish "to live in the world as it came from the Creator's hands, fresh, pure, and strong."[57] This is why, as we noted earlier, myths of creation play such a central role in so many archaic societies. It is also why so many rituals are associated with acts of creation. We have not said much about rituals so far, but Eliade does find them important, especially in association with creation accounts. Usually they involve a reenactment of what the gods did *in illo tempore* (Latin for "in that time") at the moment when the world came into being. Every New Year's festival, every myth of rebirth or reintegration, every rite of initiation is a return to beginnings, an opportunity to start the world over again. When, in archaic festivals of the New Year, a scapegoat is sent out and purifications are done to rid the community of demons, diseases, and sins, this is not just a rite of transit from one year to the next but "also the abolition of the past year and of past time." It is an attempt "to restore—if only momentarily—mythical and primordial time, 'pure' time, the time of the 'instant' of the Creation."[58] In India, coronations follow patterns set at the beginning of the world.[59] And in sacrifices as well, "there is an implicit abolition of profane time, of duration, of 'history.' "[60]

Eliade thinks it important to notice the motives that inspire this myth of return. He explains that archaic peoples, like all others, are deeply affected not only by the mysteries of suffering and death but also by concerns about living without any purpose or meaning. They long for significance, permanence, beauty, and perfection as well as escape from their sorrows. Life's minor irritations and inconveniences are not the problem; they can be borne by anyone. But the idea that the human adventure as a whole might be merely a pointless exercise, an empty spectacle with death as its end—that is a prospect no archaic people can endure. Eliade calls this experience "the terror of history," and it explains why people have been drawn so powerfully to myth, especially the myth of eternal return. Because ordinary life is not significant, because real meaning can never be found *within* history, archaic peoples choose instead to take their stand *outside* of it. In the face of life's drab, empty routine and daily irritations, they seek to overcome all in a defiant gesture of denial; through symbol and myth, they reach back to the world's primal state of perfection, to a moment when life starts over from its origin, full of promise and hope. "The primitive, by conferring a cyclic direction upon time, annuls its irreversibility. Everything begins over again at its commencement every instant."[61]

This "terror of history" was felt not only by archaic peoples but also by the great civilizations of the ancient world, where a cyclical view of time was predominant. In India, for example, the oldest teachings held that human beings were destined to live without hope in a world that passed through immense cycles of decay and decline until it was finally destroyed and again remade. The reaction to this deeply pessimistic view eventually came in the form of the classic Eastern version of eternal return—the doctrine of rebirth, or reincarnation. We find it chiefly in the famous Hindu Upanishads as well as in the teachings of Gautama the Buddha and Mahavira, the founder of Jainism. Seeing humanity as hopelessly enslaved by these endless cycles of nature, these teachers insisted that a path could be found to a purely spiritual release from history's triviality and terrors.[62] They announced that the soul, or true self, could free itself from the body, which is its main tie to history, by struggling patiently through a long series of rebirths until finally a purely spiritual escape was achieved. In different ways, all offered meaning through the doctrine of *moksha,* the soul's final release from nature and history. Elsewhere, the doctrine of return appeared in other forms. Among certain Greeks and the followers of the great prophet Zoroaster in ancient Persia, it was expressed in the belief that human history consists only of a single cycle, which has come out of eternity and will one day end forever in fire or some other great catastrophe.[63] Against this backdrop of finality, Zoroaster's followers found liberation by way of the last judgment and the reward of Heaven that came to all who had remained faithful to Ahura-Mazda, the great god of goodness and light. The pattern of these religions is thus quite clear. Though culturally more advanced than archaic peoples, the great civilizations of the Mediterranean and Near East, no less than those of India and Southeast Asia, faced the very same problem of history and labored just as strenuously to chart a path of escape.

The Revolt Against Archaic Religion: Judaism and Christianity

Almost everywhere in archaic and civilized ancient cultures, then, the problem of history was central, and the solution, the escape, was found in some form of the myth of eternal return. The pattern is so widespread, says Eliade, that only in one place—among the Hebrews of ancient Palestine—can something different be found. It is in ancient Israel that, for the first time on the world scene, a new religious outlook makes its appearance. While not entirely rejecting the idea of a mythical return to beginnings, Judaism proclaims that the sacred can be found *in* history as well as outside of it. With this, the whole equation of archaic religion is significantly altered. In Judaism, and later in Christianity, which derives from it, the idea of the meaningless cycles of nature is pushed into the background, while human events come to center stage, where they take shape along the line of a meaningful story—a history—with the sacred, in the form of the God of Israel, a participant in its scenes. In place of endless, pointless world cycles, Judaism asserts a meaningful sequence of sacred historical events. This striking innovation was fashioned chiefly by the great prophets of Israel—Amos, Isaiah, Jeremiah, and others. When disasters fell on their people, they presented these troubles not as miseries to be escaped but as punishments to be endured—*in* history—because they came from the very hand of God. In their oracles and speeches, says Eliade, the prophets affirmed the idea

> that historical events have a value in themselves, insofar as they are determined by the will of God. This God of the Jewish people is no longer an Oriental divinity, creator of archetypal gestures, but a personality who ceaselessly intervenes in history, who reveals his will through events (invasions, sieges, battles, and so on). Historical facts thus become "situations" of man in respect to God, and as such they acquire a religious value that nothing had previously been able to confer upon them.[64]

That the encounter of a people with this personal God of history is something quite new can be seen also from the famous biblical story of the patriarch Abraham, who prepares to kill his son as an offering to God. If Judaism were an archaic religion, says Eliade, this fearsome act would be an instance of human sacrifice, a killing of the firstborn to renew the sacred power of life in the gods. Within Judaism, however, the event has a quite different character. Abraham's encounter is a very personal transaction in history with a God who asks him for his son simply as a sign of his faith. This God does not need sacrifices to renew his divine powers (and indeed he does spare Isaac, the son), but what he does require from his people is a heart loyal enough to make that ultimate sacrifice if asked.[65] Christianity inherits this same perspective. The sequence of events that make up the life and death of Jesus forms a singular and historic instance, a decisive moment which, occurring once only, serves as the basis for a personal relationship of forgiveness and trust between Christian believers and their God. In celebrating the life, crucifixion, and resurrection of Christ, the Christian faithful do not engage in a ritual of seasonal rebirth; they do not act out an eternal return to beginnings. They remember a specific and final historical event, one that requires from them an equally singular and final decision of personal faith.

Of course, this new historical religion did not win an instant victory over the older, archaic attitudes, which are deeply rooted in human psychology. The tremendous attraction that fertility religions like the cult of Baal had for ordinary people in ancient Israel is proof of this in the case of Judaism. In Christian cultures also, archaic seasonal ceremonies of rebirth do survive and blend in with the more purely historical elements. And both traditions have been routinely susceptible to messianic movements. These passionate groups, which expect a return of God's chosen one, a catastrophe at the world's end, and the coming of a perfect world, bear again the marks of the archaic mind; they tolerate history, but only because they believe "that, one day or another, it will cease."[66] In consequence, both sides of the Judeo-Christian tradition have unfolded amid some considerable tension and compromise. They have found the sacred both within history and outside of it.

The Revolt Against All Religion: Modern Historicism

The Judeo-Christian turn to historical religion is for Eliade an event of momentous importance. It marks the beginning of a shift away from archaic attitudes, a first revolt against the myth of eternal return. Yet it is not the world's only great religious transformation. A second revolution, one of equal or even greater proportions, has only recently begun to take shape right in the very center of Western civilization, especially modern Europe and America. Over the last few centuries, Eliade explains, we have once again seen something quite new in human history: the wide acceptance of philosophies that deny the existence and value of the sacred altogether. Advocates of these views claim that it makes no difference where one wants to find the sacred, whether in history or beyond it, for the simple reason that human beings do not need it. The truth, they say, is that there are no gods, there are no "sacred archetypes," which can show us how to live or what ultimate purpose to live for.[67] We must now live without the sacred altogether.

We can put aside for a moment the question of whether this modern, totally unsacred view of the world is good or bad. Eliade's first concern is to show where it came from. He thinks, interestingly, that the door to this second revolution was in fact opened by the very same shift of ideas that created the first: the coming of Judeo-Christian historical religion. This seems puzzling at first sight, but for Eliade the sequence is clear. It comes into focus the moment we place everything within the original context of archaic religion and the myth of eternal return. We must remember, he tells us, that to the first archaic peoples, the world of nature was of pivotal importance. It was able at any instant to come alive with the sacred. Symbolism clothed it in the supernatural; legend and myth sang of the gods behind the storm and rain. Clues and hints of the sacred could be found in a tree, a stone, or the path of a bird in flight. Nature was the garment of the divine. This was not to be the case, however, in Judaism and Christianity. The prophets of Israel and writers of the New Testament pushed nature into the background and brought history up to the front of the stage. The seasons, storms, and trees were "desacralized," for the God of Israel and of Christian faith chose to show himself chiefly in the twists and turns of dramatic *human* events—in the Hebrews' escape from Pharaoh, in the battle of Jericho, or in the birth, death, and resurrection of Jesus Christ. In this new perspective nature still had a part to play, but only in a supporting role. Israel's prophets still saw the great wind that parted the Red Sea as a sign of the sacred, but—in the light of their historical perspective—they read it quite differently. For them it disclosed the divine not because it was a wondrous natural event—as archaic peoples would have said—but because it contributed to God's purposes. It delivered his people from the hands of their enemies.

As Eliade sees it, this change of religious sensibility is a significant one, not only on its own terms, but because of the momentous consequences that follow from it. For gradually, and almost imperceptibly, this original move from religions of nature to religions of history laid the groundwork, in the present era, for a further shift—from the newer religions of history to philosophies of history and society that discard religion altogether. Through the long passage of centuries, and especially in Western civilization, the removal of the divine from nature has slowly opened the way for entire societies to adopt a style of thought that only a few isolated individuals ever seriously considered until the coming of the modern era. That style is secularity: the removal of *all* reference to the sacred from human thought and action. Eliade explains that the logic behind this move away from religion is simple enough. Secular thinkers can argue as follows: If biblical religions like Judaism and Christianity made one great change in the world's religious consciousness, does that not license us to make another if we should so wish? If the prophets felt they had a right to take the sacred out of nature and find it only in history, why can we not follow their own example and dismiss it from nature and history alike? In short, why can we not remove it from human affairs completely? This, in essence, is the reasoning at work in nearly all of the secular, nonreligious philosophies that have come upon the world with such powerful appeal during the last three centuries of modern times. We might call them the unwelcome stepchildren of Judaism and Christianity.

Eliade describes these secular creeds as forms of "historicism," a type of thought that recognizes only things ordinary and profane while denying any reference at all to things supernatural and sacred. Historicists hold that if we want significance, if we want some sense of a larger purpose in life, we obviously cannot find it in the archaic way—by escaping history through some eternal return. But neither can we find it in the Judeo-Christian way— by claiming that there is in history some great plan or purpose of God. We can find it only in ourselves.

Examples of this historicist thinking can be found in any number of modern systems and thinkers, among them several we have already met in our chapters. Eliade notes the developmentalism of the German philosopher Hegel, the communism of Karl Marx, and the perspectives of twentieth-century fascism and existentialism. Modern capitalism might be included as well. What all of these systems share is the fundamental belief that if human beings want meaning and significance in their lives, they must create it entirely on their own—in the profane realm of history and without assistance from the realm of the sacred. This can be done in different ways, of course. Fascists and Marxists believe that even without gods or the sacred, history is still "going somewhere." It will end in the triumph of a nation or race, or in the victory of the proletariat. Existentialists tend to think that history as a whole has no central purpose; it is "going nowhere," so only the private lives and choices of individuals matter. The capitalist entrepreneur may make a similar choice by finding purpose only in money and other material goods. For such people, only personal freedom or achievement matters, and they can even argue that they are better off than archaic peoples, who do not have freedom because their lives must always conform to patterns provided by the gods.

In the contemporary world, these nonreligious philosophies have been extremely attractive, winning followers not only in Western civilization but around the world. Eliade, however, has serious doubts about all of them. Is it really the case, he asks, that they offer a greater degree of meaning than archaic religion or Judeo-Christian faith? Is the modern fascist, who must obey every command of his leader, really more free than the archaic woman, performing her household ritual of renewal? Does the life of the communist, bound absolutely to the cause of the party, really have more significance than that of the archaic tribesman or medieval Christian? Is the existentialist philosopher, whose prized individual freedom could be destroyed in a moment if a brutal army were to march into the streets, truly more content and fulfilled than the archaic villager who celebrates the seasonal feast of fertility, hoping thereby to bring life to his crops each spring?[68]

The Return of Archaic Religion

Despite his misgivings, Eliade does not carry on an extended argument with these modern philosophies. He merely voices his doubts as to whether they can ever be truly satisfying to the human personality. And he tries, by contrast, to show how, in hidden ways, archaic thinking has persisted right up to the present day. He notes, for example, that creative artists like T. S. Eliot and James Joyce display in their works a remarkable attachment to forms of the myth of eternal return.[69] Athletic events, the great public spectacles of our time, show similar affinities; they generate intense emotions and center on a single "concentrated" game time, very much like the sacred moments of primitive ritual. The dramas of theater, television, and film play out life in a compressed interval of "sacred" time that is wholly different from normal hours and days.[70] The images and stories of popular culture resemble archaic myths, creating character archetypes on which ordinary people pattern their lives: "the political or the military hero, the hapless lover; or the cynic, the nihilist, the melancholy poet." These and others play for us the same roles filled for archaic people by the heroes and gods of myth.[71] Even the modern habit of reading can be seen as a replacement for the oral traditions remembered and recited by primitive peoples; it mirrors the archaic desire to create an "escape time," free from the pressures of daily life.[72]

Finally and quite apart from its disguised modern versions, Eliade observes that even in its original form, the archaic nostalgia for paradise has never fully disappeared. Christianity, we have seen, is committed to finding the sacred only in history. Yet among the Christian peasants of Romania and other central European lands, one finds a remarkable blend in which archaic habits of mind virtually sweep aside the residue of history in the church's creeds. In this "cosmic Christianity," it is accepted that Jesus of Nazareth was a man in history, but that fact virtually disappears from view once it is taken up into the peasants' image of Christ as the great lord of nature, the eternal divinity who, in sacred folklore, continues to visit his people on the earth, just as the high god does in the myths of other archaic cultures. Significantly, the liturgies and ceremonies of this cosmic Christianity tend to celebrate not the historical Jesus, but the eternal Christ who renews the powers of nature and returns humanity to the time of beginnings. To its followers, this archaic faith offers a depth of meaning that the historical perspective inherited from Judaism can never provide.[73]

It is worth noticing that this cosmic Christianity with which Eliade concludes *The Eternal Return* bears a marked resemblance to the peasant religion he found so strongly appealing when he first encountered it in the villages of India as a young man. He is always careful not to make any open endorsements, but it seems clear that in the end his own strong sympathies lie nearest to this sort of cosmic folk religion and the satisfactions offered by the archaic frame of mind.

Analysis

Mircea Eliade follows a program of inquiry very different from the reductionist strategies we have observed, and it allows him to form a theory of religion that stands in distinct opposition to them. Among its main elements, at least three call for particular attention.

1. Critique of Reductionism

From the outset Eliade announces his strong dissent from the reductionist approaches favored in his day and still attractive in ours. In opposition to Freud, Durkheim, and Marx, he strongly asserts the independence of religious ideas and activities. He accepts that psychology, society, economics, and other forces have their effects on religion, but he refuses to see their influence as determining or even dominant. Religion, he insists, can be understood only if we try to see it from the standpoint of the believer. Like

Roman law, which we can grasp only through Roman values, or Egyptian architecture, which we must see through Egyptian eyes, religious behaviors, ideas, and institutions must be seen in the light of the religious perspective, the view of the sacred, that inspires them. In the case of archaic peoples especially, it is clearly not profane life—social, economic, or otherwise— that controls the sacred; it is the sacred that controls and shapes every aspect of the profane.

2. Global Comparativism

Another main feature of Eliade's theory is its broad and ambitious design. He is, of course, not the only theorist to try to assemble data from a wide variety of sources, places, and times, but he is certainly more ambitious in this regard than most. He takes very seriously his double mission to be both a good historian and a good phenomenologist, and he strives for a genuinely comprehensive understanding of religion in all its forms. The research that lies behind his analyses is quite remarkable in its extent. The three central texts on which we have focused here represent just a part of his labors, which include not only his several books on Indian yoga but studies as well of Australian religions, European folk traditions, and Asian shamans, or prophet-mystics. Other works focus on alchemy, initiation rituals, and witchcraft; on dreams, myths, and the occult; on symbolism in the arts; on methods of studying religion, and on a variety of other related topics. Even in retirement, he continued to work on a full-scale *History of Religious Ideas,* which was almost complete at his death. This wide-ranging global interest has won Eliade many admirers, especially among some of his students in America. Skeptical critics, on the other hand, wonder whether the problem is that it is far *too* global, and perhaps therefore superficial. In tones that hardly suggest a compliment, some see his approach as "Frazerian," a retreat to the doubtful aims and methods of *The Golden Bough.*[74]

3. Contemporary Philosophical Engagement

Third and last, as we saw in his comments on what he calls modern "historicist" philosophies, Eliade does not regard himself as a detached scholar, solely interested in the obscure customs of people from distant ages. Though his professional life is taken up with scholarship, ancient texts, and archaic ideas, he sees himself as very much a man engaged with the ideas and culture of his own time, a theorist who draws from his knowledge of the past to address important philosophical issues that confront society in the present. He is quite frank, for example, in arguing that scholars and intellectuals of the modern era have greatly underestimated the psychological merits of archaic thinking, which has sustained human endeavors for so much of the history of civilization. While, again, some greatly admire this "philosophical" side of Eliade, there are others who say it damages any claim he may have to scientific objectivity. There is undoubtedly more to be said on this matter, but as it stands, it has already taken us into the final task of this chapter, which is to turn from Eliade's theory itself to the main complaints of his critics.

Critique

Eliade's theory of religion is greatly admired in some quarters and quite strongly disputed in others. This is hardly surprising, given the bold stance he takes against reductionist approaches and the broad scope of his interests. As should be apparent from the discussion we have just concluded, Eliade is not afraid to tackle large questions and take sides on controversial matters of current interest, though both of those policies have a way of placing other scholars in a very skeptical mood right from the start. Among the charges of Eliade's detractors, it is helpful to make a distinction between minor complaints and those that are more serious. Certain misgivings expressed about his work seem quite minor or even mistaken. It has been said by some, for example, that evidence from Chinese religions and from Islam is missing from Eliade's writings, even though he claims to be a "global" comparativist. Others claim that examples which might disprove his claims can never be found in his books; that he does not carefully evaluate the texts and scholars he relies on; and that he applies our modern concepts to ancient peoples.[75] Still others have claimed that his views are a throwback to Victorian social evolutionism and that his methods are largely intuitive and speculative rather than scientific.[76] In response, we should first note that some of these criticisms could be made of almost any theory as broad as Eliade's, while others could, in part, be answered or even corrected. Failing to speak at length about Islamic or Chinese religions, for example, would not be a serious oversight unless significant evidence from these traditions could be found to contradict the general conclusions Eliade draws from his other evidence in some significant respect. After all, no one who seeks to make general observations can possibly know *all* of the available evidence. Again, it seems simply mistaken to say Eliade is some sort of old-style evolutionary thinker. He recognizes the fact of change in history, but for him change is by no means to be equated with irreversible evolutionary progress.

These points aside, however, questions about Eliade's approach still can be raised on several other, more important matters. Specifically, we must note reservations about the issues of theology, history, and conceptual precision, or clarity.

1. Theology

A number of observers have claimed that the key problem with Eliade is a religious one. Hidden within his theory, they say, are certain prior assumptions, both religious and philosophical, that undermine its objectivity; therefore it cannot be scientific. In recent years, several outspoken critics have claimed that Eliade is really a Christian theologian—or even missionary—in disguise. He believes in God and presents all religions in a favorable light, so that he can then show Christianity to be the true and best form among them.[77] As one might guess, this charge turns out to be a quite controversial matter, which, unfortunately, Eliade's own statements do not help to clarify. Though he published a journal and a long autobiography and discussed his career in a wide-ranging published interview, he has always remained evasive about his personal religious convictions. In addition, even if he were to admit to a Christian motive behind his work, we could not discredit his arguments and analyses for that reason alone, any more than, earlier on, we could dismiss the theories of Marx and Freud merely because these were inspired by decidedly antireligious motives. The question that must be asked is whether such prior beliefs, on either side of the issue, *actually enter the theory* in such a way as to make it invalid for anyone who does not accept them. Once we put the matter this way, perhaps the best that can be said is this: Although it may be true that Eliade allows his own religious sympathies to influence his science, none of his critics has so far proved that point to general satisfaction. Interestingly, one of the most objective and careful observers to write on this issue so far argues that Eliade's theory does in part depend upon what he calls a "normative" religious point of view, but this stance is closer to that of antihistorical Eastern religions like Hinduism than it is to Christianity.[78] Others argue that Eliade's personal creed is in fact the cosmic religion of the archaic peoples he so much appreciates, and that because of this he fails to do justice both to the nonarchaic, historical perspective and to the nonreligious modern perspective when he raises doubts about their value.

2. Historical Method

Another set of critics claims that troubles lie in the path not of theology but of history. As we noted above, Eliade feels he has succeeded in making the study of religion both a phenomenological and historical enterprise. He claims not only to explain the timeless symbolic forms of religion but also to show how they change with each new historical situation. His historical critics, however, are not so sure. They point out, often quite persuasively, that in reality only the timeless forms seem to count for Eliade; their special historical contexts, each with its small but significant variations of, say, the great tree, the moon cycle, or the eternal return, seem to matter very little to his interpretations. In framing his generalizations, Eliade draws examples from very distant places in space and time, lifts them out of their setting, finds surface similarities, and on that basis concludes that they form a significant pattern. Regardless of whether he turns to Vedic India several thousand years ago, to European peasants of the Middle Ages, or to primitive people living today, he finds in all religions the same basic categories of thought. Everywhere, it seems, he is able to find the same types of symbol and the same forms of myth, all expressing the same core of ideas: the reality of the sacred, a reliance on its archetypes, the escape from history, and the symbolism of return. The conclusion easily drawn from this argument is that Eliade's entire program is subject to just the sort of criticism first leveled at Frazer more than half a century earlier. It may well be that some method of this kind must be followed by anyone who attempts a truly universal theory of religion, but that does not necessarily mean Eliade's is sound. As was the case with Frazer, each time a careful anthropologist or historian who has closely studied a certain society shows that one of its symbols or myths cannot be fitted into Eliade's grand patterns, another crack appears in the theory's foundation. One or a few may not weaken the structure, but the effect of such cumulative weakening is likely to be serious.

3. Conceptual Confusions

Alongside both these problems, there is finally the matter of certain key concepts that seem, if not confused, at least somewhat imprecise and unfocused in Eliade's discussions. It is troubling that at just those moments when we want him to be very clear, Eliade's discussions can turn out to be rather disappointingly vague and elusive. Instead of sharp, clear lines, we tend to find a mist. On the question of symbolism, to give just one example, anthropologist Edmund Leach has pointed to a significant confusion. Eliade tells us that myths often present the division between the sacred and the profane and then introduce a third thing that connects them: a boat, a bridge or ladder, a pole, or "great tree." What is important, Eliade explains, is not the content of the symbols but their structure, the linkage they make between the sacred and profane. Whether the connecting object is a boat rather than a bridge does not really matter, since the important thing is the form, or framework, of the symbols—the relationships between them—rather than the actual character of the symbols themselves. At the same time, we are in other places told with equal emphasis that certain connecting symbols—like the great tree as *axis mundi*—must be considered superior to others. But surely that can be true only if the content of the symbol *does*, in fact, matter after all. So we have a confusion. Could it be, Leach asks, that Eliade has from the start decided—perhaps for his own religious reasons—that some symbols, which he personally prefers, must come out of the analysis as better than others? Could it be that content is more important than formal relationships after all? Whether or not Leach is correct, the matter of symbols and their precise significance is too important in Eliade's theory to be left in this kind of uncertainty.

A similar point can, in a sense, even be made about the concept of the sacred itself. Whenever we try to say just what the sacred is for archaic peoples, that task turns out to be extremely difficult. Eliade says it can be symbolized by the image of a center that is hard to reach, but also by a center that is easy to reach.[79] He says that stones represent the sacred because they are rugged, solid, and changeless; yet the moon, with its changing phases—its cycle of birth, death, and reappearance—is said also to represent it because "the *real* is not only what *is* indefinitely the same, but also what *becomes* in organic but cyclic forms."[80] Elsewhere we learn that "all divinities tend to become *everything* to their believers."[81] In other words, the content, or character, of the sacred as Eliade conceives it would seem to be subject to considerable change. But if this is so, if the concept of the sacred must be this formless and changeable to do its job, how useful can it really be? How instructive is it to build a theory on the notion of the sacred if, in the end, there is relatively little that is very definite about it other than the fact that it is the opposite of the profane?

Despite these problems, Eliade certainly deserves admiration for being one of the few thinkers of his age to assert boldly the independence of religious behavior over against the various forms of functionalist reductionism. He can also be commended for at least *attempting* an approach that draws its data from almost every world religion and tries to account for all the evidence within the framework of a single comprehensive system. Whether he has succeeded or ever could succeed with such an ambitious program is, of course, another matter. Interestingly, among those who think not, it is sometimes suggested that a more promising approach would be simply to abandon Eliade's hopes of a "global" theory and refocus the aims of inquiry altogether. They claim that just as much can be learned not by looking for general patterns but by doing the very opposite: by centering upon the religion of a single place or people and exploring it in painstaking depth and detail. As we shall see next, that is precisely the approach of the renowned English anthropologist E. E. Evans-Pritchard.

Notes

1. Mircea Eliade, *Journal III: 1970–1978,* tr. Teresa Lavender Fagan (Chicago: University of Chicago Press, 1989), p. 179.

2. This designation is an equivalent of the term *Religionsgeschichtliche Schule,* which was used by a prominent group of German scholars who did work in the comparative study of religions around the turn of the twentieth century.

3. On Eliade's opposition to reductionism see Carl Olson, *The Theology and Philosophy of Eliade: A Search for the Centre* (New York: St. Martin's Press, 1992), p. 32; this work also has an informative, brief account of Eliade's life and career, on which I have drawn in part for the sketch that follows.

4. *Autobiography: Volume 1, 1907–1937, Journey East, Journey West,* tr. Mac Linscott Ricketts (San Francisco: Harper & Row, 1981), p. 94. In addition to Eliade's own autobiography and journals, accounts of his life include Ioan Culianu, *Mircea Eliade* (Assisi, Italy: Cittadella Editrice, 1977) and Ivan Strenski, *Four Theories of Myth in Twentieth-Century History: Cassirer, Eliade, Lévi-Strauss and Malinowski* (Iowa City, IA: University of Iowa Press, 1987), pp. 70–128. The most extensive account of Eliade's early years is Mac Linscott Ricketts, *Mircea Eliade: The Romanian Roots, 1907–1945,* 2 vols. (New York: Columbia University Press, 1988).

5. Mircea Eliade, *Ordeal by Labyrinth: Conversations with Claude-Henri Roquet* (Chicago: University of Chicago Press, 1978), pp. 6–8.

6. Eliade, *Ordeal,* pp. 54–56.

7. Since Eliade's death, the University of Chicago Press has published English translations of both *Bengal Night* and his lover's account of the affair that led to the book. See Maitreyi Devi, *It Does Not Die* (Chicago: University of Chicago Press, 1993) and Mircea Eliade, *Bengal Night* (Chicago: University of Chicago Press, 1993). I am grateful to Professor Douglas Allen for his informative comments on this matter and for noting as well that an earlier English translation of Devi's account has been in existence since 1976.

8. It must be noted here that some of Eliade's critics think he was more active politically, and more involved with the Iron Guard, than he was ever willing to admit. That he was clearly a fervent Romanian nationalist is beyond dispute, but the extent of his sympathy for the Iron Guard and his involvement with Romanian fascism is currently a matter of heated debate. For further exploration of this controversy, see Ivan Strenski, *Four Theories of Myth,* pp. 70–103; Adriana Berger, "Fascism and Religion in Romania," *Annals of Scholarship* 6, no. 4 (1989): 455–65; and "Mircea Eliade: Romanian Fascism and the History of Religions in the United States," in Nancy Harrowitz, ed., *Tainted Greatness: Antisemitism and Cultural Heroes* (Philadelphia: Temple University Press, 1994), pp. 51–74; also Russell T.

McCutcheon, "The Myth of the Apolitical Scholar: The Life and Works of Mircea Eliade," *Queen's Quarterly* 100, no. 3 (Fall 1993): 642–63. I am grateful to Douglas Allen for referring me to the articles by Berger and McCutcheon.

9. Eliade, *Ordeal,* pp. 162–63. Unfortunately, the association with Jung has also been a source of confusion to students of Eliade's work, mainly because of a coincidence. Because the concept of "archetypes" figures prominently in Jung's theories and Eliade also uses this term in some of his writings, it could easily be supposed that Eliade borrowed both the term and the concept from Jung. But he did not, and what he means by "archetype" is something different from what it means for Jung. On this, see *Ordeal,* p. 164, as well as the preface to the English translation of *The Myth of the Eternal Return: Or, Cosmos and History* (New York: Harper Torchbooks [1949], 1959), pp. xiv–xv.

10. Olson, *Theology and Philosophy of Eliade,* p. 6.

11. Eliade, *Ordeal,* p. 105.

12. Eliade, *Ordeal,* p. 98.

13. *Patterns in Comparative Religion,* tr. Rosemary Sheed (New York: Meridian Books [1949] 1963), p. xiii.

14. Important studies of Eliade's interpretive methods include Robert Luyster, "The Study of Myth: Two Approaches," *The Journal of Bible and Religion* 34 (1966): 235–43; David Rasmussen, "Mircea Eliade: Structural Hermeneutics and Philosophy," *Philosophy Today* 12 (1968): 138–46; Mac Linscott Ricketts, "In Defense of Eliade," *Journal of Religion* 53 (1973): 13–34; and Guilford Dudley III, *Religion on Trial: Mircea Eliade and His Critics* (Philadelphia: Temple University Press, 1977). The most thorough and comprehensive study in English of issues relating to Eliade's method is Douglas Allen, *Structure and Creativity in Religion: Hermeneutics in Mircea Eliade's Phenomenology of Religion and New Directions* (The Hague, Netherlands: Mouton Publishers, 1978).

15. The best introduction to Eliade's view of this distinction as employed by archaic peoples can be found in the first two chapters of *The Sacred and the Profane: The Nature of Religion,* tr. Willard R. Trask (New York: Harcourt, Brace & World [1956 French], 1957), pp. 8–113.

16. On the differences between Eliade and Durkheim on "the sacred" and "the profane," see Olson, *Theology and Philosophy of Eliade,* p. 31.

17. Tr. J. W. Harvey (London, 1923); see Eliade, *Sacred and Profane,* pp. 8–10.

18. Eliade, *Sacred and Profane,* pp. 12–13.

19. Mircea Eliade, *Autobiography, Volume II: 1937–1960: Exile's Odyssey,* tr. Mac Linscott Rickets (Chicago: University of Chicago Press, 1988), pp. 188–89.

20. Eliade, *Patterns,* p. 148 and n. 1.

21. Genesis 28:17.

22. Eliade, *Sacred and Profane,* pp. 20–65.

23. Eliade, *Sacred and Profane,* pp. 55–56.

24. A few of Eliade's more notable works that carry analyses of symbolism but which we have no space to consider here are *Images and Symbols: Studies in Religious Symbolism,* tr. Philip Mairet (New York: Sheed and Ward, [1952 French] 1969); *Myths, Dreams, and Mysteries,* tr. Philip Mairet (New York: Harper Colo-

phon Books, [1957 French] 1975); *The Two and the One,* tr. J. M. Cohen (Chicago: University of Chicago Press, [1962 French] 1965). There are also discussions of symbolism in the lengthy study *Shamanism: Archaic Techniques of Ecstasy,* tr. Willard R. Trask (New York: Bollingen Foundation, [1951 French] 1974).

25. Eliade, *Patterns,* p. 11.

26. Eliade does not point this out in *Patterns* so much as in other, later works; see especially *Images and Symbols,* pp. 12–21. Interestingly, this book and others that speak quite explicitly about symbolism and dimensions of the personality beneath or beyond reason were written after Eliade began his conversations with Jung, who may well have been the one to push him along in this direction.

27. Eliade, *Patterns,* pp. 40, 47, 73.

28. Eliade, *Patterns,* pp. 54, 56.

29. Eliade, *Patterns,* p. 91.

30. Eliade, *Patterns,* p. 96.

31. Mircea Eliade, "Methodological Remarks on the Study of Religious Symbolism," in *The History of Religions: Essays in Methodology,* Mircea Eliade and Joseph Kitagawa, eds. (Chicago: University of Chicago Press, 1959), p. 103. This point is also noted by Douglas Allen in an unpublished manuscript entitled "Symbolism and Myth," pp. 30–32; see n. 52 below.

32. Eliade, *Patterns,* pp. 98–99.

33. Eliade, *Patterns,* p. 124.

34. Eliade, *Patterns,* p. 183.

35. Eliade, *Patterns,* p. 170.

36. Eliade, *Patterns,* p. 158.

37. Eliade, *Patterns,* p. 158.

38. This is a major theme of one of Eliade's more important essays, "Mephistopheles and the Androgyne, or the Mystery of the Whole," in *The Two and the One,* pp. 78–124.

39. Eliade devoted an early work in Romanian, still untranslated, to this entire theme: *Mitul Reintegrarii* (The Myth of Reintegration) (Bucharest, 1942). On the great importance of this theme to Eliade's theory, see Allen, *Structure and Creativity,* pp. 190–200, 231–46.

40. Eliade, *Patterns,* pp. 188–89.

41. Eliade, *Patterns,* p. 216.

42. Eliade, *Patterns,* p. 241.

43. Eliade, *Patterns,* p. 261.

44. Eliade, *Patterns,* p. 265.

45. Eliade, *Patterns,* p. 267.

46. Eliade, *Patterns,* p. 346.

47. Eliade, *Patterns,* p. 315.

48. Eliade, *Patterns,* pp. 302–303.

49. Eliade, *Patterns,* pp. 314–15.

50. Eliade, *Patterns,* p. 361.

51. On Eliade's view that symbols always tend toward a system, see Rasmussen, "Mircea Eliade: Structural Hermeneutics," pp. 138–46, especially pp. 141–42.

52. I am grateful to Douglas Allen for providing me with two helpful chapters—"Religion and Myth" and "Symbolism and Myth"—from an unpublished manuscript on Eliade, which have guided this discussion of Eliade's approach to sacred symbols. Equally helpful are the thorough discussions he provides of myth, symbol, and other key elements of Eliade's theory in *Structure and Creativity,* pp. 144–69 especially; see also n. 31 above.

53. On this point, see Stephen J. Reno, "Eliade's Progressional View of Hierophanies," *Religious Studies* 8 (1972): 153–60.

54. Eliade argues that this is, in fact, what happened in the case of Hebrew monotheism. The Hebrew prophets declared the superiority of the sky-god Yahweh, who had given them his truth, to the fertility gods of the neighboring countries.

55. Eliade, *Patterns,* p. 322.

56. In the preface to the English edition of the book, written in 1959, Eliade commented, "I still consider it the most significant of my books." See *The Myth of the Eternal Return,* p. xv. Edmund Leach, in a very critical review of Eliade's works, "Sermons by a Man on a Ladder," in *The New York Review,* October 20, 1966, p. 31, refers to *The Myth* as the one book that "still seems the most worthwhile."

57. Eliade, *Sacred and Profane,* p. 92.

58. Eliade, *Eternal Return,* p. 52.

59. Eliade, *Eternal Return,* p. 29.

60. Eliade, *Eternal Return,* p. 35.

61. Eliade, *Eternal Return,* p. 89.

62. Eliade, *Eternal Return,* p. 118.

63. Eliade, *Eternal Return,* pp. 124–27.

64. Eliade, *Eternal Return,* p. 104.

65. Eliade, *Eternal Return,* p. 108.

66. Eliade, *Eternal Return,* p. 111.

67. Eliade, *Eternal Return,* pp. 154–56.

68. Eliade, *Eternal Return,* pp. 155–59.

69. Eliade, *Eternal Return,* p. 153.

70. Eliade, *Myths, Dreams, and Mysteries,* pp. 34–35.

71. Eliade, *Myths, Dreams, and Mysteries,* p. 33.

72. Eliade, *Myths, Dreams, and Mysteries,* p. 36.

73. On this, see Mircea Eliade, *Myth and Reality* (New York: Harper & Row, 1963), pp. 170–74. I wish to thank Douglas Allen for referring me to this passage and correcting an earlier misunderstanding of this issue.

74. William A. Lessa, review of *The Sacred and the Profane,* in *American Anthropologist* 61 (1959): 1147.

75. For a full accounting of these criticisms and their merits, see John A. Saliba, *"Homo Religiosus" in Mircea Eliade: An Anthropological Evaluation* (Leiden: E. J. Brill, 1978); I am partly indebted in this section to Olson, *Theology and Philosophy of Eliade,* pp. 9–13, for a thorough and recent compilation of major criticisms raised against Eliade's theory.

76. On the claim that he is an evolutionist, see Dorothy Libby, review of *Rites*

and Symbols of Initiation, in *American Anthropologist* 61 (1959): 689. On the other criticisms, see Anthony F. C. Wallace, *Religion: An Anthropological View* (New York: Random House, 1966), p. 252; and Annemarie de Waal Malefijt, *Religion and Culture: An Introduction to Anthropology of Religion* (New York: Macmillan, 1968), p. 193.

77. Among the most vocal of these critics is Canadian scholar Donald Wiebe, who, in a number of articles and books, repeats the claim that Eliade's opposition to reductionism is not a scientific principle but a religious prejudice; see, among several of his writings that make this point, *Religion and Truth* (The Hague, Netherlands: Mouton Publishers, 1981); "Theory in the Study of Religion," *Religion* 13 (1983): 283–309; "The Failure of Nerve in the Academic Study of Religion," *Studies in Religion* 13 (1984): 401–22; and more recently, "Postulations for Safeguarding Preconceptions: The Case of the Scientific Religionist," *Religion* 18: 1 (1988): 11–19. In the United States, the same position has been taken by Robert Segal; see his "In Defense of Reductionism," *Journal of the American Academy of Religion* 51, 1 (March 1983): 97–124; similar arguments are made also in several of the essays in *Religion and the Social Sciences: Essays on the Confrontation* (Atlanta: Scholars Press, 1989); and *Explaining and Interpreting Religion: Essays on the Issue* (New York: Peter Lang Publishing, 1992). In his critical review, "Sermons by a Man on a Ladder," pp. 28–31, Leach, the well-known English anthropologist, alludes to what seems to him a religious agenda in Eliade's work, but he does not develop the point; see also n. 56 above.

78. Allen, *Structure and Creativity,* pp. 221–45, especially pp. 221–22.

79. Eliade, *Patterns,* p. 382.

80. Eliade, *Patterns,* pp. 314–15.

81. Eliade, *Patterns,* p. 262.

Suggestions for Further Reading

Allen, Douglas. *Structure and Creativity in Religion: Hermeneutics in Mircea Eliade's Phenomenology of Religion and New Directions.* The Hague: Mouton Publishers, 1978. A substantive analysis, difficult in places, but written by a scholar with an exceedingly wide and deep knowledge of Eliade's life and works.

Cave, David. *Mircea Eliade's Vision for a New Humanism.* New York: Oxford University Press, 1993. A sympathetic, but not uncritical, discussion of the humanist perspective which in the author's view guides all of Eliade's thinking about religion.

Dudley, Guilford, III. *Religion on Trial: Mircea Eliade and His Critics.* Philadelphia: Temple University Press, 1977. An instructive discussion, and critique, of the assumptions and major themes in Eliade's works.

Eliade, Mircea. *Autobiography: Volume 1, 1907–1937: Journey East, Journey West.* Translated by Mac Linscott Ricketts. San Francisco: Harper & Row, 1981. *Autobiography: Volume 2, 1937–1960: Exile's Odyssey.* Translated by Mac Linscott Ricketts. Chicago: University of Chicago Press, 1988. In these volumes Eliade himself provides a narrative of his life and thought up through his first years at the University of Chicago.

Eliade, Mircea. *Images and Symbols: Studies in Religious Symbolism*. Translated by Philip Mairet. New York: Sheed and Ward, [1952 French] 1969.

Eliade, Mircea. *The Myth of the Eternal Return: Or, Cosmos and History*. Translated by Willard R. Trask. New York: Harper Torchbooks [1949 French], 1959.

Eliade, Mircea. *Myths, Dreams, and Mysteries*. Translated by Philip Mairet. New York: Harper Colophon Books [1957 French], 1975.

Eliade, Mircea. *Ordeal by Labyrinth: Conversations with Claude-Henri Roquet*. Chicago: University of Chicago Press, 1978. A revealing interview in which Eliade discusses his own understanding of his life and his work.

Eliade, Mircea. *Patterns in Comparative Religion*. Translated by Rosemary Sheed. New York: Meridian Books [1949 French], 1963.

Eliade, Mircea. *The Sacred and the Profane: The Nature of Religion*. Translated by Willard R. Trask. New York: Harcourt, Brace & World, 1957.

Leach, Edmund. "Sermons by a Man on a Ladder." *The New York Review*, October 20, 1966. A sharply critical review of Eliade's works from the perspective of professional anthropology.

Olson, Carl. *The Theology and Philosophy of Eliade: A Search for the Centre*. New York: St. Martin's Press, 1992. A good recent introduction to the major themes in Eliade's work.

Ricketts, Mac Linscott. *Mircea Eliade: The Romanian Roots, 1907–1945*. 2 vols. New York: Columbia University Press, 1988. The most extensive account of Eliade's earlier years in Romania, Italy, India and other places.

Saliba, John A. *"Homo Religiosus" in Mircea Eliade: An Anthropological Evaluation*. Leiden: E. J. Brill, 1978. A modern anthropological assessment that mixes appreciation and criticism.

Strenski, Ivan. *Four Theories of Myth in Twentieth-Century History: Cassirer, Eliade, Lévi-Strauss and Malinowski*. Iowa City: University of Iowa Press, 1987, pp. 70–128. Contains a perceptive and provocative exploration of Eliade's ties to Romanian culture and its nationalist movement between the wars.

6

Society's "Construct
of the Heart":
E. E. Evans-Pritchard

"If he could alter the categories of his own generation's universe so
that primitive peoples would rank in it as fully rational beings, that
change would entail others, among them a higher status for religious
knowledge."

Mary Douglas, *Edward Evans-Pritchard*[1]

E. E. Evans-Pritchard is one of the great figures in modern anthropology, a
field he claimed as his profession for a period of nearly fifty years, from the
1920s to his death in 1973. Were he to have seen his name alongside the
others in this book, this modest Englishman undoubtedly would have expressed some surprise and insisted that if theories of religion are the subject,
he proposed no such thing. Certain observers, in fact, might even prefer to
describe him as an "antitheorist" of religion, for in one of his most widely
noticed books, *Theories of Primitive Religion* (1965), he takes it as his mission to dismantle the ambitious schemes of explanation put forward by the
pioneering figures in anthropology and the study of religion, including several of the theorists already discussed in these pages. It may be recalled that
on occasion in earlier chapters we noted some of his perceptive criticisms of
their views. Evans-Pritchard's role in the enterprise of explaining religion,
however, has been much larger than that of a critic whose main interest is
to find the faults in the work of others. His considerable reputation rests on
the very impressive work he was able to do "in the field"—as anthropologists prefer to say—through the studies he carried out as a trained, professional observer of actual tribal peoples.

Of the theorists we have so far met in this book, almost all have readily
offered an opinion on the nature of primitive, or tribal, religion, yet only
one—Eliade in India—records even so much as a passing contact with peo-

ple living in circumstances remotely similar to a real primitive culture. This is emphatically not the case with Evans-Pritchard, who did far more than just meet or speak with a few "native" peoples. He is a theorist of religion who actually entered two primitive societies, learned their languages, lived for a time by their customs, and carefully studied them in action. The significance of his work can therefore hardly be underestimated. His approach differs from that of earlier "armchair" theorists just as experimental science does from speculation. Further, while he was critical of most theories he had encountered, Evans-Pritchard was by no means opposed to them in principle. He felt that among anthropologists, in fact, not enough effort had been put into this enterprise, and he saw his own work among tribal peoples of Africa as, if not a way of framing a full theory of his own, at least a necessary step in the right direction.

Life and Career

Edward Evan Evans-Pritchard was born in 1902, the second son of a Church of England clergyman, Rev. John Evans-Pritchard, and his wife Dorothea.[2] The parish his father served was at Crowborough, Sussex, in the southeast of England. He took his secondary education at Winchester College, one of England's elite public schools, and then entered Exeter College, Oxford University, where he studied for four years and graduated with an M.A. in modern history. At this time his interests had already begun to turn in the direction of anthropology, so in 1923 he began graduate study at the London School of Economics. As we noted earlier, the study of anthropology in England had evolved from the older armchair-and-library sort of research practiced by Müller, Tylor, and Frazer into a discipline that required at least one apprenticeship of study devoted to a society very different—meaning "primitive" usually—from those of modern Europe and America.[3] This was precisely the kind of work Evans-Pritchard was determined to do. In London he was able to study with C. G. Seligman, who had been the first professional anthropologist to do fieldwork in Africa. At the same time, Bronislaw Malinowski came to London and became a second mentor to him. Malinowski, a noted figure, had spent four years studying the people of the Trobriand Islands, where he was the first anthropologist to do his research in a native language and immerse himself fully in the daily life of a primitive community. He strongly encouraged Evans-Pritchard to do what he had done, studying the culture of a single people in great depth; Seligman encouraged him to choose a culture in Africa.

Taking the advice of both his tutors, Evans-Pritchard traveled to the Sudan region of East Africa, the area where both the Nile and Congo rivers find their source. Under the joint control of Egypt and Britain at the time, this area was known as the Anglo-Egyptian Sudan. Between 1926 and 1931, while encountering a number of tribal communities, he made several visits to a people known as the Azande in the southern Sudan. In all, he spent almost two years with them and learned their language thoroughly, all the while writing his doctoral dissertation and other articles on their social life. Between 1930 and 1936 he did further fieldwork among the Nuer people of the Sudan. In 1935 he became Research Lecturer in African Sociology at Oxford, and four years later he married a South African, Ioma Nicholls, with whom he had a family of three sons and two daughters. In 1937 he published his first major work, *Witchcraft, Oracles, and Magic among the Azande*. Though it made little impact at first, this book acquired great importance in the years after World War II, being called by at least one authority "the outstanding work of anthropology published in this century."[4] It was followed by the first of three volumes he was to publish on the other tribe he had studied in depth. *The Nuer: A Description of the Modes of Livelihood and Political Institutions of a Nilotic People* appeared in 1940.

During World War II, Evans-Pritchard served in the British army, leading a Zande (this is singular; "Azande" is the plural) band of warriors on a campaign against certain Italian army defenses in East Africa.[5] Later, while serving at a post in Cyrenaica, Libya, he did further research that led to a study of a Muslim Sufi religious order known as the Sanusi. It was at this time, in the year 1944, that he converted to Roman Catholicism. After the war, he returned to England, where he settled first at Cambridge and then became professor of social anthropology at Oxford, taking the chair occupied by the noted advocate of functionalist theory, A. R. Radcliffe-Brown, on his retirement.

At Oxford Evans-Pritchard rose to even greater prominence as perhaps the leading figure in British social anthropology. During these years he published, alongside numerous articles on anthropological subjects, the results of his work in Libya, *The Sanusi of Cyrenaica* (1949); the second and third of his Nuer studies, *Kinship and Marriage among the Nuer* (1951) and *Nuer Religion* (1956); and major books on the methods and history of the field, including *Social Anthropology* (1951), *Essays in Social Anthropology* (1962), and *A History of Anthropological Thought* (1981); the last of these appeared a number of years after his death. Evans-Pritchard's worldwide renown in anthropology was almost matched by his fame in and about Oxford as one of the university's most delightfully eccentric characters. Unassuming, shy, and often dressed in clothes that allowed him to be easily mistaken for a handyman, his close associates marveled at his acid tongue and what one described as his "awesome, Celtic prowess at drinking."[6] In 1970 Evans-Pritchard retired from his post, and the following year, against his wishes, he was knighted. He died two years later, in 1973.

Intellectual Background

Evans-Pritchard's approach to anthropology—and consequently religion—took shape against the background of three earlier traditions. The first might be called older Victorian anthropology, the second was French sociology, and the third was the newer British school of fieldwork anthropology. We have already met the last of these, at least briefly, in the form of his teachers Seligman and Malinowski, with their emphasis on close study of a foreign culture, but we can understand why this type of research was important only if we introduce the two other traditions and the view Evans-Pritchard took of them as he began his work.

Older Anthropology

As we noticed earlier in the case of such figures as Tylor, Frazer, and their associates, the Victorian founders of anthropology were inspired by the vision of a science of human affairs. They felt they could study such things as religion and the rise of human culture in a scientific manner by methodically collecting, comparing, and classifying facts. They felt further that this science led to evolutionary conclusions. Through their inquiries, they would bring out the "laws of development" according to which humanity had made progress from its primitive beginnings to its modern achievements. And though they were less aware of this than the other principles, they preferred an approach to their field that was intellectualist and individualistic. As we noted earlier in the case of Tylor, when these scholars sought to understand primitive or religious people, they always envisioned "the savage philosopher"—an ancient man standing quite alone before his cave, puzzling over problems and devising explanations of things around him, just like a modern scientist.

Looking back on this enterprise, Evans-Pritchard, like others in the early years of the twentieth century, gave it a quite mixed review.[7] The ideal of science he found the easiest to accept, and even improve upon, chiefly by using the Victorians' research, gathering more facts, and refining the methods for studying them. The evolutionary conclusions, however, were another matter. He recognized that certain technical improvements in history were obvious: a better plough, a faster loom, a stronger wheel. Cultural progress as a whole, however, was a much larger, more elusive issue. And though it may have seemed self-evident to Tylor and Frazer, Evans-Pritchard insisted that such a theory contradicted the very scientific principles upon which it supposedly was based. Darwin, after all, had provided *evidence* to prove the physical evolution of animal species; unfortunately, evidence was precisely what the older anthropologists did *not* have for their broad theories of cultural progress, including their views on the origin and development of religion. Most theorizing about the first humans—what their marriage customs were, what their religion was, and so forth—consisted mainly of speculation about an era from which there were no historical records, nor could there ever be. The ideas were interesting, but there was no way they could be proved or, for that matter, even disproved. So in Evans-Pritchard's eyes, any theory of social evolution was bankrupt from the start.

With regard to the other feature of older anthropology, its individualist intellectualism, Evans-Pritchard had a more divided mind. Insofar as Tylor and Frazer explained primitive belief as the ideas of isolated ancient thinkers, they had clearly failed to see that humans always live *in society,* which conditions and colors their thought in a fundamental way. Insofar as they explained religion intellectually, their emphasis was rather one-sided; however, they were partly correct. All human beings, even uneducated ones, do approach life to some extent in intellectual terms; they frame concepts, connect them to other concepts, and relate both to the activities and rituals of daily life.[8]

French Sociology

Evans-Pritchard felt strongly that the proper corrective to the individualism of Tylor and Frazer could be found in the field of sociology as it had recently developed in France. As we saw in discussing Durkheim, the French tradition of interpreting human affairs in social terms went back to the period before the Revolution and could be seen in the works of the Baron de Montesquieu, especially his *Spirit of the Laws* (1748). It had been developed by men like Saint-Simon and Auguste Comte in the early nineteenth century and further refined at its close by Durkheim and his disciples. Evans-Pritchard had great admiration for Durkheim, whom he called "the central figure" in the development of social anthropology, not just because of his own work but because of the way in which he formed a circle of talented associates and students to work with him.[9] He was the leader of the French school, which had shown definitively that human social life, which included religion, could never be understood merely as what individuals think and do, though in associations and numbers; there was more to the formation of social groups than merely private thoughts and emotions in assembled form. Durkheim's disciples demonstrated that the framework of life is fixed for every person by society even before birth and remains in place through the generations. Accordingly, in their view, it was society that created much of the individual. A child born in France will speak the French language, feel obliged to obey French laws, and observe French customs. So too in thought: A French child will understand the world with French ideas.[10] Everyone knows these things, but until Durkheim not everyone knew their importance.

The colleague and sometimes critic of Durkheim who sought to explain the influence of these social factors on how people think, religiously and in other ways, was Lucien Lévy-Bruhl (1857–1939), a philosopher who was very much aware of social considerations and took a special interest in the thought of primitive peoples. When they were translated into English in the 1920s, two of his books, *How Natives Think* (1926) and *Primitive Mentality* (1923), drew considerable attention in Britain.[11] Evans-Pritchard thought these works, like Durkheim's, were extremely important for anthropology. Unlike Tylor and Frazer, whom we have seen referring to early peoples as rational but also as ignorant, superstitious, and childish, Lévy-Bruhl sought to show how primitive thought is not weaker or more immature than ours but simply different from it. It is a reflection of an entirely different social system, which places value on a type of thinking best described as "prelogical." Primitive people live in a world of "mystical participations" that do not follow our rules of logical connection or our law against contradiction. Because they obey these different rules of thought, primitive people can quite literally think of themselves as one thing and something else at the same time. When, in the report of a European explorer, a South American native declared, "I am a red parakeet," those words were meant literally, yet the native was not demonstrating that he was deranged or even weak in reasoning power; he was demonstrating a different kind of thought, a type that is irrational to us because it accepts as normal the "mystical participation" of one thing in another.[12]

Evans-Pritchard thought the work of Lévy-Bruhl to be brilliant, even though, on the key point of the primitive prelogical mind, it would need correction. Not only had it shown that the ideas and attitudes of nonliterate peoples must be understood within the context of the whole world—the whole sea of values, habits, and assumptions in which they swim—it also marked a most important change in the attitude of modern thinkers toward primitive people. In Lévy-Bruhl's perspective, early peoples were not mentally deficient, subhuman, or childish; they were equally but differently mature, human, and intelligent beings. To Evans-Pritchard, this was a perspective every anthropologist should take with him into the field.[13]

British Empirical Anthropology

Evans-Pritchard was not the only one in the Britain of his day to appreciate French sociology. Its importance had already been recognized by A. R. Radcliffe-Brown, whose ideas dominated anthropological discussion at the time. From Durkheim and his colleagues, Radcliffe-Brown had borrowed and then further developed the functional theory of society as a complete, interconnected, working organism. No part of it could be understood without the whole. Explaining primitive religion without addressing primitive class divisions or economic needs was like explaining the human heart without ever referring to the blood or lungs. It was this new view that passed a final judgment, if any were needed, on the ways of the older Victorian anthropology. From the functional standpoint, nothing could be more inappropriate than to take a custom out of one culture and a belief out of another and then connect them, as Frazer would have done, to make some general statement about "the primitive mind" in general. Evans-Pritchard, along with almost every other aspiring younger anthropologist of the time, heartily endorsed this view, as well as the important practical conclusion that followed from it. To do his work, the anthropologist could no longer stay in a library or read the reports of missionaries about this strange notion or that odd habit. He must go out into the field and make a *complete* study of a single culture, observing not just its religion, its law and economics, its class structure or kinship connections, but all of these as they come together in a unitary, organic whole. It was this conclusion, endorsed and practiced by all of his most important mentors, that led Evans-Pritchard in 1926 to the interior of the Sudan—and to his first major anthropological study.

Witchcraft, Oracles, and Magic among the Azande

In this chapter as in the others, our plan of action requires that we focus our attention on the two books in which Evans-Pritchard developed his main ideas on religion: chiefly *Nuer Religion* (1956) and, to a lesser degree, his critical study *Theories of Primitive Religion* (1965). Before doing so, however, we must take note of his extremely important earlier work on the

Azande people, in part because of its great significance for anthropological research as a whole but also because it provides the key link between the initial assumptions we have just noted and Evans-Pritchard's views on religion as they were developed in his later years.

As its title indicates, *Witchcraft among the Azande* (1937) deals with a topic that anthropologists since Tylor and Frazer had taken to be closely related to religion: namely, magical thought. For Evans-Pritchard, magic is the belief that certain aspects of life can be controlled by mystical forces or supernatural powers. Since most educated members of modern Western societies—and Evans-Pritchard includes himself in this group—think the belief in such forces is wholly mistaken, the natural question that arises is: Why then do the Azande believe in them? Evans-Pritchard found it unacceptable, as we have seen, to say with Tylor and Frazer that primitive people are partly irrational and childish. And outside of the realm of magic, there was abundant evidence to support him. On their own terms, he wrote, the Azande are very logical, curious, and inquiring. In social and practical affairs, they are clever and perceptive. They are skilled craftsmen; they are poetically imaginative, and in matters of survival and daily living extremely resourceful. On the whole "they are unusually intelligent, sophisticated, and progressive."[14] At the same time, a surprisingly significant part of life among the Azande is given over to oracles, magic, and other ritual performances. They refer to mystical ideas and ritual practices on a daily basis; they speak freely about them and without fear, even though commonsense discussion of practical matters still takes up the vast majority of their conversation and effort.

The precise nature of Zande witchcraft seems strange to a Westerner, but it is not difficult to describe. The term "witchcraft" actually refers to a physical substance that some people have in their bodies, unknown to themselves. It is inherited and can be discovered in their bodies after death. Evans-Pritchard states his own belief that this substance, which the Azande find as a dark mass in the small intestine, is nothing more than undigested food.[15] Yet the Azande believe that while this substance looks to be merely physical and natural, it operates in a mystical fashion to bring misfortune, and especially sickness, on other people. It is a mistake, Evans-Pritchard cautions, to suppose the Azande are so obsessed with witchcraft that they spend most of their time making and responding to accusations that they have it in their bodies. They do not. But references to it are made in every aspect of their life, especially in connection with almost any unfortunate turn of events that cannot be directly explained by ordinary mistakes or misjudgments.

Evans-Pritchard observes that if a blight hits one of the crops, if animals are not found in the hunt, if a wife and husband quarrel, if a commoner is turned away by his prince, there are always mutterings of witchcraft, though very little is done about it.[16] Nonetheless, when a truly serious misfortune makes an appearance—say, the presence of a wasting disease that seems to be taking the life of an individual—there is no doubt in the Zande mind that such occurrences must be due to witchcraft. The person whose witchcraft is their cause must be found—and confronted—before it is too late.

In such cases the Azande regularly consult what they call the poison oracle. In this—again, to us quite strange—procedure, a man forces poison into the throat of a chicken while at that very moment asking a question which can be answered with a yes or no. The death or survival of the chicken then determines the answer. For example, concerning the sick friend: "If x has caused his illness, poison oracle, kill the fowl."[17] If the bird dies of the poison, the person whose witchcraft has caused the illness has been found. There then follows a procedure of accusation, a ritual of "blowing water," in which the accused agrees to "cool" his witchcraft, which is devouring the soul of the sick person, and all is considered to be at an end—unless of course the victim of the witchcraft dies after all. In that case, vengeance must be taken. Evans-Pritchard points out that at one time in the Zande past, this act might have involved the murder of the accused witch. Now, however, it is usually a matter of offering compensation to the family or, even better, of discovering, again through oracles, that another person in the community, now deceased, was in fact the witch and has thus already suffered a fitting punishment for his witchcraft. Vengeance, moreover, cannot be claimed until the verdict of one's private oracle has been confirmed by the secret poison oracle of the local prince, for Zande society is an aristocracy in which the ruling class makes all final decisions. If the logic of these oracles, deaths, and acts of vengeance were analyzed publicly, Evans-Pritchard notes, it would reduce itself to an absurdity, because every new death would have to be attributed to yet another act of witchcraft in an endless circle.[18] The Azande—significantly—choose not to address this problem in any abstract or theoretical manner.

Alongside witchcraft and the poison oracle, there is a whole collection of associated magical practices. There are minor oracles that function like the poison oracle but are less accurate and need its confirmation in important matters.[19] There are all sorts of medicines that witch doctors can apply as good magic to ward off the effects of witchcraft. And there is sorcery, which is done in secret and regarded as a crime if discovered. In addition, Evans-Pritchard notes that the class of the nobility is largely exempt from the entire business of witchcraft. Commoners do not accuse the ruling class; conversely, the poison oracle of the prince, which gives the final determination on all serious witchcraft charges brought by commoners, is the anchor of the society's entire legal system. It is both constitution and supreme court.[20]

The great and painstaking detail with which Evans-Pritchard describes these magical practices is one reason for the extraordinary praise *Witchcraft* came to receive from experts in the field. It is a classic piece of what anthropologists call scientific ethnography.[21] The details have great theoretical importance, for through them Evans-Pritchard is able to show how, from the Zande perspective, the seeming absurdities of witchcraft and magic not only make a completely coherent and rational system but one that plays a central role in social life. It offers a plausible account of all personal misfortunes. It also works alongside what we would call explanation through natural causes, for the Azande also believe in these and appeal to them often as well. In certain cases, witchcraft helps to explain why natural causes act as they do. It does not explain why fire burns, but it does explain why, on this particular unfortunate occasion, fire, which never bothered me before, now has burned my hand.[22] The Azande, therefore, see no competition between science on the one hand and their system of magic, oracles, witchcraft, and religion on the other. Significantly, the notion of a struggle between these two forms of knowledge—which is so central to views of Tylor, Frazer, Freud, Lévy-Bruhl and so many other theorists of the primitive mind—seems totally foreign to their experience. Magic and religion are not replaced by science; they simply operate alongside and with it.

In addition to its task of explaining misfortune, witchcraft works along with magic to serve other useful social purposes as well. It not only serves as the foundation of legal affairs but also governs Zande morals and softens the rough edges of social life. The chances of violence, for example, are reduced because there is a routine procedure for determining the identity of those who are believed to have caused misfortune and an expectation that, in the appropriate way, they will be punished. Again, since witches are thought to be naturally disagreeable, uncooperative, unhappy people, there is a strong incentive not to behave this way lest other people suspect you are a witch and bring your name before their oracle after the next bad event.[23] As Evans-Pritchard puts it in concise form: "The concept of witchcraft . . . provides them [the Azande] with a natural philosophy by which the relations between men and unfortunate events are explained and a ready and stereotyped means of reacting to such events. Witchcraft beliefs also embrace a system of values which regulate human conduct."[24]

All of this also puts Evans-Pritchard in the position to make a clear statement about how the Azande reason as compared with thinking in a modern scientific culture, and here it is worth quoting him at length. Although the

Azande clearly do not see the theoretical weakness in their system of witch-craft belief,

> their blindness is not due to stupidity, for they display great ingenuity in ex-plaining away the failures and inequalities of the poison oracle and experimen-tal keenness in testing it. It is due rather to the fact that their intellectual ingenuity and experimental keenness are conditioned by patterns of ritual be-haviour and mystical belief. Within the limits set by these patterns they show great intelligence, but it cannot operate beyond these limits. Or, to put it in another way; they reason excellently in the idiom of their beliefs, but they cannot reason outside, or against, their beliefs because they have no other idiom in which to express their thoughts.[25]

Having said this, Evans-Pritchard then turns the argument around. He states that if we look closely at Zande witchcraft in the context of the society in which it functions, we find it a system of thought that shows certain quite striking similarities to our own nonmagical system. Certain beliefs—like the idea that there is such a thing as witchcraft—are fundamental and beyond dispute. Once these are accepted, other inferences, connections, and ideas follow from them quite logically and consistently. Moreover, the fundamen-tal ideas are always affirmed in a way that allows for certain adjustments and protections of them if they *do* happen to be contradicted by the facts.

Toward the end of *Witchcraft*, Evans-Pritchard provides a long list of considerations that affect Zande thinking and of the defenses they readily adopt to "save the system" when needed. When a poison or type of magic does not work, they declare that it may have been inappropriately used or that it was applied against mystical powers whose action is beyond the natu-ral realm and so cannot be contradicted by events within nature. If a medi-cine fails, the Azande set against it the apparent successes of others. They may also claim that magic seldom produces a result by itself but acts only in combination with other actions. Moreover, their medicines are never actu-ally tested and some are always used, so there is no way to tell what would happen if they were not. These are only a few examples of the way in which the fundamental assumptions of the Zande world view are very well pro-tected against facts that might disprove them; indeed, they form a system of belief impossible to shake. From our perspective the Azande may be wrong, but from theirs it is clear that they think quite rationally within the limits their culture chooses to allow. Their small beliefs rest very logically on certain large ones, and these important basic principles are extremely well guarded. The attachment to the major beliefs is so fundamental to their life that the Azande cannot imagine their being wrong. Without them, their en-tire social order would be inconceivable, and no one could endure that.

As philosophers, anthropologists, scientists, and theologians have gradually come to realize, what Evans-Pritchard shows to be true for the Azande has momentous consequences for the assessment of belief and doubt in our own society. The case of the Azande suggests that in any culture, certain fundamental beliefs *must* at all costs be preserved. They are too precious to lose.

Nuer Religion

In 1930 Evans-Pritchard began a series of visits to the land of the Nuer, a people living just to the north of the Azande but very different in character, culture, and traditions. He at once set upon the difficult work of learning their language and began questioning his hosts, a task that proved more difficult than with the Azande, who had volunteered information freely. Over a period of about six years, to 1936, he put together the equivalent of a year in the Nuer camps, questioning, observing, and writing. This research led in time to three impressive books—and numerous articles—which were published between 1940 and 1956. The first, entitled *The Nuer,* focused on the community's economic and political life. Like the work on the Azande, it now has the status of a classic in anthropology.[26] Among its notable features are an examination of the central place of cattle in economic life and an emphasis on the role they play in people's personal affections, as well as a fascinating discussion of the way the Nuer have constructed their ideas of time and space in relation to their way of life. In 1951 *The Nuer* was followed by a more specifically social study of the community's patterns of kinship and marriage. The trilogy was brought to completion in 1956 with *Nuer Religion,* the book that calls for our attention here.

The Concept of "Kwoth"

Evans-Pritchard begins *Nuer Religion* at the very center of its subject. On a first look, he notes, one would almost say that the Nuer are a people without religion. They seem to have no formal dogma, no developed liturgy or sacraments, no organized worship, not even a system of mythology. But those appearances are misleading. In a sense, the Nuer actually do have all of these things, though they appear in the culture in such an informal, almost hidden way that the casual observer could easily miss them.

Nuer religion centers almost totally on the concept of *kwoth,* or spirit (in the plural, *kuth:* "spirits"). First and foremost in their thought is God, the being they know as *Kwoth nhial*, the "spirit of (or in) the sky." He is the creator of all things, invisible and present everywhere, the sustainer—and taker—of life, the upholder of *cuong*, or what is morally upright, good, and true. A being with qualities of human personality, *Kwoth nhial* is also, and preeminently, a God who loves unselfishly the human beings he has created.[27] Nuer are keenly aware of God's control of their lives, often uttering quiet prayers to the effect "God is present." And though proud in their attitudes to other people, the Nuer regard themselves as nothing before him. They are dumb and small, like tiny ants in his sight.[28]

The Nuer have a strong sense of God's complete control over the great natural events that happen in the world. Floods, storms, drought, and famine—all of these are in his hands and must be accepted as they may come. If, as happens often, someone is killed by lightning in a thunderstorm, they do not mourn or hold a normal rite of burial. They accept that God has just taken back what is his own. At the same time, the lesser, if still significant, misfortunes that arise in the course of daily social life are another matter. Unlike the Azande, the Nuer do not see them as caused by witchcraft, which must be discovered through oracles so the witch can be pointed out; they feel strongly that such things should be seen as their own fault, as reversals caused by their own wrongdoing. And they believe that life cannot go on, nor can their community prosper, until matters have been made right before God—until the pollution of their wrongs has been purged. To this idea we will return shortly.

Spirits of the Above

In addition to God, the spirit of the sky, the world of the Nuer does embrace other, lesser spirits. They fall into two main groups: the "spirits of the above," that is, spirits who live primarily in the air, and "spirits of the below," those associated strictly with earth.

Spirits of the above include *deng*, the son of God; *mani*, the spirit who leads in war; *wiu*, the god of the clan assembled; and *buk*, a female spirit, called the mother of *deng*, who is associated especially with rivers and streams. Though their primary dwelling is the air, these spirits can seize and enter the bodies of human beings. When this happens in a temporary way, the sign of it in the person possessed is sickness. But there is also a more lasting kind of possession experienced by those who are recognized as prophets. Such persons are actually described as permanent possessors, or owners, of a spirit. Historically, the main role of these figures was to serve as inspired leaders in battle, especially during cattle raids upon the neighboring Dinka tribe. But in the modern era, Evans-Pritchard notes, that duty is seldom carried out. In no case does the spirit of the sky, *Kwoth nhial,* ever stoop to possess a human being. He is far, far above anything like that.

If we ask what is the relation of these secondary *kuth,* or spirits, to God, we meet one of the most complex and subtle points in the whole of Nuer theology. Typical of his approach, Evans-Pritchard makes a very close comparative analysis of Nuer speech patterns in order to determine exactly how, and in exactly what contexts, they use the terms *Kwoth nhial* (God) and *kuth nhial* (spirits of the air). The usage patterns show that in certain contexts the Nuer clearly think of the air spirits as beings with their own identity, separate and distinguishable from each other. Just as clearly, they fall between God and humanity; they are lesser spirits, beings whom the people often regard more with annoyance than fear. At the same time, being *kuth,* they are in other respects thought of as inseparable from *Kwoth nhial,* the supreme God. In other words,

> they are many but also one. God is manifested in, and in a sense is, each of them. I received the impression that in sacrificing or in singing hymns to an air-spirit Nuer do not think that they are communicating with the spirit and not with God. They are, if I have understood the matter correctly, addressing God in a particular spiritual figure or manifestation. . . . They do not see a contradiction here, and there is no reason why they should see one. God is not a particular air-spirit but the spirit is a figure of God. . . . Nuer pass without difficulty or hesitation from a more general and comprehensive way of conceiving of God or Spirit to a more particular and limited way . . . and back again.[29]

Among other things, this short sample of Evans-Pritchard's analysis shows why his work has been so much admired. He was an anthropologist who worked with great discipline, precision, and determination. Not content to find out in a general way what the Nuer think, he can be seen here, as in many other places, striving to catch each connection, sort out any confusion, and make clear each shade of difference or emphasis. In the process, of course, he was also able to win from Western scholars a respect for Nuer thought that had rarely been given to primitive peoples in the past. Instead of a culture marked by savagery and superstition, he presents a people whose material life may be very simple but whose theology is abstract and sophisticated, in certain respects strongly resembling both Jewish monotheism and Christian mysticism.[30]

Among the spirits of the air, those called *colwic* are a special class; they are the spirits created directly from the souls of human beings struck down by lightning. When lightning strikes a hut and kills its occupants, the Nuer regard this awesome event as a direct act of God, who has chosen to take back these souls for his own use. The bodies of such people, as we noted, are not buried in the normal way, for they have been instantly transformed into spirits. In their air-spiritual form, however, they often keep their connection to their original human families, serving as their patrons and protectors.

Spirits of the Below

As family guardians, the *colwic* spirits provide the Nuer with a link between one form of their gods and one part of their social structure: the family, or lineage. We find further connections of this sort the moment we turn to the other main class of divinities: the "spirits of the below," whose natural ties are to the earth rather than the sky. These spirits are held in much lower regard than those of the air; in fact, they seem hardly even to qualify as *kwoth,* though that is what they are called. It is interesting to notice that after all the attention lavished on the topic by earlier theorists of religion, this is where the controversial phenomenon of totemism finally appears in Nuer religion—much farther down the scale of importance than Frazer, Durkheim, or Freud could ever have imagined. The Nuer do recognize totem spirits, which they associate with animal species, such as the crocodile, lion, lizard, snake, egret, and even plants, gourds, rivers, and streams. Consistent with totemic customs elsewhere, members of a specific tribe or clan are said to give "respect" to their totem animal. They do not eat it; they acknowledge it when seen; and they bury it if they should happen to find it dead in the wild. The totem animal, however, is not the same as the totem spirit. The Nuer clearly think of these two as separate, though they are, of course, closely related. They take the totem animal to be a physical symbol of the totem spirit, which is a manifestation of *Kwoth.* The totem animal is always less important than the totem spirit. But totem spirits, in turn, are always less important than spirits of the air; unlike the air spirits, they must remain connected to their physical symbol, the totem animal.

Nuer theology holds finally that there are mystical objects, persons, and powers on a still lower level than spirits of the air—so low, in fact, that they take us to the margins of tribal life. There are diviners, and there are healers of a sort. The concern of these people is with minor ailments and anxieties, like fortune-tellers in our own society. In the same class are the people who control fetishes and nature sprites. These are mystically charged objects or natural occurrences that are thought to fall under the control of an individual person. The owner of a fetish, for example, may use its mystical power to avenge an injury to himself, or, then again, just to make himself feel important. In general, however, the Nuer have a dislike or at least a healthy low-grade fear of these things. Though called "spirits," they regard them as hardly deserving of the name. And there is a general suspicion that they are not genuine; there is a feeling (probably correct) that they are alien things, which have come into Nuer culture from other tribes that they dislike, especially the Dinka.

Religion and Refraction in the Social Order

Totemic and *colwic* spirits both exhibit what Evans-Pritchard calls the "social refraction" of religion. As white light is split by a prism into different colors, so the Nuer seem to think of Spirit, or God, as in these cases "refracted" into different bands, or levels, of divine power that apply in a particular way to different clans or social groups. In these cases, though the Nuer feel they are still worshipping God, they worship him as figured, or symbolized, in association with one lineage, clan, or social group in particular. Spirits of the air sometimes also assume this role when they possess a prophet who becomes a public spokesman for a clan, or when they are called upon in a special way by a certain lineage. So too with fetishes and nature sprites, which often are quite literally owned and inherited through families. Interestingly, Evans-Pritchard notes that the lower we travel down the scale of Nuer spirits, the nearer we come to the kind of elaborate and ritualized ceremonies that are normally associated with religion in the West. God, the spirit of the sky, is worshipped through simple prayer and sacrifice, while such things as hymns, possessions, and divination become more common as we descend through the spirits of the air and down to the spirits of the below.

This hierarchy of spirits tends to show itself in other ways as well. There is a political dimension, with God conceived as ruler and spirits of the air as aristocracy; below them come the totem spirits, which, as we saw, fill a middle rank, in essence spiritual but on display mainly in animals and plants; and last, fetishes fall into the undesirable position of outcast or largely foreign objects, however mystical their powers. In similar fashion, the Nuer trace a persistent contrast between the light and darkness, the first belonging always to the spirits of the air, the second always associated with those of the below. Even age comes to figure in the contrast. God is the eldest of the spirits; spirits of the air are his children; totemic spirits are the children of his daughters, and so on.

It is only natural to think of Durkheim when we follow these connections between layers of divinity and levels of society. In some respects, Nuer spirits obviously mirror social groups and attachments. But to Evans-Pritchard, this is hardly the complete picture. "An interpretation in terms of social structure," he writes, "merely shows us how the idea of Spirit takes various forms corresponding to departments of social life. It does not enable us to understand any better the intrinsic nature of the idea itself."[31] In language that recalls Eliade's strong opposition to reductionism, we are told that the value of a sociological model "is limited, for it does not help us to understand the specifically religious facts any better." Evans-Pritchard then adds,

> Were I writing about Nuer social structure this is the feature of the religion
> that it would be most necessary to stress. But in a study of religion, if we
> wish to seize the essential nature of what we are inquiring into, we have to
> try to examine the matter from the inside also, to see it as Nuer see it.[32]

Symbolism

After discussing spirit in its multiple forms, Evans-Pritchard turns to an important—and now famous—discussion of Nuer symbolism. He points out that this is the subject on which the primitive mind has been most commonly misunderstood. He begins with a very careful analysis of language, particularly what the Nuer mean when they say one thing "is" another. When a bird, for example, perches on top of a hut, they are known to say, "It is *kwoth*," or spirit. Or they may say that a crocodile is spirit, meaning that it has the significance of spirit for people who call the crocodile their totem and give reverence to the crocodile totem spirit. Again, they sometimes say that an ox is a cucumber, but only in situations where an ox must be sacrificed and none can be found or spared, so custom allows for a cucumber to be substituted—to be placed, that is, in the role of the ox. To all appearances the cucumber is still a fruit, and no one would pretend to deny it. Conceptually, however, it is in this situation given a new role, that of a (substitute) ox in sacrifice.

Again, in words remarkably like the phrase "I am a red parakeet," which so interested Lévy-Bruhl, the Nuer will say, "A twin is a bird." Lévy-Bruhl believed that such contradictory phrases show the prelogical, primitive mind at work. But do they? In a miniature masterpiece of explication, Evans-Pritchard shows what this phrase really means in Nuer culture. Birds, as the only creatures that fly in the air, are regarded as particularly close to spirit, which as we have seen is also associated with the air in the cases of both the spirits of the air and God, the "spirit of the sky." On the other hand, the birth of twins, because it is a quite unusual event, is in its way also a sign that spirit is present in a special form. Twins are given special treatment in Nuer culture, being thought of on some occasions as one personality even though they are two separate physical individuals. Twins do not receive the same sort of funeral as ordinary people, for they are said to be "people of the air" rather than, like all others, "people of the below."[33] Both twins and birds, in other words, are in an unusual way *gaat Kwoth,* "children of God," and it is in that respect that they are identical.

Against the full background of Nuer theology, then, it is clearly true, and not in the least a contradiction, to say that twins are birds. But if so, then there is also no need to claim, as Lévy-Bruhl did, that people like the Nuer have a prelogical mentality; their thought, in their terms and in ours, is quite logical enough.

Evans-Pritchard tells us further that Lévy-Bruhl was not the only one to fall into this kind of error. Earlier investigators like Müller and Tylor tended to make the same mistake when they claimed that primitive people believed the sun or moon was a divinity. Being insufficiently informed about the larger context in which primitive or ancient peoples might have made such statements, they failed to make enough allowance for metaphors, figures of speech, and multiple meanings of words. When some primitives name the sun a divinity or spirit, they may mean no more than that such an object *suggests* or *symbolizes* divinity to them, or that it simply shares one of the qualities of divinity—its grandeur or brightness or beauty. In Evans-Pritchard's view, most anthropological writers have been sorely deficient in appreciating the richly poetic habits of speech adopted by primitive peoples. In their imaginative way of describing the world, analogies, figures, symbols, and metaphors are the rule of language, not the exception.

Ghosts and the Soul

The Nuer believe that there are three parts to the human being: the flesh, the life (or breath), and the soul (or intellect). At death, the first of these goes into the ground and decays; the second goes back to God, who gave it; and the third lingers for a time near the realm of the living until it eventually disappears. The Nuer are not happy if it stays for long. They have a true horror of death, in part because all of their attention is centered on this life, which they wish to have and enjoy in abundance. Says Evans-Pritchard, "They neither pretend to know, nor, I think, do they care, what happens to them after death. There is an almost total lack of what in Western religions falls into the category of eschatology."[34] The Nuer prefer not even to talk about death. Their main concern at funerals is to make sure that the souls of the dead are given their full status as ghosts, so that they can be separated completely from the affairs of those who remain on earth. The only way a ghost can trouble the living is through *cien*, or vengeance, which may come if a person were wronged while alive and then died before a reconciliation could be made. When this situation occurs, it is necessary to make a sacrifice to God and a gift of reparation to the ghost. Since only wrongs done in life can lead to *cien*, the living can at least rest assured that only the recently dead will ever try to bother them. The dead, and their ghosts, are rather quickly forgotten in Nuer life.

For the Nuer, "soul" is something that only humans possess, and Evans-Pritchard notes that this fact bears directly on Tylor's famous animistic theory of religion.[35] Tylor, as we saw earlier, thought that early peoples developed their idea of spirits and demons out of the idea of the human soul, which they got from dreams and visions. This primitive concept of a soul led naturally to that of a spirit and thence to gods. If we look closely, however, that is not the case with the Nuer, who find these two to be very different and even opposed things. Soul is a part of all human beings, and it is created; spirit exists outside of human life, and when it enters a person, it always does so as an invasion from the outside. Even in the case of the *colwic* spirits, those persons taken by lightning, the Nuer are careful to say that their souls must be replaced by spirit at the moment they are taken. The one is so different from the other that any idea of derivation seems impossible. And in that Evans-Pritchard finds a lesson. We should notice, he warns, how Tylor's theory, which seems perfectly reasonable and natural when it is pieced together out of scattered fragments of mythology and folklore, looks very different when brought up against the concrete evidence of an actual system of primitive religious thought.

Sin and Sacrifice

The idea of sin—including the suffering that is associated with it—is central to understanding the human side of Nuer religion. The Nuer conceive of wrongdoing in two basic forms, both of which are defined by the concept of *thek*, or "respect." Among the Nuer as in other tribal cultures, various things are prohibited out of respect for others. A man, for example, ought not to be seen naked by other women in his wife's family; a new wife avoids her husband's parents; engaged or newly married couples ought never to eat in each other's presence, and so on. When these rules are broken, even unintentionally (as they most often are), the acts are considered faults, and they bring a measure of shame upon those responsible for them. In other cases, however, breaches of *thek* are more serious; they may involve such things as adultery or incest, and they are known as *nueer,* acts regarded as "death." These are usually intended actions, and they are not just shameful but sinful. Their consequence is sickness, which in Nuer thought will lead to death unless there is an appropriate sacrifice to God, who is the guardian of the entire moral order.

Though it has its human effects, all sin ultimately is sin against God, and its main consequence is to bring God, by way of his punishments, into the affairs of the community. This is a dangerous situation, for, ideally, the Nuer want God to rule but at a safe distance, looking after his world and his creatures with pleasure and not needing to enter it with punishments. The only way the danger of such divine involvement can be cleared is through sacrifice. The ceremony of sacrifice is almost the only element of Nuer religion that might qualify as a full-scale religious sacrament, though even here the most important instances are largely personal affairs—transactions between one or a few persons and God.

Sacrifice in Nuer life is of two kinds: personal and collective. The second of these—group sacrifice—seems to be the less clearly religious and perhaps less important. It occurs in connection with rites of passage, especially weddings and funerals, and its purpose is to make sacred an otherwise secular event. "It sacralizes the social event and the new relationships brought about by it. It solemnizes the change of status or relationship, giving it religious validation. On such occasions sacrifice has generally a conspicuously festal and eucharistic character."[36] The level of attention given to sacrifice on these occasions, and the emotions on exhibit, vary greatly from one person to the next; some are indifferent and almost bored, others are serious, while still others may be happy and jovial.[37] Their attitudes do not offer much support, Evans-Pritchard observes, for the views of those theorists who find the essence of religion in some unique feeling of awe, ecstasy, or fear. All kinds of emotions seem acceptable.

Unlike the group rites, personal sacrifices are more seriously religious occasions. When properly done, they require the death of an ox—the most precious possession any Nuer can claim. The ceremony, which can be held in almost any location, is conducted normally by an older male, preferably the head of a family, and occurs in four stages. There is a presentation of the designated victim to God; a consecration, in which ashes are rubbed on the back of the animal; an invocation, in which the celebrant "states the intention of the sacrifice and matters relevant to it"; and finally the immolation, in which the ox is killed, usually with a quick single spear thrust from the side into the heart.[38]

The roles of the ox and of the spear in this ritual are quite important, for the Nuer identify themselves closely with both. For the Nuer man, the spear in his right hand communicates power, virility, authority, and goodness. It is "a projection of the self and stands for the self"; by extension, it also serves to represent the clan or lineage group, which is, in fact, called by its spear name.[39] The spear represents the clan in its unity and strength—the clan as prepared for war. The ox, on the other hand, represents a more strictly personal attachment. From the moment of initiation, when each Nuer boy is given his own ox, it is an animal he becomes extremely close to, an animal he identifies with, almost as a second self. And that identification is particularly important when, later in manhood, the occasion arises for personal sacrifice, for then the ox may have to be killed. In the rite of sacrifice, the rubbing of ashes on the back of the ox seems to fix the identification of the man with the beast. It is done always with the right hand, the spear hand, symbolizing the whole self, which is thus united to the animal in the last moments before it is slain. In the gesture of sacrifice to God, a man may be said to be enacting, through the victim, his own personal death.

It is not sufficient, in Evans-Pritchard's view, just to describe the procedure of Nuer sacrifice for his readers. Turning once again to a close analysis of language, he probes and explores to discover its meaning. In this connection, he notes that anthropology has in general proposed two main views of primitive sacrifice: the gift theory and the communion theory. The latter was put forward in connection with totemism by Robertson Smith, who by now has become a familiar name in our discussions. Smith believed that by killing the animal and eating it, people engaged in an act of social communion, or solidarity—a sacred sharing of food and friendship with each other and with God. There were no "bargains" or trade-offs involved. The gift theory, on the other hand, proposes just that: an exchange, or trade, in which something is given to God, who gives his favor in return. Nuer ceremonies, Evans-Pritchard tells us, clearly belong in some sort of "gift" category. Their central purpose is to give something very precious to God, even though God, of course, does not get anything he does not already have. The important thing is that a human being, responsible and at fault, undergoes a loss, a denial of the self, that connects deeply with a personal sense of guilt for wrong and expresses the desire for evil to be purged, expiated, cleansed, and expelled. It is not a case of God being angry and needing to be pleased. It is a case of the human need to make a transfer of that which is evil in oneself to the ox as a representative, "so that in its death that part may be eliminated and flow away with the blood."[40] Dramatic as the ceremony may be, the key thing is not the ritual but inward intention. In this serious and necessary transaction, the person who sacrifices—and the community about him—finds a release from the dangerous visit of spirit to human affairs. With the atonement complete, God can at last "turn away" and be finished with the entire matter. The family, clan, or tribe can again feel out of danger.

Evans-Pritchard closes his discussion with a short account of prophets and priests, none of whom is central to Nuer religion in the way that they are for religions like Judaism and Christianity. The most important is the leopard-skin priest, who performs his role mainly in connection with a murder or some other circumstance in which a human life is taken. His task is to provide sanctuary for the killer, to begin a process of reconciliation with the victim's family, and to arrange compensation for the act, so as to prevent any one such terrible event from spiraling into a destructive blood feud. He is thus a valuable figure, but more for social than religious reasons. Other figures include the cattle man, or cattle priest, and the prophet. In the past these figures, who claim to possess (or be possessed by) certain spirits of the air, acquired political significance among the Nuer clans and therefore were suppressed by colonial authorities. They are not rivals of the priests, but the keen interests of some in material things, and the unusual behavior of most, have caused the Nuer people as a whole to view them with mixed feelings.

As with *Witchcraft among the Azande* and the other Nuer books, one cannot read *Nuer Religion* without coming to appreciate the careful and thorough work of its author. Only the most patient study in the field could yield the precise, sympathetic, and systematic account of primitive beliefs and rituals that appears in its pages. From its narrative two things clearly emerge: (1) a picture full of correctives for nearly every one of those theorists who has formed a personal image of "primitive religion" without ever having come into contact with the real thing and (2) the portrait of a complex, well-ordered religious system, one that seems almost surprisingly Western and even "modern" in character.[41]

Theories of Primitive Religion

Early in the 1960s, Evans-Pritchard was invited to give a short series of lectures at the University College of Wales. He took the occasion as an opportunity to revisit several issues first raised in the conclusion of *Nuer Religion* and expand them into a general discussion of lectures theories of primitive religion. In 1965 the lectures were published as *Theories of Primi-*

tive Religion, one of Evans-Pritchard's shortest but most enjoyable books—a work whose pages not only sparkle with clear analyses and penetrating criticisms but are often adorned with choice exhibits of his stinging wit. In addition, by way of its judgments on others, the analyses in this book indirectly say much about his own fully ripened views on the matter of explaining religion. Though we have space here to look at this work only briefly, we can at least trace the general lines of its argument.

Evans-Pritchard opens *Theories of Primitive Religion* with a word of caution and some candid comments about earlier approaches to the subject. Most of the interpretations he considers were developed at a time when little was known and a great deal was misunderstood about the actual facts of primitive religion. Few people who engaged the issue had even seen a primitive culture, let alone studied one. But not for a moment, he declares, did that stop them from writing on the subject, with all the confusion and distortion one would naturally expect in the process. He further observes that nearly all of these thinkers start with the premise that most of religion, like most of magic, is something quite strange to modern people, who think scientifically, but quite normal to primitive people, who have no difficulty accepting absurd and incredible ideas. They see primitives as "quite irrational" people, "living in a mysterious world of doubts and fears, in terror of the supernatural and ceaselessly occupied in coping with it."[42] The challenge they thus find themselves facing is to give a reasoned and plausible explanation of why early peoples held these beliefs, and why, despite the progress of science, so many other people still do. The explanations they propose, which include those considered or mentioned in our own earlier chapters, are of two main types: psychological and sociological. Those taking the path of psychological explanation include Müller, Tylor, Frazer, Freud, and others. Numbered among the sociological theorists are Marx and Durkheim, naturally, as well as Durkheim's disciples, Lévy-Bruhl, and a sequence of others.

In framing their psychological accounts of religion, Evans-Pritchard notes that theorists have almost without exception resorted mainly to clever guesswork. Each has simply asked himself how he, an educated Westerner, might have come to hold a religious or magical belief if he were walking in the footsteps of some primitive person who one day put his hand to his chin to reflect upon the world around him. Müller, a sentimental and romantic gentleman, says he would have been dazzled and intrigued by nature's great displays of power; accordingly, he finds the origin of religion in nature worship. Tylor, a flinty rationalist, thinks he would have been puzzled by the human figures he sees in dreams; so he produces the animistic theory. Frazer, both a rationalist and evolutionist, thinks he would have started with magic, then changed to religion, and finally adopted science. Being intellectuals, they all offer psychological explanations we can call intellectualist. They think that primitive people, like themselves, wanted to explain everything and so settled upon religious beliefs as a way of showing how the world works.

Other psychological interpreters, alert to the fact that while not all people are thinkers, all do have feelings, have put forward a type of theory best called emotionalist. Freud, for example, imagines that early people were gripped by anxieties and fears that could be eased only by concluding there was a divine Father above them. The English scholar Marett and the anthropologists Lowie and Malinowski suppose that primitives felt a certain profound awe and wonder about life and took this as a sign of some awesome Being or Power who had created it. Regardless of the specifics, however, one common feature is apparent in every one of these theories: They are pure speculation. Evans-Pritchard calls them examples of the "If-I-were-a-horse" mistake. Because these interpreters do not really know how a primitive person thinks, they imagine he or she would think as they do. Some make matters even worse by supposing that they can actually reconstruct the thoughts not just of today's primitives but of the very people who thousands of years ago first created religion, even though these ancient believers have left us not a single written word about anything in their lives, let alone their thoughts about a god or gods! Needless to say, the unsparing verdict Evans-Pritchard renders on such psychological theories is that they are for the most part worthless.

Sociological thinkers, Evans-Pritchard continues, have done a somewhat better job, but not by much. The most important theories framed along these lines are those of Robertson Smith, the French scholar Fustel de Coulanges, and of course Émile Durkheim. These scholars have noticed, quite correctly, that however primitive people think, they do not do it on their own, any more than civilized people do. They are part of a culture, a society, which shapes their language, values, and ideas. Yet even with this insight at their disposal, sociological theorists have been no less inclined to guesswork than their psychological rivals. Because none of them actually knows a real primitive society, each simply chooses to create one in his imagination out of the scraps of evidence about totemism, sacrifice, or some other custom that happens to float in conveniently from Australia or other remote parts of the globe. As a result, even the most brilliant of the sociological theorists, Durkheim, constructs a theory that, however fascinating, begins to crumble the moment new evidence comes along to show that totemism is something very different, and much more diverse in kind, than he thinks it is. For all their promise, then, sociological theories come in the end to something only slightly better than psychological ones; they still tend toward the fallacy that begins, "If I were a horse."

By contrast with these efforts, Evans-Pritchard finds it refreshing to note the achievement, limited as it is, of Lucien Lévy-Bruhl. He, too, scarcely left the comfort of his study, and he was mistaken to think that the primitive mind is prelogical while the modern mind is not. But he was a penetrating thinker, who, almost alone among modern theorists, recognized the crucial principle that we cannot understand the culture or religion of primitives until we concede that their whole world may be a very different one from ours, and that this world cannot be properly explained until we have worked very hard and very long to understand how it functions *from the inside*.[43]

With so many failures and only Lévy-Bruhl to admire, one is inclined at this point to ask whether even attempting to explain religion is any longer worth the effort. Interestingly, and despite the record, Evans-Pritchard very much thinks it is. He believes, in fact, that more explanation, not less, should be offered, so long, of course, as theorists are ready to learn from the mistakes of their predecessors. There is, after all, at least a grain or more of truth in these earlier theories. There can be no question that religion involves the intellect, that it engages the emotions, and that it is closely associated with social organization. But it cannot be explained by any one of these factors alone. It must be explained comprehensively, in terms of its relations with all other factors and activities in a given society. In addition, though the guesswork of the past has compelled current anthropology to turn toward careful, specialized studies of specific cultures like the Azande and the Nuer, interpreters do need to move beyond specialized work. At some point, theorists need to "take into consideration all religions and not just primitive religions."[44] In this connection, Evans-Pritchard notes, one promising general path of inquiry has already been charted by the Italian social theorist Vilfredo Pareto, the French philosopher Henri Bergson, and the German sociologist Max Weber, all of whose writings seem to converge on a common theme. Instead of regarding religion and magic as forms of primitive thought, while science is assumed to be modern, they suggest that these two types of thinking are perhaps best seen as complementary configurations—forms of understanding that are clearly different but equally necessary in all human cultures, primitive and modern alike. No society can survive without something like science *and* something like religion; all cultures will always need both science's constructs of the mind and religion's "constructs of the heart."[45]

Evans-Pritchard does not completely commit himself to this last view, but he does suggest that it ought to be pursued as a hypothesis and that it should be confirmed or disproved through further work in the comparative study of religion, which has been sadly lacking to date. Moreover, such study should center not on theological writings, which carry the ideas of elites and leaders, but on encounters with ordinary people, on religious faith as it is actually lived and practiced. That is a difficult enterprise, he notes in conclusion, and the scholar without any personal religious commitment is unlikely to succeed in it. For the study of religion is not entirely like other disciplines. Scholars who reject all religion will inevitably be looking for some explanation that reduces it, some theory—biological, social, or psychological—that will explain it away. The believer, on the other hand, is a person much more likely to see religion—including other people's religions—from the inside and to try to explain it on terms that are its own.

Analysis

One way to measure Evans-Pritchard as a theorist of religion is to place his work next to that of Eliade, who is almost his exact contemporary. Both men began their work in the decades between the two world wars, at a time when functionalist interpretations were dominant and when, in European culture as a whole, reductionist Freudians and the followers of Marx were regarded as the most impressive thinkers of the age. Both men came to reject this dominant perspective and anchor their work in a more sympathetic approach to the religion of primitive (in Eliade's word, "archaic") peoples. Both also insist that there must be no more lapses into evolutionary thinking, which is useless for the study of human cultural activities; besides, it never fails to put primitives at the bottom and beginning of history while Western culture is placed at the end and the top. Finally, both men—it is not irrelevant to add—exhibit a natural sympathy for religion that arises out of personal heritage or commitment: Eliade to Romanian "cosmic" Christianity, Evans-Pritchard to Catholic Christianity after his conversion in 1944.[46]

Agreed as they are against certain attitudes of the age, Eliade and Evans-Pritchard nonetheless choose to carry out their programs of opposition in quite different ways. Starting from a resolute rejection of all reductionism, Eliade sets out to draw a global portrait of "the religious mind" in all, or at least most, places and times. He is also a man of the library, who thinks religion can still best be understood through its recorded history and mythology. Evans-Pritchard's course is quite noticeably different. He too comes to reject functionalism, at least in its more extreme reductionist form, and the whole thrust of his research is to show that there really is no need for it.

After all, if primitive magical and religious systems are in their terms just as rational as ours, we certainly do not need a reductionist theory to explain why people believe irrational things. At the same time, he is not nearly so emphatic about all of this as Eliade, especially in the case of sociologically functional approaches to religion, which played a strong role in his training and earlier work. He opposes any sociological determinism, to be sure, but, as we have seen, he also has the keenest appreciation for the merits of the French school—for Durkheim and especially Lévy-Bruhl.[47] In addition, he has no wish to make claims about "the archaic mind" on some sort of world-wide, all-embracing scale. In his view, theories of that sort give us just another instance of "If-I-were-a-horse" speculation. Not that there is anything necessarily wrong with the *ideal* of a broad, general theory embracing all of religion. At the close of *Nuer Religion,* Evans-Pritchard describes his own work as a step toward "building up a classification of African philosophies" that will make for the even wider comparisons needed to construct a theory of religion as a whole.[48] But to be done right, such things take time, patience, and a great deal more research. They simply cannot be done as effortlessly as theorists like Eliade, and those of the past century, have supposed. Nor can they be done in the same way. Regardless of whether it is a world religion or primitive cult one studies, Evans-Pritchard insists that in the future the real work must be done outside of libraries and theological texts. A valid theory will have to explain religion as it is lived by ordinary people, not as it is taught by priests and theologians. That is where the real source of its power and remarkable resilience will ultimately be found.

If we draw a comparison with economics, we can see that Evans-Pritchard's great achievement lies on the plane not of macro- but micro-theory of religion. In his detailed account of Nuer belief and practice, he is able to show, just as he did for Zande magic, how religion "makes sense" for a specific people, in a specific kind of tribal society, at a specific point in time. He shows how this religion is intellectually coherent, how it "fits together" within itself. And he shows that it is culturally connected; it fits into the patterns of Nuer life in ways that answer both personal and social needs. When we compare Evans-Pritchard's own very solid, small-scale achievement in *Nuer Religion* with the grand, theoretical balloons he floats by us from the past, puncturing them as he writes, it is not hard to see which kind of work, in his eyes, carries the greater weight. On the issue of how best to construct theories that reflect a true "science" of religion, his work represents an unmistakable turning point. No subsequent interpreter can afford to ignore his achievement.

Critique

As Freud's theory of religion depends in part on the strength of his psychology, so the value of Evans-Pritchard's theory rests in part on the nature and quality of his anthropology. As we have noted above, the judgment of most anthropologists on the value of his fieldwork and his interpretation of cultures is extraordinarily high. He is regarded by some as the greatest ethnographer ever to have worked in the field. Though there have been criticisms of him, the most important ones do not seem to bear on the religious dimensions of his work.[49] So we can perhaps pass over these and note for our purpose the following points, which more specifically address his approach to religion.

1. Assessments of Other Theories

There are places where Evans-Pritchard shows considerably less patience with the theories of his fellow scholars than he does with the thought of the Azande and the Nuer. In discussing Nuer sacrifice, for example, he criticizes as "inept" those thinkers—like Rudolf Otto—who find the origin of religion in a distinctive emotion of awe or solemn wonder. The crowds at Nuer collective ceremonies show all kinds of emotions: attention, indifference, solemnity, amusement, whatever.[50] Having said this, however, Evans-Pritchard in the very same context also points out that these collective sacrifices occur on occasions that are barely religious at all; they are largely social events, where one would expect a great variety of emotions, including, of course, at least a few serious moments.[51] When, on the other hand, he discusses personal sacrifices, which by his own account are more purely religious occasions, the emotional state of the participants seems to be quite different. They are expected to show a sincerity and solemn disposition that seem not at all unlike the emotions Otto calls religious. They show a mood of solemnity and awe, a sense—one might almost say—of the numinous. This is not to say that Nuer religion offers a confirmation of theories like Otto's; it is meant only to suggest that when dealing with other theorists Evans-Pritchard shows an occasional rush to judgment. The same tends to be true when he demolishes other theories with his favorite hammer: the "If-I-were-a-horse" fallacy. In a sense, the method of "If-I-were-so-and-so" is the only one we have when we wish to understand the motives and actions of other people, as the detective does when trying to rethink the actions of a person who has committed a crime. The real problem with this kind of argument, which Evans-Pritchard does not strive very hard to detect, is not *that* it is used (we really have no other) but *how* it is used, especially when people merely guess about how tribal peoples think instead of carefully reconstructing their thought on a solid foundation of evidence.

2. The "Primitive" Mind

Evans-Pritchard's great achievement has been to give theorists of both religion and human society a greater appreciation for what we can call "the normality" of the primitive mind. In the light of his work, we can say that the world of non-Western, tribal thought seems to make sense; it seems to us no longer absurd or childish, as it once seemed to Tylor, Frazer, and others. But even so, we can legitimately ask whether Evans-Pritchard has solved as much of the problem of the primitive mind as he may seem to think. It is interesting, in the case of the Azande, for example, that after analyzing a particular item of witchcraft, he will write something on the order of the following: "Azande have little theory about their oracles and do not feel the need for doctrines."[52] Or in another connection he will observe that the idea of testing general beliefs against actual experience is simply foreign to them. On reading this, the question that naturally comes to the mind of the reader is: Why not? *Why* do the Azande fail to test their beliefs? Evans-Pritchard's answer to this question is well known. He says magic is something too fundamental, and too important, in Zande life ever to be questioned—*as are* some of the inconsistent and seemingly illogical notions that many ordinary people hold in our culture as well. In short, they and we are the same, neither of us being in the sum of things either fully rational or wholly irrational. But here there is a further question to be asked. We and they do not seem to be *exactly* the same, for our culture is quite clearly a divided one. Some people in it—scientists, philosophers, mathematicians, even philosophical theologians—*do* stress theoretical understanding of the world, while others of us do not. Zande culture, on the contrary, seems curiously *un*divided. In it, we seem unable to find *anyone* who wants to defend theoretical knowledge and testing, or *anyone* who believes in critical, logical, and experimental thought. In that sense, this society *is* different, and we would very much like to know why. Evans-Pritchard does not really pursue this question, even though it is clearly important to the defense of his view that our culture and theirs stand on intellectually equal footings.[53]

3. The Need for Theory

The last complaint we might bring against Evans-Pritchard is in some ways the most obvious and important—and yet the one to which he would most readily plead guilty. He does not really have a full theory of religion, or

even of primitive religion, but only a theory of *a* religion—that of the
Nuer—along with a few suggestions as to how thoughtful scholars can begin
to work so as one day actually to arrive at something more general. Far
better, he tells us, to do the small-scale foundational work that in the future
will yield a solid general theory than to rush once again into the groundless
speculations that were the trademark of theories past. This is a point no one
can dispute. Yet true as it may be, Evans-Pritchard himself recognizes that
this is not an entirely satisfactory way to leave things. A revealing comment
comes in the concluding pages of *Theories of Primitive Religion:*

> During [the] last century . . . general statements were indeed attempted . . .
> in the form of evolutionary and psychological and sociological hypotheses,
> but since these attempts at general formulations seem to have been abandoned
> by anthropologists, our subject has suffered from loss of common aim and
> method.[54]

We could almost wonder, in light of these comments, whether Evans-
Pritchard's weakness is just the opposite of his predecessors'. Could the
study of religion have been done an even greater service if someone as well
grounded as he in the evidence were perhaps *more* willing to generalize—
even if only on the order of suggestion and hypothesis? Could he not himself
have possibly contributed something to this much-needed "common aim and
method"? At the very least, a book from his hand with a title such as "Notes
Toward the Construction of a General Theory of Religion" would certainly
not have gone unread.

Even without such an effort, however, Evans-Pritchard's influence on
thought about religion, especially in anthropological circles during the last
half of our century, has been enormous. We shall see an instructive parallel
to it in the next and last of our theorists, Clifford Geertz, the contemporary
American advocate of interpretive anthropology.

Notes

1. *Edward Evan Evans-Pritchard* (1980), p. 93; see n. 2 below.
2. There is no complete biography of Evans-Pritchard. T. O. Beidelman, *A Bibliography of the Writings of E. E. Evans-Pritchard* (London: Tavistock Publications,
1974), pp. 1–4, provides a brief biographical note, and he gives a more substantial
account in "Sir Edward Evans-Pritchard, 1902–1973: An Appreciation," *Anthropos*
69 (1974): 553–67. There is also a measure of biographical information in a critical
study by anthropologist Mary Douglas, who has been strongly influenced by Evans-
Pritchard; see her *Edward Evans-Pritchard,* Modern Masters Series (New York: Viking Press, 1980), pp. 1–22 et passim.
3. Evans-Pritchard himself gives an account of this important development in an

introduction to anthropology that he provided in a series of lectures given for the BBC in 1950. They were later published under the title *Social Anthropology;* see his *Social Anthropology and Other Essays* (Glencoe, IL: The Free Press, [1951] 1962), pp. 43–85.

4. John Middleton, "E. E. Evans-Pritchard," *The Macmillan Encyclopedia of Religion,* 8: 198.

5. He gives a fascinating account of this campaign in "Operations on the Akobo and Gila Rivers, 1940–41," *The Army Quarterly* 103, no. 4 (July 1973): 1–10; Clifford Geertz, *Works and Lives: The Anthropologist as Author* (Stanford, CA: Stanford University Press, 1988), pp. 49–72, uses this account as the basis for an interesting appraisal of Evans-Pritchard's personality and work.

6. Beidelman, "Appreciation," p. 556.

7. For his judgments on this older, evolutionary tradition, see *Social Anthropology and Other Essays,* pp. 21–42 especially.

8. For Evans-Pritchard's assessments of Tylor and Frazer, see *Social Anthropology and Other Essays,* pp. 31–33; also *Theories of Primitive Religion* (Oxford, England: Clarendon Press, 1965), pp. 24–30; and portions of *A History of Anthropological Thought,* ed. Andre Singer (New York: Basic Books, 1981). For his specific address to Frazer's theory of magic, see "The Intellectualist (English) Interpretation of Magic," *Bulletin of the Faculty of Arts* (Egyptian University, Cairo) 1 (1933): 282–311.

9. See his comments in *Social Anthropology and Other Essays,* pp. 51–53; also in *Theories of Primitive Religion,* pp. 53–69, where he is, however, also severely critical.

10. Evans-Pritchard felt that this sociological premise was supported by philosophers like the Italian Eugenio Rignano (1870–1930) and confirmed by recent research in the psychology of perception. Most notably, the Cambridge experimental psychologist Frederick Bartlett had shown how people screen what comes to their senses and choose to accept or reject impressions based on their prior social conditioning. On this, see Douglas, *E. E. Evans-Pritchard,* pp. 6–24.

11. In its French original, *How Natives Think* appeared first, in 1910; it was not translated, however, until after the success of *The Primitive Mentality,* whose French original appeared in 1922 and received an English translation the very next year.

12. For a brief discussion of this example, which was to become famous in philosophical discussions of epistemology, see Douglas, *Evans-Pritchard,* pp. 8–12. Two of the more interesting discussions of the issue are Jonathan Z. Smith, "I Am a Parrot (Red)," *History of Religions* 2 (1972): 391–413; and Clifford Geertz, "Religion as Cultural System," in *Anthropological Approaches to the Study of Religion,* ed. Michael Banton (London: Tavistock Publications, 1966), pp. 37–38.

13. I am indebted to Professor Robert Segal for calling my attention to the long, thoughtful letter that Evans-Pritchard received from Lévy-Bruhl in November 1934 and for providing me with a copy of the published translation of it, which appeared in 1952: L. Lévy-Bruhl, "A Letter to E. E. Evans-Pritchard," *British Journal of Sociology* 3 (June 1952): 117–23. I have also benefitted greatly from Segal's perceptive comments in his review of Evans-Pritchard's *History of Anthropological*

Thought in *Annals of Scholarship* 2 (Winter 1981): 119–28. In his letter, Lévy-Bruhl was responding to an article Evans-Pritchard had published on his theory earlier that year; see "Lévy-Bruhl's Theory of Primitive Mentality," *Bulletin of the Faculty of Arts* (Egyptian University) 2 (1934): 1–36.

14. E. E. Evans-Pritchard, *Witchcraft, Oracles, and Magic among the Azande* (Oxford, England: Clarendon Press, 1937), p. 13.

15. Evans-Pritchard, *Witchcraft, Oracles, and Magic*, p. 63.

16. Evans-Pritchard, *Witchcraft, Oracles, and Magic*, p. 63.

17. Evans-Pritchard, *Witchcraft, Oracles, and Magic*, pp. 299–312.

18. Evans-Pritchard, *Witchcraft, Oracles, and Magic*, pp. 28–29.

19. Evans-Pritchard, *Witchcraft, Oracles, and Magic*, p. 378.

20. Evans-Pritchard, *Witchcraft, Oracles, and Magic*, p. 343.

21. Beidelman, "Evans-Pritchard: An Appreciation," p. 560, writes, "The Azande book is unquestionably the greatest single monograph ever written on an African people and one of the truly great books in anthropology."

22. Evans-Pritchard, *Witchcraft, Oracles, and Magic*, p. 69.

23. Evans-Pritchard, *Witchcraft, Oracles, and Magic*, p. 117.

24. Evans-Pritchard, *Witchcraft, Oracles, and Magic*, p. 63.

25. Evans-Pritchard, *Witchcraft, Oracles, and Magic*, p. 338.

26. On the importance of this book to current anthropology and the small "industry" of interpretation and evaluation it has produced, see Ivan Karp and Kent Maynard, "Reading *The Nuer*," *Current Anthropology* 24, no. 4 (August–October 1983): 481–92; comments on the article and a response from the authors can be found on pp. 492–503.

27. Douglas, *Evans-Pritchard*, pp. 91–113, points out that Evans-Pritchard prepared himself for writing on Nuer religion by reading extensively in the Western theological literature he found in his father's parsonage study. She adds that the description of *Kwoth nhial* as a god of selfless love seems to draw upon *Agape and Eros* (1936), a classic study of the concepts of love in Western religious thought by the Lutheran theologian Anders Nygren; Evans-Pritchard acknowledged this book and its influence in other works.

28. E. E. Evans-Pritchard, *Nuer Religion* (Oxford, England: Clarendon Press, 1956), p. 12.

29. Evans-Pritchard, *Nuer Religion*, pp. 51–52.

30. To those familiar with the mystical theology of the early and medieval Eastern church, the Nuer hierarchy of spirits reflecting God, but not identical to him, resembles the modalistic language used by the theologian Sabellius to explain the Trinity. Their beliefs about the *kuth nhial* also bear a likeness to the mystical doctrine of the heavenly angelic hierarchy as presented in the widely read early medieval treatises of Pseudo-Dionysius the Areopagite.

31. Evans-Pritchard, *Nuer Religion*, p. 121.

32. Evans-Pritchard, *Nuer Religion*, pp. 121–22.

33. Evans-Pritchard, *Nuer Religion*, p. 131.

34. Evans-Pritchard, *Nuer Religion*, p. 154.

35. Evans-Pritchard, *Nuer Religion*, p. 158.

36. Evans-Pritchard, *Nuer Religion*, p. 199.
37. Evans-Pritchard, *Nuer Religion*, pp. 207–208.
38. Evans-Pritchard, *Nuer Religion*, p. 208.
39. Evans-Pritchard, *Nuer Religion*, p. 239.
40. Evans-Pritchard, *Nuer Religion*, p. 281. It is worth noting, in connection with this discussion of sin and atonement, the classic study by Meyer Fortes, *Oedipus and Job in West African Religion* (Cambridge, England: Cambridge University Press, [1959] 1983). The work of Fortes, another fieldworking African anthropologist, is often mentioned in conjunction with Evans-Pritchard's; see Jack Goody, "Introduction," *Oedipus and Job*, p. vii.
41. In the preface to *Nuer Religion*, p. vii, Evans-Pritchard notes and agrees with the comment of Miss Ray Huffman, an American Presbyterian missionary who after many years among the Nuer observed that "the missionary feels as if he were living in Old Testament times." Douglas, *Evans-Pritchard*, p. 105, notes the strong similarities of this religion, with its emphasis on God as the upholder of the moral order and on inward conviction rather than ritual, to the most distinctively modern form of Christianity—Protestantism.
42. Evans-Pritchard, *Theories of Primitive Religion*, p. 10.
43. Evans-Pritchard, *Theories of Primitive Religion*, pp. 78–99.
44. Evans-Pritchard, *Theories of Primitive Religion*, p. 113.
45. Evans-Pritchard, *Theories of Primitive Religion*, p. 115.
46. It should not be assumed that Evans-Pritchard was especially nonreligious before his conversion, which for him was not a startling reversal or dramatic event. Douglas, *Evans-Pritchard*, p. 43, notes that he regarded it as "no sudden break with his past but the latest step in the steady development of one who had always been a Catholic at heart." See his "Fragment of an Autobiography," *New Blackfriars*, January 1973, pp. 35–37.
47. Douglas, *Evans-Pritchard*, p. 44, points in this connection to his study on *The Sanusi of Cyrenaica* (Oxford, England: Clarendon Press, 1949), which we have not been able to consider here. "Better than anything else he wrote," she observes, this book "explains his recurrent shafts of criticism against reductionist theorizing and against sociological determinism."
48. Evans-Pritchard, *Nuer Religion*, p. 314.
49. For a discussion of some of these criticisms, see Adam Kuper, *Anthropologists and Anthropology: The British School 1922–1972* (New York: Pica Press, 1973), pp. 111–19, et passim; see also the extensively revised edition, *Anthropology and Anthropologists: The Modern British School* (London: Routledge & Kegan Paul, 1983), pp. 88–98; for a thorough analysis of Evans-Pritchard's work on the Nuer, see Karp and Maynard, "Reading *The Nuer*," pp. 481–92, and the ensuing discussion, pp. 492–503.
50. Evans-Pritchard, *Nuer Religion*, p. 207.
51. Evans-Pritchard, *Nuer Religion*, p. 199.
52. Evans-Pritchard, *Witchcraft, Oracles, and Magic*, p. 314.
53. It should be noted, however, that in a famous article, "Understanding a Primitive Society," first published in the *American Philosophical Quarterly* in 1964, the

British philosopher Peter Winch persuasively argued precisely the opposite. Evans-Pritchard, he claimed, felt he had grounds to appreciate that the Azande, though wrong about magic, were nonetheless still rational. In fact, argues Winch, his sympathy for them did not go far enough. Evans-Pritchard should have said that not only were the Azande rational, but that he as an Englishman, starting from an entirely different set of assumptions about the world which the Azande did not accept, was not even justified in saying that they were wrong. Winch's provocative article became part of an extended and subtle debate over the nature of human rationality which engaged some of the most sophisticated minds in the circles of British analytical philosophy. For an introduction to this discussion, which continues to the present, see the collection of essays in Bryan R. Wilson, ed., *Rationality* (Oxford, England: Basil Blackwell, [1970] 1984), including pp. 78–111, where Winch's article is reprinted.

54. Evans-Pritchard, *Theories of Primitive Religion*, p. 114.

Suggestions for Further Reading

Beidelman, T. O. *A Bibliography of the Writings of E. E. Evans-Pritchard*, pp. 1–4. London: Tavistock Publications, 1974. Provides a brief biographical note on Evans-Pritchard's career. There is no comprehensive biography.

Beidelman, T. O. "Sir Edward Evans-Pritchard, 1902–1973: An Appreciation." *Anthropos* 69 (1974): 553–67. An account of Evans-Pritchard's achievements and importance in his chosen field of anthropology.

Douglas, Mary. *Edward Evans-Pritchard*. Modern Masters Series. New York: Viking Press, 1980. A short but informative analysis, combining biographical information with critical assessment, by a well-known anthropologist strongly influenced by Evans-Pritchard's research.

Evans-Pritchard, E. E. "Fragment of an Autobiography." *New Blackfriars*, January 1973, pp. 35–37. The author's own brief account of his life, centering on his mid-life conversion to Catholicism.

Evans-Pritchard, E. E. *The Nuer: A Description of the Modes of Livelihood and Political Institutions of a Nilotic People*. Oxford, England: Clarendon Press, 1940.

Evans-Pritchard, E. E. *Nuer Religion*. Oxford, England: Clarendon Press, 1956.

Evans-Pritchard, E. E. *Theories of Primitive Religion*. Oxford, England: Clarendon Press, 1965.

Evans-Pritchard, E. E. *Witchcraft, Oracles, and Magic among the Azande*. Oxford, England. Clarendon Press, 1937.

Geertz, Clifford. *Works and Lives: The Anthropologist as Author*. Stanford, California: Stanford University Press, 1988. Observations on Evans-Pritchard's works and his personal style alongside essays on other great figures in anthropology.

Karp, Ivan, and Kent Maynard. "Reading *The Nuer*." *Current Anthropology* 24, no. 4 (August–October 1983): 481–503. A wide-ranging discussion of the impact of Evans-Pritchard's research among the Nuer in Africa; comments on the article and on Evans-Pritchard by other anthropologists are included.

Kuper, Adam. *Anthropology and Anthropologists: The Modern British School.* London: Routledge & Kegan Paul, 1983. Examines Evans-Pritchard's important role in the British tradition of fieldwork anthropology.

Lienhardt, Geoffrey. "Evans Pritchard: A Personal View." *Man,* n.s. 9, no. 2 (June 1974): 299–304. Comments on Evans-Pritchard's career by a distinguished fellow anthropologist who did similar fieldwork on a different African tribe.

Wilson, Bryan R., ed. *Rationality.* Oxford, England: Basil Blackwell, [1970] 1984. Essays by a number of distinguished philosophers debating the same questions of rational thought and behavior raised by Evans-Pritchard's study of the Azande.

Winch, Peter. "Understanding a Primitive Society." In *Rationality,* edited by Bryan R. Wilson, pp. 78–111. Oxford, England: Basil Blackwell, [1970] 1984. A celebrated controversial essay which begins from Evans-Pritchard's analysis of magic and witchcraft and challenges it by claiming that he did not take his sympathy for Azande ideas and customs far enough.

7

Religion as Cultural System: Clifford Geertz

Cultural analysis is not "an experimental science in search of a law but an interpretive one in search of meaning."
Clifford Geertz, *The Interpretation of Cultures*[1]

The last theorist in our sequence, the American cultural anthropologist Clifford Geertz, is still living and writing today. If, until his death, Evans-Pritchard was the leading figure in British anthropology, there are many who would say that Geertz currently holds a similar place among American scholars, not only in anthropology but in all of social science.[2] Like Evans-Pritchard, Geertz has taken a keen interest in religion, even though it is only one of many issues in cultural analysis that have drawn his close attention. The themes he has addressed in numerous essays and books published over the last 30 years fall across the entire spectrum of human social life: from agriculture, economics, and ecology to kinship patterns, social history, and the politics of developing nations; from art, aesthetics, and literary theory to philosophy, science, technology, and, of course, religion. The phrase "Renaissance man" is seldom used in the contemporary world of specialized learning, but it is not too far from accurate in describing Geertz's remarkably wide circle of interests and investigations. His chief concern has been to press for a serious rethinking of fundamentals in the practice of anthropology and other social sciences—a rethinking that bears directly on the enterprise of understanding religion. With keen insight and considerable eloquence, he has argued that human cultural activities are quite unusual and distinctive things, and that we will therefore get nowhere if we try to "explain" them in the way scientists explain everything else we meet in the natural world. Whether we like it or not, human beings are different from atoms and insects. They live within complicated systems of meaning, which anthropologists call "cultures." So if we wish to understand these cultural activities, one of the most important of which is certainly religion, we have no choice but to find a method that suits them. And that method is "interpretation." In matters human, we are far better off if we abandon the "explanation of behaviors" approach that a natural scientist might apply to a colony of bees or species of fish and turn instead to the "interpretation of cultures."[3] Not surprisingly, that phrase stands as the title of Geertz's most famous book.

Although Geertz has recommended this new approach for all of anthropology and social science, he himself has led the way in applying it specifically to the study of religion, which he has helped to revitalize in the process. Indeed, with perhaps the sole exception of Mircea Eliade, there is probably no American scholar who has done more than Geertz to show how valuable a well-crafted study of religion can be to an understanding of other aspects of human life and thought. It is perhaps needless to add that this interpretive stance, which strives to see all religions through the eyes and ideas of the people who practice them, marks a further step on the path already entered by Eliade and Evans-Pritchard. It is the path that leads away from functionalism and reductionism and toward an appreciation of religion's distinctively human dimension: the ideas, attitudes, and purposes that inspire it.

Life and Career

Clifford Geertz was born in San Francisco, California, in 1926.[4] After completing his high school education, he attended Antioch College in Ohio, where in 1950 he received his B.A. degree in philosophy. From Antioch he went on to study anthropology at Harvard University. By this time, of course, fieldwork had become the cornerstone of anthropological training both in Britain and the United States and, while still a graduate student, Geertz chose to take his plunge. During his second year at Harvard, he and his wife Hildred traveled to the island of Java in Indonesia and remained there for two years, studying the complex multiracial, multireligious society of a single town. After returning to Harvard, Geertz took his doctorate in 1956 from Harvard's Department of Social Relations with a specialization in anthropology. With his wife, he then set out on a second term of fieldwork in Southeast Asia, this time on the island of Bali. Like Java, Bali was a part of the new Indonesian Republic, which had been established late in the 1940s, shortly after World War II had put an end to Dutch colonial rule. Unlike Java, where Islam was the dominant faith, Bali possessed its own religion, which consisted of a colorful and fascinating network of beliefs and rituals derived mostly from Hinduism. In both Bali and Java, Geertz's first mission as an anthropologist was to do ethnography—to prepare detailed and systematic descriptions of these non-Western societies, noticing especially how the different aspects of life blended into a cultural whole. In the same way that Evans-Pritchard's work among the Nuer and Azande formed a basis for his theoretical writing, so, for Geertz, this work in Java and Bali has provided the foundation for most of his later essays and analyses. In terms of religion especially, his close contact with these Indonesian communities has served as both source and stimulus for many of his most original ideas. It led him early on to the view that if, as functionalists claim, a religion is always shaped by its society, it is no less true that a society is also shaped by its religion.

In 1958, after the completion of his fieldwork in Bali, Geertz briefly joined the faculty of the University of California at Berkeley; he then moved to the University of Chicago for ten years, from 1960 to 1970. In 1960 he published *The Religion of Java,* a thorough and lively account of the beliefs, symbols, rituals, and customs found in the town where he had conducted his first term of fieldwork.[5] This study exhibited an attention to detail which rivaled that of Evans-Pritchard, but it also attempted to be more wide-ranging—and needed to be, for the society Geertz had chosen was considerably more complicated by the collision of cultures than were the largely isolated African communities of the Azande and the Nuer in the interior of the Sudan. In Java's culture, Islam, Hinduism, and native animist traditions all claimed a place in the social system. Alongside his work on Javan religion, Geertz pursued research that led to several other books as well. *Agricultural Involution* (1963) examined the ecology and economics of Indonesia and assessed its troubles and prospects in the postcolonial era. *Peddlers and Princes,* published in the same year, compared the economic life of a town in Java with another in Bali. And *The Social History of an Indonesian Town* (1965) told the story of the community in which Geertz had done most of his fieldwork—Modjokuto in Java—noting the close connections between economics, politics, and social life as the community moved from colonial rule to independence.

We may recall that Evans-Pritchard's one venture outside of tribal Africa occurred during his stay in Libya, when he studied the Muslim community of the Sanusi. Interestingly, after his work in Indonesia, Geertz made a similar move to expand his base of field research by doing further work in the Islamic culture of Morocco in North Africa. Beginning in the 1960s, he made five field trips to this area, which enabled him to observe a second Muslim religious community in a part of the world decidedly different from Southeast Asia. As a result, he was able, in *Islam Observed* (1968), to make a comparative study of a single major religion—Islam—as it had taken shape in two completely different cultural settings. This is a book we shall look at more closely in this chapter. In later years, this North African fieldwork led to a further study, *Meaning and Order in Moroccan Society* (1980), to which Geertz contributed along with other authors.

In 1970 Geertz became the only anthropologist ever named a Professor at the famous Institute for Advanced Study in Princeton, New Jersey, where at present he continues to carry on his research. This singular honor, which brought him to the institution where Einstein once worked, did not come to him mainly because of his ethnographic research; that could have been done—if not quite as well—by a number of other professionals in the field. It came because in the decade of the 1960s, while doing his ethnography, Geertz caught the attention of thoughtful people in many fields with a series of striking critical essays that addressed some of the most important theoretical issues in modern anthropology. It was in these penetrating, analytical discussions that he first set out his reservations about most earlier social science, claiming that many of its aims and methods were seriously misguided. In the same breath he was able to make a forcible argument for his newer style of "interpretive" anthropology. In America especially, Geertz's theoretical writings have been read with interest not only by other anthropologists but by scholars across all fields in the academy and by not a few thoughtful general readers as well. Though some have left their mark individually, most of these critical essays have made their greatest impression in gathered form, chiefly in the collection entitled *The Interpretation of Cultures* (1973), a work that was widely acclaimed, and in *Local Knowledge* (1983), a more recent assemblage which has earned similar approvals. A proper appreciation of Geertz's approach to religion requires that we pay attention to both sides of his work: the ethnographic and the theoretical.

Background: American Anthropology and Social Theory

To understand Geertz's position among theorists of religion, we must notice first his background in anthropology, where perhaps the most important fact is that he was educated neither in Durkheim's Paris nor Evans-Pritchard's Oxford but at Harvard University in the United States. His ideas on both culture and religion were thus developed under two main influences: a strong and independent American tradition of anthropology and a perspective on social science he encountered while studying at Harvard under the prominent theorist Talcott Parsons.

Since about the turn of the twentieth century, a truly professional style of research in anthropology had been established in the United States under the leadership of the German immigrant scholar Franz Boas (1858–1942) and his younger contemporaries Alfred Louis Kroeber (1876–1960) and Robert Lowie (1883–1957). At the time when Tylor and Frazer in England were still promoting grand theories built on the comparative method, these pioneering figures had already seen its error and abandoned its ways.[6] Ahead of their time and, like Evans-Pritchard, sharing the view of Bronislaw Malinowski (1884–1942), one of the great and pioneering fieldwork anthropologists, they insisted that any general theory must be rooted in rigorous "particular" ethnography, the kind of study that centers on one community and may take years or decades to complete. In America, these men had natural access to the many tribal cultures of native American communities, and they used it to good advantage, learning tribal languages and doing fieldwork in their communities. Boas made a lifelong study of the peoples along the Canadian Pacific coast; Kroeber and Lowie worked among the tribes of the American plains.

In addition to fieldwork, Boas, Kroeber, and Lowie placed an emphasis on "culture" as the key unit of anthropological study. They insisted that, in their field studies, they were investigating not just a society—as some European scholars preferred to think—but a wider system of ideas, customs, attitudes, symbols, and institutions, of which society was only one part. "Society," the Americans tended to think, was a term weighted too heavily toward the purely material and structural components of human communities, while the appropriate term for their more comprehensive concept, which searched for hidden attitudes and emotions that lay behind and within the social order, was "culture." In fact, however, at least some of the difference appears to have been verbal. For the most part, Europeans seem to have meant by "society" and "social anthropology" something rather close to what American anthropologists meant by "culture" and "cultural anthropology."

In her widely read *Patterns of Culture* (1934), Ruth Benedict, a remarkable and talented student of Kroeber and Boas, explained that culture was the key to understanding even individual human personality traits.[7] When, in fieldwork, she noticed a difference of temperament between the gentle, restrained Pueblo Indians and more combative tribes like the Pima and Kwakiutl, she traced it to the fundamental character of Pueblo culture, which stressed harmony, while the others did not. Such a view departed significantly from that of theorists in the school of Durkheim, who had considerably less interest in the psychology of individuals because it was not something concrete and objective in the way social facts like families and clans are. Benedict found individual psychology important, for it showed that a culture was a pattern, a kind of "group personality," which each of its members held in the mind.

While still a student, Geertz seems to have absorbed most of the main ideas of Boas, Kroeber, and Benedict quite naturally into his own anthropological perspective. Though he chose Indonesia rather than any of the native American communities as his locale, he immediately enlisted, as we have seen, in two solid terms of fieldwork. In addition, he fully endorsed the American commitment to particular studies; they were much to be preferred over the bad science of general theories built on poorly gathered evidence. Anthropology, Geertz heartily agreed, must be ethnography before it can be anything else. Its focus must fall on specific places and peoples, so that general conclusions come, if at all, only from these closely studied single instances. Further, and finally, he embraced the American view that the objects of anthropologists' inquiries are "cultures," not "societies." He recognized that the door to other people's lives could not be unlocked only by examining such social units as the family, kinship patterns, clan structures, or legal systems; it was necessary to search beyond these for the entire interconnected pattern of ideas, motives, and activities that we call a culture.

With regard to this last point, we should notice that Geertz did have some reservations about the newer stress on culture and showed rather more sympathy for the sociological approach of the French school than did others. For if, as Benedict claimed, culture was nothing more than a kind of group attitude, a communal "personality" passed on in the minds of individual persons, then there was really nothing very objective about it for the social scientist to study. In the American view, one tended to argue that individual behavior is an expression of culture, while defining culture merely as the way in which individuals have learned to behave.[8] Such circular statements might be true, but they were not very enlightening. If the concept of culture was to serve as a useful guide for scientific research, the French were right in saying that it had to refer to something objective, not just to elusive psychological states like the Pueblo "feeling of harmony" or another tribe's attitude of aggression. In addressing this difficulty, Geertz found help in the work of Talcott Parsons, his Harvard teacher and at the time one of the leading sociologists in America.

American Social Theory: Parsons and Weber

It is hard to know how direct his influence was, but Talcott Parsons seems to have affected Geertz in two ways.[9] First, Parsons himself had been influenced by the great German sociologist Max Weber, who in the early 1900s had published several brilliant and original studies of the relationship between religion and society. At a time when few Americans knew who Weber was, Parsons translated some of his works and explained his key ideas. Weber was a man of enormously wide learning, able to write intelligently about German Lutherans in one book and Chinese Confucians in the next. In addition, he had the remarkable ability to connect specific facts in ways that led to striking abstract concepts and theories. Many people know that it was Weber who first connected Protestantism with capitalist economics in the essays of his well-known book *The Protestant Ethic and the Spirit of Capitalism* (1904–05), but this was only one of many suggestive ideas he offered in the fields of sociology and comparative religion. He was also one of those responsible for introducing the much-debated method of *Verstehen* (German for "understanding"), which stressed the role of human ideas and attitudes in any explanation of social systems. Corresponding to this is the idea that cultures are products of human "action" (in German, *Handeln*); they come about because humans do things in accord with certain ideals, attitudes, and values. Consequently, only when we understand the meaning (in German, *Sinn*) of an action to the people who engage in it can we really grasp and explain what is going on.

It seems hardly an accident that, in translated and updated form, each of these main concepts of Weber's, which were transmitted to America by Parsons, finds its way also into Geertz's interpretive approach to culture. Throughout his theoretical essays and even some of his ethnography, there is probably no single social theorist whom Geertz refers to more often, or in a more kindred spirit, than Max Weber.

In addition to serving as a channel for the ideas of Weber, Parsons provided Geertz with something else: a way of resolving the problem of culture as it had been left by anthropologists like Ruth Benedict. In *The Structure of Social Action* (1934), his most important book, Parsons built upon Weber and developed the view that all human groups exist on three tiers, or levels, of organization: (1) individual personalities, which are shaped and governed by (2) a social system, which is, in its turn, shaped and controlled by (3) a separate "cultural system." The last of these, which is a complex network of values, symbols, and beliefs, interacts with both the individual and the society, but for purposes of analysis it can be separated from them. To many, this thesis was a breakthrough. If Benedict's idea of culture as a group personality was too vague and subjective to be of much scientific use, Parsons' concept was not. A "cultural system" was an objective thing, a collection of symbols—objects, gestures, words, events, all with meanings attached to them—that exists outside the minds of individual people yet works inwardly to shape attitudes and guide actions. In brief, if Weber had shown how to understand a culture, Parsons had shown where to find it. For him, a culture was not just a set of elusive emotions or changeable impressions inside individual minds; it was something real and permanent—something objective—which has an effect on private emotions but maintains an existence apart from them. This concrete symbolic system is recognized by all the people within a society; it can therefore also be known by anthropologists and others who stand outside of it. As we shall see below, Geertz clearly shares this idea of a culture as an objective system of symbols, so much so that some observers prefer to call his approach not interpretive but "symbolic" anthropology.[10]

Interpretive Social Science: Principles and Precepts

Weber, Parsons, and the tradition of American anthropology all provide components of Geertz's perspective. To see how he assembles them into a complete program of interpretive anthropology, we can now turn to his own writings, especially the theoretical essays and other works published mostly in the two key decades of his career, the 1960s and 1970s. Since we obviously cannot cover all of these in our discussion and since some are theoretical and others ethnographic, it will be best if we work in stages. We begin by looking at two of Geertz's best-known theoretical essays: the first explains his interpretive anthropology in general terms, and the second directs it specifically to religion. With these in hand, we then turn to some samples of the way in which Geertz applies his perspective to actual religions.

Culture and Interpretation: The Method of "Thick Description"

In 1973 Geertz published his award-winning collection of essays entitled *The Interpretation of Cultures*. Most of these pieces had first appeared in various scholarly journals during the previous decade. But as an introduction to the others, Geertz provided a new essay that has since become the classic statement of his point of view. He entitled it "Thick Description: Toward an Interpretive Theory of Culture." In it, he points out first that although the term "culture" has tended to mean many different things to previous anthropologists, the key feature of the word is the idea of "meaning" or "significance." Man, he says, quoting Max Weber, is "an animal suspended in webs of significance he himself has spun."[11] If therefore we wish to do what anthropologists are paid to do, namely, explain the cultures of other human beings, we have no choice but to use a method that is described by the English philosopher Gilbert Ryle as "thick description." We must describe not only what actually happens but what people *intend* by what happens. Ryle gives the example of two boys, one of whom experiences an unintended nervous twitch of his eye while the other winks at a friend. In a purely physical, or "thin," description, both of these movements can be identically described. But the minute we take into account the element of meaning, the *significance* of the physical motion, no two actions could be more different. The one means nothing, the other means a great deal. "Thick" description, which includes the meaning of the motion, shows the wink to be decidedly different from the twitch. It must be clearly understood, says Geertz, that ethnography, and so all of anthropology, is always a matter of thick description. Its aim is never just to describe the mere structure of a tribe or clan, the bare elements of a ritual, or, say, the simple fact that Muslims fast in the month of Ramadan. Its task is to discern meanings, to discover the intentions behind what people do, the *significance* for all of life and thought of their rituals, structures, and beliefs.

It is important to notice than when we speak of "meanings," most people think of something quite private—an idea in an individual person's head. But a moment's further thought makes it clear that there is nothing necessarily private at all about meaning. I cannot wink privately at you unless there is something public—a context of meanings—shared by both of us that enables you to take from the wink the same meaning I give to it. We should therefore understand that the culture of any society is just this shared context of meanings. Or, to use Geertz's own words, "culture consists of socially established structures of meaning in terms of which people do such things as signal conspiracies and join them or perceive insults and answer them."[12] A culture is not something physical, but it is there—objectively there—nonetheless. And it is the one thing that, more than any other, anthropologists must try to reconstruct when they study a community or people of any place or time.

By the same token, however, it is equally important to notice that a culture is not *just* about meanings, as if it were a purely self-contained system of symbols, like mathematics. Behavior, or action, must also be observed "because it is through the flow of behavior—or, more precisely, social action—that cultural forms find articulation."[13] This may mean that on some occasions an anthropologist's description of a culture will not always be completely consistent. People sometimes behave in ways that seem to clash with the system of meaning prescribed by their own culture; or, perhaps more accurately, cultural systems sometimes present multiple and conflicting patterns within which people choose courses of action. It also means that anthropologists can never do more than *re*construct what other people really think and do by writing down their own best interpretation of it. Cultural analysis is, for the interpretive anthropologist as for every other careful theorist, always a matter of "guessing at meanings, assessing the guesses, and drawing explanatory conclusions."[14]

Now none of this difficult work can be done well unless it is done, so to speak, microscopically. Interpretive anthropology attends to "ethnographic miniatures," small-scale subjects like clans, tribes, or villages, whose cultural systems can be mapped out in all the minute detail characteristic of each and amid the great diversity evident among all. For Geertz, this means too that any attempt to make broad, general statements about all of humanity must be viewed with the strongest suspicion. In the past, he notes, anthropologists have tended to say things like "Middletown, which I have studied, is the United States in miniature." The answer to that is: In some respects it may be; in others it most probably is not. So such general statements are just as likely to mislead as to inform. Again, it is sometimes said that a certain society is a "test case" through which we can prove something about all others. (Durkheim, we might recall, even though Geertz does not mention him, thought of Australian totemism as a "crucial experiment" to prove his thesis about religion.) But here again, what kind of laboratory test case can we really make when almost none of the important conditions can be controlled? We can never compare two human cultures the way we can control two laboratory cultures, placing them in identical dishes and adding a chemical to one and nothing to the other. The findings of any one such cultural test case, says Geertz, are "as inherently inconclusive as any others."[15]

In light of all this, anyone interested in explaining human activities must understand that the day when scholars set as their goal some "general theory of cultural interpretation" is now past—and most likely gone forever. For the unavoidable fact is that analysis of culture is not "an experimental science in search of a law but an interpretive one in search of meaning."[16] Does this mean that the interpretation of cultures can never at all give us wisdom that is of any general value? Well, not quite, Geertz tells us; but what we can learn from it is probably more like the diagnosis a doctor makes in determining a type of illness from certain symptoms. Anthropology is never fully predictive, never able to offer the certainty that is available in fields like physics or chemistry, which center only on physical processes that follow the laws of motion or the rules of molecular reactions. The anthropologist cannot say with certainty what will happen in a culture, any more than a doctor can definitely predict that a child will come down with measles. But like a diagnosis, a theory can and should try to *anticipate* what will happen. In interpreting one culture, a theory ought in some way to be capable of being "tried out" on another, and then be either kept for more use or discarded. In that connection, anthropologists do have a variety of general ideas at their disposal—abstract concepts expressed in words like "structure," "identity," "ritual," "revolution," "world view," "integration," and so on. These allow a theorist to stretch a single example into an idea that might apply in several or many cases. They may not seem like much, but in fact such concepts are extremely valuable, and in any case, they form the only kind of general observation a good theorist would ever want to make. Anything more ambitious might be interesting, but it is also likely to mark the return of the old mistakes: bad science pretending to be anthropology.

Cultural Interpretation and Religion

If interpretive anthropology is a matter of seeking out the system of meanings and values through which people live their lives, then it stands to reason that in any culture religion will command serious anthropological attention. That Geertz firmly believes this is evident in the first study that came out of his fieldwork—and for that matter the first of his career—*The Religion of Java* (1960). This book is an ethnography in the best tradition of American anthropology; it is a particular study of a specific people whom Geertz came to know in depth through his immersion in their language and culture. It explores in detail the complex interweaving of Muslim, Hindu, and native animistic (the Javan name is *abangan*) religious traditions. And it looks at religion as a cultural fact in its own right, not as a mere expression of social needs or economic tensions (though these are certainly noticed). Through its symbols, ideas, rituals, and customs, Geertz finds the influence of religion to be present in every crevice and corner of Javan life. His study is so microscopically detailed, so closely tied to the particulars of Javan culture, and so careful to avoid generalizations that he might well have used it as the very model for the kind of "thick description" anthropology we have just seen him recommend. For that very reason, however, the book does not try to tell us very much of a theoretical nature about the aims of an interpretive approach to religion. Typically for him, Geertz chooses to do that instead with an essay, "Religion as a Cultural System," first published in 1966 and later included in *The Interpretation of Cultures*. Though almost as celebrated as "Thick Description" and just as widely noted or commented upon, this is not the easiest essay to understand or to summarize. But it is important, so we must try to notice at least its main ideas.

Geertz begins by telling us, as his title indicates, that he is interested in considering "the cultural dimension" of religion. Here he also helps by providing a fairly clear and complete idea of what he means by a culture. He describes it as "a pattern of meanings," or ideas, carried in symbols, by which people pass along their knowledge of life and express their attitudes toward it.[17] Now as there are within a culture many different attitudes and many different forms of knowledge to pass on, so there are also different "cultural systems" to carry them. Art can be a cultural system, as can "common sense," a political ideology, and things of a similar nature.[18]

What does it mean to say religion is a cultural system? Geertz offers an answer to this question in a single, heavily packed sentence. Religion is:

> (1) a system of symbols which acts to (2) establish powerful, pervasive, and long-lasting moods and motivations in men by (3) formulating conceptions of a general order of existence and (4) clothing these conceptions with such an aura of factuality that (5) the moods and motivations seem uniquely realistic.[19]

Anthropologists, of course, are not obligated to be brief, clear, and simple. Yet though it is forbidding on a first look, this description is not quite as dark as it first may seem. In the rest of his essay, Geertz actually does us the service of breaking down his account (which serves as both a definition and theory) by explaining in detail each of its elements. We can start with the first. By "a system of symbols" Geertz means just about anything that carries and conveys to people an idea: an object like a Buddhist prayer wheel, an event like the crucifixion, a ritual like a bar mitzvah, or a simple wordless action, like a gesture of compassion or humility. A Torah scroll, for example, conveys to Jews the idea, among others, of God's revelation. The image of a saint in a hospital room may convey the idea of divine concern for the sick. As we have seen before, the important thing about these ideas and symbols is that they are not purely private matters. They are public—things that exist outside ourselves in the same way that, say, a computer program can exist outside a computer as well as within it. As programs can be examined and understood objectively apart from any physical machines into which they are installed, so religious symbols, though they enter into the private minds of individuals, can be grasped apart from the individual brains that think them.

When it is said, secondly, that these symbols "establish powerful, pervasive, and long-lasting moods and motivations," we can abbreviate this by saying that religion makes people feel things and also want to do things. Motivations have goals, and they are guided by an enduring set of values—what matters to people, what they think is good and right. The Buddhist monk feels a strong negative motivation, an aversion, when presented with a generous midwestern American steak dinner. For him, it is wrong both to eat meat and eat in such quantity, because attachments to food weigh him down in his struggle for a better rebirth and ultimate escape from life in the natural world. His motivation here is a matter of morals, of choosing for himself the good over the evil. Jews wishing to see Jerusalem and Muslims hoping to visit Mecca will also arrange things so as to reach their goal, which is to attain the morally good experience of being in the space that is sacred to their traditions. Moods, on the other hand, are less defined and less clearly directed. When the Hindu pilgrim arrives at Benares or the Christian at Bethlehem, he or she may well experience, even unexpectedly, a feeling of joy or an inner peace that possesses the spirit for a time and then leaves, giving way naturally, at a later time, to a different mood.

The power of these moods comes from the fact that they are not occasioned by trivial or minor things. They arise because religion occupies itself with something very important; it formulates "conceptions of a general order of existence." By this Geertz simply means that religion tries to give ultimate explanations of the world. Its main interest is not to tell us about stocks and bonds, sports and games, or fashions in clothing and entertainment. Its intent is to provide an ultimate meaning, a great ordering purpose to the world. Everyone knows when the disorder, the chaos of the world makes itself felt. It does so when people face things that, intellectually, they just cannot comprehend; when, emotionally, they face sufferings they cannot bear; or when, morally, they encounter evil, which they cannot accept. At these moments they see what is, but it collides with what ought to be.

On the one side, then, stand conceptions of the world, and on the other a set of moods and motivations guided by moral ideals; taken together, these two lie at the core of religion. Geertz abbreviates the two elements by referring simply to "world view" and "ethos"—to conceptual ideas and behavioral inclinations. Going further, he then adds that religion "(4) clothes these conceptions with such an aura of factuality that (5) the moods and motivations seem uniquely realistic." In simpler terms, this means that religion marks out a sphere of life that has a special status. What separates it from other cultural systems is that its symbols claim to put us in touch with what is "really real"—with things that matter to people more than anything else. And it is in rituals, above all, that people are seized by the sense of this compelling reality. In rituals, the "moods and motivations" of religious believers coincide with their world view in such a way that they powerfully reinforce each other. My world view tells me I must feel this way, and my feelings tell me, in turn, that my world view must be right; there can be no mistake about it. In ritual, there occurs "a symbolic fusion of ethos and world view"; what people want to do and feel they should do—their *ethos*— joins with their picture of the way the world actually is.

Geertz explains that a vivid example of this fusion, this blending of ethos

and world view, can be found in one of Indonesia's most remarkable ceremonies.[20] On certain occasions the people of Bali stage a colorful performance of a great battle between two characters from their mythology: the
fearsome witch Rangda and the comical monster Barong. As these two
struggle, the audience itself gradually comes into the great spectacle, with
some members taking the parts of the supporting characters and others
swooning into states of trance. As the performance proceeds, it becomes
clear that for the Balinese this drama is "not merely a spectacle to be
watched but a ritual to be enacted."[21] At its height, the great drama of the
performance, the intense emotion, and the crowd involvement bring the
whole scene almost into chaos. The struggle always ends without a clear
winner, but that is largely irrelevant. What is important is the way this
theatrical event evokes from the Balinese people the attitudes and emotions—a mixture of playfulness, exhibitionism, and fear—that are most distinctive of their culture. In and through the turbulent, emotion-filled process
of observing and joining this ritual, they come to experience a deep confirmation of their view of the world as an always uncertain struggle between
the evil and the good. Further, these religious moods and motivations, fitted
to the world view, carry over from the ceremony into the rest of society and
give all of Balinese life the characteristics that set it apart from the lives led
in other cultures.[22]

From all of this, we should be able to see again how unwise it is, in
religion no less than any other sphere of culture, to leap toward quick general conclusions. Balinese religion is so distinctive, so specifically its own
sort of thing, that there is hardly anything about it which we could turn into
a general rule for all religions—other than the fact that all traditions somehow manage to combine, like the Balinese, both a world view and an
ethos.[23] Accordingly, as Geertz explains in his conclusion, any useful study
of religion will always require a two-stage operation. One must first analyze
the set of meanings found in the religious symbols themselves—a difficult
task in itself. Then comes the even more difficult but equally important
second stage: since the symbols are tightly connected to both the structures
of the society and the psychology of its individual members, those connections must be traced along a continuous circuit of signals given, received,
and returned.[24] If we think of wires strung in a triangular configuration
among three poles, one standing for symbol, another for society, and a third
for individual psychology, we have a fitting image of the steady flow of
influences and effects that pass among and between all three in any religious
cultural system.

Interpreting Religion: A Balinese Example

If this is what Geertz's approach to religion looks like on its theoretical side, what shape does it take when actually applied to individual cases? Although his writings on Bali, Java, and Morocco give us more than enough examples to choose from, we have space here to consider just two: one, a short essay on religion in modern Bali, and the other, as noted, Geertz's comparative study of Muslim culture in Indonesia and Morocco, which he published as *Islam Observed* (1968).

The article " 'Internal Conversion' in Contemporary Bali," published in 1964, begins with an idea proposed (not surprisingly) by Max Weber. In one of his interesting comparative studies, Weber makes a distinction between two types of religion that can be found in world history: the "traditional" and the "rationalized." Traditional religions, which he also calls "magical," are more characteristic of primitive people, whose lives are steeped in polytheism. They see a new divinity in every tree or rock, and they perform a new ritual at almost every turn in their lives. They are so immersed in dealings with this spirit or that demon that they are hardly even aware they "have" a religion; it is just what they always do. Encounters with the gods saturate every aspect of their society. Rationalized religions, on the other hand, are different. These are the so-called great world religions like Judaism, Confucianism, and the Hinduism of India's philosophers. Instead of many spirits, they tend to see divinity in the form of one or two, or just a few, great spiritual principles: Israel's one God; China's Tao, or Way of Nature; and India's Brahman, or Supreme Spirit. Rationalized religions are in general abstract and logical; their God or spiritual principle stands "apart from" or "above" the little things of life that the spirits of magical religions are always attending to. And their removal of divinity from nearby things leaves ordinary life "disenchanted"—left bare—of its little gods, so that in order to bring people back into contact with the sacred, they must often introduce new ways of reaching the divine. Instead of the countless everyday rituals of magical religion, rationalized religions propose encounters with the divine through mystical experience, as Hindu sages recommend, or through moral codes like Judaism's Ten Commandments. Unlike the adherents of traditional cults, the followers of such religions are very much aware of what they are doing; they know well that they have chosen a single, well-organized system of belief.[25]

Rationalized and traditional religions also differ in one other important respect: the way in which they deal with the great problems of life. Traditional religions, as Evans-Pritchard explained in the case of Zande witchcraft, address these great questions—what life means, why there is pain, why there is evil—in very particular, specific ways. They do not ask, "Why do people suffer?" They ask, "Why is my father sick?" And they look for very particular answers as well: "Father is sick because his enemy has used witchcraft." Rationalized religions, however, always raise such questions to a cosmic scale; they include the whole world. In the case of suffering, they point not to a single witch but to Satan, who brought sin into the world, or to the dark, cool side of the Tao; they appeal, in short, to great realities that affect everyone.

After pointing out these differences, Weber goes on to say that most of the rationalized world religions seem to have appeared at times of great social upheaval, at moments when the traditional religions of the villages and fields no longer met people's needs. Christianity, for example, arose amid the great social turmoil caused in the ancient Mediterranean world by the rise and spread of Greco-Roman civilization. Confucianism appeared amid the chaos of China's destructive ancient civil wars.

Granting the value of this broad conceptual framework, says Geertz, let us now apply it to modern-day Bali. Anyone who approaches its culture with these contrasts of Weber's in mind will at once notice several interesting things. Though in name it is Hindu, the religion of Bali is not the mysticism of India's intellectuals but the everyday polytheism and mythology of its villagers; that is to say, it fits Weber's category of a traditional religion. There is in it almost no rationalized theology, whereas rituals and a sense of nearby divinity can be found everywhere. There are thousands of temples in the landscape, and a person can belong to dozens of them at the same time. Often people have no idea which gods are worshipped in them, but for each one they insist that an appropriate ritual be performed exactly according to a set plan. The ceremonies, moreover, are also tightly woven into the social structure. Local priests who belong to the Brahmin caste find their high social rank reinforced by their special spiritual status; each "owns" a group of lower-caste followers who associate him with divinity, while he calls them his "clients." In addition, one of the main enterprises of the various princes, kings, and lords on the island is to hold large-scale religious festivals, spectacles which require time-consuming labor, sometimes from hundreds of peasants and other subjects. The ceremonies symbolically remind all people of their proper place on the social scale; the highborn host the celebrations, while the lowborn do the work. Finally, in the true manner of magical religions, the cult of death and witches, which we saw above in the great combat of Rangda and Barong, penetrates to almost every aspect of Balinese life. Over the years, moreover, though they have encountered both Christianity and Islam, the Balinese have never seriously considered conversion to either of these outside faiths.[26] So their traditional religion has been able to survive the centuries largely untouched by the influence of any rationalized world religion.

As Geertz viewed it in 1964, however, Bali was an island confronted with dramatic social changes, many brought on by the coming of independence to all of Indonesia in 1949. Modern education, political consciousness, and improved communication had opened the channels of contact with the outside world. The growth of cities and of population had added to the pressure, so that what happened in the ancient societies when social turmoil brought the disenchantment of the world and the end of magical religion seemed very similar to what was happening in modern Bali. If one were to look closely, in fact, it would seem that the people of modern Bali were at that very moment engaged in Weber's process of "internal conversion," transforming their traditional ways of worship into something that, gradually, was beginning to assume the features of a rationalized world religion. Geertz notes that in the course of his fieldwork, he was particularly struck one evening when, at a funeral, an intense philosophical discussion of the meaning and purpose of religion broke out among certain young men of the town. Almost unknown in traditional cultures, such discussions are the hallmark of rationalized religion; yet here just such a vigorous exchange was taking place on the street in Bali. Almost as unheard of in a traditional situation is the development of scriptures, doctrines, religious literacy, and an organized priesthood. Yet again, there were signs that every one of these things was now coming into Balinese culture. Interestingly, too, the nobles and princes, perhaps seeing their old privileges threatened by the coming of democratic government, had actually put themselves behind this initiative, hoping they could keep their status by being in the forefront of a new, more defined and self-conscious Balinese religion. The new movement, says Geertz, had only recently acquired the most visible badge of any rationalized faith: an organization. In opposition to the Indonesian government's Muslim-dominated Ministry of Religion, Bali had recently chosen to establish its own, locally supported, purely Balinese ministry, which had assumed the task of certifying Brahmana priests and creating an authorized class of professional clergy.

In sum and essence, Geertz explains, all of those processes and changes that Weber discovers behind the growth of the great rationalized religions of the world could be found in evidence on the island of Bali in the postwar era. Bali in 1964 seemed to stand where Rome did in the time of Jesus and China did in the days of Confucius. That being so, the natural question that comes to mind is: Can any more general conclusions be drawn from Bali's experience? Is there a theory to connect ancient Rome with modern Bali, and perhaps other places as well? Geertz does not propose one. What will happen in the future, he concedes, is something no one can predict. None-theless, if there is no theory, there is clearly much insight to be gained from applying general conceptions such as Weber's, along with the promise that the case of Bali may help us further to apply and refine them. In conclusion Geertz observes, "By looking closely at what happens on this peculiar little island over the next several decades, we may gain insights into the dynamics of religious change of a specificity and an immediacy that history, having already happened, can never give us."[27]

Islam Observed

Our second example of Geertz's interpretive approach in action takes us into a larger subject, his comparison of two kinds of Islam. At the outset of *Islam Observed* (1968), he states, ambitiously enough, that his aim is to lay out a "general framework for the comparative analysis of religion" and apply it to one faith, Islam, as it exists in the two quite different countries that his fieldwork has enabled him to know best: Indonesia and Morocco.[28] In addi-tion to being Muslim, he notes, both of these cultures have in modern times passed through great social change. At one time traditional societies of rice farmers in the one case and herdsmen in the other, both became colonies of Western powers (the Dutch and the French) and have only recently won independence (Indonesia in 1949, Morocco in 1956). Religion, needless to say, has often been at the center of the social transformations that have come over both of these nations.

The Classical Styles of Islam

Morocco took shape as a Muslim nation during four important centuries from about 1050 to 1450 A.D., when the society was dominated by aggres-sive tribesmen from the desert and strong-minded merchants in the towns. The two main figures in this culture were the warrior, or strongman, and the mystic, the Muslim holy man, who sometimes came together in the ideal form of the warrior-saint. Idris II, who built the city of Fez in the ninth century and was the first Moroccan king, cut such a figure; he was a fierce fighter and reformer who claimed direct descent from the Prophet Muham-mad. Later in time, holy men so devout that they were known as mara-bouts—from the Arabic word *murabit:* "lashed" or "shackled" to God—attracted bands of followers who split the land into militant sects, each fiercely loyal to its sacred leader. In Indonesia, by contrast, Islam arrived later and took a rather different form. Long a prosperous farming culture whose abundant rice fields supported peasant, prince, and merchant alike, Indonesia had little use for the boldness and nerve that were key to survival in Morocco.[29] The virtue prized above all others was quiet diligence in the fields, a personality trait supported for centuries by Hindu-Buddhist religious ideals, which stressed meditation, inwardness, and personal composure. Not until the 1300s did Islam begin to reach the Indonesian islands, and then it came quietly through trading contacts and in a tolerant Indian form that allowed it, at first, to blend with the Hindu, Buddhist, and animist peasant beliefs already in place. Indonesian Islam accordingly developed flexible features; it was "adaptive, absorbent, pragmatic, and gradualistic"—very different from the "uncompromising rigorism" and "aggressive fundamental-ism" of Morocco.[30] While the one evolved into something gradualist, lib-eral, and accommodating, the other took a shape that was perfectionist, puri-tanical, and uncompromising.

These characteristic religious attitudes, rigorous in the one case, relaxed in the other, Geertz calls "the classical styles" of Islam in each nation. Both are "mystical," because they find religious truth through immediate contact with God, but there are significant differences, which Geertz chooses to explain through the stories of two legendary religious leaders. In Indonesia's sacred legends, Sunan Kalidjaga is the hero said to have brought Islam to the island of Java. He was born to an official in the court of a ruling family during the age of the great Hindu-Buddhist "theater states"—that is, at a time when the ruling classes, as members of the highest caste, were regarded as the spiritual elite of the country. In the royal and princely courts, elabo-rate religious ceremonies were held to demonstrate both the political power and religious authority of the kings. As a young man, however, Kalidjaga cared little for religion until one day he met a Muslim mystic whose precious cane and jewels he tried to steal. The holy man only laughed at his foolish desire for material things and suddenly transformed a nearby banyan into a tree of gold, hung with jewels. Kalidjaga was so astounded by this miracle and the man's indifference to wealth that he asked to become a Muslim as well, then proved his Islamic self-discipline by remaining in one place, in a state of obedient meditation, for an interval that stretched to several decades! He thus became a Muslim without ever seeing the Koran or visiting a mosque. Significantly, however, after embracing Islam, Kalidjaga did not abandon the theater-state culture of his childhood. Instead, he helped to establish a new royal city at Mataram, and there used his own high position and the ceremonies of the king's court to promote Islam, just as these had once served the purposes of the older Hindu-Buddhist religion.

The legend of Kalidjaga is, of course, more than the tale of a man. It is the story of all Islam as it came to Indonesia, merged with the older religions, and adapted itself to the culture of the theater states. Such syncretism, or blending, of religions was very typical of Indonesia, but it did not last. It began to break down in the modern era, as Islam came to be the dominant faith of the merchants, whose power grew stronger, and as the Dutch, who arrived at the same time to colonize the islands, pushed the ruling class out of power. Under pressure from the European conquerors, the delicate mixed religion of these earlier days broke up into the three separate traditions— Hindu-Buddhist, Muslim, and native animist—that we find in Java today.

In a fashion similar to Kalidjaga in Java, the features of Islam in Morocco can best be seen in the life of the Muslim holy man known as Sidi Lahsen Lyusi, one of the last of the marabouts, who lived in the 1600s. Like the others, Lyusi too saw himself as "tied to God." A wandering prophet, scholar, and pilgrim, he was a man of intense morality and great learning, a mighty figure who, in Moroccan stories, is revered as the saint who faced down a sultan. It happened that while a guest of none less than the Sultan Mulay Ismail, founder of the great Alawite dynasty, Lyusi one day began to insult his host by breaking all of the serving dishes in the palace. The purpose of this ungrateful display was actually a noble one: to protest against the backbreaking labor the sultan imposed on his slaves. For this, the sultan expelled Lyusi from the palace and later took action personally to kill him. But when he charged the holy man's tent, his horse miraculously began to sink into the ground. Immediately, the sultan admitted his wrongs, acknowledged Lyusi's demand to be recognized as a holy man and a *sherif,* or descendant of the Prophet, and allowed him to go his way.

The extraordinary quality that Lyusi triumphantly demonstrated in this confrontation was *baraka,* a kind of spiritual charisma. His supernatural power to stop the sultan's horse was a sure sign that he possessed this divine blessing. Yet in Islam there has always been a second way of proving one's divine authority—that is, to be accepted as a *sherif,* a descendant of the prophet. Even though Lyusi performed a miracle, he required that the sultan recognize in him this second proof of his holiness as well. We thus find centered in this one holy man the great question that faced all of Islam in Morocco: How is the spokesman for God to be known? Does *baraka* come simply through a holy man's personal charisma and miraculous powers? Or must one be a *sherif,* a descendant of the Prophet Muhammad? Or are both required? In the tension between these two principles, Geertz tells us, we can see one of the key issues that animated Moroccan Islamic culture throughout its history. Over time, the ruling families of the country established descent from the Prophet as the dominant principle, but the idea of *baraka*—as expressed in the charismatic qualities of holiness, moral intensity, and wonder-working power—never disappeared. It remained very much alive in various cults of the saints and—significantly for later history—in popular opinion. The people tended to hold that the sultan should possess both qualities: personal religious charisma *and* descent from the Prophet's line. As a result, both heredity and spirituality had to be in evidence if the sultan were to rule with any real power.[31]

In both Indonesia and Morocco, then, the classical styles of Islam are "mystical"; they try to bring people into the immediate presence of God. But the stories of the Muslim saints show how different in form even mystical Islam can be. The passive "illuminationist" mysticism of Kalidjaga stands in sharp contrast to the aggressive "maraboutist" piety of Lyusi. To borrow from Geertz's own definition, the religions of Indonesia and Morocco, though both Islamic, show decidedly different "moods and motivations." On the Indonesian side, there is "inwardness, imperturbability, patience, poise, sensibility, aestheticism, elitism, and an almost obsessive self-effacement . . . ; on the Moroccan side, activism, fervor, impetuosity, nerve, toughness, moralism, populism, and an almost obsessive self-assertion."[32]

The Scripturalist Revolt

Whatever these differences, Islamic Indonesia and Morocco have in recent times had to cope with two common major problems: their colonial rulers and the challenge of modernization. In both countries, says Geertz, the high point of colonial domination fell roughly in the century between about 1820 and 1920. And in both, this experience made people much more aware that they were Muslim while their Christian masters were not. Islamic religion became identified with protest, nationalism, and the hope of independence. In the process, however, the faith itself began to change. The classical styles—Indonesian illuminationism and Moroccan maraboutism—found themselves now under challenge from a powerful new movement which claimed to be recovering something very old. This was "scripturalist" Islam. In the case of Indonesia, this scripturalist revolt took shape in the 1800s, at the high point of Dutch control and at a time when national sentiment turned strongly against colonial powers. Inspired by new opportunities for pilgrimage to Mecca, Indonesians began to discover in Arabia a different, more rigorous and militant Islam, which soon came to be taught in newly founded schools. In these *santri* (Javanese for "religious student") institutions, the older and more flexible illuminationist Islam was pushed aside to make room for the "purer," original tradition, which centered on the example of the Prophet, the first caliphs, and above all the literal truth of every word of the Koran. Mosque and marketplace, moreover, were always natural allies, and so, in the growing number of trading centers throughout Indonesia, this new-style, scripture-based Islam rapidly spread, all the while contributing its strength to a growing nationalism and the cause of resistance to colonial rule. Interestingly, says Geertz, at almost the very same moment, scripturalism also made its appearance in Morocco. Known as the cause of the Salafi, or "righteous ancestors," and led by fierce, passionate nationalists such as Allal Al-Fassi, this new movement had by 1900 come into open conflict with the older style of maraboutist—or "holy man"—Islam. As in Indonesia, these new scripturalists opposed both the French and the older, classical Muslim style.

Scripturalist Islam in both Indonesia and Morocco thus provides a background to the struggle for national independence that engaged both countries throughout the middle years of the twentieth century. This struggle can be followed in the careers of the two national leaders at the time, Sultan Muhammad V in Morocco and President Sukarno in Indonesia. Muhammad V rode to power on the strength of the nationalism inspired by the scripturalist revolution in his country. Personally devout as he was, Muhammad V found himself nonetheless uneasy with the fundamentalism of the scripturalists. He preferred the older-style maraboutist Islam, which recognized the sultan as the chief holy man of the country. When, in the course of the 1950s, the French took a number of unpopular measures, Muhammad V refused to be their puppet and resisted. He was deposed and exiled, but two years later managed to return in triumph as head of the new, independent Moroccan state. In Muslim eyes, his defiance and devotion were clear proof of divine favor; he had shown the same *baraka* as Lyusi, and he measured up fully to the prized maraboutist ideal of the warrior-saint.[33] Nonetheless, says Geertz, it is hard to see his success in uniting the old religious ideals with the new postcolonial age as more than a holding action.

Sukarno's story in Indonesia is a less happy one, since it ends with his overthrow by the military in 1965. Yet in the long struggle that he led from the 1920s to the year of independence in 1949 and then as president of the new nation, we can see a similar mix of religious and political concerns. Sensitive to the religious diversity of his people and resisting both communism on the left and the Muslim scripturalists on the right, he tried to unify all parties with his famous Pantjasila (Five-Point) Creed: nationalism, humanitarianism, democracy, social justice, monotheism. When this eventually failed, he made a last effort at unity that seemed to turn the clock back to the time of the hero Kalidjaga. He tried to revive in modern form the ancient "theater state," building the world's largest mosque, a colossal sports stadium, and a national monument. He also instituted a number of grand state ceremonies.

In the last analysis, both Sukarno and Muhammad V knew well the power of religion in their societies; both sought to harness it constructively to the national cause. Significantly, both decided that an Islam of the classic rather than scripturalist style offered the best hope of success. Just as significantly, neither was completely successful. Although Muhammad V achieved more than Sukarno, Geertz claims that in neither case could the older forms of faith survive unchanged in the modern circumstance.

Conclusion: World View and Ethos

What, then, is the significance of the parallel Islamic histories that can be traced in Indonesia and Morocco? That question can be answered by recalling the central point of "Religion as a Cultural System": religion consists of a world view and an ethos that combine to reinforce each other. A set of beliefs people have about what is real, what gods exist, and so forth (that is, their world view) supports a set of moral values and emotions (that is, their ethos), which guides them as they live and thereby confirms the beliefs. In both of these cultures up to at least the year 1800, world view and ethos supported each other in this natural way and met people's religious needs. In Morocco, Islamic belief gave support to the ethos of maraboutism, which "projects a style of life celebrating moral passion," and this ethos, in turn, reinforced the Muslim creed.[34] In Indonesia, the same balance seems to have held; the world view of blended Islam and Hinduism supported the gentle, meditative mysticism of figures like Kalidjaga, while the ideal of conduct and emotion he provided gave support to the world view. During the last century, however, and in both lands, the arrival of nationalism and the protests of scripturalism have brought serious challenges. Doubts of the world view and changes in ethos have appeared in ways that leave people uncertain about each and dimly aware that the one is often at odds with the other.

With regard to world view, the root problem is a clash of ideas. In both lands, secular attitudes have entered the scene with the spread of science in industry, the universities, and professional classes. At the opposite extreme, the determined "ideologization" of religion in the hands of the scripturalists, who either isolate the Koran from all other knowledge or claim that all knowledge is somehow already in the Koran, has had the same unsettling effect. Collisions between these two seemingly incompatible perspectives have fostered deep uncertainty of belief where once there was only quiet assurance.

The effect of modern developments on the ethos component of religion in both countries has also been significant. To prevent misunderstanding, Geertz notes that a distinction must first be made between the *force* a religion may have and the *scope* of its influence in any given culture. Moroccan Muslims regard the encounter with God as an extremely intense, all-consuming experience; yet for them, most of ordinary life in the marketplace, recreation, or politics seems decidedly unreligious. Conversely, in Indonesia, few religious experiences are as intense, as full of force, as those that are prized in Morocco, but the range of religiosity is far wider. There is scarcely a single aspect of life that is not in some way tinged with a sense of the supernatural.[35] Still, despite these differences, it is clear that in both countries a significant erosion of ethos is under way. In small, hidden ways, the hold of religious moods and motivations on both cultures has begun to weaken. People may still be "religious-minded," wishing to keep their sacred symbols, but they are less immediately religious. They are moved less by the direct presence of their gods than by the more indirect feeling that they would like their gods to be present. More and more, we could almost say, theirs is becoming a religion once removed from the Reality it claims to worship.

Islam Observed offers a particularly good illustration of Geertz's approach to religion precisely because of what it does *not* do. It does not offer a crisp logical argument in defense of a definite thesis about religion, Islamic or otherwise. It is instead a kind of exploration, a journey into cultural systems led by a guide who is too interested in describing landscapes and comparing one with another to care whether the path he is traveling will ever reach a destination. As he walks, we notice three things. First, Geertz has a keen interest in the particularity of each culture he interprets. While Morocco and Indonesia are both Islamic nations, a central theme of his discussion is the marked difference in the flavor, the character, and the texture of the two forms of Islam they present.

Second, there is the characteristic stress on meaning, the "thick description" of the religion in terms of what is significant to those who live it. The Islam of Morocco and Indonesia is governed by the same formal theology in both places, but within that common system, the ideas that are emphasized and the attitudes and emotions that are treasured differ in marked degree. In Morocco, the stress on the holy man, on moral passion, and on intensity of experience creates a pattern of meaning and values distinctively different from the more passive, tolerant, widely diffused sense of the supernatural found in Indonesia. Thus, although both nations are Muslim and both encounter the identical challenges of nationalism and scripturalism, each responds in its own way, and with varying degrees of success in the outcome. Morocco's Muhammad V succeeds in preserving a style of classical Islam in the new age of nationalism; Indonesia's Sukarno does not.

Third and finally, despite all of the attention to specifics and differences, Geertz does venture to suggest at least the prospect of more general conclusions. He notices, for example, that whatever their differences, neither Morocco nor Indonesia seems able permanently to reverse the tide of doubt created by the rise of secularism and scripturalism. For him, this is the kind of similarity which may serve, like the categories of Max Weber, as at least the beginning of a theorem that could be "tried out" elsewhere, in the hope it will apply more widely to religions in other places and times.

Analysis

We can best measure Geertz's achievement as an interpreter of religion by noticing two things: (1) where he stands among theorists of religion we have considered in this book and (2) what he stands for as the most eminent spokesman for interpretive anthropology.

1. Geertz and Other Theorists

In the sequence traced in this book, Geertz clearly holds a place in the pattern of thought embraced by both Evans-Pritchard and Eliade. He is the most recent and widely applauded opponent of functionalist reductionism—rejecting it not only as an explanation of religion but as an account of any human cultural system. Contrary to Marx, Durkheim, and Freud, Geertz insists that a general reduction of all religion to the product of hidden neurosis, social need, or economic conflict can claim no more credibility than any other grand theory—which is to say, very little. To explain a religion without trying to grasp the system of meanings it conveys is not unlike trying to explain a computer without mentioning a program, or a book without referring to words. It cannot be done.

While Geertz thus stands close to Eliade and Evans-Pritchard on the key matter of reductionism, there are nonetheless other issues on which he plainly stands apart. We noticed, for example, that Evans-Pritchard cherishes the thought of one day having a general science of religion whose theories can be built up from small, specific studies that ethnographers in the present and in the future still need to complete. Geertz thinks that time spent in pursuit of such a dream is wasted, for what it imagines will simply never happen. Eliade's program is, of course, quite different from Evans-Pritchard's, but he too is inspired by the hope of finding something universal: the human response to the sacred as expressed in certain enduring images and symbols shared by religious people of all times and places. Geertz, in sharp contrast, is a declared and passionate particularist; to him, a theory of the "universal forms" of religion is as much a mirage as any "general science" of it. Though a friend of anyone who opposes reductionism, Geertz is nonetheless a theorist of his own quite independent stripe.

2. The Interpretive Anthropologist

In assessing Geertz the anthropologist, we must first recall again the two sides of his remarkable career. He has been from the beginning both an ethnographer and a theorist: on one side, a careful student of quite specific cultures in Indonesia and Morocco; on the other, a talented conceptual thinker, intrigued by the broad issue of how to understand and explain human behavior. His ethnography, though not of first interest to us here, is praised and admired on all sides. Ordinary readers and most professional scholars marvel alike at the sensitivity, insight, analytical skill, and intricate style of his essays on Balinese religion and field studies like *The Religion of Java,* as well as the other works. We can point to almost any page of these writings and notice a subtle turn of phrase, a striking observation, or the discovery of an important idea hidden in a seemingly trivial detail.

Ethnography of such high quality is interesting in its own right, but in Geertz's case it also supports—in a sort of indirect way—the central point of his interpretive theory. Most scholars of any kind—not just theorists of religion, anthropologists, and social scientists—make an effort to know one or a few things in great depth, so that from this foundation they can speak intelligently on broader subjects as well. Freud's psychoanalysis started with single patients and led in time to a theory of all human personality. From the specific case of Australian totemism, Durkheim produced an account of religion in all societies. In Geertz's case, however, this relationship between the specific and the general is quite clearly different. Except in certain very limited ways, he does not, like Durkheim or Freud, move from the specifics of religion in Bali or Morocco to general pronouncements on religion in all or even most other places. He very nearly does the precise opposite. He as much as states that his ethnography—and that of others as well—cannot and should not be made into a general theory. The point of his method is to celebrate the opposite: particularity. In the interpretive approach, no two instances of humanly created meaning can ever be fitted into one iron rule.

We might almost say that the better the ethnography, the worse its chance of becoming science, at least in the traditional sense of that term. Geertz produces his finely etched accounts of Bali's rituals and Java's feasts much as a great painter does a portrait—to show us that the features and temperament of this duchess or that queen are truly individual; there is not, and will never be, another like her. Thus, after reading *The Religion of Java* or *Islam Observed,* we find ourselves saying that we now know a great deal about Indonesian and Moroccan religion. But if we then look further in Geertz's pages for some sort of general idea or thesis that ties things together, it is very difficult to find anything more than cautious suggestions, the hint at a possible connection here, a possible comparison there. Beyond that we cannot go. For the fact is that in Geertz's opinion distinctive cultural expressions simply *cannot* be tied together, at least not the way experimental scientists place under a single rule the facts of cell division or planetary motion. In human affairs, as he puts it in the title of his second essay collection, all knowledge is "local knowledge." That phrase is well chosen. It can stand as both the motto for the entire approach of interpretive anthropology and the mark of Geertz's distinctive contribution to the field.

Critique

It would seem that the first step in presenting any critique of Geertz on religion or any other subject would be to admit that this is not an easy thing to do. Geertz's stature in American social science, and well beyond it, may not be quite beyond criticism, but it is certainly imposing enough. His critics are few; his admirers legion. Minor complaints have been raised about his abundant vocabulary and a literary style so decorated with metaphors, analogies, and allusions that it can on occasion obscure what would otherwise be clear and distinct. But these do not seem to be serious charges; they may even arise from the kind of professional envy that is actually a form of compliment.[36]

There are, however, at least two more substantive issues that can be raised: one about Geertz's rather confusing view of anthropology as "science"; the other about the clash between his principles and his practice in interpreting religion.

1. Anthropology as Science

In promoting his program of interpretive anthropology, Geertz insists that he has no intention of abandoning the belief that his discipline is a science.[37]

Yet, as a number of anthropological critics have noticed, that is, in fact, just what he seems to be doing. For example, in "Thick Description," the very same essay that states his commitment to science, he just as forthrightly declares that his form of cultural analysis is "not an experimental science in search of a law, but an interpretive one in search of meaning."[38] Some anthropological critics have shown an understandable bewilderment with such conflicting statements on such a fundamental issue. In the view of Paul Shankman, one of his sternest professional critics, some of Geertz's claims reduce themselves to mere gamesmanship with words.[39] Shankman and others contend that if interpretive anthropology is only looking for "meanings," whatever those are, and not striving to develop scientific theories to explain what it finds, then Geertz's ideas may be interesting, but they certainly are not the products of a science.[40] Theoretical laws, after all, are what science is all about. So, say what he may, Geertz the interpreter of meanings is not recommending science; he is recommending the end of science, at least in anthropology.

It should be clear from what we have seen of Geertz's position that these critics are partly right. Geertz *is* proclaiming the end of science in anthropology if by "science" we mean the making of ironclad predictive laws about human behavior in the way physicists speak of the law of gravity and biologists describe the laws of cell division. But Geertz undoubtedly would go on to add that this is not the only form a science can take. For "science," from the Latin term *scientia,* can just mean a systematically acquired body of knowledge. Consider a comparable field of study like history. There is a sense in which historians are scientists. In evaluating a document, they work quite rationally to determine such things as the specific dates before and after which it could not have been written. In constructing the story of a battle or a parliament, they proceed quite critically, weighing the importance of different events and decisions. In explaining the rise of a nation or the fall of a king, they are always proposing theories, testing them with evidence, and then discarding or revising them as the case requires. All of these procedures are things we call science; they are rational, critical, and evidential. And as far as anthropology goes, those are precisely the things that good ethnographers do on every day of their field research. In that respect, ethnographers plainly work as scientists, even though their conclusions will always be stated in the probabilities that apply in human affairs, not in the necessary laws of physical nature.

Understanding that there can be two kinds of science, then, clears up some of the confusion. But even so, anthropologists who cherish the natural sciences as their model of study still have their misgivings. They note that a further problem of the interpretive approach is its disabling effect on our motivation to explain. Another critic of the interpretive approach, Richard Franke, observes that, in one of his articles, Geertz addresses the fact that tens of thousands of Balinese peasants were massacred after the fall of President Sukarno in 1965. In seeking to account for this atrocity, Geertz refers it to a deep contradiction in the Balinese sensibility, a combination of a love for high art and a darker love of extreme cruelty. But in the process, says Franke, he never really tries to find out

> who was killing whom, who benefited from the massacre. . . . Instead of asking about the possible roles of . . . foreign business elements, the United States CIA, wealthy Indonesian military officers and their business allies . . . [and others], Geertz offers the "goal [of] understanding how it is that every people gets the politics it imagines."[41]

Other scholars have shown that there was, in fact, nothing uniquely Balinese about the sensibility that led to this slaughter at all. The killing arose from a power struggle between the communists and the military—a struggle quite depressingly typical of what has occurred elsewhere in Asia. At times Geertz has seemed aware of this tendency to overinterpret.[42] But in the view of the critics, the stronger tendency of his thought has been quietly to forget the cautions that arise from his own better moments.[43]

2. Interpreting Religion

In the case of matters more specifically religious, we must keep in mind Geertz's central idea: that religion is always both a world view and an ethos. It consists of ideas and beliefs about the world and an inclination to feel and behave in accord with those ideas. Its peculiar chemistry comes from the support that each of these two elements gives to the other. Although Geertz throughout his discussions reminds us often of this point, it is not very clear, at least on the face of it, why such a statement should be regarded as particularly new, original, important, or illuminating. It seems to be not only true but almost too obviously true. It is a kind of truism. One is inclined to ask how religion can ever be anything *but* a set of beliefs and behaviors that relate to each other. Can we really even imagine a religion that announces to its followers, "God exists" as part of its world view but then recommends that they live as if there were no God, or makes no recommendation on a pattern of life? Can we really conceive of an ancient Chinese sage who might have said, "The Tao holds the secret of life," but then recommended that people live as if no such thing as the Tao existed?[44]

In this same connection it is interesting to observe that when Geertz actually interprets religious behavior, only one of the two elements he thinks central to it ever gets detailed and thorough scrutiny. He tends to say a great deal about ethos—about conduct, values, attitudes, aesthetics, temperament, and emotions—but very little actually about world view. Henry Munson, Jr., a recent critic, has very perceptively noted that in his discussion of the dramatic Balinese spectacle of Rangda and Barong, Geertz writes eloquently and at length about the Balinese ethos, the combined emotions of horror and hilarity that are on display, the moods of dark fear and playful comedy that ebb and flow through the entire performance.[45] But he passes over almost entirely the native myths upon which the story is based. When it is said, for example, that the audience fears the witch Rangda, what is it precisely that they are afraid of? Her ugliness? Her threat to children, whom she is known to eat? Death in itself, which she symbolizes? Or something horrible that happens *after* death? Is it perhaps just one of these or several? Or could it be all? From Geertz's account, we just do not know. The "world view" side of the religious equation, which in his theory of interpretation is just as important as "ethos," is, in his practice of it, often curiously neglected.

In *Islam Observed,* the same thing tends to happen. While tracing very closely the relationship between the social context and religious life in both Indonesia and Morocco, Geertz writes at length about differences in ethos: the divergent values, moods, and temperaments that appear in the contrast between the activist self-assertion of the Moroccans and the inward self-effacement of Indonesia. But in all of this we are told almost nothing about the Islamic world view: its belief in Allah, the five pillars of Muslim practice, the doctrines of fate and the last judgment, and so on. And that omission leaves behind it a substantial trail of questions: Without any reference to world view, how do we know the "temperaments" are even religious? Political revolutionaries are often self-assertive, while addicts of certain drugs can be quite inward and self-effacing. We would also like to know if the different social contexts, which have had such a strong impact on ethos, have made any similar impression on world view. Are there some things Moroccan Muslims believe which Indonesians do not? Or are the basic beliefs about God and the world, for example, still the same? If they are in fact the same, then is there not a serious problem to be addressed? If world view and ethos reflect and "reinforce" each other, and if the Moroccan ethos differs sharply from the Indonesian one, why are the world views not different as well?

All of these questions point to a rather curious feature of Geertz's interpretive approach, particularly in the case of religion. Though in theory he continually asserts that the trademark of his method is the way it addresses "meanings," the way it attends to the social symbols that carry ideas, he often seems to be quite surprisingly uninterested in these meanings. In practice, he seems much more excited about actions and feelings—feelings unattached to the beliefs that would seem to be necessary to inspire and shape them.[46] What is especially puzzling about this stress on emotion and ethos—especially if we recall Geertz's American anthropological background—is that in some ways it brings his view of culture back to the subjective notion of a "group personality" found in the theory of Ruth Benedict—a theory which, under the influence of his teacher Parsons, he would seem to have rejected. Even in his much praised ethnographic writings, for all their attention to detail, there seems a noticeable hesitance on Geertz's part to track down the inner relationships between the specific beliefs in Islamic or Balinese theology. A comparison here with Evans-Pritchard's meticulous reconstruction of Nuer theology is instructive. If we truly wish to look at a religion in terms of its meanings and want to avoid the vagueness of concepts like the "group personality," then an attention to such particular beliefs, a tracking of their minute connections and shades of difference, would seem to a central part of the anthropologist's mission.

None of these questions, of course, is likely to tarnish the sheen on any of the numerous personal tributes paid to Geertz and his work by his colleagues in modern anthropology and the wider circle of the social sciences, as well as by sundry admirers and observers from other fields of study. His success in establishing the great "interpretive turn" in anthropological research, and in pointing that path out to students of religion as well, has left his reputation quite secure. The doubts do suggest, however, that other and future theorists who see promise in his approach—as indeed there is—would be quite mistaken to suppose that there is no need still to assess, revise, and improve it.

Notes

1. Clifford Geertz, "Thick Description: Toward an Interpretive Theory of Culture," in Geertz, *The Interpretation of Cultures: Selected Essays* (New York: Basic Books, 1973), p. 5.

L. Peacock, "The Third Stream: Weber, Parsons, Geertz," *Journal of the Anthropological Society of Oxford* 7 (1981): 122. When in 1970 Geertz was appointed to the Institute for Advanced Study in Princeton, New Jersey, he was the only anthropologist, and one of the first social scientists, to be included among the mathematicians and physicists who make up the majority of its membership. The inclusion of social scientists in this circle of brilliant theoretical minds did not come without considerable controversy. See Landon Jones, "Bad Days on Mt. Olympus," *Atlantic*, February 1974, pp. 37–53.

3. Geertz is, of course, not the only recent thinker to move toward an interpretive approach to social science. For an overview of the broader movement, with comments on Geertz's importance, see Paul Rabinow and William Sullivan, "The Interpretive Turn: A Second Look," in Rabinow and Sullivan, eds., *Interpretive Social Science: A Second Look* (Berkeley, CA: University of California Press, 1979), pp. 1–30; for examples, see the essays reprinted in this collection.

4. There is, to my knowledge, no biography of Geertz or full-dress critical study of his life and work, though there are, of course, many shorter, critical essays on his interpretive anthropology. Some particulars of his career can be found in Adam and Jessica Kuper, eds., *The Social Science Encyclopedia* (London: Routledge & Kegan Paul, 1985), under "Geertz, Clifford." Other particulars, and a good step in the direction of a thorough critical study, can be found in Kenneth A. Rice, *Geertz and Culture* (Ann Arbor, MI: University of Michigan Press, 1980). Much of this work, however, consists of lengthy summaries of Geertz's works with heavy use of extended quotations.

5. This research was undertaken by Geertz as part of a team project in Java that involved a number of other scholars (including his wife Hildred), each of whom was assigned to write on a different feature of life in the town. Geertz's study of Javan religion was the first in the series to be published. The project was funded by a grant from the Ford Foundation and administered by the Center for International Studies of the Massachusetts Institute of Technology. On this research, see Douglas Oliver, "Foreword," and Geertz's "Acknowledgements," in Clifford Geertz, *The Religion of Java* (Glencoe, IL: The Free Press, 1960), pp. vii and ix–x.

6. On this tradition, see Paul Bohannon and Mark Glazer, eds., *High Points in Anthropology* (New York: Alfred A. Knopf, 1973), pp. 81–142.

7. On Ruth Benedict, see Bohannon and Glazer, *High Points in Anthropology*, pp. 174–83.

8. This was a criticism made by Talcott Parsons, which Geertz cites with approval in an essay entitled "After the Revolution: The Fate of Nationalism in the New States," in *Interpretation*, pp. 249–50.

9. A thoughtful reconstruction of the influence that Parsons probably had upon Geertz can be found in Peacock, "The Third Stream," pp. 122–29; the same connection is made by Adam Kuper, *Anthropology and Anthropologists* (London: Routledge & Kegan Paul, 1983), p. 188.

10. See, for example, Sherry Ortner, "Theory in Anthropology since the Sixties," *Comparative Studies in Society and History* 26 (January 1984): 126–66, especially 128–32.

11. Geertz, "Thick Description," p. 5.

12. Geertz, "Thick Description," p. 12.

13. Geertz, "Thick Description," p. 17.

14. Geertz, "Thick Description," p. 20.

15. Geertz, "Thick Description," p. 23.

16. Geertz, "Thick Description," p. 5.

17. Geertz, "Religion as a Cultural System," in *Interpretation of Cultures*, p. 89.

18. Geertz has, in fact, written essays on each of these; see "Ideology as Cultural System," in *Interpretation of Cultures*, pp. 193–233; "Common Sense as a Cultural System" and "Art as Cultural System," in Clifford Geertz, *Local Knowledge: Further Essays in Interpretive Anthropology* (New York: Basic Books, 1983), pp. 73–93 and 94–120.

19. "Religion as a Cultural System," p. 90.

20. "Religion as a Cultural System," pp. 114–117.

21. "Religion as a Cultural System," p. 116.

22. "Religion as a Cultural System," p. 119.

23. "Religion as a Cultural System," p. 122.

24. "Religion as a Cultural System," p. 125.

25. Geertz's summary of Weber's theory appears in " 'Internal Conversion' in Contemporary Bali," in *Interpretation of Cultures*, pp. 171–75; the full article covers pp. 170–89.

26. " 'Internal Conversion,' " pp. 181–82.

27. " 'Internal Conversion,' " p. 189.

28. Geertz, *Islam Observed* (Chicago: University of Chicago Press, 1968), p. v.

29. Geertz, *Islam Observed*, p. 11.

30. Geertz, *Islam Observed*, p. 16.

31. Geertz, *Islam Observed*, pp. 52–54.

32. Geertz, *Islam Observed*, p. 54.

33. Geertz, *Islam Observed*, p. 81.

34. Geertz, *Islam Observed*, p. 98.

35. Geertz, *Islam Observed*, p. 112.

36. For one example of this complaint, see Paul Shankman, "Gourmet Anthropology: The Interpretive Menu," *Reviews in Anthropology* 12 (Summer 1985): 247.

37. He reaffirms this often, but see especially "Thick Description," p. 24: "For a field of study which, however timidly (though I, myself, am not timid about the matter at all), asserts itself to be a science. . . ."

38. Geertz, "Thick Description," p. 5.

39. See "Gourmet Anthropology," pp. 241–48, and for a more extended critique, "The Thick and the Thin: On the Interpretive Theoretical Perspective of Clifford Geertz," *Current Anthropology* 25 (June 1984): 261–79.

40. Others who argue that Geertz's approach represents an unwise departure from scientific ideals include Richard Newbold Adams, "An Interpretation of Geertz," *Reviews in Anthropology* 1, no. 4 (November 1974): 582–88; William Roseberry "Balinese Cockfights and the Seduction of Anthropology," *Social Research* 49 (Winter 1982): 1013–28; and Robert A. Segal, "Interpreting and Explaining Religion: Geertz and Durkheim," and "Clifford Geertz and Peter Berger on Religion: Their Differing and Changing Views," in Segal, *Explaining and Interpreting Religion: Essays on the Issue* (New York: Peter Lang, 1992), pp. 77–101, 103–22.

41. Richard W. Franke, "More on Geertz's Interpretive Anthropology," *Current Anthropology* 25 (1984): 692–93.

42. See, for example, his caution, in "Thick Description," p. 30, that interpretive

Seven Theories of Religion

anthropology must always stay in touch "with the hard surfaces of life—with the political, economic, and stratificatory realities . . . and with the biological and physical necessities on which those surfaces rest."

43. See Paul Rabinow, "Humanism as Nihilism: The Bracketing of Truth and Seriousness in American Cultural Anthropology," in *Social Science as Moral Inquiry*, ed. Norma Haan et al. (New York: Columbia University Press, 1983), p. 73.

44. The only thing that comes close to this is the unusual philosophy of the "As if" proposed by the late-nineteenth-century philosopher Hans Vahinger, who said that though God does not exist, people must behave "as if" he did.

45. Henry Munson, Jr., "Geertz on Religion: The Theory and the Practice," *Religion* 16 (January 1986): 19–25. There is unfortunately no space in this chapter to consider another quite different line of criticism advanced by Talal Asad, "Anthropological Conceptions of Religion: Reflections on Geertz," *Man*, n.s. 18, no. 2 (June 1983): 237–59, who attacks Geertz's definition of religion and his concept of religious symbols. A very instructive collection of studies is to be found in *Soundings: An Interdisciplinary Journal* 71 no. 1 (Spring 1988), where the entire number, with contributions from Ralph V. Norman, William G. Doty, Bradd Shore, Robert A. Segal, Stephen Karatheodoris, Ruel W. Tyson, Jr., and Walter B. Gulick is addressed to Geertz and his work, including his views on religion.

46. Munson, "Geertz on Religion," p. 24, pointedly shows how this omission creates a serious problem for Geertz in his discussion of the Islamic concept of *baraka*, which he explains as either a fact of heredity or a kind of personality trait, while passing over any discussion of the meaning of the word in Islamic theology. This leads to some results that are quite strange. It turns out that *baraka*, which Geertz thinks of as "personal presence, force of character, or moral vividness," can also be possessed by places and objects.

Suggestions for Further Reading

Asad, Talal. "Anthropological Conceptions of Religion: Reflections on Geertz." *Man*, n.s. 18, no. 2 (June 1983): 237–59. An unconventional discussion of Geertz, which is obscure in places, but focuses critically on his assumptions about the nature of religion and religious symbolism.

Geertz, Clifford. *The Interpretation of Cultures: Selected Essays.* New York: Basic Books, 1973.

Geertz, Clifford. *Islam Observed.* Chicago: University of Chicago Press, 1968.

Geertz, Clifford. *Local Knowledge: Further Essays in Interpretive Anthropology.* New York: Basic Books, 1983.

Geertz, Clifford. *The Religion of Java.* Glencoe, Illinois: The Free Press, 1960.

"Geertz, Religion, and Cultural System." Special issue of *Soundings: An Interdisciplinary Journal* 71, no. 1 (Spring 1988). A set of essays by seven authors from different fields addressing Geertz's research, methods, and theories as well as his views on religion and other topics.

Kuper, Adam, and Jessica Kuper, eds. *The Social Science Encyclopedia.* London: Routledge and Kegan Paul, 1985. Under "Geertz, Clifford." A brief account of Geertz's career. For Geertz, as for Evans-Pritchard, there is at present no full-length biography or critical study.

Munson, Henry, Jr. "Geertz on Religion: The Theory and the Practice." *Religion* 16 (January 1986): 19–25. A thoughtful analysis, with some compelling criticisms of Geertz's actual practice as distinct from the principles of his interpretive approach.

Peacock, James L. "The Third Stream: Weber, Parsons, Geertz." *Journal of the Anthropological Society of Oxford* 7 (1981): 122–29. Traces the intellectual roots of Geertz's interpretive anthropology through his Harvard mentor to Max Weber's ideas and methods.

Rabinow, Paul, and William Sullivan. *Interpretive Social Science: A Second Look.* Berkeley: University of California Press, 1979. Essays by various scholars assessing the movement in anthropology for which Geertz is the foremost spokesman.

Rice, Kenneth A. *Geertz and Culture.* Ann Arbor, Michigan: University of Michigan Press, 1980. A first step in the direction of a full-scale study of Geertz and his program, though it relies heavily on summaries of Geertz's works and extended use of quotation.

Roseberry, William. "Balinese Cockfights and the Seduction of Anthropology." *Social Research* 49 (Winter 1982): 1013–28. An analysis of Geertz against the background of the opposing approach to anthropology taken by the school of "cultural materialism."

Segal, Robert A. "Interpreting and Explaining Religion: Geertz and Durkheim," and "Clifford Geertz and Peter Berger on Religion: Their Differing and Changing Views." In Robert A. Segal, *Explaining and Interpreting Religion: Essays on the Issue,* pp. 77–122. New York: Peter Lang, 1992. Terse, analytical, and critical essays on Geertz which shed light on his view of religion through comparisons of his approach with those of other leading social theorists.

Shankman, Paul. "Gourmet Anthropology: The Interpretive Menu," *Reviews in Anthropology* 12 (Summer 1985): 241–48. A stringent critique of Geertz by a younger professional in the field.

Shankman, Paul. "The Thick and the Thin: On the Interpretive Theoretical Perspective of Clifford Geertz." *Current Anthropology* 25 (June 1984): 261–79. Another aggressive critique of Geertz's interpretive approach, with responses from other anthropologists.

8

Conclusion

An old story tells of a theological school that taught its students to reject all modern ideas, especially those of German philosophers. Each year the final examination included a question asking: "What do you know about the philosophy of Immanuel Kant?" To which the approved answer was: "That he was wholly in error." As anyone acquainted with the difficult writings of Kant well knows, this convenient response did not just assure students of a passing grade; it gave them an escape from a great deal of hard intellectual labor. So far as we know, the seminarians never protested.

In somewhat the same way, it would be convenient here at the end of our survey if we could issue a simple verdict of "right" or "wrong" on each of our theorists, just as a jury decides a case in court. We could accept some, reject the others, and end our inquiry with that. In matters of explanation and interpretation, however, things are never quite so simple. Categorical judgments plainly save effort, but at a severe price in understanding. Consider for a moment the fact that most of the theories discussed in these chapters could be declared failures just by applying the most common test of the natural sciences, in which a single contrary example counts as a disproof. In almost every case we have observed, from Freud's psychological reductionism all the way over to Eliade's affirmations of the irreducible sacred, it is not hard to find somewhere a lone piece of evidence—a single religious belief or ritual—that will offer up a contradiction and destroy even the most finely crafted of generalizations. One pointed counterexample would allow us to dismiss almost any of our theorists as "wholly in error." The only problem is that, in the process, we would also lose any chance of noticing the most important thing about their work. For as the history of research in most fields abundantly shows, the value of theories goes far beyond the simple fact of their being true or false. "Wrong" explanations that discover an entirely new way of seeing a subject or break open a new path of investigation can be much more important than "right" ones that do little more than restate what everyone already claims to know. In addition, and as should now be plain to all, the matters taken up by most theorists of religion are far too complicated to yield a direct "up-or-down" vote of confidence on any theory in its most general form. It is much more likely that parts of an interpretation will be rejected and pieces of its argument questioned, while in other respects it may be accepted, amended, or even usefully combined with other views. As a rule, the central thesis of every theorist we have considered (with the possible exceptions of Evans-Pritchard and Geertz) is much too broad in scope to be either accepted or rejected in its total form. Each approach must be broken down into specific components and theorems, some of which will probably persuade while others will not.

All of that being so, we will do best to end our survey not with a set of verdicts but with a sequence of comparisons, bringing together all of the views we have so far considered separately and measuring them in collected form against certain general principles applicable to all. In that connection, we must ask of any theory the following questions: (1) *How does it define the subject?* What concept of "religion" does it start from? (2) *What type of theory is it?* Since explanations can be of different kinds, what kind of account does the theorist offer, and why? (3) *What is the range of the theory?* That is, how much of human religious behavior does it claim to explain? All of it? Or just some? And in that light, does it actually do what it claims? (4) *What evidence does the theory appeal to?* Does it try to probe deeply into a few facts, ideas, and customs or does it spread itself widely to embrace many? Is the range of the evidence wide enough to support the range of the theory? (5) *What is the relationship between a theorist's personal religious belief (or disbelief) and the explanation he chooses to advance?* An exploration of these questions should not only show us where our theories converge and where they part ways; it should also help us to take a reading of their historical importance and perhaps frame a guess about their future as well.

Defining Religion

It is often said that religion is something so individual, so elusive and diverse that it defies definition. It can mean almost anything to just about anyone. That is not the view of the theorists considered here. Although, as has been shown, they disagree sharply on explaining religion, they differ much less than one might suppose on the matter of defining it. If we look closely—and in one or two cases between the lines—it is apparent that they

all come near the view that religion consists of belief and behavior associated in some way with a supernatural realm, a sphere of divine or spiritual
beings. This is a point worth demonstrating in some detail.

Tylor and Frazer both choose to define religion in quite straightforwardly
supernaturalist terms, as does Eliade with his concept of the sacred, which
is the realm of the gods, ancestors, and miracle-working heroes. Tylor puts
it perhaps most simply when, in his well-known minimum definition, he
refers to "belief in spiritual beings."[1] Durkheim, on the other hand, seems
at first glance to take a quite different view, for he explicitly rejects the
concept of the supernatural. He defines religion instead as that which concerns the sacred, then further identifies the sacred with what is social.[2] For
him, society is worshipped as divine. Nonetheless, his view is actually
closer to the others than he admits, for the whole argument of *The Elementary Forms* depends on the premise that in the eyes of those who subscribe
to it, a religion normally consists of beliefs (in his language, "representa-
tions") and behavior associated with a realm of reality which, even if the
believers themselves do not so see it, we with our modern concept of nature
clearly *would* call supernatural. When Durkheim turns to his primitive Australians, he does not discuss their trading habits or techniques of husbandry;
he starts with beliefs and ceremonies that refer to the supernatural, the rites
required by the gods, and the stories of the ancestral spirits. To be sure, he
differs from a theorist like Eliade in claiming that though his inquiry *starts*
with such rites and beliefs, that is not where it ends. His aim is to show that
once the issue has been explored, the Australians' worship of the totem god
will turn out to be, in fact, their concern for the clan. But he cannot get to
this conclusion without at least beginning his investigation at almost the
same place it starts for Tylor, Frazer, and Eliade—with the general notion
of the supernatural.

The views of Freud and Marx on this issue need considerably less explication. Both are quite content with a conventional definition. They see religion
as belief in gods, especially the monotheistic Father God of the Judeo-
Christian tradition, though like Durkheim they insist that this is only religion
on its surface. Underneath the appearances lies humanity's obsessional neurosis or the pain of economic injustice that requires the opium of belief.

Evans-Pritchard and Geertz, finally, can be seen to follow convention as
well, though both have their problems with the term "supernatural." Evans-
Pritchard prefers the term "mystical" because, unlike the cultures of the
modern West, the tribal societies he explores have no clear concept of an
opposition between a "natural" world and a "supernatural" one.[3] Nonetheless, he makes it clear that the overriding concern of both Nuer religion and
Azande witchcraft is always to arrange a proper relationship with this "mys-

tical" realm that lies behind and beyond ordinary life. Before they can be at peace with themselves or at home in society, the Nuer feel deeply that they must have a clear conscience before the gods, while the Azande must always locate the source of the witchcraft that is causing their troubles. Geertz's position is similar. The word "supernatural" does not appear in his well-known definition of religion as a cultural system, where he speaks in abstract terms of "a system of symbols" that conveys "conceptions of a general order of existence."[4] Moreover, his main interest is in the *ethos,* the "moods and motivations" of religious people, rather than in the supernatural beings they fear or love. But when we turn to the actual accounts of religion provided in his ethnographies of Java, Bali, and Morocco, it is clear that the key feature of religion, as he sees it, lies in the emotional and social responses people make to their world view: that is, to the supernatural beings they believe in, whether that be Allah and the angels of Islam or the spirits, deities, and demons of Balinese and Javan traditional cults.

Thus, while the theorists we have examined may disagree on any number of things, the definition of religion is, in the main, not really one of them. Though some say it less directly than others, all tend to find religion, initially at least, in those beliefs and practices associated with spiritual or supernatural beings. Even in the cases of Durkheim, Evans-Pritchard, and Geertz, each of whom does have reservations, the differences turn out to be chiefly a matter of terminology and emphasis, not substance. Defining religion is thus the single issue on which all seven theorists can be said to stand, broadly speaking, on common ground.

Types of Theory

Needless to say, the moment our theorists turn from definition to explanation, all consensus rather quickly disappears, as we have had ample occasion to notice in the preceding pages. By their very nature, of course, explanations come in different kinds, and that fact in itself is a ready source of confusion. As we noted at the outset of this survey, the same fact, event, or behavior can often be explained in multiple ways, some of which can easily be mistaken for others. In *Theories of Primitive Religion,* Evans-Pritchard observes that when, in the later 1800s, the first spokesmen for the science of religion presented their work as a search for "origins," they were not always very clear on the meaning of that term.[5] Assuming we can ever find it, the *historical* origin of religion is one thing; its *psychological* or *social* origin is another. The first would be found in certain specific events belonging to the earliest ages of civilization; the second is rooted in conditions characteristic of human life in all times and places. The one is a past occurrence; the other refers to timeless features of all human existence.

The search for religious origins in the first sense of the word was carried on especially by Max Müller, Tylor and Frazer, Freud, and even (to a degree) Durkheim. It is closely connected with the doctrine of human social evolution. It holds that religion is the result of a process that began with events—like Freud's "murder of the first father"—lodged deep in the human past. Like civilization itself, it then slowly developed through stages of ever greater complexity till it reached the beliefs and practices we know today. Such evolutionary theories naturally take a keen interest in primitive peoples, because they are thought to display religion, as well as civilization, in its earliest, simplest, and purest form. In the words of perhaps the most well-worn of evolutionist analogies, they show us the acorn from which the oak of religion has grown. In addition, the primitive form is regarded almost without exception as inferior to what is modern. "Crude," "childish," "barbaric," and "savage" are favorite words of theorists like Tylor and Frazer.

As we have had several occasions to note, this once fashionable doctrine of social evolution in time came to be rejected on almost all sides. Its chief problem was that it claimed knowledge of things that no modern inquirer could ever hope to know; the "earliest forms" of human religion and social life are subjects we can only guess about—and not with much skill.[6] With the failure of this historical evolutionism, theory in the twentieth century has turned almost exclusively to the other sense of the term "origins." Religion, it is held, is ultimately traceable to the human *psychological* needs or *social* circumstances that we find in every age and place of human existence. But that is not all. Within this second style, as we have often noted above, one must further distinguish purely functional and even reductionist explanations, such as we find in Freud, Marx, and Durkheim, from the antireductionist positions of Eliade, Evans-Pritchard, and (in his unique way) also Geertz. The thrust of the reductionist approach is quite clear. Since, in the modern scientific world, religion cannot be considered either a rational form of belief or a normal type of behavior, we must appeal to something subconscious or irrational to explain why it still persists. For Freud that "something" is obsessional neurosis, for Marx it is economic injustice, and for Durkheim it is "society" and its compelling demands on the individual.

The opponents of reductionism insist that such theories rest on a serious misunderstanding. Eliade and Evans-Pritchard argue that when seen in its own terms, there is nothing at all irrational or abnormal about religion; so there is no point in seeking to "explain it away" through appeals to the subconscious, the social, or the purely material. Evans-Pritchard shows that even when they seem absurd to outsiders, religious beliefs form part of a coherent, orderly system that is neither barbaric nor crude but just different from the systems that underlie modern, nonreligious societies. Eliade takes the challenge to reductionism even further, arguing that the archaic mode of thought we find in religion is actually more meaningful, and thus more "normal," than modern secular attitudes because it answers more fully to the deep human need for order and significance in a world of disorder, evil, and suffering. So too for Geertz. From his interpretive position in anthropology, which appreciates the particular, self defining character of every culture, he contends that religious societies stand on a footing of coherence and normality equal to any other, including our own scientific one.

All things considered, this antireductionist position can be said to have gradually gained strength throughout the century, aided, of course, by the rather sudden and steep decline in the stature of both Freud and Marx. We can even note as a further contribution to this shift the surprising revival of Tylor's intellectualist theory, though now stripped of its discredited evolutionary assumptions. We saw in Chapter 1 how both Tylor and Frazer insist that religion, though mistaken, represents an attempt to be rational; its main purpose is to explain what goes on in the world. In recent years that theme has been rediscovered by the "neo-Tylorian" anthropologist Robin Horton, who claims that this sort of intellectualism is just what he finds in the religious systems of the African peoples he has studied. Their gods and spirits explain the world to them in quite the same way that the concept of an atom or the law of gravity explains things to people living in cultures shaped by modern science.[7] Clifford Geertz, incidentally, comes near in places to the same opinion. Though he thinks that religion is, of course, much more than a purely intellectual exercise and that it fills an assortment of emotional and social needs, he observes that more than anything else, the people he met in Indonesia appealed to their gods simply to explain events they otherwise could not understand.[8] Needless to say, then, the debate between reductionist and antireductionist theory, between the irrationalists and the intellectualists, remains very much alive to the present day, with the main tide of opinion moving somewhat away from reductionism and toward the opposition.

The Range of Theories

As we have noticed throughout the preceding chapters, all seven of our theories address themselves in some measure to the question of religion in general—religion taken as a whole. But they do so in quite different ways. Like their predecessor Max Müller, Tylor and Frazer feel they can explain the entire history of religion as it first appeared and then developed through the long span of the human centuries. This strikes us today as an astonishingly unrealistic goal, though for their part a commitment to the principle of social evolution gave these early anthropologists all the inspiration they needed. For Tylor, the spirit worship of primitive peoples, the polytheism of the Greeks and Romans, and the monotheism of the higher religions can all be explained as steps on the staircase of civilization; they mark the ascent of humanity to ever more rational forms of religion—the most rational step, however, being the modern one: the choice for no religion at all. Frazer's view, which includes magic as a preliminary stage, follows the same grand, global pattern. Nor are these two alone. From their very different perspectives, the three major reductionists—Freud, Durkheim, and Marx—show the same sort of general ambition. When they explain religion, they mean to explain all of religion, and they refer to Judeo-Christian monotheism as a sort of paradigm case, the supreme instance of what is also found in numerous other, lesser forms. For Freud, the idea at the center of humanity's universal obsessional neurosis is the Judeo-Christian belief in God as Father. For Marx the opiate of capitalism's masses is the Christian hope of Heaven, where God will reward all of the impoverished innocents who have suffered in the present life. As it happens, Durkheim also puts his focus on a single religion, which can be taken as a sort of paradigm for all others. For his archetypal instance, he chooses the totemism of the Australian aborgines, the earliest and simplest of religions, which puts on display "the elementary forms" from which all others can be derived. In his view, the results of his study thus apply not just to Australia but to religion wherever we may find it.

Eliade, as we have seen, clearly opposes the ways of these reductionists, but he nonetheless shares their hope of finding a way to explain all of religion as we know it. He rejects the evolutionism of Tylor and Frazer, but he carries out his inquiries, which search for the sacred in the patterns of symbolism and myth that are common to all human societies, on the sort of worldwide scale that bears a close resemblance to their early anthropological approach. Eliade draws his evidence from every age and every locale of human civilization; in his search for the universal patterns of symbolism and myth, he moves freely from Hindu writings on yoga and the shamanism of Asia to the aborigines of Australia, the "cosmic Christianity" of European peasants, and to many other times, places, and peoples, whether ancient or modern, Eastern or Western, simple or sophisticated. His aims are genuinely global.

If Eliade's universalist ambitions bring him together with the reductionists he otherwise distrusts, they tend at the same time to separate him from the position of his fellow anti-reductionists, Evans-Pritchard and Geertz. As we have seen, both of these theorists have serious misgivings about any theory that aspires to universal claims about all of religion. From their perspective, Eliade's methods are essentially a throwback to an era anthropologists have long since left behind. He knows only the discredited "Frazerian" style of comparative research. While he is right, they would say, to try to explain religion on its own terms, it is hopeless to think that this can be done with the method he chooses—by searching through all of the world, and all of history, to find nothing more than surface similarities between the symbols, myths, and rituals of one culture and those of others. There may indeed be certain symbolic themes—like that of rebirth associated with the cycles of the moon—shared by peoples of many times and places, but each of these must be explored in depth and within the context of its own culture if its character is to be correctly understood. On their view, we cannot casually cruise across societies as if we were tourists, noticing only surface resemblances between one myth or symbol and another. Nor can we, like Freud, Marx, and Durkheim, allow one tradition to represent all others. For Evans-Pritchard and Geertz, the focus of the religionist, like that of the anthropologist, must be on the particular, for the simple reason that myths and symbols are always things embedded in societies and cultures.

Evidence and Theory

An explanation is one thing; the way one tries to prove it is another. If we look at all seven theories in light of their approach to the evidence, certain clear differences of strategy are not hard to notice. Because they believe that a truly global theory of religion requires an equally global array of evidence, Frazer, Tylor, and Eliade all set out with great determination to collect the widest possible range of information. The strength of this approach lies in its honest attempt to make a complete "fit" between theory and evidence. It assumes that if claims about all of religion are to be made, then evidence from all (or as close as we can come to all) of religion ought to be assembled. Nevertheless, its disadvantages are obvious. It is a program that cannot be pursued without extreme dependence on second-order information which cannot easily be tested; it relies heavily, and usually uncritically, on the reports and investigations of others. Second and more seriously, such global theories almost by definition must make their arguments by pulling facts and ideas out of their natural context in the cultures that generate them. When that happens, the risks of distortion and misunderstanding are very real.

These difficulties with evidence are rather neatly escaped by Freud and

Marx, even though, as we have seen, the claims they make about religion are in a sense just as universal as any made by Tylor, Frazer, or Eliade. Marx and Freud feel no need to search the world for data because they have found something better—the fundamental mechanism in human beings that everywhere generates religion, regardless of the specific form it takes in one culture or the next. It makes little difference to Marx whether we explore the tribal religions of New Guinea or the Christianity of Europe. Beneath the particulars, we will find everywhere the same fundamental dynamic of struggle between the classes that generates the hope of another, better world for the poor and produces gods who, by their moral laws, protect the interests of the rich. Similarly for Freud, there is no need to gather facts from around the world when the source of all rites and beliefs can be traced directly to the oedipal tensions and neuroses that are characteristic of every human personality. If we have in hand the principle that generates all religion, we have no need for all the many labors of anthropology and comparative religion other than to supply us with instructive supporting details.

The problem with both of these theories, of course, is that they must *show* just how all religions arise from the Oedipus complex or the class struggle; they cannot just assume it. Since religions differ tremendously in both form and substance around the world, it is the obligation of both Freud and Marx to show us just *how* Chinese folk religion, let us say, or Australian totemism is generated by the same psychological and social forces that have produced Judeo-Christian monotheism. Certainly there are possibilities for doing this, as we noticed above. The Hindu doctrines of caste and reincarnation would seem almost to beg for a Marxist analysis. But Marx and Freud are too busy with other matters to show an interest. Both are content to apply their theories chiefly to Judeo-Christian monotheism and let their verdict on it stand for all other religions as well. Unfortunately, though, such simple strategies cannot substitute for genuine comparative religious research. The sharp focus of both Freud and Marx on Western monotheistic religion places an unavoidable limit on the value of their explanations. Universal claims are made to rest on largely provincial arguments. The range of the evidence is insufficient to support the range of the theories.

The remaining three theorists—Durkheim, Evans-Pritchard, and Geertz— think that the matter of theory and evidence can be settled only by some form of compromise. They find the comprehensive approach of Tylor, Frazer, and Eliade unacceptable and the Western focus of Marx and Freud too narrow. The truth, they say, must be found somewhere in between. In this connection Durkheim's solution, though different, still somewhat resembles that of Freud and Marx. He too thinks he has found the mechanism that generates all of religion—not in the individual psyche or the class struggle but in the needs of society. He also thinks he can illustrate this mechanism through an account of a single religious tradition that serves as his test case—in his own words, the "one well-made experiment" which is "valid universally."[9] The religion he chooses, however, is not Judeo-Christian monotheism but primitive Australian totemism, for it better shows the "elementary forms" of all religion. As we noted in the chapter discussion of Durkheim, however, his critics have been quick to point out that Australian clan cults alone offer no better foundation for a general theory than does any other religion taken in isolation. So here again, though Durkheim does try to be more genuinely scientific about his procedure than either Marx or Freud, he nonetheless faces the same problem. The very specific nature of his Australian evidence is insufficient to support the universal claims of his theory.

Durkheim's example enables us to see just why theorists like Evans-Pritchard and Geertz have moved so decisively away from any general claims about the nature of religion. The problem is in the evidence, which in their view must be quite patiently studied in individual cases before any general statements can even begin to be made. In that connection, Evans-Pritchard does express a kind of deferred hope that at some later time other scholars, building on studies done in the present, may eventually be able to frame well-founded general interpretations. In the conclusion of *Nuer Religion,* he describes his own careful work in the Sudan as little more than a small first step on the way to comparative studies that, in the future, will examine African systems as a whole.[10] From there, presumably, he would encourage interpreters to go on to even wider theories that embrace other continents and cultures, though all of that would no doubt occur well in the future. Geertz, by contrast, is decidedly more skeptical. As we have already seen, the position he takes brings him very near to announcing the end of all general theories in both anthropology and religion. He thinks the fault of earlier theorists from Tylor and Frazer to Eliade and the reductionists lies not, as Evans-Pritchard claims, in the method or manner of reaching their goal but in the goal itself. His contention is that the evidence does not, and probably will never, allow for any scientifically generalized claims about religions or cultures as we find them in anthropological research. Given the deep and sharp particularity of separated societies around the world, the whole idea of a general theory applied to something so culture-bound as religion must be called into question. Accordingly, says Geertz, we cannot frame a general explanation of religion any more than we can create a general theory of culture, sports, architecture, or world literature. What we can develop, as the title of his most important book states, is the interpretation of *cultures,* plural; what we cannot achieve is some generic theory of culture in the singular. And what is true of culture is equally true of religion. We can investigate and interpret individual cults, creeds, and even emotional states, but we cannot reach some comprehensive theory of *religion* in general. The range of our evidence will always be insufficient to support the range of such a theory.

In sum, then, the cautions of Evans-Pritchard and the renunciations of Geertz stand out in rather sharp relief against the backdrop formed by the earlier and far more ambitious designs of their predecessors and rivals. Nor are they alone. If anything, the course of the most recent discussions in the theory of religion has only deepened doubts and multiplied hesitations about all general formulations. Current theorists wonder aloud whether the term "science," insofar as it stands for a coherent system of generalized assertions, can any longer even be used in relation to the field of religious studies.[11]

Theory and Belief

None of the thinkers we have met in this book should be considered a purely detached scholar, writing on a subject of no immediate interest to himself or his times; each is a human being who, in addition to his theory, holds certain personal religious convictions as well. The relationship between those beliefs and the explanations proposed is a subtle and complicated matter, which we can hardly explore in any complete way here. Nonetheless, a few general comments on this problematical issue may turn out to be useful.

First, we must recall a point made early on in this book. There is a sense in which all of the theories we have considered offer at least a possible challenge to religious belief because, from the start, they rule out all supernatural explanations of religious endeavors. The devout Christian explains his or her faith as a gift of God; the Muslim explains the power of the Prophet through direct inspiration from Allah. By contrast, the theorist of religion appeals only to what are described as "natural causes." This difference of approach need not necessarily create a conflict. Max Müller, a devoutly religious man, saw no reason why natural and supernatural explanations of religion should ever come into conflict; in his view, the two could nicely converge.[12] But that was not the view of Tylor and Frazer, who set the terms for so much of the theoretical discussion we have followed here. Both were antireligious rationalists who took considerable pleasure in announcing that supernatural explanations of religion lose their purpose once we grant that belief in spirits and gods arises from a natural, but mistaken, way of approaching the operations of the world. That Muhammad believed

Conclusion   279

himself inspired by Allah, they would say, is a fact no one need doubt; that he actually was so inspired is a claim no rational person can accept. Religion for Tylor and Frazer is thus a form of thought suitable to those ages when people lived in relative ignorance of natural causes. Now that civilization has evolved to a higher stage and the ways of science are known to all, such crude explanations of events are no longer needed.

The decidedly antireligious uses that Tylor and Frazer found for the comparative study of religion opened the way to the even more aggressive attacks of the three great reductionists we have considered—Freud, Durkheim, and Marx. Like Frazer and Tylor, they, too, personally reject religion and dismiss it as a relic left over from ages of ignorance. Going a step farther, however, they proceed to explain how it has survived by tracing its origin to irrational or subconscious causes—the neurotic psychology of the individual, economic injustice in the social order, or the idealization of community interests. Since religion cannot possibly be a normal and rational thing, such functional and reductive accounts of its survival appear to be the only ones available. Atheism in this connection seems to lead naturally to reductionism.[13]

Even so, not all of these reductionisms are exactly the same. Among the three we have examined, there is one significant point of difference. Both Marx and Freud think religion is not only false but, by their standards of morality and normalcy, also evil. It is something unhealthy and dysfunctional, a kind of disease people must try to be cured of. Durkheim, however, sees this matter differently. Though just as much an atheist as Freud or Marx, religion from his perspective is not in the least abnormal or dysfunctional, for societies have not been able to exist without it. In fact, if one day it does disappear, he thinks some other system of beliefs and ideas will have to be found to replace it. Thus, even though he is a reductionist, Durkheim's more affirmative attitude toward religion in terms of its constructive social function must be separated from the scorn of Freud and Marx. His view is more deliberate and impartial, and in that respect it bears an interesting, if rather faint, resemblance to the antireductionism of Eliade, Evans-Pritchard, and Geertz.

It is not hard to see why Eliade and Evans-Pritchard, both of whom were possessed of a lifelong sympathy with religious belief, would take a stand in opposition to reductionism. Reductionist explanations, even in the less militantly antireligious form developed by Durkheim, tend to be so fundamentally opposed to the normal stance of faith that it is hard to see how believers could find them acceptable. To the eyes of the believer, reductionism seems an inescapably alien form of explanation. Yet if all believers tend to oppose reductionism, it does not follow that *only* believers will oppose it, even though current theorists of religion sometimes make the mistake of supposing this must be so.[14]

On this point Geertz, the last of our seven theorists, provides a most instructive example. He describes his own stance as agnostic; he has no personal religious commitments. Yet in his work he opposes reductionist theories just as vigorously as Eliade and Evans-Pritchard. He obviously does not do so because reductionists present any challenge to his personal beliefs, but simply because in his view they do not adequately explain the subject of religion. For him, their appeal to a single circumstance or process that explains all forms of belief—whether it be Marx's class struggle or Freud's personal neurosis—simply cannot do justice to the extraordinarily diverse forms of religion that we actually encounter in the world. The concept of the class struggle may explain some aspects of some religions; it cannot begin to explain what lies behind all of them.

Behind the scenes, then, it is apparent that personal commitments have played at the very least a strong motivating role in the development of modern theories of religion. To those who, like Freud and Marx, have written from a personal stance of antipathy toward religion, aggressive reductionism seems only natural and right. To those who, like Eliade, have been moved by sympathy with the religious perspective, it can only be misguided and mistaken.

Theories Past and Present

While personal commitments have thus played their role in the theoretical enterprise, it would be a mistake to think that the influence of any of our theorists has been limited only to those who share his beliefs. Theories are, of course, affected by the belief or disbelief of their authors and audiences, but neither their shape nor their fate is wholly determined by either. Though Tylor and Frazer were anti-Christian agnostics, readers of all persuasions were drawn to their evolutionary intellectualism because of the compelling portrait it presented of religion's place in the history of ideas. Today, readers are drawn to neo-Tylorian theory for parallel reasons.

A somewhat similar judgment can be applied in the case of the key spokesmen for reductionism. Though Marx and Freud were militant atheists, the influence of their theories, which probably reached its apex just after the middle decades of our century, has extended far beyond the narrow circles of psychoanalysis, communist "true believers," and academic atheists. And the reason for that is clear. As we noted in the chapter discussions, the theories of both Marx and Freud are particularly aggressive forms of functionalist explanation; they claim *fully* to explain religion by reducing it to the dynamics of class struggle or a personality disorder. Few thoughtful observers today or in the past have ever made a purchase of these views in their full-dress reductionist form. But many have found them to be extraordinarily useful simply by scaling back their claims from the whole to the part. As reductionists who claim a complete explanation of religion, Freud and Marx both have been largely discredited. But in the more modest role of functionalists whose penetrating partial insights into the nature of personality and the dynamics of the social struggle have thrown a bright light on certain hidden dimensions of religious experience, their impact has been enormous. Although confidence in their theories has been shaken in the last decades especially, their interpretations are unlikely to fade completely from view.

In the case of the somewhat less militant reductionism of Durkheim, we can say even more. Few people of his time and fewer still in ours have ever accepted the highly imaginative derivation of all religion from Australian totemism that appears in *The Elementary Forms of the Religious Life*. But that issue aside, his demonstrations of the close, seemingly inseparable connection between the religious and the social have yielded perhaps the most fruitful interpretive theorem of our entire century. While the influence of Marx and Freud once soared and has now fallen, that of Durkheim and his sociological school has remained steady and strong. Even today it continues to grow.

Though he has left his main mark as the outspoken opponent of reductionism, Eliade's impact on the debates over religion offers an intriguing parallel to that of Durkheim. His defense of archaic thought and its vision of the sacred is in itself a thesis worth serious consideration. But not unlike Durkheim, Eliade greatly increased his influence on modern discussion by establishing himself at a great university and assembling, if not quite a school, then at least an extended family of younger scholars who have largely shared his general perspective. Moreover, because his own religious sympathies were muted, his antireductionist stance never became tied to personal belief in the way that would have turned it into a theological confession rather than, as it certainly is, an independent theoretical stance. Thus many scholars even of agnostic temperament are drawn to Eliade's antireductionist perspective on purely theoretical grounds; in their view, and quite apart from personal beliefs, it is simply a better way to explain religion.

New chapters on Eliade and reductionism undoubtedly remain to be written. In the meantime the two sides in the debate have seen their quarrel gradually eclipsed by a larger issue that has come to overshadow them both. That is the question whether *any* general theory of religion, reductionist or not, can continue to claim serious scientific attention. The question that the intellectual heirs of both sides in this debate must face in the present is whether the day of such ambitious, all-embracing explanatory schemes as both Eliade and his reductionist adversaries devised has perhaps finally come to an end. However convincing they may have seemed in earlier times and places, universalist theories now draw fire from critics on almost all sides. They are dismissed as superficial in some cases, as speculative and unprovable in others, and as vague, arbitrary, or subjective in still others. Though harsh and on occasion even unfair, these attacks have come to carry real weight.

In the more skeptical environment of the present, therefore, it is difficult to avoid the conclusion that the future belongs not to the general theories of either Durkheim or Eliade but to the new particularist approaches, to the disciples of Evans-Pritchard and Geertz. Evans-Pritchard has been doubly significant in this connection. Not only has he published one of the more incisive critiques of generalist theories; his own works on both the Azande and the Nuer have succeeded in showing how much deeper and richer explanations of religion can be when they are rooted in a close, careful, and detailed study of the entire culture that is their home. The same sort of argument by example is to be found in the work of Geertz. As we have seen above, his splendid and detailed ethnographic studies of religion in Bali and Java, as well as Morocco, have left all theorists of religion with an intriguing dilemma. What happens when the first mission of a science—to acquire precise, accurate, and specific information—is done so thoroughly that its second task—the formulation of a general theory based on similarities between cases—becomes almost impossible to accomplish? Until some usable path through this dilemma is found, the day of the general theory is not likely to make a quick return. Thus, for the foreseeable future at least, the detailed and thorough but sharply circumscribed studies of Evans-Pritchard and Geertz are the models most likely to be followed by others.

This emphasis on particular studies does not mean that no statements at all of a more general sort can be made about the role of religion in human culture. Attempts to make connections, find similarities, or suggest abstract principles of comparison always remain useful. But these are principles outlining what is plausible, not what is certain. And they suggest what some observers have always expected: that the future of theoretical study in religion belongs most likely to the humanities rather than the sciences, even though the ideals of the latter remain a part of its inspiration. This is decidedly not because humanist inquiry has been found to be in some way better than scientific, but simply because the human arts and sciences now seem more appropriate to the subject. For religion in the end seems to be a matter not of impersonal processes that can be known with certainty because they have been scripted by the laws of nature, but of personal beliefs and behaviors that can only be plausibly explained because they have arisen from complex, partly free and partly conditioned choices of human agents. In the late 1800s, when the new study of anthropology first captured the interest of the Victorians, the great legal historian F. W. Maitland made an interesting prediction. Anthropology, he said, will one day become history, or it will become nothing at all. Though it is now a full century since they were spoken, these words have about them an uncanny ring of prophecy, which applies just as fully to the scientific study of religion. The age of supposedly scientific general theories seems to have passed—perhaps forever. Insofar as they managed to misread or misunderstand the nature of religion in human affairs, it is all to the good that they should now be left behind. As they go, however, we should note their legacy. They were, and still remain, impressive exhibits of the way in which theoretical inquiry, even in error, serves as a powerful incentive to further exploration and deeper understanding.

Notes

1. *Primitive Culture: Researches into the Development of Mythology, Philosophy, Religion, Language, Art, and Custom*, 2 vols., 4th ed., rev. (London: John Murray, [1871] 1903), 1: 424.

2. *The Elementary Forms of the Religious Life: A Study in Religious Sociology*, tr. Joseph Ward Swain (London: George Allen & Unwin, Ltd., 1915), pp. 24–29, 47.

3. See *Witchcraft, Oracles and Magic among the Azande* (Oxford, England: Clarendon Press, 1937), pp. 80–83; for his definition of "mystical notions," see p. 12.

4. Geertz, "Religion as a Cultural System," in *The Interpretation of Cultures* (New York: Basic Books, 1973), p. 90.

5. Evans-Pritchard, *Theories of Primitive Religion* (Oxford, England: Clarendon Press, 1965), pp. 101–102.

6. Evans-Pritchard, *Theories of Primitive Religion*, p. 101.

7. Horton has outlined his views in a number of well-known articles; see "The Kalabari World View: An Outline and Interpretation," *Africa* 32 (1962): 210–40; "Ritual Man in Africa," *Africa* 34 (1964): 85–104; and "Neo-Tylorianism: Sound Sense or Sinister Prejudice?" *Man*, n.s. 3 (1968): 625–34. His most recent work is *Patterns of Thought in Africa and the West: Selected Theoretical Papers in Magic, Religion, and Science* (Cambridge, England: Cambridge University Press, 1993).

8. See "Religion as a Cultural System," in *Interpretation of Cultures*, p. 101, where he writes, "Certainly, I was struck in my own work, much more than I had at all expected to be, by the degree to which my more animistically inclined informants behaved like true Tyloreans. They seemed to be constantly using their beliefs

to "explain" phenomena: or, more accurately, to convince themselves that the phenomena were explainable within the accepted scheme of things."

9. Durkheim, *Elementary Forms,* p. 415.

10. E. E. Evans-Pritchard, *Nuer Religion* (Oxford, England: Clarendon Press, 1956), p. 314.

11. For comment on some of these issues, see the essays of Robert Segal in *Explaining and Interpreting Religion: Essays on the Issue,* Toronto Studies in Religion, vol. 16 (New York: Peter Lang, 1992); see also the stance taken by Robert Segal and Donald Wiebe in their essay "Axioms and Dogmas in the Study of Religion," *Journal of the American Academy of Religion* 57 (Fall 1989): 591–605 and my response in "Axioms without Dogmas: The Case for a Humanistic Account of Religion," *Journal of the American Academy of Religion* 59, no. 4 (Winter 1991): 703–709. See also my "Explaining, Endorsing, and Reducing Religion: Some Clarifications," in *Religion and Reductionism,* eds. Thomas Idinopoulos and Edward Yonan (Leiden: E. J. Brill, 1994): 183–97, along with the other essays in this volume.

12. See above, Introduction, pp. 7–9; chapter 1, pp. 18–20.

13. On this, see Robert A. Segal, "In Defense of Reductionism," *Journal of the American Academy of Religion* 51, no. 1 (March 1983): 97–124.

14. See my "Reductionism and Belief," *Journal of Religion* 66, no. 1 (January 1986): 18–36.

Index

Geertz, Clifford (*cont.*)
  Evans-Pritchard, comparison with, 234–
    35, 247–48, 257–58, 263
  explanation, 233–34. *See also* Geertz:
    anthropology, interpretive
  fieldwork, 234
    in Bali, 234–35
    in Java, 234–35, 264n. 5
    in Morocco, 235–36
  Frazer, comparison with, 237
  Freud, comparison with, 257–58
  functionalism, 235. *See also* Geertz:
    anthropology, interpretive
  illuminationism, Indonesian, 253
  interpretation. *See* Geertz: anthropology,
    interpretive
  Islam, Muslims, 250–57, 262–63
    baraka (spiritual charisma), 252–54,
      266n. 46
    Holy man in, 250–54, 256–57
    marabout (Muslim mystic, holy man),
      250–55
    Muhammad, the Prophet, 250, 252
    pilgrimage to Mecca, 245
    Ramadan, fasting in, 241
    scripturalists, 253–57
    and the "ideologization" of religion,
      255–56
    sherif (descendant of the Prophet
      Muhammad), 252–53
  life and career, 234–36, 263n. 2
  magic, 247–49
  marabout. See Geertz: Islam
  Marx, comparison with, 257
  "meaning," 233, 260–61
    in culture, 233–35, 238, 240–43
    in religion, 243–46, 255–57, 262–63.
      See also Geertz: anthropology,
      interpretive
  moods, 244–45
  motivations, 244–45
  Rangda and Barong, myth of, 245–46,
    262
  reductionism, 257
  religion, study of, 233–34
    force of, distinguished from *scope* of,
      256
  ritual, 245–46
  santri (religious) schools, 253–54
  science. *See* Science: natural, Geertz and;
    Science, social
  secularism, 255–57
  sherif. See Geertz: Islam
  sociology, French, 238
  symbols, system of, 244–45

  symbolic fusion of world view and
    ethos, 245–46
  theater states, of Indonesia, 251, 254–55
  thick description, 240–43
  Tylor, comparison with, 237
  world view and ethos, 245–46, 255–57,
    261–63, 266n. 44
Gennep, Arnold van, 117
Gillen, F. J., 40, 101, 116. *See also*
  Spencer, Baldwin
Goethe, Johann Wolfgang von, 3, 162
Grünbaum, Adolf, 82–83

Haeckel, Ernst, 63
Hegel, Georg Wilhelm Friedrich von, 184.
  See also Marx: Hegel, Georg
  Wilhelm Friedrich von
Herodotus, of Halicarnassus, 4
Hinduism
  Eliade and, 159–60, 165, 180, 189
  Geertz and, 235, 245, 247–48, 251–52
  Marx and, 147, 276
  Müller and, 3, 8, 19
Holy Man. *See* Geertz: Islam
Horton, Robin, 49n. 35, 273, 280
Hume, David, 6, 7

Idris II, King of Morocco, 250
Indians, American, 237–38
Ionesco, Nae, 160
Iron Guard, 160
Islam, Muslims, 7, 158–65, 170, 200. *See
  also* Geertz: Islam
Ismail, Sultan Mulay, of Morocco, 252–53

Jefferson, Thomas, 6
Jones, Ernest, 57
Joyce, James, 185
Judaism, 126, 139, 181–82. *See also* Freud:
  Jewish family and heritage
Jung, Carl, 11, 57, 77, 160–61, 193n. 9

Kalidjaga, Sunan, 251–52, 254–55
Kant, Immanuel, 268
Kautsky, Karl, 143
Kennedy, John F., funeral of, 110
Kroeber, Alfred Louis, 237–38

Lamarck, Jean, 81
Laws of Development, 8, 20–21, 342, 343
Legion of the Archangel Michael, 160,
  192n. 8
Lenin, Vladimir, 124
Lessing, Gotthold, 6